AIDS TO
ENGLISH-JAPANESE TRANSLATION

山 崎 貞
# 新々英文解釈研究

東京大学教授
佐山栄太郎 改訂

新訂新版

東京 研究社 発行

# は　し　が　き

　英文を読む者——ことに受験者——のぜひ一通り心得ておらねばならぬと思われるような構文成句の一般を説きたいという考えで編まれたのが本書の前身「英文解釈研究」であった。

　同書は幸い学生諸君の求めるところに適したと見え、大正元年秋初版を出してから三年間に十数版を重ね、大正四年秋改訂増補の上書名に「新」の字を冠して発行してから数年間さらに数十版を重ね、なお需要増加の勢いであるという。

　今回再び全部にわたり改訂を施し、旧版例題中比較的実用に遠いものを省き、最新試験問題を加え、「新々英文解釈研究」と命名して発行することにした。例題の大部分は明治三十五年より大正十二年に至る諸学校の入学試験問題から採り、その他は主として現行英語教科書に材を求めた。

　収録した構文成句の数は数百にのぼるけれど、比較研究に便にし、記憶を助けるため、形の似たもの、意味の似たものなどは一括して同所に集めて、百十余章に分かち、配列も文法的の順序によらず、やはり形や意味の類似をたどって脈絡を通ずるようにした。

　解説は紙面をおしまず、なるべく平易詳細に、かつ各章に簡単な類例数個ずつを加え理解を助けるようにしたから、これを誦読暗記すれば、ただに英文解釈のみならず、和文英訳にも資するところ少なくないと信ずる。

　近年発音のゆるがせにすべからざることが識者間に高調せられ、高等学校、商大等の入学試験には Accentuation の問題が加えられるようになった、これまことにしかるべき事であって、他の諸学校も漸次これにならうようになるだろうと思う。本書はこの趣

勢(せい)にかんがみ、毎ページ重要な単語の発音と訳語とを脚註として付することにした。

大正十四年一月

山　崎　　貞

## 改訂にあたって

　今日すでに相当の年輩の人たちのうちには、彼らの中学時代、あるいはもっと上級の学校の学生時代に、山崎貞先生の「英文解釈研究」のご厄介になったものが、ずいぶんたくさんあるであろう。この書物のおかげで高校の入学試験を突破した人もあるであろうし、この指導によって、英文理解の目を明けてもらった人もあるに違いない。そういう人たちにはなつかしい書物である。しかし、この研究書が単に過去の、思い出の書にとどまらないことは、現在、年々きわめて多数の若い読者を引きつけている事実がよくこれを証明している。実に親子二代にわたってお役に立っている参考書である。しかし、なんと言っても、最初の出版以来、四半世紀以上の時の経過は、社会生活全般の変化と共に、英語そのものにも、またその学習方法にも、種々の変遷をもたらした。もしこれが服装の流行を扱ったものであったとすれば、とうの昔に全く役に立たなくなっているはずである。ところが、今日もその利用者がますます多くなりつつあることは、この書物が英語学習の基本となる大綱を正しく把握しているからに相違ない。けれども、卒直に言えば、根幹は依然として健全であるけれども、枝葉に至ると、すでに枯れて役に立たなくなったもの、あるいは、時代の趣好に全然合わないものなど、剪定(せんてい)や植え替えを必要とする部分が生じていることは否定できない。今回の改訂は、要するに、この剪定であり接木であり、時に移植であると言えよう。その改訂の要旨を具体的に述べれば、次のようになる。

　第一、項目別解説の部分は、これはこれとして完璧に近いものであると考えられるから、ほとんど筆を入れない。ただごく少数

の箇所を注意事項のような形で補っている。

　第二、問題のさし替えと追加、これに最も多くの努力が払われている。語法そのものの練習としてはさしつかえないものでも、内容が今日の事情と全然合わないもの、または好ましくないものを省き、内容の上からも表現の上からももっとも適切なものを入れ替えた。また、ことに必要な項目には思い切って多数を追加した。入れ替え、追加の数は全部で二百題前後、つまり総数の二割程度であろうと思う。その資料は、現代作家の文、特にまた、近ごろの大学入試問題から採った。

　第三、解説、解答の全般にわたって、和文の表現を現在の利用者の便宜に合うように徹底的に改訂した。

　第四、問題の出典を示す指示は、原著執筆当時の教科書名や、今日は既にその名を失ってしまった出題校の名などが多いので、これらは抹消することにした。出典は文の性質上必要と認めるもののみを残した。ただし、最近の入学試験問題は出題校を入れたが、これは読者に便宜であろうと考えたからである。出典を示していない問題は、従来のもので出典を抹消したものと、新たに加えたものとがまじっているわけである。

　このように改訂者としては相当に努力したつもりであるから、この名著が、これまでの真価を維持していき、その上に、多少にせよ、新しい利用価値が加えられることになるならば、改訂者の幸いはまことに大きいと言うべきである。

　　　　1958年　初秋

　　　　　　　　　　　　　　　佐　山　栄　太　郎

## 再改訂について

　前回の大改訂からすでに7年の歳月を経た。この著書を利用される読者の数は年々ふえると言っても、けっして減るようには見えない。しかし読者はその質において変化して来たように思われる。今回の改訂の目標は、これらの読者の便宜に一段とよく応じることにあった。すなわち、前回の改訂版の序文の中で示された第三の項目を、さらに徹底して押し進めたわけである。他の項目についても、でき得るかぎりの改善を試みたことはもちろんである。この新装の書物のために、さらに多くの読者の愛顧を請うしだいである。

　　　1965年　秋

　　　　　　　　　　　　　　　　　　佐　山　栄　太　郎

# CONTENTS

|   |   | PAGE. |
|---|---|---|
| 1. | A man **of learning** is not always a man **of wisdom** | 1 |
| ,, | Such meanness does not become a man **of his means** | ,, |
| 2. | He is **an oyster of a man** | 3 |
| ,, | **That fool of a John** has forgotten to clean my boots | ,, |
| 3. | The bamboo is a kind of grass | 5 |
| ,, | What is learned in **the cradle** is carried to **the grave** | ,, |
| 4. | **The rich** are not always happy | 8 |
| ,, | **The good** and **the beautiful** do not always go together | ,, |
| 5. | He is **honesty itself** | 11 |
| ,, | He is **the incarnation of avarice** | ,, |
| ,, | I am **all attention** | ,, |
| 6. | Carbonic acid (gas) is not a poison **in itself** | 14 |
| 7. | I live all **by myself** | 16 |
| ,, | I cannot finish it **by myself** | ,, |
| 8. | I like to do everything **for myself** | 18 |
| ,, | He loves labour **for itself** | ,, |
| 9. | I did not call him; he woke up **of himself** | 23 |
| ,, | The boy ran away from school, but returned **of his own accord** | ,, |
| 10. | He often **talks to himself** when he is alone | 25 |
| ,, | I **have** this big room all **to myself** | ,, |
| 11. | He did it **himself** | 27 |
| 12. | He is **the very** man for you | 28 |
| 13. | **The wisest** man cannot know everything | 31 |
| 14. | He is **the last person** to do such a thing | 32 |

| | | |
|---|---|---|
| 15. | Nothing can be **simpler** | 34 |
| 16. | **The sooner the better** | 36 |
| 17. | I do **not** love him **the less for** his faults | 39 |
| ,, | I love him **all the better for** his faults | ,, |
| 18. | He can $\begin{cases}\textbf{no more} \text{ swim} \\ \textbf{not} \text{ swim } \textbf{any more}\end{cases}$ **than** $\begin{cases}\text{a hammer can (swim)} \\ \text{I can fly}\end{cases}$ | 42 |
| 19. | The book has **few** faults | 46 |
| ,, | The book has **a few** faults | ,, |
| 20. | He **seldom** goes out | 51 |
| ,, | It is **hardly** possible | ,, |
| 21. | You are **too** young **to** understand such things | 53 |
| ,, | He is **too** wise **not to** know it | ,, |
| 22. | He is **too** ready **to** speak | 56 |
| ,, | I am **only too** delighted **to** accept your kind invitation | ,, |
| 23. | We **cannot** praise him **too** much | 59 |
| ,, | It is **impossible to overpraise** him | ,, |
| 24. | We have two dogs; **one** is white, and **the other** black | 62 |
| ,, | We have two dogs, a white one, and a black one; **the one** is larger than **the other** | ,, |
| 25. | Health is above wealth, for **this** cannot give so much happiness as **that** | 64 |
| 26. | To know is **one thing,** to practise is **another** | 65 |
| 27. | The tail of a fox is longer than **that of** a hare | 67 |
| 28. | The ship was built in less than a year, **and that** in the midst of the war | 69 |
| 29. | **What with** teaching, and **what with** writing, my time is fully taken up | 71 |
| ,, | **What by** policy, and **what by** force, he always accomplishes his purpose | ,, |
| 30. | I do **what** is right in my own sight | 73 |
| 31. | He has had no regular education; he is **what you call a** | |

| | | |
|---|---|---|
| | self-made man . . . . . . . . . . . . . . . . . . | 75 |
| 32. | Coal and iron made England **what she is** . . . . . . . . | 77 |
| 33. | He is handsome, clever, and **what is better** still, very rich . | 78 |
| 34. | This is **all** the money (that) I have . . . . . . . . . . | 80 |
| „ | I will give you **what** money I have . . . . . . . . . . | „ |
| 35. | Leaves **are to** the plant, **what** lungs **are to** the animal . . | 83 |
| 36. | **As** the lion is king of beasts, **so** is the eagle king of birds . | 86 |
| 37. | **It is in** studying **as in** eating; he who does it gets the benefits, and not he who sees it done . . . . . . . . | 88 |
| 38. | He is **as** brave **as any** man alive . . . . . . . . . . . . | 89 |
| „ | He is **as** brave a man **as ever** breathed . . . . . . . . . | „ |
| „ | He is **the bravest** man **that ever** lived . . . . . . . . . | „ |
| 39. | **Who in the world** are you? . . . . . . . . . . . . . . | 93 |
| „ | He **had not** a penny **in the world** . . . . . . . . . . . | „ |
| „ | **The greatest** naval power **on earth** . . . . . . . . . . . | „ |
| 40. | He is **something of** a lawyer . . . . . . . . . . . . . | 96 |
| 41. | You shall want for nothing **as long as** I live . . . . . . . | 98 |
| „ | Any book will do, **so long as** it is interesting . . . . . . | „ |
| 42. | I got up **so** early **as to** be in time for the express . . . . | 102 |
| „ | I got up early **so as to** be in time for the express . . . . | „ |
| 43. | I got up **so** early **that** I was in time for the express . . . | 104 |
| „ | I got up early (**so**) **that** I **might** be in time for the express . | „ |
| 44. | I work hard (**for fear**) **lest** I **should** fail . . . . . . . . . | 108 |
| „ | I work hard **for fear** (**lest**) I **may** fail . . . . . . . . . . | „ |
| 45. | He **had the kindness to** show me the way . . . . . . . | 112 |
| „ | He **was so kind as to** show me the way . . . . . . . . | „ |
| 46. | Do not trust **such** men **as** praise you to your face . . . . | 115 |
| „ | He is **such** a fool **that** no one will keep company with him . | „ |
| 47. | He is **not so much** a scholar **as** a writer . . . . . . . . | 119 |
| „ | He can**not so much as** read his own name . . . . . . . | „ |
| 48. | He is rather hot-tempered, and owns **as much** . . . . . . | 123 |

## CONTENTS

48. What takes you only three hours, takes me **as many** days . 123
49. Apples are sold at **so much** a piece . . . . . . . . . . . 126
,, Apples are sold at **so many** for a hundred yen . . . . . . ,,
50. They worked hard **like so many** ants . . . . . . . . . . 127
51. It was very cold last evening—**so much so** that I could not stir out of doors . . . . . . . . . . . . . . . . . . . . 129
52. He is an Edokko, **if ever** there was one . . . . . . . . . 131
,, He can do it, **if any** one can . . . . . . . . . . . . . . . . ,,
,, **If** you do it **at all,** do it well . . . . . . . . . . . . . . . ,,
53. He has **ever so** many children . . . . . . . . . . . . . . 135
,, Home is home, be it **ever so** homely . . . . . . . . . . ,,
54. You seem to be a physician. —**So** (*indeed*) **I am** . . . . 137
,, I am a physician. —**So** (*also*) **am I** . . . . . . . . . . . ,,
55. I had waited an hour **before** he appeared . . . . . . . . 139
56. I had **not** waited **long before** he appeared . . . . . . . . 141
57. We had **scarcely** got on shore **when** it began to blow hard . 143
,, We had **no sooner** got on shore **than** it began to blow hard . ,,
,, **As soon as** we got on shore it began to blow hard . . . . ,,
58. I shall see him **before long** . . . . . . . . . . . . . . . 148
59. People do **not** know the blessing of health **till** they lose it . 149
60. **Persevere, and** you will succeed . . . . . . . . . . . . . 151
,, **Persevere, or** you will fail . . . . . . . . . . . . . . . . ,,
61. **One more effort, and** you will succeed . . . . . . . . . 154
62. I love you more than he **does** . . . . . . . . . . . . . . 155
,, He **does** work hard, but somehow he remains as poor as ever . . . . . . . . . . . . . . . . . . . . . . . . . . . ,,
63. He **goes** to school . . . . . . . . . . . . . . . . . . . . 158
,, He **will** *often* sit for hours together, absorbed in deep thoughts . . . . . . . . . . . . . . . . . . . . . . . . ,,
,, I **used to** take the "Yomiuri," but not now . . . . . . . ,,
,, He **would** *often* come home drunk, and beat his wife . . ,,

| | | |
|---|---|---|
| 64. | I **am used to** hardships | 161 |
| 65. | I **have a liking for** that man | 162 |
| „ | I **have a dislike to** that man | „ |
| „ | He **has a genius for** poetry | „ |
| 66. | He **took** me **by the hand** | 165 |
| „ | He **struck** me **on the head** | „ |
| „ | He **looked** me **in the face** | „ |
| 67. | "I will **ease** you **of** your burden." So saying, the highwayman **robbed** the traveller **of** his money | 168 |
| 68. | I went to the station **to see** a friend off | 172 |
| „ | He lived **to see** his son a great man | „ |
| „ | She wept **to see** her son in such a plight | „ |
| 69. | I **saw him enter** the room | 176 |
| 70. | I will **have** some one **come** | 178 |
| „ | I shall **have** some one **come** | „ |
| 71. | I shall **have** my watch **stolen** | 181 |
| „ | I will **have** my watch **mended** | „ |
| 72. | **To tell the truth**, I am tired of teaching | 185 |
| 73. | He knows German and French, **to say nothing of** English | 189 |
| „ | He does **not** know English, **to say nothing of** German or French | „ |
| 74. | **There is no staying** at home in this fine weather | 191 |
| „ | It is **no use crying** | „ |
| 75. | He **is possessed of** great wealth | 193 |
| „ | I saw on every side faces **expressive of** anxiety | „ |
| 76. | The watch I lost was **of** great **value** | 197 |
| 77. | This pheasant is **of my own shooting** | 199 |
| „ | I sent him a pheasant **of my own shooting** | „ |
| 78. | I will **make** a man **of** you | 201 |
| 79. | **Writing** something on a card, he gave it to me | 204 |
| „ | **Written** in an easy style, the book is adapted for beginners | „ |

| | | |
|---|---|---|
| 80. | **Written, as it is,** in an easy style, the book is adapted for beginners | 208 |
| ,, | **Living, as I do,** so remote from towns, I rarely have visitors | ,, |
| 81. | **Generally speaking,** girls make better linguists than boys | 210 |
| 82. | **Brave as he was,** a tremor passed through him | 212 |
| 83. | He **may well** be proud of his son | 215 |
| ,, | He is proud of his son, and **well he may** | ,, |
| 84. | You **may as well** call a cat a little tiger **as** call a tiger a big cat | 217 |
| ,, | You **might as well** call a horse a fish **as** call a whale one | ,, |
| 85. | Accidents **will** happen | 220 |
| ,, | This cork **will not** come out | ,, |
| 86. | **You shall** live | 222 |
| ,, | **He shall** die | ,, |
| 87. | Why **should** I **not** succeed? | 225 |
| 88. | **What a pity** that things **should** have come to this! | 227 |
| ,, | **I am surprised** that you **should** say so! | ,, |
| ,, | **Who** are you that you **should** speak thus to me? | ,, |
| 89. | One **should obey** the dictates of one's conscience | 229 |
| ,, | You **should have obeyed** your father | ,, |
| 90. | **It is right that** one **should** speak well of the absent | 231 |
| 91. | I **would rather** die than live in dishonour | 232 |
| ,, | You **had better** go to the seaside | ,, |
| 92. | If you **would** be happy, be virtuous | 235 |
| ,, | **Would** that I were young again! | ,, |
| 93. | **Whatever** the matter **may be,** do your best | 236 |
| ,, | **No matter what** the matter **may be,** do your best | ,, |
| ,, | **Let** the matter **be what it may** (or **will**), do your best | ,, |
| ,, | **Be** the matter **what it may** (or **will**), do your best | ,, |
| 94. | If I **were** a bird, I **would** fly to you | 242 |
| ,, | **I wish** (that) I **had** wings, and **could** fly to you | ,, |

| | | |
|---|---|---|
| 95. | The child talks **as if** it were a man | 244 |
| ,, | He talks **as though** he knew everything | ,, |
| 96. | **Should I fail** this time, I would try again | 248 |
| 97. | He worked very hard, **otherwise** he would have failed | 250 |
| 98. | I **might have been** a rich man | 254 |
| ,, | **A wise man would** not do such a thing | ,, |
| ,, | **Without water**, nothing **could** live | ,, |
| ,, | **To hear him speak English**, one **would** take him for an Englishman | ,, |
| 99. | I **cannot but** laugh to hear such a story | 256 |
| ,, | I **cannot help** laughing to hear such a story | ,, |
| 100. | **No one but** a fool would do such a thing | 258 |
| ,, | He is **nothing but** a student | ,, |
| 101. | **Who should** come in **but** the man we were talking of? | 262 |
| 102. | He is **anything but** a scholar | 264 |
| ,, | He is **all but** dead | ,, |
| 103. | There is **no** rule **but** has exceptions | 266 |
| 104. | There is **nothing so** difficult **but** it becomes easy by practice | 268 |
| 105. | I **never** see you **but** I think of my brother | 269 |
| ,, | I **never** see you **without** thinking of my brother | ,, |
| 106. | There is **no** rule that has **not** exceptions | 272 |
| 107. | **But for** his idleness, he would be a good student | 274 |
| ,, | **But that** he prevented me, I would have replied | ,, |
| 108. | I *do not deny* **but that** I know him | 276 |
| 109. | **It is true** its flower is beautiful, **but** it bears no fruit | 278 |
| 110. | He has **both** experience **and** scholarship | 280 |
| ,, | He has experience **as well as** scholarship | ,, |
| ,, | He has **not only** scholarship, **but also** experience | ,, |
| 111. | **Not that** I dislike the task, **but that** I am unequal to it | 284 |
| ,, | The mountain is **not** valuable **because** it is high | ,, |

**112.** It is an ill wind that blows nobody good . . . . . . . . . 287

解　答　篇 . . . . . . . . . . . . . . . . . . . . . . . 289
索　　　引 . . . . . . . . . . . . . . . . . . . . . . . 457

# 新々
# 英文解釈研究

## (1)

(a) A man **of learning** is not always a man **of wisdom**.
(b) Such meanness does not become a man **of his means**.

【訳】(a) 学者が必ずしも賢い人とはかぎらない。
(b) そんなけちな事をするとはあの金持にも似合わない。

〔解説〕「**of**＋抽象名詞＝形容詞」のように言いなおしてよいことが多い。その場合の of は通例ある性質の所有を示すいわゆる属性の of (attributive "of") である。すなわち

a man **of learning**＝a **learned** man （学問を有する人＝学者）
a man **of wisdom**＝a **wise** man （知恵のある人＝賢い人）

類例：―

a woman **of beauty**＝a **beautiful** woman （美人）
a man **of ability**＝an **able** man （有能な人、敏腕家）
a man **of benevolence**＝a **benevolent** man （なさけ深い人）
a man **of sense**＝a **sensible** man
　（常識のある人、物のわかった人）

---

(1) **wisdom** [wízdəm] 知恵。　**meanness** いやしい行為。　**means** 資力。**become** 似合う。　**ability** [əbíliti] 才能。　**benevolence** [binévələns] 慈悲心。

〖注 意〗 **a man of his word** （約束を守る人）
**a man of the world** （世間なれた人、世才にたけた人）

などのばあいの word や world は抽象名詞ではないが、それに準ずるものとみることができる。前者は a man of character (人格者)に類し、後者は a man of worldly wisdom (世渡りの知恵を持った人)の意味である。

(b) 「**a man of one's＋抽象名詞**」のように his とか my とか代名詞がはいると、「彼のような」「私のような」を加えて訳せばよい。類例：—

Such conduct does not become *a man of his years*.
(あの人があんなことをするとは年がいもない)

I should not have expected such folly from *a man of his experience*.
(あの経験家がそんなばかなことをするとは意外だ)

**a man of his means** （あの人のような金持）
**a man of his wisdom** （あの人のような賢い人）

---

**1.** It is the laborious and painstaking men who are the rulers of the world. There has not been *a statesman of eminence* but was *a man of industry*.

**2.** To the *man of strong feelings and passions* the only real safeguard for chastity is an habitual and instinctive shrinking from personal contact with what is common.

**3.** The true genius is *a mind of large general powers*, accidentally determined to some particular direction. （東京芸術大）

**4.** He grew improvident as he grew poor; and though he

---

**world** [wəːld] 世間。 **character** [kǽriktə] 品性、人格。 **worldly** 世間的な、世俗的な。 **become** 似合う。 **folly** 愚かなこと。
**1. laborious** [ləbɔ́ːriəs] 勤勉な。 **painstaking** [péinztèikiŋ] 骨折りをおしまない。 **eminence** [émínəns] 卓越。 **but**=that...not. **industry** [índəstri] 勤勉。 **2. safeguard** [séifgɑːd] 保護。 **chastity** [tʃǽstiti] 清純。 **habitual** [həbítjuəl] 平素の。 **instinctive** [instíŋktiv] 本能的な。 **shrinking** しりごみ。 **contact** 接触。 **3. general** 一般に通じる。 **accidentally** [æ̀ksidéntəli] 偶然に。 **determined** [ditə́ːmind] 限定された。 **4. improvident** [imprɔ́vidənt] 無思慮な。

talked like *a man of sense*, his actions were those of a fool.

(*Goldsmith*)

**5.** No *man of science* is likely to achieve anything great, unless he brings to his work a zeal comparable with that of religion, and unless he is prepared to follow truth wherever it leads him. But zeal without strict discipline of the intellect will get him nowhere.

**6.** The watch was by no means low-priced, and was too expensive for *a person of my limited means;* still it was cheap at the price asked, for as to its action it defied all comparison.

---

## (2)

(a) He is **an oyster of a man.**
(b) **That fool of a John** has forgotten to clean my boots.

【訳】（a）彼はかき（牡蠣）みたいな（寡黙な）人だ。
　　　（b）あのばか者のジョンのやつが私の靴をみがくのを忘れた。

〚解　説〛（a）「名詞＋of a…」が形容詞に代用されて「～のような…」の意味となる。すなわち

　an **oyster of a** man＝an **oysterlike** man＝a man **like an oyster**
　　（かきのような人）
　an **angel of a** wife＝an **angelic** wife＝a wife **like an angel**
　　（天使のような［姿も心も美しい］妻）

---

5. **is likely to** …しそうだ。　**achieve** なしとげる。　**zeal** 熱心。　**discipline** [dísiplin] 統制、規律。　6. **expensive** 高価の。　**limited** 限られた、あまり多くない。　**asked** 求められた。　**as to** …については。　**defy** [difái] 物ともせぬ。
　(2) **oyster** [ɔ́istə] かき。　**angelic** [ændʒélik] 天使のような。

類例:—

   a **saint of a** man （仏様［聖人］みたいな人）
   a **mountain of a** (=*mountainous*) wave （山のような波）
   a **pig of a** (=*piggish*) fellow （豚のようなやつ）
   a **palace of a** house （御殿のようなりっぱな家）

（b）「名詞＋**of a**」が形容詞に代用されても「…のような」を入れずに訳してよい場合がある。類例:—

   that **fool of a** John＝that **foolish** John
     （あのおろかなジョン）

こういうのはもとの句の口調をそのまま日本語に移して「あのばか者のジョン」「あのジョンのばか者」などと訳すのもよい。類例:—

   her **brute of a** (=*brutelike*) husband
     （けもののような彼女の夫）
   that old **villain of a** (=*villainous*) landlord
     （あの亭主の悪党じじい）

〖注　意〗 of の次に来る名詞には、それが普通名詞であっても、固有名詞であっても、必ず不定冠詞がつく。

―――――――

**7.** Jack Harmon had shut up his cat below, but poor puss escaped somehow, for all at once a shrill cry was heard, and there was Jumbo clinging to a rail, with *a great mountain of a wave* coming right down upon her.

**8.** A boy of a captain.
   A captain's boy.

**9.** It is as I have said *a labyrinth of an old house*.   (*Doyle*)

**10.** *You darling of a Jane!* how kind in you to bring me the shawl!

―――――――

**brute** [bru:t] けもの、畜生。　**villain** [vílən] 悪党。　**villainous** [vílənəs] 兇悪な。　**7. puss** [pus] 猫。　**all at once** 突然。　**shrill** 鋭い。　**cling** しがみつく。　**9. labyrinth** [lǽbərinθ] 迷宮。　**10. darling** [dá:liŋ] かわいい者。

**11.**　Railway accidents are rare, marvellously rare, when one thinks of *those networks of railroads* that are enough to make one's head swim to look at them.　　　　　　　　　(*Max O'Rell*)

**12.**　She was *a fine figure of a woman* and I could well believe that in youth she had been beautiful.　　　　　　　　(*Maugham*)

**13.**　Hitherto he had been in *a perfect barrack of a dormitory* that contained at least twenty beds.　　　　　　　　　(東大)

**14.**　The other day, when Typhoon No. 11 battered the Kanto area, we had *a devil of time*, what with two of the windows blown in, and the roof leaking in half a dozen places.

**15.**　"Look here, madam," he cried out, "*that idiot of a maid of yours* has only packed one silk stocking for my two legs."　　　　　　　　　　　　　　　　　　　　　　(九州工大)

---

( 3 )

(a)　**The bamboo** is a kind of grass.
(b)　What is learned in **the cradle** is carried to **the grave**.

【訳】　(a)　竹は草の一種である。
　　　 (b)　赤ん坊のときに覚えたことは死ぬまで忘れない。

〖解 説〗　the は「この」「あの」「その」など特定のものを指すのが本来であるが、転じて特別の意味に用いられる場合が二つある。

(a)　「**the ＋ 単数形の普通名詞**」の形が その類全体を代表することが

---

11. **marvellously** [máːviləsli] ふしぎなほど。　**head swim** 頭がくらくらする。　13. **barrack** 兵舎。　**dormitory** 寄宿寮。　**contain** 入れている。　14. **batter** たたく。　**what with ... and ...** や～何やで。　**leak** [liːk] 雨もりがする。

(3)　**bamboo** [bæmbúː] 竹。　**cradle** [kréidl] ゆりかご。　**grave** [greiv] 墓場。

ある(いわゆる代表単数)。たとえば上例 the bamboo はこの竹とか、あの竹とかある特定の竹をさすのではなく、「一般に竹というもの」の意味である。類例:—

　**The horse** is a useful animal.＝Horses are useful animals.
　　(馬は有用な動物だ)
　**The wise man** does not court danger.
　　(君子は危きに近よらず)
　By whom was **the phonograph** invented?
　　(蓄音機はだれが発明したか)

　(b)　「**the＋単数形の普通名詞**」の形はまた抽象の観念をあらわすことがある。すなわち

　**the cradle＝infancy**
　**the grave＝death**

というような意味で「ゆりかご」「墓」という具体のものをもって「幼年時代」、「死」という抽象観念をあらわしたものである。しかし訳す場合に普通名詞のまま直訳しても意味のよく通じることもある。類例:—

　**The pen** is mightier than **the sword**.
　　(筆は剣より強い＝文は武にまさる)
　He gave up **the sword** for **the plough**.
　　(彼は剣をなげうって犂($\frac{1}{2}$)を執った＝軍人をやめて農夫となった)
　When one is reduced to poverty **the beggar** (＝the mean side of human nature) will come out.
　　(人は貧乏すると乞食根性が出るものだ)
　He has very much of **the diplomatist** in him.
　　(彼にはひじょうに外交家肌がある＝策士だ)

　**the heart** (情)　　　　　　**the head** (知力)
　**the ear** (聴覚)　　　　　　**the father** (父としての情)

　〚注　意〛　この the が分量をあらわす much, some などに変わること

---

**court** [kɔːt] (危険など)を求める。　**phonograph** [fóunəɡræf] (古い蠟($\frac{3}{5}$)管式の)蓄音器。今のは gramophone.　**infancy** [ínfənsi] 幼年期。　**sword** [sɔːd] 剣。 **plough** [plau] すき(農具)。　**be reduced to poverty** 貧窮におちいる。　**diplomatist** [diplóumətist] 外交官。

がある。類例:—

 There is **much beast** and **some devil** in man.
 （人間には獣的なところがたぶんにあり、また悪魔的なところもいくぶんある）

---

**16.** *The man on the street* has heard that this second industrial revolution (*i.e.* the Automation Revolution) will refashion his life, but rumors about "push-button factories" cause him to worry about the future of his job. 　　　　　　（日本女子大）

**17.** If *the boy* sows the seeds of moral or physical ill health, *the man* will reap the bitter harvest.

**18.** When promises have been made, fulfil not only *the letter*, but the spirit of that which they agreed to perform.

**19.** *The novelist* is dead in the man who has become aware of the triviality of human affairs. 　　　　　　(*Maugham*)

**20.** I look upon indolence as a sort of suicide; for *the man* is effectually destroyed, though the appetite of *the brute* may survive. 　　　　　　(*Chesterfield*)

**21.** "Philadelphia?" said she, and all *the mother* suffused her eyes. "If you live in Philadelphia, perhaps you know our Ben."

**22.** His pity and sympathy were awakened by the eloquent words of compassion and the strong appeal for mercy; and forgetting *the judge* in *the man and father*, he sprang from his chair.

---

**16. refashion** 造りかえる。 **push-button** 押しボタン式の。 **worry** 心配する。
**17. sow** [sou] 蒔(ま)く。 **reap** [riːp] 刈り取る。 **18. letter** 字句。 **perform** [pəfɔ́ːm] 遂行する。 **19. triviality** つまらないこと。 **20. indolence** [índələns] 怠惰。 **suicide** [sjúisaid] 自殺。 **effectually** 効果的に、実際的には。 **appetite** [ǽpitait] 欲望。 **survive** [səːváiv] 生き残る。 **21. suffuse** [səfjúːz] 満たす。
**22. eloquent** [éləkwənt] 雄弁な。 **compassion** [kəmpǽʃən] あわれみ。

**23.** At a crisis of this sort, *the beggar* was uppermost in him, and *the man of genius* hid his head with confusion. (*Stevenson*)

**24.** Reading is essential, and a practical book can help; but unless you have the germ of *the writer* in you, the unbreakable will to write, you will get nowhere.

**25.** There was enough of *the schoolboy* still in Mallinson to make him respond to the curt command of a senior, though he was obviously in poor control of himself. (*Hilton*)

---

## (4)

(a) **The rich** are not always happy.
(b) **The good** and **the beautiful** do not always go together.

【訳】 (a) 富んでいる者必ずしも幸福とはかぎらない。
(b) 善と美とは必ずしも相伴うわけではない。

〖解 説〗 (a) 「the＋形容詞＝複数の普通名詞」と見るべき場合。

**the rich**＝rich men　　　**the learned**＝learned men
**the wise**＝wise persons　　**the ignorant**＝ignorant people

類例：—

**The old** cannot enter into the feelings of **the young**.
　(老人には若い人の感情を酌(く)むことはできない)

〖注 意〗 この形が単数の意味に用いられる場合も二、三ある。例：—

**the accused** （告訴された人、刑事被告）
**the unknown** （知られていない人、または事実）

---

23. **crisis** [kráisis] 危機。 **uppermost** 一番上に、まっ先きに。 **confusion** [kənfjúːʒən] 狼狽(ろうばい)。 24. **germ** [dʒəːm] 萌芽。 **will** 意志。 **get nowhere** なんの結果も得られない。 25. **respond** [rispónd] 応答する。 **curt** [kəːt] ぶっきらぼうな。 **obviously** あきらかに。 **poor control** 不十分な抑制。

比較:—
- **the dead**＝死んだ人々。(複数)
- **the deceased**＝死んだ人、故人。(単数)

None but *the brave* deserve *the fair*. (*Dryden*)
(勇者のみが美人を得るにふさわしい)

(b)「**the**＋形容詞＝抽象名詞」と見るべき場合。
- **the true**＝truth (真)
- **the good**＝goodness (善)
- **the beautiful**＝beauty (美)

類例:—
There is but a step from **the sublime** to the ridiculous.
(荘厳と滑稽(訟)とはただ一歩のへだたり[紙一重]である)

〖注 意〗 この形が具体的な物の一部分を示すことがある。類例:—
**the yellow** of an egg＝卵の黄身。

---

**26.** Among the many problems facing our modern civilization, the fate of *the aged* is certainly one of the foremost in the public mind, judging by the number of articles on this subject carried by magazines and newspapers. (九州大)

**27.** Never speak ill of *the absent* or of anybody else unless you are sure they deserve it; and, not then, unless it is necessary for their amendment.

**28.** In a totalitarian state these questions lead directly to a control of the entire educational process; *the capable* are to be sorted out and educated for the different professions according to the nation's need for these professions. (*J. Conant*)

---

(4) **sublime** [səbláim] 荘厳な。 **ridiculous** [ridíkjuləs] こっけいな。 **26. facing** 直面する。**foremost** まっ先きの。 **27. deserve it** 悪口に値する。**not then** その場合でも...するな。 **necessary** [nésisəri] 必要な。 **amendment** [əméndmənt] 悔い改め。 **28. totalitarian** [toutælitéəriən] 全体主義の。 **be sorted** えり分けられる。 **according to** ～に応じて。

**29.** In all ages it (*i.e.* poetry) has been especially the concern of *the educated, the intelligent, the sensitive*, though it has appealed also, in its simpler forms, to *the uneducated* and to children. (日本女子大)

**30.** Among the objectives which the new legislation sought to achieve was the widening of opportunity for children of *the less well-to-do*.

**31.** By moral power we may sway the hearts of men in thousands of millions through thousands of years, as *the great and good* have done and will do.

**32.** *The active* commonly do more than they are bound to do; *the indolent* less.

**33.** The truth was that she had found a great many sad things in the course of her work among *the poor* of the little village that appeared so picturesque when it was seen from the hillside.

**34.** A youth strives after *the impossible*, and he is apt to break his heart because he has never even touched it, but nevertheless his whole life is the sweeter for the striving. (東京女子大)

**35.** He would often leave *the right* to pursue *the expedient*.

---

29. **concern** 関心事。 **sensitive** 感じやすい。 **appeal to** ~に訴える、好かれる。 30. **Among** one of と考える。 **legislation** [lèdʒisléiʃən] 立法。 **sought** seek の過去。 **well-to-do** 暮しが楽な。 31. **sway** 動かす、感動させる。 33. **in the course of** ...しているうちに、...を通じて。 **picturesque** [pìktʃərésk] 絵のように美しい。 34. **strive after** 求めて努力する。 **break one's heart** 落胆する。 **the sweeter** の the は「それだけ」の意味。 35. **pursue** [pəsjúː] 追求する。 **expedient** [ikspíːdiənt] 便宜な。

(5)

- (a) He is **honesty itself.**
- (b) He is **the incarnation of avarice.**
- (c) I am **all attention.**

【訳】 (a) 正直とはああいう人間をいうのだ。
(b) あいつは欲の固まりだ。
(c) 私は一心不乱に注意しています。

〖解説〗 (a) 「抽象名詞＋**itself**」の形は、形容詞に very; extremely; exceedingly などをつけて強めたものと同じ意味になる。たとえば

He is **honesty itself.**

(彼は正直そのもの＝正直の権化(ごんげ)＝ひじょうに正直だ)

のような関係で、つまり He is *extremely honest.* の意味となる。類例：—

He is **cruelty itself.**

(残忍きわまるやつだ)

She is **neatness itself.**

(彼女はほんとにさっぱりしたふうをしている)

(b) He is **the incarnation of avarice.**＝He is *avarice itself.*

(彼は欲の権化＝ひじょうに欲が深い)

という関係になる。なお incarnation とほぼ同じ意味の抽象名詞を用いて the embodiment of; the personification of; the perfection of; the image of など、それからまた普通名詞を用いて a paragon of; a prodigy of; a model of; a picture of など、あるいは形容詞にして incarnate; personified; embodied などを用いた例もたくさんある。例：—

He is *the personification of* patriotism.＝He is *patriotism personified.*

(彼は愛国心の権化だ)

---

(5) **incarnation** [ìnkɑːnéiʃən] 化身(けしん)。 **avarice** [ǽvəris] 貪(どん)欲。 **cruelty** [krúː(ː)əlti] 残酷。 **embodiment** [imbɔ́dimənt] 具体化物。 **personification** [pəːsɔ̀nifikéiʃən] 擬人。 **perfection** [pəfékʃən] 典型。 **image** [ímidʒ] 像。 **paragon** [pǽrəgən] 模範。 **prodigy** [prɔ́didʒi] 奇才。 **incarnate** [inkɑ́ːnit] 体現した。 **patriotism** [pǽtriətizm] 愛国心。

（c）「**all**＋抽象名詞」の形は(a)の形とまったく同じ意に用いられる。
　I am **all attention**.＝I am *full of attention*.
　　（私は全身ことごとく注意だ＝注意に満ちている）
という関係で、つまり I am *very attentive*. ということになる。類例：—
　He is **all kindness**.＝He is *kindness itself*.＝He is *extremely kind*.
　　（彼はひじょうに親切だ）
　The children are **all eagerness** to go to the festival.
　　（こどもたちはしきりにお祭りに行きたがっている）
　I shall be **all anxiety** till I hear from you.
　　（おたよりのあるまでは、まあ私どんなに心配でしょう）

〖注　意〗　（c）の形にならって、複数普通名詞に all を付けて用いることがある。
　He was **all eyes and ears**.＝He was **all attention**.
　　（体じゅうを眼と耳にして注意していた）
　She was **all smiles**.
　　（満面に笑みをたたえていた、笑みこぼれるばかりであった）

---

**36.**　The officers were *all attention* as Fritz, holding his father's hand, related his story.

**37.**　From the crown of his head to the sole of his foot, he is *all mirth*.
(*Shakespeare*)

**38.**　Perhaps I ought to remember that she is very young, a mere girl, and make allowances.　She is *all interest, eagerness, vivacity;* the world is to her a charm, a wonder, a mystery, a joy.
(*Mark Twain*)

**39.**　At that very moment Marie and Pierre came into the workshop, *all chatter and laughter*, delighted with their excursion.
(*Zola*)

---

**anxiety** [æŋzáiəti] 心配。　**36. relate** [reléit] 語る。　**37. crown** [kraun] 頭のてっぺん。　**sole** [soul] 足の裏。　**mirth** 歓喜、陽気。　**38. allowances** 斟酌(しんしゃく)、手心[を加える]。　**vivacity** [vivǽsiti] 活発さ。　**39. excursion** 遠足。

**40.** When I was a boy, I knew an old gentleman who used to say the most ferocious things about his landlady behind her back, but who was *all smiles and obeisance* as soon as she came into the room. (*Lynd*)

**41.** When I spoke to him kindly he was *all smiles* in a moment.

**42.** Just at present I have got no use for that tongue of yours. You may be *all eyes and ears*, the more the better.

(*L. Linch*)

**43.** While she was waiting for the tinkling of the bell *all nerves*, suddenly he stood before her. (*Maugham*)

**44.** Washington was *discretion itself* in the use of speech, never taking advantage of an opponent, or seeking a short-lived triumph in a debate.

**45.** Seated in his hereditary elbow chair, and looking around him like the sun of a system, beaming warmth and gladness to every heart, the old squire was *hospitality itself*. (*Irving*)

**46.** Francis I, *the incarnation of strong ambitions and weak convictions*, was sovereign of France at the age of twenty.

**47.** Mothers-in-law are forever a target for men's sarcasms. Step-mothers are supposed to be *the embodiment of everything that is mean*. (*Max O'Rell*)

**48.** The Scotchman, still more than the Englishman, is *common sense personified*. (*Max O'Rell*)

---

40. **ferocious** [fəróuʃəs] ひどい。 **behind one's back** 陰で。 **obeisance** [oubéisəns] おじぎ。 42. **tongue** [tʌŋ] 舌。 43. **tinkling** チンチン鳴ること。 44. **discretion** [diskréʃən] 分別。 **take advantage of** つけこむ。 **opponent** [əpóunənt] 相手。 **triumph** [tráiəmf] 勝利。 **debate** [dibéit] 討論。 45. **hereditary** [hiréditəri] 世襲の。 **system** 系、系統。 **beam** [bi:m] (*v.t.*) 発散する。 **squire** 郷士。 **hospitality** [hɔ̀spitǽliti] 歓待。 46. **conviction** [kənvíkʃən] 信念。 **sovereign** [sɔ́vrin] 君主。 47. **forever** [fərévə] 永久に。 **target** [tá:git] 標的。 **sarcasm** [sá:kæzm] 冷評。 48. **personify** 具体化する。

**49.** Falkland and Caleb Williams are *the mere impersonation of the unbounded love of reputation and irresistible curiosity.* (*Lamb*)

**50.** In every relation of life he was not only above reproach, he was much more than that: he was *a model of what men ought to be*, yet seldom are, in their conduct towards others.

## ( 6 )

Carbonic acid (gas) is not a poison **in itself.**

【訳】 炭酸ガスはそのものは本来毒ではない。

〖解 説〗 **in itself**＝in its own nature; apart from its surroundings (その物自身の性質において、周囲の関係を離れて)

上の例でいえば炭酸ガスというものはなるほどそれを呼吸すれば窒息するということもあるが、そういう関係を離れて炭酸ガスその物本来の性質においては有毒でないという意味である。「その物本来は」とか「その物だけで」などと訳して当たることが多い。類例：——

A thing good **in itself** may become harmful by its use.
(本来は善いものでも用い方によっては悪くもなる)

---

**51.** To do anything because others do it, and not because the thing is good, or kind, or honest *in itself*, is to give up all moral control upon yourself, and go in great haste to the devil with the majority.

**52.** A fine courtesy is a fortune *in itself*. The good man-

---

49. **unbounded** 無限の。　**reputation** [rèpjutéiʃən] 名声。　**irresistible** [ìrizístibl] 抵抗しがたい。　**curiosity** [kjùəriɔ́siti] 好奇心。　50. **reproach** [ripróutʃ] 非難。　**are** 主語は men。
(6) **carbonic** [kɑ:bɔ́nik] 炭素の。　**acid** [ǽsid] 酸。　**poison** [pɔ́izn] 毒。
51. **give up** 放棄する。　**in great haste** 大急ぎで。　**devil** [dévil] 悪魔。
**majority** [mədʒɔ́riti] 大多数(の人間)。　52. **courtesy** [kə́:tisi] 礼節。

nered can do without riches, for they have passports everywhere.

(*Chesterfield*)

**53.** The carriage stopped, and the voice of Mrs. Squeers was heard, ordering a glass of spirits for somebody, which was *in itself* a sufficient sign that something extraordinary had happened.

**54.** Agriculture is one of the most exhausting forms of toil, and *in itself*, by no means conducive to spiritual development; that it played a civilizing part in the history of the world is merely due to the fact that, by creating wealth, it freed a portion of mankind from the labour of the plough.

**55.** It was 'only one thing, one simple thing; that some hundreds of millions of men and women should set themselves to do good instead of evil and reap therefrom blessings instead of curses.' If that is really all we need we are saved. For we have it, or almost have it, already. But alas, *in itself* it is not enough.

(*Gilbert Murray*)

**56.** Our society is founded not upon the cold and bloodless "economic man" of the Marxist but upon a faith in man as an end *in himself*.

---

**do without** なしですます。 **passport** [páːspɔːt] 旅行免状。 **53. order** 命じる、注文する。 **spirits** 火酒、強酒。 **extraordinary** [ikstrɔ́ːdinəri] 異常な。 **54. exhausting** [igzɔ́ːstiŋ] 疲れさせる、骨の折れる。 **toil** 労役。 **by no means** けっして...でない。 **conducive** [kəndjúːsiv] みちびく、助成する。 **that it played ...** (名詞節)。 **is due to ...** による。 **mankind** [mænkáind] 人類。 **plough** すき[農具]。 **55. set themselves to do** するつもりになる。 **reap** 刈りとる。 **therefrom** そこから。 **curses** [kə́ːsiz] 災禍。 **56. Marxist** [máːksist] マルクス主義者。 **is founded** 建てられている。

## (7)

(a) I live all **by myself.**
(b) I cannot finish it **by myself.**

【訳】（a）ぼくはまったくの<u>ひとり</u>住まいだ。
　　　（b）<u>ぼくひとりでは</u>仕上がらない。

〖解説〗（a）**by oneself**=separated from others; alone （別に離れて；ひとりで）

**by** は元来「そば」「かたわら」の意味であるから I sat **by him.** は「私は彼のかたわらにすわった」である。こんどは I sat **by myself.** というと「自分で自分のかたわらにすわった」、つまり、No one sat **by me.** (だれもぼくのかたわらにすわらなかった)、すなわち自分ひとり離れてすわったことになるのである。類例：—

With whom did you go?—I went all **by myself.**
　　（君はだれと行ったか——ぼくはまったくひとりで行った）

注意すべきことは alone が必ずしも「ひとり」の意味でないと同様に、「**by＋再帰代名詞**」の形式にも by ourselves とか by themselves とか複数の場合の有り得ることである、たとえば

We were left **alone.** （私たちだけ後に残った）

というのは、他の者はみな去って自分たちだけ残ったという意味で、残ったのが二人の場合ならば、「二人さし向かいに」などと訳してよい。同様に

The Chinese like to live **by themselves.**
　　（中国人は好んで自分たちだけ別に住む）

といえば、他国人を交えず自分たちだけ別に、いわゆる南京町を作ることをいう。

（b）**by oneself**=without others' help （他人の助力なしに）

この場合には次の章に述べる for oneself と相通じて、はっきりと区別がつけにくい。比較：—

---

(7) **separate** [sépəreit] 分離する。**Chinese** [tʃainíːz] 中国人。

(a) I often take a walk **by myself.**
  (ぼくはよくひとりで散歩する)
(b) I did it all **by myself.**
  (ぼくは全然ひとりでそれをやった)

**57.** "George, I am going to eat my supper *by myself*, after this," said little Harry.

"I don't believe you will," replied his brother.

"Then I wish every one would stop scolding me at table."

**58.** One morning he had to go ashore in his boat to get food and oil. He did not like to leave his daughter *by herself;* but the sea was calm, and he was sure that he would soon be back.

**59.** Frequently, when the weather was calm, immediately after dinner, I jumped *by myself* into a little boat and rowed out into the middle of the lake. (北海道大)

**60.** The land *by itself* would have produced a race of peasants and landowners, but the sea, by adding imagination and the spirit of adventure, has made sailors, traders, adventurers, conquerors, colonizers and empire-builders of them, and turned their little island into the mother country of the Empire which this same sea holds together.

**61.** I want you to make me responsible for some of the work of the house. I shall be so pleased to feel that you can trust

---

57. **reply** [riplái] 答える。 **scold** [skould] 叱る。 58. **be back** もどる。
59. **frequently** しばしば。 **immediately** じきに。 60. **peasant** [pézənt] 百姓。farmer はむしろ「地主」に近い。**adventurer** [ədvéntʃərə] 冒険家。**conqueror** [kóŋkərə] 征服者。 **colonizer** [kólənaizə] 植民地開拓者。 **empire** [émpaiə] 帝国。 **of them** は made~of them と続く。them=peasants and landowners. **hold together**=keep united 結合しておく。 61. **responsible** [rispónsibl] 責任ある。

me to do something *all by myself*.

**62.** How is modern Man going to fill the spiritual vacuum in his soul? This vacuum has been created by the rise of modern science. Science has expelled religion in its traditional forms; yet science, *by itself*, is incapable of filling the void. (*A. Toynbee*)

**63.** Letters in themselves are not language, but merely symbols which are used for the sounds of which language is composed. There is no life or meaning in written symbols *by themselves;* but they must be translated, as it were, into the sounds for which they stand before they become language or have any meaning.

---

## (8)

(a) I like to do everything **for myself.**
(b) He loves labour **for itself.**

【訳】 (a) ぼくは何でも自分ですることが好きだ。
　　　(b) 彼は労働そのものを愛する＝働くのが好きで働く。

〖解 説〗 (a) **for oneself**＝**independent of others' help; by one's own efforts** (他人の力を借りずに、独力で)

**for** は目的を示すから、I will do it **for you.** は「私がお前のためにしてやろう」あるいは「お前にかわってしてやろう」などの意味である。そこで、I will do it **for myself.** は「自分で自分のためにする」意味でとりもなおさず「人にしてもらわず、独力でする」ことである。参考：—

---

62. **vacuum** [vǽkjuəm] 真空、空虚。 **rise** ぼっ興。 **expel** 追い出す。 **traditional** 伝統的な、従来の。 **void** 空虚。 63. **symbol** [símbəl] 記号。 **is composed of ...** で成り立っている。 **meaning** [míːniŋ] 意味。 **as it were** いわば。 **stand for** 表象する。

Shall I do it **for you**?
＝ぼくがしてあげましょうか。
No, I will do it **for myself**.
＝いや、自分でします。
He can do everything **for himself**.
＝彼は何でも自分ですることができる。
He can cook **his own food** and make **his own clothes**.
＝自分で自分の食物をこしらえられるし、自分で自分の着物を縫うことができる。

〖注 意〗 his と for himself と重複して「自分で自分の...」の意味となるような場合に his own の構文に変わるのである。すなわち

He can cook **his own** food. [＝He can cook **his** food **for himself**.]

類例：—

I will simply state the facts, and leave every one to **judge for himself**.
（私は単に事実を述べるにとどめ、あとは各人の判断に任せる）
Now you **see for yourself**. Are you convinced?
（さあごらんのとおりです。納得(なっとく)が行きましたか）
The fact **speaks for itself**.
（事実がものをいっている）
Look after the boy till he can **shift for himself**.
（子供の自活のできるまで世話を見てやりなさい）
He is old enough to **do for himself**.
（彼はもう独立してもよい年だ）

to judge for oneself は他人の意見などを採用するのでなく自分自身で判断すること。to see for oneself は見た人の話など聞くのでなく自分自身で実際に見ること。The fact speaks for itself. は事実みずから語る、すなわち self-evident (自明) の事実などという意味。to shift for oneself (＝to provide for *or* take care of oneself) は一つの成句になっている。

---

(8) **clothes** [klouðz] 着物。 **state** 述べる。 **leave** まかせる。 **judge** 判断する。 **convince** [kənvíns] 説得する、納得(なっとく)させる。 **look after** めんどうをみる。 **shift** やりくりする。 **evident** [évidənt] 明白な。

どうにかして自分で自分の世話をする、すなわち「みずから身を処する」「自活する」などの意味である。

[注意] for oneself が上述のような意味とはならず、「自分のために」と訳されるべき場合ももちろんある。類例:—

You may keep the money **for yourself.**
(その金は自分のにして取っておきなさい)

(b) **for itself**=**for its own sake**

He loves labour **for itself.** は「彼は労働のために労働を愛する」、すなわち金がほしいとか、運動のためにするとか他に目的があるのではない、ただ働きたいから働く、働くのが道楽(どうらく)という意味である。類例:—

She loves him **for himself.**
([その人の金を愛するのでもない、権力を愛するのでもない] その男を愛するのである)

We should practise virtue **for its own sake.**
([ほめられたさにするのではいけない] 徳のために徳を行うべきである)

---

**64.** He was a very ingenious boy, and resolved to manufacture paintbrushes *for himself*.

**65.** The boy who did it *for himself* has taken a stride upward, and what is better still, has gained strength for other and better ones.

**66.** There was no time to consult his mother. She was now some little way off. He must act *for himself* and on his own judgment for the first time in his life. (*Florence Montgomery*)

**67.** Children need a stable framework for their lives; they

---

**practise** [præktis] 実行する。
64. **ingenious** [indʒíːniəs] 器用な、発明の才ある。 **resolve** 決心する。 **manufacture** [mænjufǽktʃə] 製造する。 65. **a stride upward** 向上の一歩。 **what is better still** もっとよいことには。(副詞節) 66. **consult** [kənsʌ́lt] 相談する。 **off** 離れて。 67. **stable** 安定した。 **framework** わく組。

like to know where they are and know what is expected of them; they do not want to decide everything *for themselves*.

(大阪学芸大)

68. I want you know that the decision I have made has been mine and mine alone. This was a thing I had to judge entirely *for myself*.

69. The best help is not to bear the troubles of others *for them*, but to inspire them with courage and energy to bear their own burdens *for themselves*, and meet the difficulties of life bravely.

70. Each man *for himself* and God for us all. (*Proverb*)

71. The various Russian dictators, Lenin, Trotsky, Stalin, might be at war with one another, but each made the same claim *for himself* and for Russia. (*Gilbert Murray*)

72. Mr. Larkin sprang forward and seized the deserted oar. "Lie down in the bottom of the boat," said he to the man; "and, captain, take the other oar; we must row *for ourselves*."

73. Mr. Larkin had received the glass from my hand to take a look *for himself*.

74. The whole spirit in which education is conducted needs to be changed, in order that children may be encouraged to think and feel *for themselves*, not to acquiesce passively in thoughts and feelings of others.

75. If, instead of finding *for ourselves* the words that will

---

68. **decision** [disíʒən] 決定。 **entirely** [intáiəli] まったく。 69. **bear** [bɛə] 堪える。 **inspire** [inspáiə] 吹きこむ、鼓舞する。 71. **various** いろいろの。 **dictator** 独裁者。 **be at war with** 相争う。 **claim** 要求、主張。 72. **desert** [dizə́:t] 棄てる。 **oar** [ɔ:] オール。 **row** [rou] 漕ぐ。 74. **conduct** [kəndʌ́kt] 行う。 **encourage** 奨励する。 **acquiesce** [æ̀kwiés] 甘んじて服する。 **passively** 受身に。

precisely and exactly and truly express our ideas, we simply adopt the words and phrases of other writers, we are like a man who goes to the slop-dealer for a suit of clothes, instead of being properly fitted by an intelligent clothier. Ready-made clothes fit everybody; and nobody.

**76.** You have opened *for yourself* the way to success. You must persevere if you desire to reach your goal; otherwise be assured that the more splendid the beginning, the darker will the end be.

**77.** Some creatures cast their eggs as chance directs them, and think of them no farther;...others hatch their eggs and tend the birth, till it is able to shift *for itself*. (*Addison*)

**78.** The elder boys had been well educated while the father lived, but at his death the younger members had to shift *for themselves*.

**79.** The best lover of boating follows it *for itself*, as a lover of reading does not read only for a degree. (*Hamerton*)

**80.** In short, so far from practising honesty *for its own sake*, he has not yet learned that honesty is, even from a selfish point of view, the best policy.

**81.** He wanted to make use of his apprentice's talents *for*

---

75. **precisely** 精密に。**adopt** [ədɔ́pt] 採り入れる。**slop-dealer** [slɔ́pdi:lə] 出来合い服屋。**be fitted** 仮縫いをして体に合わせてもらう。**intelligent** そう明な。**clothier** [klóuðiə] 洋服屋。76. **persevere** [pə̀:sivíə] 忍耐する。**goal** [goul] 決勝点、目的。**otherwise** そうでなければ。**be assured** 信じなさい。**the more...the darker** the more, the better の公式の応用。**splendid** [spléndid] 光輝ある。77. **creature** [krí:tʃə] 生物。**cast** 生む。**chance** 運、偶然。**hatch** 卵からかえす。**tend** 世話する。**shift** やりくりする、やって行く。79. **follows** 従事する。**degree** [digrí:] 学位。80. **in short** 要するに。**so far from...** どころでなく。**point of view** 見地、立場。**policy** [pɔ́lisi] 政策。81. **make use of** 利用する。**apprentice** [əpréntis] 年期小僧。

*himself.*

**82.** With greater pressure on their resources the Icelandic fishermen have shown an increasing desire to keep as much of these fishing grounds as possible *for themselves.*

(9)

(a) I did not call him; he woke up **of himself.**
(b) The boy ran away from school, but returned **of his own accord.**

【訳】(a) 私が起こしたのではない、彼はひとりでに眼をさましたのだ。
(b) 子供が学校から逃げたが、またひとりで帰って来た。

〖解説〗(a) **of oneself**=without external cause; spontaneously
=ひとりでに；自然に
(b) **of one's own accord**=of one's own free will
=自分が承知で；自分の意志で

前者は無意識の自発を示し、後者は自由意志を示す。すなわち (a) の例では眼をさまそうと思ってさましたのではない、自然にさめたのである。(b) の例においては子供が自分で帰ろうと思って帰ってきたので、人からしいられたのではないという意味である。類例：—

The door opened **of itself.**
（戸がひとりでに開いた）
I did not put out the light; it went out **of itself.**
（私が灯火を消したのではない、ひとりでに消えたのだ）
Weeds grow **of themselves.**
（雑草は蒔(ま)かないのにひとりでにはえる）

---

**82. pressure on their resources** 資源に対する圧迫。**fishing ground** 漁場。
(9) **one's own accord** [əkɔ́ːd] 自発。**spontaneously** [spɔntéinjəsli] 自然に。

The man has left **of his own free will,** so I am not bound to keep to my agreement.

（彼は自分の勝手で去ったのだから、私は契約を守る義務はない）

〖注　意〗　無生物の主語に of its own accord を用いた例を往々見るがそれは主語を擬人化して意志あるもののように見たのである。類例：—

The wind blew the door to, or it shut **of its own accord**; one or the other.

（風が吹いて戸を閉めたのか、戸が勝手に閉まったのか、どちらかである）

〖注　意〗　この **to** は to its place のような気持で、push *or* shut the door to などと使われる。**one or the other** は The case was either the one or the other. のように考えればよい。

---

**83.**　The old dame set the mill upon the table, and said very slowly:—

*Grind O Mill! do grind away!*
*Grind out some rolls, I beg and pray!*

The Mill began to turn round and round *of itself*, and soon ground out a roll hot from the oven.

**84.**　When we are not too anxious about happiness and unhappiness, but devote ourselves to the strict and unsparing performance of duty, then happiness comes *of itself*.

**85.**　Ali Baba went boldly into the cave, and gathered as much of the gold coin, which was in bags, as he thought his three asses could carry. When he had loaded them with the bags,

---

83. **dame** [deim] 婦人。**mill** ひきうす。**grind** [graind] ひく、つぶす。**away** せっせと。**rolls** 巻きパン。**oven** [ʌvn] 窯(かま)。 84. **anxious** [ǽŋkʃəs] 気にかける。**devote oneself to** 〜に身をささげる。**unsparing** [ʌnspέəriŋ] 骨身を惜しまない。**performance** [pəfɔ́:məns] 遂行。 85. **boldly** [bóuldli] 大胆に。**as much** は as he thought... にかかる。**load** 荷を積む。**pass in and out** はいったり出たりする。

he laid wood over them in such a manner that they could not be seen. When he had passed in and out as often as he wished, he stood before the door; and on his pronouncing the words, "Shut, Sesame!" the door closed *of itself*.

**86.** The scientist looks for order in the appearances of nature by exploring likeness. For order does not display itself *of itself*, it is not there for the mere looking. (横浜市立大)

**87.** You know the toy made like a mouse, which, when you touch it in particular place, runs away apparently *of its own accord*, as if it were alive.

**88.** French people do it when forced by necessity, but they do it with a sad heart; English people *of their own free will* have the courage to sever old ties and begin new experiments of life. (*Hamerton*)

**89.** Some persons thought that, after its fright had passed over, the animal would return *of its own accord*.

**90.** He must have done it at somebody's instigation; he is not the man to do such a thing *of his own head*.

## (10)

(a) He often **talks to himself** when he is alone.
(b) I **have** this big room all **to myself**.

---

**laid** [leid] lay の過去および過去分詞。 **pronounce** [prənáuns] 発音する。 **sesame** [sésəmi] ごま。 **86. order** 秩序。 **appearances** 現象。 **explore** 探し求める。 **likeness** 類似。 **display** 表示する。 **87. particular** [pətíkjulə] 特別の。 **apparently** [əpǽrəntli] 外見上。 **as if** あたかも...のように。 **88. when forced** しいられた時。 **sever** [sévə] 切り離す。 **tie** きずな。 **experiment** [ikspérimənt] 実験。 **89. fright** [frait] 恐怖。 **pass over** すぎ去る。 **90. instigation** [ìnstigéiʃən] 扇動。

【訳】 (a) 彼はひとりでいるときに、よくひとりごとを言う。
(b) 私はこの大きいへやをまったく独占している。

〖解 説〗 (a) **to talk to oneself** は「自分に向かって話をする」、すなわち「ひとりしゃべり」で、いささか気ちがいじみているが、**to say to oneself** は「自分に向かっていう」で、「ひとりごと」の意にもなるが、通例は「心中で言う」「ひとり思うに」など訳して当たる。類例：—

　**to laugh to oneself** (ひとり笑う)
　**to chuckle to oneself** (ひとりほくそえむ)
　**to picture to oneself** (心にえがく)
(b) **to have to oneself** (独占する)

類例：—
　**to keep** the secret **to oneself**
　　(秘密を自分ひとりに守る；秘して言わない)
　**to leave** a person **to himself** (放任しておく)
　**to take credit to oneself** for... (...を自分のてがらとする)

---

**91.** "How beautiful she looks!" *said* Ben *to himself*.

**92.** "What an iron race, these Scots!" I have often *exclaimed to myself*. "Who could hope to compete with them?"
*(Max O'Rell)*

**93.** There (*i.e.* in the hospital) I *had* a room *to myself*, as each officer had, and to lie there in that sweet sunny room and hear no groans but my own was almost like being in heaven. *(Max O'Rell)*

**94.** I drifted into the sitting-room, and *had* our guest *all to myself* for I don't know how many hours.

**95.** I knew all about the affair, but I *kept* the knowledge *to myself*.
*(T. B. Aldrich)*

---

92. **iron** [áiən] 鉄のような。 **compete** [kəmpíːt] 競う。 93. **officer** 士官。 **groans** うめき。 **but**=except。 94. **drift** ぶらっと行く。 **guest** [gest] 客。 **for** ...の間。 95. **knowledge** [nɔ́lidʒ] 知識。

**96.** If *left to himself*, he would have whistled his life away in perfect contentment. (*Irving*)

---

(11)

> He did it **himself.**

【訳】 彼は<u>自分自身で手を下して</u>した。

【解説】 自分で自分をとやかく言う場合に用いられる oneself は再帰目的語であるからセンテンスの構成上はぶくことはできない、たとえば He killed himself. (彼はわれとわが身を殺した; 自殺した)において himself を除いてはセンテンスを成さない。しかし oneself が単に語勢 (emphasis) の目的で用いられることがある、そういう場合にはそれをはぶいても文法上別にさしつかえない。He did it himself. の himself は単に He の意を強めるために用いられたのであるから、はぶいて He did it. だけでも完全なセンテンスである。

ここには oneself が意味を強めるために用いられた例をあげる。その場合にはいろいろ訳し方がある、**even** (さえも), **also** (もまた) など解すべき場合のほか、「そのもの自身」「自分自身で手を下して」「他ならぬそのもの」「他は知らずそのものだけは」など。類例:—

No man but has his faults; Confucius **himself** was not free from faults.

(だれ一人欠点のないものはない、孔子で<u>さえ</u>欠点を免れなかった)

I am going the same way **myself.**

(私<u>も</u>同じ方へ行くのです)

You had better go **yourself.**

(君は<u>自分で</u>行く方がよい)

---

**96.** whistle away 口笛を吹いて...すごす。 contentment [kənténtmənt] 満足。
(11) emphasis [émfəsis] 語勢。 Confucius [kənfúːʃiəs] 孔子。

**97.** On went the fire rushing and crashing through the woods. The heavens *themselves*, I thought, were frightened.

**98.** Sir William Thornhill, content with a little *himself*, permits his nephew to enjoy the rest. (*Goldsmith*)

**99.** Now an apple is, of course, an inanimate object; and therefore it could not move *itself*.

**100.** Yes, he found that there was some force outside of the apple *itself*.

**101.** Any piece of knowledge which the pupil has *himself* acquired, any problem which he has *himself* solved, becomes by virtue of the conquest much more thoroughly his than it could else be.

---

( 12 )

> He is **the very** man for you.

【訳】 彼は君にはおあつらえ向きの人物だ。

〖解 説〗 very が名詞の前につく場合はもちろん形容詞である。形容詞の very は (a) the, this, that, the same などに伴なって、「他のものでなくて、このもの、そのもの」など強くそのものをさすのに用いる場合と、(b) 名詞の意味を強めて、「...までも」「...がかえって」などの意味を示す場合とある。

( a ) **very=the same** すなわち同一物 (identity) を強調する場合。

---

97. **On went ...** 主語と述語の順をかえて、強勢の文としたもの。 98. **content** [kəntént] 満足して。 **permit** [pəmít] 許す。 **nephew** [névju] 甥(##)。 **the rest** 残りの財産。 99. **inanimate** [inǽnimit] 無生の。 **object** [ɔ́bdʒikt] 物体。 101. **pupil** [pjú:pil] 生徒。 **by virtue of** ...の力で、...のおかげで。 **conquest** [kɔ́ŋkwest] 征服。 **thoroughly** [θʌ́rəli] 徹底的に。 **else** そうしない場合に。 **be** の次に his を入れて解する。

(12) **identity** [aidéntiti] 同一なること。

類例:—

I started on **that very** day.
(私はちょうどその当日出発した)
This is **the very** purse that I lost.
(これがすなわちぼくのなくしたさいふだ)
He was killed on **the very** spot.
(その場を離れずず即死した)
（b） **very=even** or **oneself** と見られる場合。類例:—
The **very** stones cried out.
([無心の]石までさえも声を立てて叫んだ)
His **very** defects came to be held in esteem.
(彼の欠点まで尊重されるようになった)
His **very** vigour causes him to stumble.
(彼の勇気がかえって彼をつまずかせるようなことになる)

---

**102.** *The very* base of national feeling is respect for the past; for the best possessions of the people of a country are the memories they have in common. These memories constitute a sacred treasure that each individual ought to consider more precious than anything else he possesses.

**103.** The circumstances of which so many complain should be regarded as *the very* tools with which we are to work, the stepping stones we are to mount by. They are the wind and tide in the voyage of life, which the skilful mariner generally either takes advantage of or overcomes.

---

**defect** [difékt] 欠点。　**be held in esteem** 尊敬される。　**vigour** or **vigor** [vígə] 気力。　**102. base** 基盤、土台。　**possession** [pəzéʃən] 所有物。　**in common** 共通に。　**constitute** [kɔ́nstitjuːt] 構成する。　**sacred** [séikrid] 神聖な。　**precious** 貴い。　**103. circumstances** [sə́ːkəmstənsiz] 境遇。　**complain** [kəmpléin] **of** ...について泣き言を言う。　**be regarded as** ...と見なされる。　**stepping stones** 踏み石、踏み台。　**mount** 上へ昇る。　**mariner** [mǽrinə] 船乗り。　**take advantage of** 利用する。　**overcome** うち勝つ。

**104.** Ah, here's the thing I am after. Please get those things off, sir, and throw them in the fire. Do me the favor to put on this shirt and this suit; it's the thing, *the very thing*— plain, rich, modest, and just ducally nobby. (*Mark Twain*)

**105.** *The very* excellences of his character unfitted him for the conduct of a war. He was in fact a Peace Minister, forced into war by a panic and enthusiasm which he shared in a very small degree.

**106.** She stood grandly defiant, a queenly figure, her eyes fixed upon his as if she would read his *very* soul. (*Doyle*)

**107.** That person, old or young, who tries to be other than himself, makes a failure of life, yet many do *this very* thing.

**108.** It is now many years ago—but for *that very* reason the story is better worth hearing before it is quite forgotten.

**109.** *The very* difference in their characters produced an harmonious combination.

**110.** Through mathematics we learn on *the very* threshold a lesson which, if universally known and applied, would prevent most of the ills the world is liable to. (九州大)

**111.** *The very* things that Horace looked upon as hateful

---

104. **be after** 求める。 **favor** 親切な行為、好意。 **do me the favor to** どうぞ...してください。 **ducally** 公爵のような。<duke. **nobby**=smart. 105. **excellence** [éksələns] 卓越、長所。 **unfit** [ʌnfít] 不適当にする。 **conduct** 指揮。 **forced into** 無理に...へ押しやられた。 **panic** 恐怖、恐慌。 **enthusiasm** [inθjú:ziæzm] 熱狂。 **share** 分ちもつ。 **degree** 度合。 106. **defiant** [difáiənt] 反抗的に、ごうまんに。 **a queenly figure** これは defiant と同じく補語の役。 **fixed** 過去分詞の形。 **soul** [soul] 魂。 108. **worth hearing** 聞くだけの価値がある。 109. **harmonious** [ha:móunjəs] 調和した。 **combination** [kɔmbinéiʃən] 結合。 110. **threshold** [θréʃhould] しきい。 **universally** あまねく。 **applied** 適用される。 **prevent** 防止する。 **be liable to** おちいりやすい。 111. **look upon** 見なす。

were, in fact, the sources of his friend's most permanent enjoyment.

---

(13)

> The wisest man cannot know everything.

【訳】 どんな賢い人でも何でも知るということはできない。

〖解 説〗 最上級に even の意を加えて「どんな…でも」と訳してよい場合がしばしばある。類例：—

(Even) **the best** workman will blunder sometimes.
（どんな名工でも時に失策はあるものだ＝弘法にも筆の誤り）

---

**112.** "*The weakest* living creature," says Carlyle, "by concentrating his powers on a single object, can accomplish something; whereas *the strongest*, by dispersing his over many, may fail to accomplish anything. The drop, by continually falling, bores its passage through *the hardest* rock. The hasty torrent rushes over it with hideous uproar and leaves no trace behind."

**113.** There are circumstances in which *even the least energetic* of mankind learn to behave with vigor and decision; and *the most cautious* forget their prudence and embrace foolhardy resolutions.

---

source [sɔːs] 根源。 permanent [pə́ːmənənt] 永久の。
(13) blunder [blʌ́ndə] 大失策。 112. concentrate 集中する。 whereas [hwɛərǽz] しかるに、ところが。 disperse [dispə́ːs] 分散する。 accomplish 達成する。 bore [bɔː] 孔をあける。 passage 通路。 hasty torrent 急流。 hideous [hídiəs] おそろしい。 uproar [ʌ́prɔː] 騒ぎ。 trace 跡。 113. circumstance [sə́ːkəmstəns] 事情。 energetic [ènədʒétik] 活動的。 mankind [mǽnkáind] 人類。 behave 行動する。 vigor 元気。 decision 決断。 cautious [kɔ́ːʃəs] 用心深い。 prudence 慎重さ。 embrace [imbréis] 抱く。 foolhardy [fúːlhɑːdi] 無鉄砲な。 resolution 決心。

**114.** Poetry is as universal as language, and almost as ancient. *The most primitive* peoples have used it, and *the most civilized* have cultivated it. (日本女子大)

**115.** *The most important* ideas in the world can be printed and sold for a few cents, and if you get the ideas they are exactly as useful to you as if they had come out of a costly volume printed on fine paper and bound in silk.

**116.** *The best* teacher in *the best* college in the world cannot give a student an education. He can lead the way to the mine from which it can be dug, provide him with the proper tools, and show him how to use them. He can encourage him when disheartened, and spur him to more vigorous effort, but the student will own only so much of the precious metal as he digs for himself. (長崎大)

---

### (14)

> He is **the last person** to do such a thing.

【訳】 あの人はけっしてそんなことをしそうな人じゃない。

〖解 説〗 last＝least likely

そんなことをしそうな人をだんだんと指を折って数えてみると、彼はその最後の人、すなわち、「彼は最もそんなことをしそうもない人」ということになる。つまり一種の強い打消しである。類例：—

---

114. **universal** 普遍的。 **ancient** 古代からある。 **primitive** 原始的。 **cultivate** 発達につとめる。 115. **print** 印刷する。 **for** の代金で。 **costly** [kɔ́stli] 高価な。 **exactly** 正確に。 **come out of** から出てくる。 **bound** [baund] bind (綴じる)の過去分詞。 116. **mine** 鉱山、鉱坑。 **dig** 金銀などを掘る。 **provide** 提供する。 **proper** 適当な。 **disheartened** 落胆した。 **spur** 激励する。 **vigorous** 精力的な。 **own** 自分のものとする。 **precious metal** 貴金属。

Breach of promise is **the last thing** that he is likely to commit.
（破約などということはけっしてあの人のしそうなことじゃない）
This is **the last place** where I expected to have met you.
（まさかこんな所で君に会おうとは思わなかった）
You are **the last man** whom I expected to have met here.
（まさか君にここで会おうとは思わなかった）

---

**117.** Lord St. Vincent had lost none of his old energy and was *the last man* in the world to suffer his authority to be set at nought.

**118.** The pretext was *the last thing* that Hastings was likely to want. *(Macaulay)*

**119.** In this house I saw,—*the last thing* one would have expected to find in the heart of Lapland—a piano. *(B. Taylor)*

**120.** It is a well-known fact that the care of their health, or, what is the same thing, the rational treatment of their own flesh and blood, is *the very last thing* that these people seriously think of.

**121.** The suddenness of his appearance, in *the very last place* under heaven in which I should have expected to see him, took me completely by surprise.

---

(14) **breach** [briːtʃ] break（破る）の名詞。　**117. energy** [énədʒi] 元気。**authority** [ɔːθɔ́riti] 権威、権力。 **suffer**＝allow 黙認する。　**set at nought** [nɔːt] 無視する。　**118. pretext** [príːtekst] 口実。 **want** 欠如する。　**119. in the heart** 奥地で。 **120. what is the same thing** 同じことだ[が]。 **rational** [rǽʃənəl] 合理的。 **treatment** 処理。 **flesh and blood** 肉体。　**121. under heaven** 天が下で。これは強意の用法。　**take a person by surprise** びっくりさせる、不意打ちをくらわせる。

## (15)

> **Nothing** can be **simpler.**

【訳】　こんな簡単なことはない。

〖解　説〗　「否定語＋比較級＝最上級」としてよいことが多い。すなわち

 **Nothing** can be **simpler than** this.

 =**Nothing** can be **so** simple **as** this.

 =This is the **simplest** thing of all.

類例:——

 A **greater** man **never** lived.

 =He is the **greatest** man that **ever** lived.

 =あんな偉い人はいまだかつてなかった。

 I never saw a **more** beautiful garden [**than** this].

 =I **never** saw **so** beautiful a garden [**as** this].

 =This is the **most** beautiful garden I **ever** saw.

 =こんなりっぱな庭園は見たことがない。

 **Nothing** is **farther** from my intention **than** to speak ill of you.

  (君のことを悪く言おうなどということはもっともぼくの心から遠いことだ——そんな心はすこしもない)

---

**122.**　*Nothing* is *less* common *than* commonsense.

(Max O'Rell)

**123.**　*Nothing* in this world is *more* hopeless *than* aimlessness. It matters not how the individual is, or how favourable his surroundings are.　If he has no purpose, he is destined to misery.

**124.**　*Nothing* is *more* detestable *than* the man who courts

---

(15) **intention** [inténʃən] 意向。　122. **commonsense** 常識。　123. **aimlessness** [éimlisnis] 目的のないこと。　**It matters not** 重要でない、どうでもよい。**favourable** [féivərəbl] 都合がよい、順境である。　**surroundings** [səráundiŋs] 環境。**destine** [déstin] 運命を定める。**misery** [mízəri] 不幸。124. **detestable** [ditéstəbl] 憎むべき。　**court** [kɔːt] 求める。

popularity.

**125.** Whang, the miller, was naturally avaricious; *nobody* loved money *better than* he, or *more* respected those that had it.

**126.** *Nothing* can be *more* beautiful *than* the clumps of trees and the woods and the long lines of hedges along the fields and lanes, clad in their spring garment of freshly opened leaves. In the orchards pear trees and cherry trees seem like a cloud of white and pink against the clear blue of the sky.

**127.** Do not spend your time so now that you will reproach yourself hereafter. There are *no sadder* thoughts *than* "Too late," and "It might have been." Time is a trust, and for every minute of it you will have to account. Be spare of sleep, spare of diet, and sparest of time.

**128.** *Nothing* could be *more* contrary *than* the causes underlying the crisis in the two countries. In America, supply is far in excess of effective demand; in Russia, demand is much greater than available supply.

**129.** There is *nothing so* unpleasant *as* to meet a man who assumes an attitude of superiority. What is true in the relations of individuals is even truer in the case of international

---

**popularity** [pɔ̀pjulǽriti] 人望。 **125. avaricious** [æ̀vəríʃəs] どん欲な。 **those** =people. **126. clump** [klʌmp] 群、木立。 **hedge** [hedʒ] 生垣。 **lane** 小道。 **clad** [klæd] clothe (着せる、まとわせる) の過去分詞。 **garment** [gáːmənt] 衣。 **orchard** [ɔ́ːtʃəd] 果樹園。 **against** ...を背景にして。 **127. reproach** [ripróutʃ] 責める。 **hereafter** 今後、将来、これは前の now に対応する。 **trust** 預かり物、信託されたもの。 **minute** [mínit] 分(ふん)。 **account for** 使途を詳細に説明する。 **spare** [spɛə] 倹約な。 **diet** [dáiət] 食物。 **128. contrary** 相反する。 **underlying** [ʌ̀ndəláiiŋ] 基をなす。 **crisis** [kráisis] 危機。 **supply** [səplái] 供給。 **be in excess of** ...を上回わる。 **effective** 実際の。 **demand** [dimáːnd] 需要。 **available** [əvéiləbl] 利用し得る、役に立つ。 **129. assume** [əsjúːm] 取る。 **attitude** [ǽtitjuːd] 態度。 **superiority** [sjùpiərióriti] 優越。

gatherings, where a great number of people from countries of different traditions, sentiments, and customs, get together.

**130.** Certain it is that *no* bread eaten by man is *so* sweet *as* that earned by his own labour.

**131.** It is the very joy of man's heart to admire, where he can; *nothing so* lifts him from all his mean imprisonments, were it but for moments, *as* true admiration.

**132.** *No* one of his day *more clearly* foresaw the future dangers to which America would be exposed, or showed *more distinctly and forcibly* how they were to be avoided, *than* Washington.

**133.** There is *no* effect of the subtle operation of the association of ideas *more* universal and *more* curious *than* the manner in which the most trivial circumstances recall particular persons to our memory. (東大)

**134.** *No one* was capable of *harder* work, when it had to be done, and few could *better* shoulder responsibility; but the facts remained that he was not passionately fond of activity, and did not enjoy responsibility at all. (新潟大、*J. Hilton*)

---

( 16 )

## The sooner the better.

**gathering** [gǽðəriŋ] 集会。 **sentiment** [séntimənt] 感情。 **get together** 集合する。 **130. earned** 働いて手に入れた。 **131. admire** [ədmáiə] 感嘆する。 **lift** 高揚させる。 **mean** いやしい。 **imprisonment** [imprízənmənt] 束縛。 **were it but** ただ...であろうとも。 **132. foresee** [fɔːsíː] 予知する。 **be exposed to** ...に身をさらす。 **distinctly** はっきりと。 **forcibly** 力強く。 **they**＝the dangers. **Washington** [wɔ́ʃiŋtən]. **133. subtle** [sʌtl] 微妙な。 **association** 連想。 **trivial** 些細(ざい)な。 **circumstances** [sɔ́ːkəmstənsiz] 事情。 **recall** 呼びもどす。 **134. shoulder** になう、負う。 **responsibility** 責任。 **the fact remains that** という事実は依然として変わりはない。 **passionately** 情熱的に。

【訳】 早ければ早いほどよい。

〚解　説〛 「**the**+比較級…**the**+比較級…」
の形では "the" は冠詞ではなく, 前のは一種の関係副詞で by how much などの意味, 後のは一種の指示副詞で, by so much などの意味。前後相応じて「どれだけ…なるかに従ってそれだけ…＝…すれば…するほど, ますます…」の意味となる。上に掲げた例の省略された部分を補って paraphrase すると次のようになる:—

**The sooner** you do it, **the better** it will be.
=*By how much sooner* you do it, *by so much better* it will be.
=*In whatever degree sooner* you do it, *in that degree better* it will be.
=どれだけの程度に早くやるかに従ってそれだけの程度だけよろしい
=早くすれば早くするほどよい。

類例:—

**The higher** up you go, **the colder** it becomes.
（高く登れば登るほど寒くなる）

---

**135.** *The better* a man's character is, *the more* easy it will be for him to become still better; and *the worse* he is, *the more* easily he will be utterly ruined.

**136.** *The less* we fancy ourselves ill, or bother about little bodily discomforts, *the more* likely perhaps we are to preserve our health.

**137.** *The more* things a man is interested in, *the more* opportunities of happiness he has and *the less* he is at the mercy of fate, since if he loses one thing he can fall back upon another.

---

(16) **paraphrase** [pǽrəfreiz] 換言解釈する。　135. **utterly** [ʌ́təli] まったく。**be ruined** だめになる。＜ruin [rúːin] 滅ぼす。　136. **fancy** 空想する。**bother** [bɔ́ðə] (心を) わずらわす。**discomfort** 不快。**preserve** 維持する。　137. **opportunity** [ɔ̀pətjúːniti] 機会。**be at the mercy of** …に左右される、自由にされる。**fall back upon** …にたよる。

**138.** But *the more* we study the annals of the past, *the more* shall we rejoice that we live in a merciful age, in an age in which cruelty is abhorred, and in which pain, even when deserved, is inflicted reluctantly and from a sense of duty.

**139.** Music, in the highest sense, stands less in need of novelty. *The older* it is and *the more* we are accustomed to it, *the greater* the effect it produces upon us.

**140.** There are two opposite ideas of how to live wisely. According to one theory, civilization consists in multiplying wants and the means of gratifying them. According to the other, *the more* things that we can contentedly go without *the better* off we shall be.

**141.** Scholars are apt to think that by shortening sleep they can gain knowledge. It is defective knowledge that allows them to think so. *The more* sleep we get, if it be sound, dreamless slumber, *the better* we can work on waking.

**142.** *The more* the government came into the hands of the people and became in idea the government of themselves by and for themselves, *the better* was it able to command loyalty, and to appeal to sentiments of duty and devotion on which the tyrant had no call.

---

138. **annals** 年代記。 **rejoice** うれしく思う。 **merciful** 慈悲ふかい。 **abhor** [əbhɔ́ː] ひどく嫌う。 **when deserved** 当然それだけのことがある場合に。 **inflict** [inflíkt] 与える。 **reluctantly** [rilʌ́ktəntli] 不承不承に。 139. **stand in need of** ...を必要とする。 **novelty** [nɔ́vlti] 新奇。 140. **theory** 説、論。 **consist in** ...に存する。 **multiply** [mʌ́ltiplai] 増す。 **gratify** [grǽtifai] 満足させる。 **contentedly** [kənténtidli] 満足して。 **go without** なしですませる。 **be well off** 楽に暮らす。 141. **be apt to** ...しがちだ。 **defective** [diféktiv] 欠点のある。 **slumber** [slʌ́mbə] 睡眠。 **on waking** 目をさましたとき。 142. **in idea** 観念上。 **command** [kəmɑ́ːnd] 強要する。 **loyalty** [lɔ́iəlti] 忠節、愛国心。 **appeal** 訴える。 **sentiment** 感情。 **devotion** 献身。 **tyrant** [táiərənt] 暴君。 **call on** ...に対する要求。

## (17)

> (a) I do **not** love him **the less for** his faults.
> (b) I love him **all the better for** his faults.

【訳】（a）あの人には欠点があるがやはり私は好きだ。
　　　（b）あの人には欠点があるからなお私は好きだ。

〖解説〗（a）I do **not** love him **the less for** his faults.
　＝I do **not** love him **the less because** he has faults.
　＝He has faults, **but** I love him **none the less**.
　＝**Though** he has faults, I love him **none the less**.
　＝He has faults, **nevertheless** I love him.
　＝彼に欠点があるからといって、それだけ少なく彼を愛するということはない。
　＝彼には欠点があるが、しかし私はそれだけ少なく彼を愛するということはない。
　＝彼には欠点があるが、それにもかかわらず私は彼を愛する。

すなわちこの形式の「**the＋比較級**」は前章の形式の後半ということがわかる。この形式は常に打消しに伴ない、また同時に for, because, though, but などを伴なうのを普通とする。

（b）I love him (all) **the better for** his faults.
　＝**As** he has faults, I love him **the better**.
　＝He has faults, **so** I love him **the better**.
　＝彼には欠点があるからそれだけ余計私は彼を愛する。
　＝彼には欠点があるからかえって余計私は彼を愛するのだ。

この形式の「**the＋比較級**」もまた (a) と同性質のものということがわかろう。

（a）では for や because を「からといって...しない」と訳したが、(b) では for や as を「から...する」と訳すところに注意を要する。because のかわりに that を用いることがある。

---

(17)　**fault** [fɔ:lt] 欠点。　**nevertheless** [nèvəðəlés] それにもかかわらず。

**143.** The senses are no longer the supreme means of enjoyment, but the affections are engaged, and we love the things around us *all the more because* they are familiar. (鳥取大)

**144.** "You may be as neat as you please," interrupted I, "and I shall love you *the better for* it; but this is not neatness, but frippery." (*Goldsmith*)

**145.** *As* you had the better education, and the greater advantage, stupidity or neglect on your part is *much the more* culpable.

**146.** Therefore, though we admire those great works of imagination which have appeared in dark ages, we do *not* admire them *the more because* they have appeared in dark ages.

(*Macaulay*)

**147.** Even if we be busy mechanizing so many aspects of life, or rather, just because we *are* mechanizing them, there is *all the more* reason to reserve to birds a place in our scheme of things. (*J. S. Huxley*)

**148.** You have yet friends, warm friends, who will *not* think *the worse* of you *for* being less splendidly lodged. (*Irving*)

**149.** To escape from nervous fatigue in modern life is a very difficult thing. All through his working hours, and still more in the time spent between work and home, the city worker is

---

143. **supreme** [sjuprí:m] 最高の。 **means** 手段。 **affections** 情。 **be engaged** 使われる。 144. **neat** きちんとした。 **as you please** 好きなだけ。 **interrupt** [intərʌ́pt] さえぎる。 **frippery** [frípəri] 安っぽいおしゃれ。 145. **advantage** 有利な立場。 **stupidity** [stjupíditi] 愚鈍。 **on your part** お前の方で。 **culpable** [kʌ́lpəbl] 罪のある。 146. **dark ages** 暗黒時代 (中世をこう呼ぶことが多い)。 147. **mechanize** [mékənaiz] 機械化する。 **aspect** 面, すがた。 **reserve** 取っておく。 **scheme** [ski:m] 組織。 148. **worse** [wə:s] いっそう悪く。 **splendidly** りっぱに。 **lodged** 住まって。 149. **nervous** [nə́:vəs] 神経の。 **fatigue** [fətí:g] 疲労。 **work and home** 職場と家庭。

exposed to noise, most of which, it is true, he learns not to hear consciously, but which *none the less* wears him out.

**150.** Frequently, leaving my boat at the mercy of the wind and water, I abandoned myself to daydreams, which, although foolish, were *none the less* delightful. (北海道大)

**151.** A good tale is *none the worse for* being twice told.

**152.** The youth underwent the gaze of Majesty, *not the less* gracefully *that* his self possession was mingled with embarrassment.

**153.** If we knew what a man really admires, we might form some guess as to what sort of a man he is, or at least what sort of a man he is likely to be. This, of course, applies only to moral qualities; since a very plain person, for example, may admire beauty, and a weak person may admire strength, *all the more for* not possessing it.

**154.** In telling the story of my travels, as in travelling itself, I never know how to stop. My heart throbbed with joy as I drew near to my dear Mamma, but I did *not* go *any the quicker for* that.

---

**be exposed to** ...にさらされる、...の被害をうける。 **consciously** [kɔ́nʃəsli] 意識して。 **wear** [wɛə] 疲らす。 150. **leave~at the mercy of ...** ~を...のなすがままにまかせる。**abandon myself** 身をゆだねる。152. **underwent**＜**undergo** 受ける、こうむる。 **gaze** 凝視、見つめること。 **gracefully** 優雅に。 **self possession** 冷静。 **mingle** まぜる。 **embarrassment** [imbǽrəsmənt] 当惑。 153. **form guess** [ges] 推量する。 **as to** ...について。 **apply** あてはまる。 **plain** [plein] 不器量な。 154. **throb** [θrɔb] どきどきする。 **draw near** 近づく。

**(18)**

He can $\begin{cases} \textbf{no} \quad \textbf{more} \quad \text{swim} \\ \textbf{not} \text{ swim } \textbf{any more} \end{cases}$

$\quad\quad$ **than** $\begin{cases} \text{a hammer can (swim).} \\ \text{I can fly.} \end{cases}$

【訳】 彼が泳げないことは

$\quad\quad\begin{cases} 金づち(が泳げない)と同然。 \\ ぼくが飛べないと同然。 \end{cases}$

【解説】 英文の後半が打消しでないのを打消しに訳すのは不合理のようであるが、この構文はひとつのことを否定するために、明白に否定し得る他のことを引合いに出し、程度比較の形として表わしたものである。つまり上の例を直訳すれば、「彼は金づちの泳げる程度以上(もしくはぼくが飛べる程度以上)には泳げない」となり、言いかえれば

He **can** swim **as little as** $\begin{cases} \text{a hammer } \textbf{can} \text{ (swim).} \\ \text{I } \textbf{can} \text{ fly.} \end{cases}$

＝彼は金づちの泳げる程度、ぼくの飛べる程度しか、泳げない。

となる、ところが金づちの泳げる程度、ぼくの飛べる程度は明らかにゼロであるから、けっきょく

He **cannot** swim **just as** $\begin{cases} \text{a hammer } \textbf{cannot} \text{ swim.} \\ \text{I } \textbf{cannot} \text{ fly.} \end{cases}$

＝彼は、金づちが泳げないと同様、ぼくが飛べないと同様に、泳ぐことができない。

となる。これを一般の形式として次のように示すことができる：―

A is $\begin{cases} \textbf{no} \quad \textbf{more} \quad \textbf{B} \\ \textbf{not B any more} \end{cases}$ than X is $\begin{cases} \textbf{[B]}. \\ \textbf{Y.} \end{cases}$

＝A is not B, just as X is not $\begin{cases} \textbf{[B]}. \\ \textbf{Y.} \end{cases}$

＝A が B でないのは X が B (あるいは Y) でないのと同様だ。

---

(18) **hammer** [hǽmə] 金づち。

2番目と4番目が共に B である場合には4番目の B は はぶかれるのが普通である。例：—

He is $\begin{cases} \textbf{no more} \text{ a poet} \\ \textbf{not} \text{ a poet } \textbf{any more} \end{cases}$ **than** $\begin{cases} \text{I am (a poet).} \\ \text{I am a scholar.} \end{cases}$

=彼が詩人でないことは $\begin{cases} ぼくが詩人でないと同然。 \\ ぼくが学者でないと同然。 \end{cases}$

He is **no more** a god **than** we are.

=He is **not** a god, **any more than** we are.

（彼とてわれわれ同様神ではない）

I am **no more** mad **than** you are.

（君が気違いでないと同様ぼくも気違いではない）

You have **no better** right **than** I.

（ぼくにも権利はないが君にもない）

He **cannot** effect the impossible, **any more than** we can.

（彼が不可能事をなし得ないのはわれわれがなし得ないと同様だ）

〖注　意〗 no more than (*or* not any more than) と not more than との間に次のような区別がある。

$\begin{cases} \text{He is } \textbf{no more} \text{ diligent } \textbf{than} \text{ you are.} \\ \text{（君は勤勉でないように彼も勤勉でない＝2人とも不勉強）} \\ \text{He is } \textbf{not more} \text{ diligent } \textbf{than} \text{ you are.} \\ \text{（彼は君ほどは勉強しない＝彼も勤勉だが君の方がいっそう勤勉だ）} \end{cases}$

$\begin{cases} \text{A whale is } \begin{Bmatrix} \textbf{no more} \text{ a fish} \\ \textbf{not} \text{ a fish } \textbf{any more} \end{Bmatrix} \textbf{than} \text{ a horse is.} \\ \text{（くじらが魚でないのは馬が魚でないと同様だ）} \\ \text{A horse is } \textbf{not more} \text{ a mammal } \textbf{than} \text{ a whale is.} \\ \text{（馬も哺乳動物であるが、くじらもやはり哺乳動物だ）} \end{cases}$

---

**155.** Absolute justice is indeed *no more* attainable *than* absolute truth; but the righteous man is distinguished from the

---

**poet** [póuit] 詩人。　**mammal** [mǽməl] 哺乳動物。　155. **absolute justice** 絶対の正義。　**attainable** [ətéinəbl] 達し得る。　**righteous** [ráitʃəs] 正しい。 **distinguish** [distíŋgwiʃ] 区別する。

unrighteous by his desire and hope of justice, as the true man from the false by his desire and hope of truth.

**156.** A man has *no more* right to say an uncivil thing *than* to act one; *no more* right to say a rude thing to another *than* to knock him down.

**157.** As for knowledge, it can *no more* be planted in the human mind without labour *than* a field of wheat can be produced without the previous use of the plough.

**158.** If the sun were to be extinguished, in a day or two the whole earth would be fast bound in a frost so terrible, that every animal, every plant would die; we could *no more* live in such a frost *than* we could live in boiling water.

**159.** How can you make a fool perceive that he is a fool? Such a personage can *no more* see his own folly *than* he can his own ears.

(*Thackeray*)

**160.** A man can *no more* avoid looking ahead when he lives his life *than* he can when he sails his boat, and in one case as in the other, his direction is determined by his thought about what lies before him, his assurance of things hoped for.

**161.** At that distance, peacefully eating, the elephant looked *no more* dangerous *than* a cow.

(熊本大)

**162.** It still remains the truth that one *cannot* jazz through

---

true man の次に is distinguished を入れて見る。 **156. right** 権利。 **uncivil** [ʌnsívl] 無礼の。 **knock down** はりたおす。 **157. as for** …については。 **plant** 植える。 **previous** [prí:vjəs] 以前の。 **plough**=[plau] すき[農具]。 **158. were to** 万一…となれば。 **be bound in a frost** 氷結する。 **extinguish** [ikstíŋgwiʃ] 消す。 **159. perceive** [pəsí:v] 認める。 **personage** [pə́:sənidʒ] 人物[軽蔑的用法]。 **folly** [fɔ́li] 愚かな事。 **160. ahead** [əhéd] 前方へ。 **direction** 進行の方向。 **determine** [ditə́:min] 決定する。 **assurance** [əʃúərəns] 確信。 **hope for** 希望する。 **162. It remains the truth that** …ということは依然として真理だ。remain は自動詞、the truth は補語。 **jazz** 浮かれ暮す。

education *any more than* one can jazz through life. The learning must always involve a severe intellectual discipline—an enduring of hardness and a cheerful acceptance of difficult work.

**163.** Work is *not* of course, *any more than* play, object of Life; both are means to the same end.

**164.** He seemed *not* to notice the bustle *any more than* if the silence of a desert had been around him. He was wrapt in his own thoughts.

**165.** Brandt did *not* know *any more than* a child what to do with this discovery.

**166.** The sage knows *no* fear of death; *nor* does he feel anger towards those who inflict suffering on him *any more than* the mother towards the child for whom she lays down her life even when it has imposed suffering upon her.

**167.** What is absurd, however, is to say that you are always unlucky. You *cannot* always be unlucky *any more than* you can always be lucky.

**168.** There are wall-paintings in Egyptian tombs and at Rome and Pompeii which can be classed as landscape paintings because they represent rocks and plants and trees in a naturalistic manner, but they *no more* conform to our general idea of this type of painting *than*, say, a Chinese wall-paper. (*Herbert Read*)

---

**learning** [lə́:niŋ] 学問。 **involve** 伴なう。 **discipline** 訓練。 **acceptance** [əkséptəns] 引受けること。 **164. bustle** [bʌ́sl] 雑踏(ざっとう)。 **desert** [dézət] 沙漠(さばく)。 **wrapt** [ræpt] wrap (包む)の過去および過分。 **165. discovery** [diskʌ́vəri] 発見。 **166. sage** [seidʒ] 賢人。 **inflict** [inflíkt] (苦しみを)与える。 **suffering** [sʌ́fəriŋ] 苦しみ。 **the mother** の次に feels anger を入れて解する。 **lay down one's life** 命をなげ出す。 **impose** [impóuz] 負わせる。 **167. absurd** [əbsə́:d] ばかばかしい。 **168. tomb** [tu:m] 納骨所。 **Pompeii** [pɔmpí:ai]. **be classed as** ...として分類される。 **naturalistic** 写実的な。 **conform** 合致する。 **general idea** 一般の概念。 **say** たとえば。

**169.** The Goddess Diana, sir, is *not more* particular in her behaviour *than* Sophia Wackles; I can tell you that. (*Dickens*)

---

( 19 )

---

(a) The book has **few** faults.
(b) The book has **a few** faults.

---

【訳】 (a) この本には欠点が少ない。
(b) この本にも欠点が少しはある。

〖解 説〗 同じく二、三欠点ある書物を評しても (a) のように has **few** faults と言えば「欠点が少ない」とほめた言い方になり、(b) のように has **a few** faults と言えば「欠点も少しはある」とけちをつけることになる。

ただし、*quite a few* は口語では「かなり多数」の意味になるから注意を要する。

**little** と **a little** との関係もこれと同様である。ただし、few, a few は数えることのできる複数普通名詞につき、little, a little は数えられない物質名詞や抽象名詞につくという違いがある。副詞としての little, a little にも同様の区別がある。

類例:—

Are there *any* French books in the library?
(図書館にフランス語の本があるか)
  Yes, there are **a few.** (少しはある)
  But, there are **very few** German books.
  (しかしドイツ語の本はきわめて少ない)

---

169. **Diana** [daiǽnə]. **particular** [pətíkjulə] やかましい。 **behaviour** [bihéivjə] 振舞い。 **Sophia** [sofáiə].
(19) **library** [láibrəri] 図書館。

> He grows worse; there is **little hope** of his recovery.
> (だんだん悪くなる、回復の望みは少ない)
> He is not much better, but there is **a little hope**.
> (あまりよくないがまだ少しは望みがある)

〖注　意 1〗　not a few (or no few)＝many
　　　　　　not a little (or no little)＝much

比較：―

> I was **not a little** surprised at his failure.
> (彼が失敗したのに少なからずおどろいた)
> I was **not** surprised **in the least**.
> (私は少しもおどろかなかった)

> He has **not a little** (or **no little**) knowledge of the world.
> (あの人はよほど世間を見た＝なかなか苦労人だ)
> He has **not the least** knowledge of the world.
> (あの人は世間のことは少しも知らない＝まるでお坊ちゃんだ)

〖注　意 2〗　副詞の little が、動詞の前につくと強い打消し、すなわち not at all の意味となる。ただしこの慣用は know, think, dream, expect など少数の動詞に限られている。類例：―

　You **little know** what mischief you have done.
　(お前は自分がどんな悪いことをしたのかまるで知らないのだ)
　I **little thought** that it was you.
　(あれが君だとは夢にも知らなかった)

〖注　意 3〗　little はまた how, so, as, too などに伴なって打消しの意味をあらわす。

類例：―

　This anecdote shows **how little** he knows the world.
　(この逸話によっていかに彼が世の中のことを知らないかがわかる)
　He knows the world **so little that** he trusts everybody.
　(彼は世の中のことを知らないから、だれでも信用する)
　He knows the world **as little as** a baby.
　(彼は赤ん坊同様世間のことを知らない)

---

**mischief** [místʃif] いたずら。　**anecdote** [ǽnekdout] 逸話。

He knows the world **too little to** do for a lawyer.
(彼は世間のことを知らないから弁護士に向かない)

〖注 意 4〗 **only a little, only a few** は but little, but few と同様打消しの意味である。類例：—

I have **only a little** money left.
(金は少ししか残っていない)
There are **only a few** such men.
(そういう人は少ない)

---

**170.** Whatever may be said in dispraise of the telephone, there are *few* of us who would willingly be without it. There would be *few* more difficult forms of self-denial for a man who is accustomed to having a telephone in his house than to order the telephone to be taken away.

**171.** *Few* of us take the pains to study the origin of our cherished convictions; indeed, we have a natural repugnance to so doing. (名古屋市大)

**172.** With all things unfinished before him and behind, he fell asleep after many troubles and triumphs. *Few* can ever have gone wearier to the grave; none with less fear. He had done enough to earn his rest.

**173.** *Few* battles in history have a better title than the battle of Stalingrad to rank among " the decisive battles of the world." *Few* military defeats have been so complete and overwhelming

---

170. **dispraise** [dispréiz] 非難、悪口。 **be without it** それなしですませる。 **self-denial** [sélfdináiəl] 克己。 **be accustomed to** ...に慣れている。 **be taken away** とりはずす。 171. **pains** 骨折り。 **cherished** 心に抱いていた。 **conviction** 確信。 **repugnance** [ripʌ́gnəns] 反感。 172. **unfinished** 未完成で。 **triumph** [tráiəmf] 得意、成功。 **weary** [wíəri] 疲れた。 **earn his rest** 働いたむくいとして休息を得る。 173. **title** [táitl] 資格。 **rank** 列にはいる。 **decisive** [disáisiv] 決定的。 **defeat** 敗北。 **overwhelming** [òuvə*h*wélmiŋ] 圧倒的。

as that which overtook Hitler's forces at the hands of the Soviet armies in the spring of 1945. (横浜国立大)

**174.** The greatest beauty of music, as against the other arts, is that it is an international language, because it is the language of the emotions, which vary *little* all the world over, and hardly at all in Western Europe.

**175.** It was a place which there is *little* need to describe today, except that it was a vision of ruin and violence, and one might be excused on first seeing it for saying, "My thoughts troubled me." (津田塾)

**176.** Short though our stay in life may be, it is the appointed sphere in which each has to work out the great aim and end of his being to the best of his power; and when that is done, the accidents of the flesh will affect *but little* the immortality we shall at last put on.

**177.** Thousands of them perish in obscurity, *a few* are great names. They are sensitive for others as well as for themselves, they are considerate without being officious, their courage is not display but the power to endure, and they can take a joke.

(千葉大)

**178.** Among the greatest discoveries of science *not a few* have been made by accident. Setting out to reach a certain goal,

---

**overtook**<overtake 圧倒する、襲う。 **forces** 軍勢。 174. **as against** ...と対比して。 **emotion** [imóuʃən] 情緒。 **vary** 変化する。 175. **describe** [diskráib] 記述する。 **ruin and violence** 破壊と暴力。 **be excused** 許される。 176. **stay in life** この世に逗留(誂)すること。 **appointed sphere** 定められた世界。 **work out** 苦心して達成する。 **being** [bíːiŋ] 存在。 **flesh** [fleʃ] 肉体。 **affect** 影響する。 **immortality** [ìmɔːtǽliti] 不死。 **put on** 身につける。 177. **perish** 死ぬ。 **obscurity** [ɔbskjúəriti] 世に知られないこと。 **considerate** 思いやりがある。 **officious** [əfíʃəs] 差出がましい。 **display** 見せかけ。 **take** 解する。 178. **by accident** 偶然に。 **set out** 出発する。

the investigator chances in his way upon a law, or an element, that had no place in his purpose.

**179.** I'm anxious that you should be a good scholar, but I'm more anxious that you should be a good clean man. And if you graduate with a sound conscience, I shan't care so much if there are *a few* holes in your French.

**180.** We sometimes pass a house in the country where the gates are off the hinges, the fences are broken, the grounds are full of weeds, when *a little* labor would make all these things right. We think that the man who lives there takes things too easily.

**181.** Our wounds smarted *not a little*, and although we took time once more to wash them, they became so stiff that our progress was both toilsome and tedious.

**182.** The mate pointed out, with *no little* difficulty, the cake of ice floating off to the leeward.

**183.** All that he had learned only made him feel *how little* he knew in comparison to what remained to be known.

**184.** I knew *how little* John would have to live upon besides what his wife brought him.

**185.** He *little imagined* of how much consequence it might be.

**186.** They *little thought* it was Cinderella, whom they had

---

**investigator** [invéstigeitə] 研究者。 **chance upon** 偶然に出会う。 179. **conscience** [kɔ́nʃəns] 良心。 **hole** [houl] 欠陥。 180. **off the hinge** [hindʒ] ちょうつがいがはずれて。 **weeds** 雑草。 **make...right** ちゃんと整頓する。 **take** 考える。 **easily** [íːzili] のんきに、むぞうさに。 181. **wound** [wuːnd] 傷。 **smart** いたむ。 **stiff** こわばった。 **toilsome** つらい。 **tedious** [tíːdiəs] あきあきする。 182. **mate** 航海士。 **cake** 塊。 **leeward** [líːwəd] 風下。 183. **comparison** [kəmpǽrisn] 比較。 184. **live upon** それで生計を立てる。 185. **of consequence** [kɔ́nsikwəns] 重要な。 186. **Cinderella** [sìndərélə].

left at home in rags.

**187.** You *little know* in what company you will begin the march! (*Stevenson*)

**188.** They enter into undertakings with a hardihood *little dreamt of* by those living in town.

**189.** He spent *but little* on himself; but for public purposes his hand was open.

---

( 20 )

(a) He **seldom** goes out.
(b) It is **hardly** possible.

【訳】(a) 彼は<u>めったに</u>外出<u>しない</u>。
　　　(b) それは<u>ほとんど</u>あり得べから<u>ざる</u>ことだ。

〖解　説〗(a) **seldom** ⎫
　　　　　　　　**rarely** ⎭ ＝めったにない

This word is **rarely** used.
(この語はめったに用いられない)

〖注　意〗「まれにはある」の意味には **on rare occasions** を用いる。
類例：—

This plant is found **on rare occasions**.
(この植物はまれにはある植物だ)

　　　　(b) **hardly** ⎫
　　　　　　**scarcely** ⎭ ＝ほとんどない

It is **hardly** possible. [＝It is *almost impossible*.]
(ほとんど不可能)

---

in rags ぼろ服を着て。　**188.** undertaking 引きうけた仕事。hardihood ずぶとさ、蛮勇(紛)。　dreamt [dremt] dream の過去分詞。　**189.** spend on ...に金を使う。
(20) rarely [réəli] まれにしかない。　occasion [əkéiʒən] 場合。

There is **scarcely any** hope of his recovery.
[=There is *almost no* hope...]
(回復の見込みはほとんどない)
He **hardly ever** opens a book.
[=He *almost never* opens a book.]
(彼は本を開くことはほとんどない)
I kept still, **hardly** daring to breathe.
(ほとんど息もつけないで(息を殺して)じっとしていた)

---

**190.** As we looked on each other, we *scarcely* knew whether to laugh or to be frightened at the strange figures we made.

**191.** The Grecian citizens at the time of Pericles were almost all equally qualified to fill offices or discharge business; so that regulation, that greater part of the public offices should be filled by lot, *rarely* resulted in the choice of any but able and well qualified men. (*Swinton*)

**192.** As we watch the stars at night they seem so still and motionless that we can *hardly* realize that at the time they are rushing on with a velocity far exceeding any that man has ever accomplished.

**193.** The whole subject of atomic physics is in its infancy, and there is *hardly* any limit to what may be reasonably expected in the way of both theoretical and practical progress.

**194.** It is becoming more and more obvious as time goes

---

190. **be frightened** こわがる。 **figures** [fígəz] 姿。 **we made** 自分たちが示した。 191. **Grecian** [gríːʃən] ギリシアの。 **Pericles** [périkliːz]. **qualified** 資格がある。 **fill offices** 役職につく。 **discharge** はたす。 **regulation** [règjuléiʃən] 規則。 **by lot** 抽せんで。 **result in** ...の結果になる。 **any but** ...でない人。 192. **rush on** 突進する。 **velocity** 速さ。 **accomplish** 達成する。 **exceed** [iksíːd] 優る。 193. **atomic physics** 原子物理学。 **infancy** 幼児期、初期。 **in the way of** ...の面で。 **theoretical** [θiərétikəl] 理論的。 194. **obvious** [ɔ́bviəs] 明白な。

on that there is *scarcely any* department of Nature's activity, *scarcely any* useful art practised by man, in which the laws and principles of chemistry are not involved.

**195.** He was *hardly* ever angry with his servants; it shows how *seldom* this occurred, that when, as a small boy, I overheard a servant being scolded, and my father speaking angrily, it impressed me as a dreadful circumstance, and I remember running upstairs out of a general sense of awe. (滋賀大)

---

## (21)

(a) You are **too** young **to** understand such things.
(b) He is **too** wise **not to** know it.

【訳】 (a) お前はまだ若いからそんなことはわからない。
(b) 彼はそれを知らないほどばかじゃない。

〖解説〗 (a) 「too＋形容詞＋不定詞」
この形式はたいてい次のように見てよい：—

$$\text{too} \sim \text{to} \ldots = \text{so} \sim \text{that} \begin{Bmatrix} \text{can} \\ \text{do} \\ \text{will} \end{Bmatrix} \text{not} \ldots$$

＝「...するにはあまりに～」
「あまり～だから...しない」

すなわち to... という不定詞を打消すことになる。類例：—

He is **too old to** work.
＝He is *so old that* he *cannot* work.

---

**department** [dipá:tmənt] 部門。**which** department と art を指す。**principle** 原理。**involve** [invɔ́lv] 含む。 **195. it shows ...** の it は that 以下を代表する。**occur** [əkə́:] 起こる。**overhear** ふと耳にする。**scold** しかる。**impress** 印象づける。**out of** ...から、...のために。**general sense of awe** 一般的な恐怖感。

=働くには年をとり過ぎている。
=年をとりすぎて働けない。

He is **too idle to** work for his bread.
=He is *so idle that* he *does not* work for his bread.
=彼はなまけ者で働いて飯を食うことをしない。

(b) **too~not to...=so~that cannot but...**

この形は (a) の形に not が加わったのだから、「...しないにはあまりに~」「~だから...しないことはない」と否定が二つ重なって相互に打ち消し、けっきょく「~だから...する」と肯定の意味になる。ゆえに上に掲げた (b) の例は「彼はりこうだからそれを知っている」であるが、反対の意味の形容詞を用いて訳した方が日本語として適当な場合もある。

He is **too wise not to** know it.
=He is *so wise that* he *cannot but* know it.
=He is *not so foolish that* he *does* not know it.
=ひじょうに賢い男だからそれを知らないはずがない。
=それを知らないほどばかではない。

〖注 意 1〗 **too~for** の形を取ることもあるが、それは後に不定詞がはぶかれているので、for は不定詞の意味上の主語を示すものと見るべき場合が多い。類例:—

This book is **too** difficult **for** us [to understand].
（この本はぼくらが理解するにはむずかしすぎる＝むずかしくてぼくらにはわからない）

しかしまた **too~for** の for を for the purpose of の意味と見るべき場合もある。類例:—

My spirits were **too** low **for** work.
（あまり元気がなくて仕事もできなかった）

It was **too** beautiful **for** words.
（言うに言われないほど美しかった）

〖注 意 2〗 次の例では too~to をこの公式どおりに考えると誤りとなる。

In fact there are some experts who say there are physiological and psychological reasons that make such slim women better candidates for space travel than any shape of man. The plump well-rounded girl reportedly has *too much* tissue *to* nourish.

(お茶の水女大)

(事実、このようなほっそりした女性の方がどんな体格の男性よりも宇宙旅行には適任者だというには生理的、心理的理由があるという専門家もある。報ずるところではまるまると太った女子には養わねばならぬ筋肉組織が多すぎるというのだ)

ここの to nourish は tissue を修飾する不定詞である。too much に応ずるためには nourish の後に for space travel を入れることになる。

---

**196.** Every year thousands of people make their way to Switzerland to take part in winter sports or to climb the peaks in summer. No mountain is *too* high or *too* steep or *too* forbidding *to* scare the mountaineer, and one after another the peaks are conquered and mountain-climbers are now as numerous as fallen leaves in autumn.

**197.** The chains of habit are generally *too* small *to* be felt till they are *too* strong *to* be broken. (*Johnson*)

**198.** Countries which are nearly self-supporting as regards the necessaries of life and the raw materials of wealth are more secure than those which are obliged to import their food or coal or oil from abroad—unless, indeed, they are *too* weak *to* defend their natural wealth.

**199.** Though the Romans were masters of all the world, as then known, they were not *too* proud *to* learn useful lessons

---

**196. Switzerland** [swítsələnd] スイス。**take part in** 参加する。**forbidding** [fəbídiŋ] 近寄りがたい。**scare** [skɛə] おどす、おびえさす。**mountaineer** [màuntiníə] 登山家。**numerous** [njú:mərəs] 多数の。 **197. be felt** あると感じる、それと気づく。 **198. self-supporting** 自給する。**as regards** に関して。**necessaries** [nésisəriz] 必要品。**raw materials** 原料。**secure** [sikjúə] 安全な。**import** [impɔ́:t] 輸入する。 **199. as then known** 当時知られていたところの。

from the people whom they conquered.

**200.** Now certain subjects are supposed to be beneath the dignity of literary art; and some of these subjects might appear to you *too* trivial for a great poet *to* busy himself with.

**201.** He was *too* much of a man of the world *not to* know better.

**202.** One great secret of the success that has been given me is, undoubtedly, the life-long habit I have had of giving close attention to small details. Nothing has been *too* small *to* receive my attention. Things that most young people seem to think are really *too* trifling have never been *too* small *for* me.

---

( 22 )

---

(a) He is **too** ready **to** speak.
(b) I am **only too** delighted **to** accept your kind invitation.

---

【訳】 (a) あの男はしゃべりすぎる。
　　　(b) 大喜びでご招待に応じます。

〖解 説〗 (a) too~to... の形では~が ready, inclined などという語であると to... という不定詞を打消しはしないで、「あまり~で困る」という意になる。比較:—

(1) He is **too** angry **to** speak.
　　=He is *so* angry *that* he *cannot* speak.
　　=あまり立腹しているのでものも言えない。

---

conquer [kɔ́ŋkə] 征服する。 200. subject [sʌ́bdʒikt] 主題。dignity [dígniti] 威厳。 trivial [tríviəl] つまらない。 busy himself with それにかかわる。 202. secret [síːkrit] 秘訣(ひけつ)。 of giving ...は habit に続く。 close [klous] 細かな。 detail [díːteil] 細目。 trifling [tráifliŋ] つまらない。
(22) accept [əksépt] 受納する、承諾する。

(2) He is **too** ready **to** speak.
　　=He is *too* talkative.
　　=あまりおしゃべりすぎる。

(1) では too は angry だけについて「怒りすぎ」てものが言えないことを表わし，(2) では too は ready to speak 全体について，"ready to speak" ということの度がすぎることをあらわす。また不定詞から見れば (1) の to speak は too を qualify (限定)し，(2) の to speak は ready を qualify する。類例:—

　　He is **too much inclined to** give himself airs.
　　=彼はあまり気取りたがって困る。

(b) **only too~to...** の形式でも to... は打消しには解せられない。**only** (or **but**) **too=exceedingly; very much** などと見てよい。例:—

　　I am **only too glad to** do so. (大喜びでいたします)

〘注意〙 不定詞を伴なわない場合の

　　**too~**

　　**only** (or **but**) **too~**

は alas! の意味を加えて「~すぎて困る」などのように訳する。類例:—

　　What he says is **but too** true.
　　(彼のいうことは、本当でなければいいのだが、遺憾ながら本当だ；本当だからしかたがない)

　　The rest you know **but too** well.
　　(悲しいかなそのあとは君がよくご存じのとおりだ)

　　The festival was over **only too** soon.
　　(いつまでもあればよいのにお祭があまり早くすんでしまって惜しかった)

この only が all にかわって

　　It was over **all too** soon.

などとなることもある。なお

　　I arrived **none too** soon.
　　(すこしも早すぎはしない、ちょうどよい時刻に着いた)

のような用法もある。

**festival** [féstivəl] 祭礼．

**203.** If any one whom you do not know to be a person of truth, sobriety, and weight, relates strange stories, be not *too ready to* believe or report them; and yet be not *too forward to* contradict him.

**204.** One cannot correct one's faults without knowing them, and I always looked upon those who told me of mine as friends, instead of being displeased or angry, as people in general are *too apt to* be.

**205.** Philosophers have been *too ready to* suppose that question of fact can be settled by verbal considerations. Plutarch has an amusing discussion on the question: Which came first, the Hen or the Egg? and the consideration brought forward is that the hen came first, because everyone speaks of a hen's egg and no one says an egg's hen. *(Lord Avebury)*

**206.** When they hear her gentle voice calling them, they are *only too glad to* obey, and, like obedient children, come and go at her bidding.

**207.** He is near the prince's age, and will be *but too happy to* wait upon his royal highness. *(Hawthorne)*

**208.** Those individualistic nations in which the interests of the nation are *only too often* sacrificed to the selfish interests of the individual, where ministers, generals, and admirals are rarely

---

203. **sobriety** [sobráiəti] まじめ。 **weight** 重み。 **relate** 話す。 **forward** 出すぎる、生意気な。 **contradict** [kɔ̀ntrədíkt] 反ぱくする。 204. **correct** [kərékt] 誤りをただす。**look upon ~as ...** ~を...と見なす。**in general** 一般の。**be apt to** ...しがちだ。 205. **philosopher** [filɔ́səfə] 哲学者。 **question** [kwéstʃən] 疑問。**be settled** 決定される。**verbal** [və́:bəl] 言語上の。**Plutarch** [plú:tɑ:k]. **brought forward** 提出された。 206. **obey** [obéi] 従う。**obedient** [əbí:djənt] 従順な。**at her bidding** 彼女の言いつけ通りに。 207. **royal** [rɔ́iəl] **highness** 殿下。 208. **individualistic** [ìndividjuəlístik] 個人主義的。**sacrifice** [sǽkrifais] 犠牲にする。

appointed by merit only, where jobbery occurs even in time of war, and where everything is considered to be permitted that is not actually punished by law, will do well to learn from this country's example, for it cannot be doubted that the cause of this country's greatness and of its success can be summed up in the one word—patriotism.

**209.** Our own generation has known the Reign of the Lie *only too well*. We have had it from Hitler and the Nazis, and then from Lenin and Stalin. (*Gilbert Murray*)

**210.** It is good for a community to have plenty of exercise; it is very bad for it to subordinate all other interests to sports and games. Athleticism in the present generation goes, it is admitted, *too far*. Reasonable sport accumulates energy, but excessive sport wastes it.

( 23 )

> We **cannot** praise him **too** much.
> It is **impossible** to **overpraise** him.

【訳】 どんなに ほめても ほめたりない。

〘解 説〙 cannot...too much; it is impossible to over... は「あまり...しすぎるということはできない」「いくら...したとしても過ぎるということはない」などの意味である。類例:—

---

**appoint** 任命する。 **merit** 功績。 **jobbery** [dʒɔ́bəri] 汚職。 **do well** するとよい、するのが賢明だ。 **be summed up** 要約される。 **patriotism** 愛国心。
**209. the Reign of the Lie** 虚偽の治世(支配)。 **210. community** [kəmjúːniti] (一般の)社会、公共。 **exercise** [éksəsaiz] 運動。 **athleticism** [æθlétisizm] 運動第一主義。 **reasonable** 適度の。 **accumulate** [əkjúmjuleit] 蓄積する。 **excessive** 過度の。

We **cannot** be **too** careful in this world; our best friends often deceive us.

(世に処するにはいやが上にも注意すべきである、大の親友さえ人をあざむくこともある [おそろしい世の中だ] から)

**It is impossible** to speak **too** severely of his conduct.

(彼の行為はどんなにひどく評しても酷に過ぎるということはない)

〘注　意〙 too ; over に代えて enough ; sufficient などとし、cannot ; impossible に代えて他の打消しにする場合もある。

類例:—

I **cannot** thank you **too much.** ＝I **cannot** thank you **enough.**
(お礼の申しようもありません)

We **can scarcely** pay **too** high a price for liberty.
(自由を得るためにはどんな犠牲を払っても惜しくない)

---

**211.** We *cannot* be *too* strict in applying to books the rules we follow in regard to society and refusing our acquaintance to those books unworthy of it.

**212.** We are all apt, when we know not what may happen, to fear the worst. Therefore, we *cannot* be *too* careful not to make our troubles and difficulties look much greater than they really are, especially in those unfavourable times for our country.

**213.** A book may be compared to your neighbour; if it be good, it *cannot* last *too* long; if bad, you *cannot* get rid of it *too* early.

---

(23) **deceive** [disíːv] あざむく。　**severely** [sivíəli] きびしく。　**conduct** [kɔ́ndəkt] 行為。　**liberty** [líbəti] 自由。　211. **applying** あてはめる、目的語は rules. **in regard to** ...に関して。　**society** [səsáiəti] 交際。　**acquaintance** [əkwéintəns] 知り合いになること。　**refusing** こばむこと、前の方の in に続く。　**unworthy** [ʌnwə́ːði] 値しない。　212. **fear the worst** 最悪の場合を心配する。　**make...look** 見えるようにする。　**unfavourable** [ʌ́nféivərəbl] 都合の悪い。　213. **be compared to** ...にたとえられる。　**neighbour** [néibə] 隣人。　**last** 続く。　**get rid of** 除く。

**214.**　We *cannot too* often remind ourselves that freedom of the press is not intended for the convenience of those who publish newspapers, control radio or television stations or in other ways spread news and ideas abroad. Freedom of the press is for the public, the whole public, and it is inextricably connected with all other freedoms.　　　　　　　　　(慶応大)

**215.**　Some people think that they cannot spare time for exercise. They *cannot* be told *too* soon that they must find time for exercise, or they will have to find time for illness.

**216.**　As a teacher with limited time at my disposal, I *cannot* speak *too* highly of the value of the information to be obtained from the Encyclopædia Britanica.

**217.**　*It is difficult* to speak in terms of *too* high praise of the first geological maps of England, which we owe to the industry of this courageous man of science.

**218.**　Fifty years of study and labour elapsed before Galileo completed the invention of his pendulum—an invention, the importance of which, in the measurement of time and astronomical calculations, *can scarcely* be *overvalued*.

**219.**　The silkworm is an animal of such acute and delicate sensations, that *too* much care *cannot* be taken to keep its habi-

---

214. **the press** 新聞、雑誌。**intend** 意図する。**convenience** 便宜。**control** 支配する。**spread~abroad** 広く伝達する。**inextricably** [inékstrikəbli] とけないほど。 215. **spare** [時間を]さく。 216. **at one's disposal** [dispóuzəl] 自分の自由に使える。**speak highly of** ほめる。**obtain** [əbtéin] 得る。**Encyclopædia** [ènsaiklopí:diə] 百科全書。**Britanica** [briténikə]. 217. **terms** 言葉。**geological** [dʒiolódʒikəl] 地質学上の。**industry** 勤勉。**courageous** [kəréidʒəs] 勇敢な。 218. **elapse** [ilǽps] 経過する。 **Galileo** [gæliléiou]. **pendulum** [péndjuləm] 振子。**measurement** [méʒəmənt] 測定。**astronomical** [æstrənómikəl] 天文学上の。**calculation** [kælkjuléiʃən] 計算。 219. **acute** 鋭い。**delicate** せん細な。**sensation** 感覚。**habitation** [hæbitéiʃən] 住居。

tation clean, and to refresh it from time to time with pure air. I have seen them languish and die in scores, in consequence of an accidental bad smell.

**220.** The central role of free, competitive, private enterprise in the life of America *can hardly* be *exaggerated*. But the basic sources of the strength of American civilization go deeper; they are ethical and spiritual.

**221.** The selection of a place of residence, even though we only intend to pass a few short years in it, is from the intellectual point of view a matter so important that one *can hardly exaggerate* the consequence.

---

### (24)

(a) We have two dogs; **one** is white, and **the other** black.

(b) We have two dogs, a white one, and a black one; **the one** is larger than **the other**.

【訳】（a）私の家には犬が二匹いる、一つは白で、一つは黒い。
　　　（b）私の家には白いのと黒いのと犬が二匹いる。白いのは黒いのより大きい。

【解説】二つあるものをどちらとも定めず一つを取れば one で、残った方が the other である。だから

（a） **one ... the other** はどちらとも定めず「一つは...一つは...」

---

refresh [rifréʃ] 元気をつける。　languish [lǽŋgwiʃ] 弱る。　scores [skɔːz] 多数。　in consequence of ... の結果。　accidental 偶然の。　**220.** role 役割。competitive [kəmpétitiv] 競争的。enterprise [éntəpraiz] 企業。exaggerate [igzǽdʒəreit] 誇大に言う。ethical 倫理的。**221.** residence [rézidəns] 住居。intellectual [ìntiléktjuəl] 知的の。

と訳してよい。これに反して

(b) **the one...the other** は **the former...the latter** の意味だから「前者は...後者は...」と訳さなければならない。比較:—

> His brothers are both abroad; **one** in England, and **the other** in America.
> (彼の兄弟は二人とも外遊中だ、一人はイギリスに、一人はアメリカに)
> Neither my elder brother nor my younger brother is in Japan; **the one** is in Brazil, and **the other** in Argentina.
> (私の兄も弟も日本にいません、兄はブラジルに弟はアルゼンチンにおります)

〖注 意〗 三つ以上のものをどれとも定めず一つずつ取る場合は **one, another** (or **a second**), **a third** と言い、なお残り数個あればひっくるめて **the others** (or **the rest**) と言い、残りが一つなら **the other** と言う。

---

**222.** What is wanted to-day is less printing and less reading, but more thinking. Reading is easy, and thinking is hard work, but *the one* is useless without *the other*.

**223.** Public men are nearly always being overblamed or overpraised, and the more knowledge they have of themselves, the less likely they are to be unduly depressed by *the one* or to be unduly elated by *the other*. (大阪府立大)

**224.** We cannot fail to see that the connection between body and mind is a very close one, and when we note how *the one* affects *the other* we must admit that health is a moral duty

**225.** " Oh, you're a *'prentice!* " said a little boy, the other

---

(24) **Brazil** [brəzíl]. **Argentina** [ὰːdʒəntíːnə]. 222. **printing** [príntiŋ] 印刷(物)。 223. **overblame** 過度に非難する。 **likely to** ...しそうで。 **unduly** [ʌndjúːli] 過度に。 **depress** 気を落とさせる。 **elate** [iléit] 得意がらせる。 224. **connection** 関係。 **note** 注意する。 **affect** 影響する。 **admit** 認める。 225. **a 'prentice** は **an apprentice** [əpréntis] (年期小僧) の略。

day, tauntingly to his companion ... *The former*, I perceived by his dress, was of a higher class in society than his humble, yet more dignified companion. *The latter* was a sprightly, active lad, scarce twelve years old, and, coarsely, but neatly attired.

**226.** In 1783, a volcano in Iceland sent out two streams of lava; *one* forty miles long and seven miles wide, and *the other* fifty miles long and fifteen miles wide.

**227.** She ran to her closet, and pulled out a nice, clean apron and cap, and tied *the one* round her waist, and *the other* round her comely face, ... and away she ran downstairs, where stood her husband and the two gentlemen. The good woman bowed low, first to *one* and then to *the other*.

**228.** Thus *one* man commits theft in order to secure refuge in prison, *another* burns the house of a friend who refused him a little rice, *a third* flees to the south leaving his family to starve.

---

( 25 )

Health is above wealth, for **this** cannot give so much happiness as **that**.

【訳】 健康は富にまさる、これはあれほど幸福を与えることは出来ないからである。

---

**taunt** [tɔ:nt] あざける。 **perceive** 気づく。 **humble** 身分の低い。 **dignify** [dígnifai] 品位をつける。 **sprightly** [spráitli] 快活な。 **coarsely** 粗末に。 **attired** [ətáiəd] 装いをした。 **226. volcano** [vɔlkéinou] 火山。 **lava** [lɑ́:və] 溶岩。 **227. closet** [klɔ́zit] 押入れ。 **apron** [éiprən] 前掛。 **comely** [kʌ́mli] かわいらしい。 **bow** [bau] 礼をする。 **228. commit theft** 窃盗(窃)をはたらく。 **in order to** ...するために。 **secure** 確保する。 **refuge** [réfju:dʒ] 隠れ場。 **flee** 逃げる。 **starve** 飢える。

〖解　説〗　this は「これ」と近いものをさし、that は「あれ」と遠いものをさす。したがって the one...the other とは前後転倒して

　　**this＝the latter**　　（後者）
　　**that＝the former**　　（前者）

という関係にある。類例：—

　Young men, two paths lie before you, virtue and vice; **this** leads to misery, **that** to happiness.
　　（青年諸君、諸君の前に二つの途があり、善行と不善とである、これは不幸に至る道で、あれは幸福に至る道だ）

---

**229.**　Work and play are both necessary to health; *this* gives us rest, and *that* gives us energy.

**230.**　Dogs are more faithful animals than cats; *these* attach themselves to places, and *those* to persons.

**231.**　Winter and summer come to all; *this* with its flowers, and *that* with its snow.

**232.**　The poor want some advantages which the rich enjoy; but we should not therefore account *these* happy, and *those* miserable.

---

(26)

> To know is **one thing,** to practise is **another.**

【訳】　知ることと行うことは全く別な事である。

〖解　説〗　another には種々の用い方がある。ふつうは
　( a )　**another＝one more**

---

(25)　**path** [pɑːθ], **paths** [pɑːðz] 道。　230. **faithful** 忠実な。　**attach** [ətǽtʃ] 愛着せしめる。　232. **advantage** [ədvάːntidʒ] 利益。　**account** [əkáunt] はかる、考える。　**miserable** [mízərəbl] あわれな、みじめな。

と見て,「もう一つの」と形容詞に訳すか,あるいは副詞のようにして「また...」と訳せばよい。例:―

    There was **another** fire last night.
      (ゆうべまた火事があった)

(b) **another**＝**also one**

の意味に用いられる場合は「もまた」などと訳す。例:―

    He is an imposter, and his son is **another**.
      (彼は山師だ、その息子もまた山師だ)
    If I am a fool, you are **another**.
      (おれがばかなら貴様もばかだ)

(c) 転じて「別の」「変わった」という意味を生じてくる。例:―
    There is **another** meaning.
      (もう一つ別の意味がある)
    From that time he became **another** man.
      (その時から彼は生まれ変わったような人間になった)

(d) 二つのことが或る点において似ていながらまったく別であることを言いあらわすのに

    **one thing**...**another thing**...

を用いる、前の囲みの中に示した例はすなわちこの用法で、知っていたらば行ないそうなものだが、実際は知行必ずしも合一するものでないという意味。

---

**233.** We need not regret that work is *one thing* for men and *another* for animals, and that it has ceased to be a simple, natural function. Nor should we wish it to become a form of sport, for then it would be unproductive.

**234.** It is *one thing* to make great progress in curing or

---

(26) **impostor** 詐欺師(さぎし)。 **233. regret** 残念に思う。 **cease** [siːs] **to be**...でなくなる。 **function** [fʌ́ŋkʃən] 機能、働き。 **unproductive** [ʌnprədʌ́ktiv] 非生産的。 **234. progress** [próugres; *v*. prəgrés] 進歩。 **cure** 治療する。

preventing disease and *another* to say that all the afflictions of man can be overcome by human intelligence. (金沢大)

**235.** It is *one thing* to know truth about oneself; it is quite *another thing* to have it told one by somebody else.

(*Aldous Huxley*)

**236.** If you have any fault to find with any one, tell him, not others, of what you complain; there is no more dangerous experiment than that of undertaking to be *one thing* before a man's face and *another* behind his back.

**237.** All know that it is *one thing* to be rich, *another thing* to be enlightened, brave, or humane; that the questions how a nation is made wealthy, and how it is made free, or virtuous, or eminent in literature, in the fine arts, in arms, or in polity, are totally distinct enquiries.

---

(27)

> The tail of a fox is longer than **that of** a hare.

【訳】 狐のしっぽは兎のしっぽより長い。

〖解 説〗 同一名詞の反復を避けるために that of... (複数は those of...) を「the+名詞+of...」のかわりに用いることがある。このごろは「狐のしっぽは兎のそれより長い」などいう直訳体の文も見えるが、日本文としてはやはり名詞をくりかえす方がおだやかであろう。類例:—

---

**prevent** [privént] 予防する。**affliction** 苦痛。**overcome** 征服する。 **235. have it told one** 自分にそれを言われる。 **236. find fault with** ...をとがめる。 **complain** [kəmpléin] 不平をいう。 **undertaking** 企てること。 **behind one's back** かげで。 **237. enlightened** [inláitnd] 啓発された。 **humane** [hju:méin] 人情ある。 **virtuous** [vá:tjuəs] 有徳な。 **eminent** すぐれた。 **polity** [póliti] 政治形態。 **totally** 全然。 **distinct** 別な。 **enquiry** [inkwáiəri] 質問。

The climate of Japan is milder than **that** (=*the climate*) of Russia.
(日本の気候はロシアの気候より温和だ)

The ears of a hare are longer than **those** (=*the ears*) of a fox.
(兎の耳は狐の耳より長い)

---

**238.** Do not talk about dress, either your own or *that of* others. Perhaps you may see some boy or girl poorly dressed; but what of that? Cotton may be as clean as silk.

**239.** When I cast my eye on the expanse of waters, my heart bounded like *that of* a prisoner set free. I felt an inextinguishable curiosity kindle in my mind, and resolved to take this opportunity of seeing the manners of other nations.

**240.** There is nothing in any of the northern countries with which to compare the richness of tropical growth; and lovely as are the tints in a broad American landscape, they are as nothing in point of splendour to *those of* the tropical scene.

**241.** Even in America, as a matter of fact, the education of girls and women was far behind *that of* boys and men. Only in the lowest elementary schools were girls freely admitted, in order that they might learn to read and write.

**242.** Every one will admit that man is a social being. We see this in his dislike of solitude, and in his wish for society

---

(27) **climate** [kláimit] 気候。**Russia** [rʌ́ʃə] ロシア。 **238. poorly dressed** 貧しい服装をしている。**cotton** 木綿。 **239. cast** 投げた、ここは過去。**expanse** [ikspǽns] 広がり。**bound** はねる、おどる。**prisoner** [prízna] 囚人。**set free** 自由の身となった、set は過去分詞。**inextinguishable** [inikstíŋgwiʃəbl] 消しがたい。**curiosity** [kjùəriɔ́siti] 好奇心。**kindle** 点火する。**resolve** 決心する。**opportunity** 機会。 **240. northern** [nɔ́:ðən] 北の。**compare** [kəmpέə] 比する。**tropical** [trɔ́pikəl] 熱帯の。**growth** 繁茂、草木。**tint** 色彩。**landscape** [lǽndskeip] 風景。 **splendour** [spléndə] 見事さ、光彩。 **241. be behind** ...におくれている。**elementary** [eliméntəri] 初歩の。**admit** [ədmít] 入れる。 **242. solitude** [sɔ́litjù:d] 孤独。 **society** [səsáiəti] (=companionship) 交際。

beyond *that of* his own family.

**243.** The hardships or misfortunes we lie under are easier to us than *those of* any other person would be, in case we could change conditions with him.

---

( 28 )

> The ship was built in less than a year, **and that** in the midst of the war.

【訳】 この船は一年もかからずにできた、しかも戦争のまっ最中に。

〖解 説〗 こういう構文の that は前文の叙述部全部を反復するかわりに用いられたものである。すなわち、上の例においても、もしくだくだしさをいとわなければ and was built... とくりかえすところである。こういう and that は「しかもそれは」あるいは単に「しかも」など訳して当たる。類例:—

He had shown both loyalty and spirits, **and that** at a time when both were rare qualities.
(彼は忠節と気慨(がい)を示した。しかも忠節も気慨も多く見られなかった時に)

〖注 意〗 and...too はこの形の変体である。例:—
He writes English, **and** very well **too**.
(彼は英文が書ける、しかもなかなかよく書く)

---

**244.** The general impression of a man, *and that* most likely to endure, is formed largely from his ordinary everyday life,

---

243. misfortune 不幸。 lie under それで苦しむ、それをこうむっている。 in case=if. conditions 境遇。
(28) loyalty [lóiəlti] 忠節。 quality [kwóliti] 性質。 244. general impression 全般的印象。 endure [indjúə] 永くもつ。

and not from any one or more episodes, however striking they may happen to be.

**245.** King Richard was a strong, restless, burly man, with one idea always in his head, *and that* the very troublesome idea of breaking the heads of other men.

**246.** But while I do live, let me have a country, or at least the hope of a country, *and that* a free country.

**247.** We were two hours in making less than a mile, *and that* with danger, sometimes in the river and sometimes on the rock.

**248.** It is owing to the absence of character that great geniuses have been known to die in poorhouses. It is on account of character that men with little talent have died millionaires—*and* most respected ones, *too*.

**249.** "I must find a place of concealment," he thought, "*and that* within the next few seconds, or all is over with me in the world."

**250.** Let every man be occupied, *and occupied* in the highest employment of which he is capable, and die with the consciousness that he has done his best.

---

**episode** [épisoud] 挿話。 **striking** [stráikiŋ] 目立つ、いちじるしい、人の注意を引く。 **happen** たまたま...である。 245. **restless** 落ちつきのない。 **burly** [bə́:li] たくましい。 **troublesome** [trʌ́blsəm] やっかいな。 **break** たたき割る。 247. **make** 進む。 248. **absence** [ǽbsns] 欠乏。 **geniuses** [dʒí:njəsiz] 天才。 **poorhouse** 救貧院。 **on account of** ...のために、...によって。 **millionaire** [mìljənέə] 百万長者。 **respected** 人から尊敬された。 249. **concealment** かくすこと。 **all is over** 万事休す、何もかもだめになる。 250. **be occupied in** ...に従事する。 **capable** [kéipəbl] 能力ある。 **consciousness** [kɔ́nʃəsnis] 自覚。

(29)

> (a) **What with** teaching, and **what with** writing, my time is fully taken up.
> (b) **What by** policy, and **what by** force, he always accomplishes his purpose.

【訳】(a) 教えること<u>やら</u>、書くこと<u>やら</u>でぼくは少しも暇がない。

(b) 政略を<u>用いたり</u>、暴力を<u>用いたり</u>して彼は必ず目的を遂げる。

〖解 説〗 (a) what with..., and what with...

(b) what by..., and what by...

の形式では what は partly の意味の副詞であるから、どちらも「一つには...また一つには...」「...やら...やら」など訳すが、with は原因を示し、by は手段を示すという違いがある。類例:—

**What with** the high prices, and **what with** the badness of the times, they find it hard to get along.

(物価が高いやら、不景気やらでなかなかやりきれない)

**What by** threats, and **what by** entreaties, he finally had his will.

(おどしたりすかしたりして彼はとうとう自分の思いどおりにした)

〖注 意〗 二度目の what with; what by ははぶかれることがある、ことに三つ以上並べる場合には最初の一つだけ言って他は省略するのが通例である。また二つ並べる場合には what with; what by のどちらも **between** にかえることができる。例:—

**Between** teaching and writing, my time is fully taken up.

また **what between** ということもある。例:—

---

(29) **take up** (時間を)とる。**policy** [pɔ́lisi] 策略。**accomplish** [əkɔ́mpliʃ] 成就する。**purpose** [pə́:pəs] 目的。**get along** 暮して行く。**threat** [θret] 威嚇(ぃ、)。**entreaty** [intrí:ti] 嘆願。**finally** [fáinəli] 終りに。

> **What with** flirting, and **what with** quarrelling,  
> **What between** flirting and quarrelling,  
> } they had no time left for any serious occupation.
>
> (ふざけたりけんかをしたりで彼らはまじめな仕事をする時がなかった)

また原因を示す with の代わりに through を用いて **what through ... and what through ...** ということもある。

---

**251.** *What with* the hum of human voices, the lowing of cattle, the squeaking of pigs, *and* the laughter caused by the merry-andrew, the market place was in very great confusion. (*Hawthorne*)

**252.** *What with* her increasing population *and* her lack of raw materials, Japan is suffering from the high cost of living.

**253.** *What with* the high price of provisions, and *what with* the occasional sickness, the family found it very difficult to live on their income.

**254.** *What with* the joy of seeing her son back safe and sound, and *what with* their good fortune, the boy's mother got well in a few days. She began to be very proud of her son, and never tired of talking about his adventures to her visitors.

**255.** *Half through* indolence, *half through* pride, that Spaniard cannot bend to work.

**256.** *What with* official business and private business I have

---

flirt [fləːt] (男と女が)ふざける。 quarrel [kwɔ́rəl] けんかをする。 251. hum [hʌm] こまの回るときのような音。 human [hjúːmən] 人間の。 lowing [lóuiŋ] (牛の)鳴き声。 squeak キーキー鳴く。 merry-andrew [mériændruː] 道化役者。 confusion [kənfjúːʒən] 混雑。 252. population [pɔ̀pjuléiʃən] 人口。 raw materials 原料。 253. provisions 食糧。 occasional [əkéiʒnəl] 時々の。 on ... にたよって。 income 収入。 254. safe and sound 無事息災(そく)で。 get well 元気になる。 be tired of ... にあきる。 adventure 冒険。 255. indolence 怠惰。 Spaniard [spǽnjəd] スペイン人。 bend 屈する。 256. official [əfíʃəl] 公務の。 private [práivit] 私の。

no leisure.

**257.** Sitting down there in the dark, *what with* the sound of waters *and* rocking movement of the ship, I had fallen asleep.

(Stevenson)

**258.** He was at the head of the customhouse, and *what by* bribes, and *what by* extortions, he made enormous sums of money.

**259.** I stript myself, put my clothes into the vessel, and drawing it after me, *between* wading *and* swimming arrived at the royal port of Blefuscu. <div align="right">(<i>Swift</i>)</div>

---

( 30 )

> I do **what** is right in my own sight.

【訳】 私は自分で見て正しいと思うことをする。

〔解 説〕 what=the thing which; that which
こういう what は 先行詞(Antecedent) と 関係代名詞(Relative Pronoun) とを兼ねたものである。類例：—

Do you understand **what** I say?
　(ぼくのいうことがわかりますか)
I am sorry for **what** I have done.
　(自分がしたことを悲しむ＝とんだことをしてすみません)

---

**260.** Anyone who has kept up his interest in his education after graduation knows that *what* is learned in school and college

---

leisure [léʒə] 暇。　**257.** rocking 揺れる。　**258.** customhouse 税関。 bribe [braib] わいろ。 extortion [ikstɔ́:ʃən] 強請(ホッ)。 enormous [inɔ́:məs] 巨大な。　**259.** strip 着物を脱ぐ。 vessel 船。 wade [weid] (川などを)歩いて渡る。
　(30) antecedent [æntisí:dənt] 先行詞。 sorry [sɔ́ri] 悲しい。 **260.** keep up もち続ける。 graduation [grædjuéiʃən] 卒業。

is at best a small part of it—merely beginning of an education.

**261.** *What* is most important is that in America *what* is right matters to the average citizen, and the truth matters.

**262.** Away went the horse full gallop, and before Hans knew *what* he was about, he was thrown off, and lay in a ditch by the roadside.

**263.** Resolve to perform *what* you ought, and perform without fail *what* you resolve.

**264.** By working night and morning for a neighbor, he had amassed, *what* seemed to him, a large sum of money, and this was expended in books.

**265.** But after all, *what* interests us most in a foreign city is not the ruins or the churches or the pictures or the scenes of historical and legendary happenings, but the ordinary life of the place—the crowds in the streets, the traffic, the shopfronts.

**266.** A remembrance of *what* is past and an anticipation of *what* is to come seem to be the two faculties by which man differs most from other animals. He endeavours to derive his happiness, and experiences most of his miseries, from these two sources.

**267.** *What* the final verdict of history will be on the English nation and on the Anglo-Saxon race, it is not for us to antici-

---

**at best** よくても、せいぜい。 261. **matter** 重要である。 **average** ふつうの。 262. (at) **full gallop**=at a gallop 疾駆して。 **about**=doing. **throw off** 投げ落とす。 **ditch** 溝。 263. **resolve** 決心する。 **ought** の次に to perform を補う。 **without fail** まちがいなく、必ず。 264. **amass** [əmǽs] 集める。 **expend** [ikspénd] 費す。 265. **after all** 結局。 **ruins** [rúːinz] 廃墟。 **scene** [siːn] 古跡。 **legendary** [lédʒəndəri] 伝説的な。 **happenings** [hǽpniŋz] 出来事。 **traffic** 人通り。 **shopfront** 店頭。 266. **remembrance** [rimémbrəns] 記憶。 **anticipation** [æntìsipéiʃən] 予想。 **faculty** 能力。 **endeavour** [indévə] 努力する。 **derive** [diráiv] 引き出す。 267. **verdict** [vɔ́ːdikt] 裁決、判断。 **anticipate** [æntísipeit] 予想する。

pate; but our linguistic test, our examination of *what* we have so far added to the language of civilization, enables us at least to form an opinion about the past achievement of our race.

**268.** It is clear that *what* this generation needs is not increase of material resources or knowledge and skill, but the motive and will to utilise them not selfishly for the profit of some, but unselfishly for the good of all.

(31)

He has had no regular education; he is **what you call** a self-made man.

【訳】 彼は正規の教育を受けなかった。あれがいわゆる「自力で仕上げた男」である。

〖解説〗 what you call
what we call
what is called

はいずれも「いわゆる」と訳してよい。この場合も **what=that which** であるが便宜のために別に一項を設けたのである。類例:—

He is **what is commonly called** a bore.

(あれが世間で言ううるさい[うんざりさせる]やつだ)

She is **what** people **call** a "glamour girl."

(ああいう女がいわゆるグラマー・ガールだ)

【参考】 **so-called** も「いわゆる」であるが、speaker (話し手)がその

---

linguistic [liŋgwístik] 語学上の。**so far** これまでに。**form an opinion** 意見を出す。achievement 功績。268. generation [dʒènəréiʃən] 世代。resources [risɔ́:siz] 富源。**will to utilise** 利用しようという意志。selfishly [sélfiʃli] 利己的に。profit 利益。good 利益、幸福。

(31) regular [régjulə] 規則正しい、正規の。 bore [bɔ:] うるさい人。**glamour** [glǽmə] 魅惑(ミゎ)。

名前を真正のものと認めないような場合に用いられる。
That is **so-called** naturalism.
(あれがいわゆる自然主義だ)［真の自然主義はあんなのじゃない］

---

**269.** Read, consider well what you read, form your own judgment, and stand by that judgment in spite of the sayings of *what are called* learned men, until fact or argument be offered to convince you of your error.

**270.** The travelers, camels, and camel drivers, together, form *what is called* a caravan.

**271.** His principle was to live simply and always below the amount one has earned. This, he pointed out, was the one way to freedom from anxiety about poverty and to provide the means for fresh enterprises, or *what we call* capital.

**272.** *What is commonly called* peace is not peace at all; mere absence of fighting is not peace; on the contrary, if you want peace, you will have to fight for it.

**273.** The water in all these rivers, lakes, and oceans is constantly rising into the air in *what is called* moisture or vapor.

**274.** It is pleasant to smell a sweet rose or violet; and I believe, smelling really **forms a good part of** *what we call* tasting.

**275.** Their impression of Radio Liberation was wholly

---

**naturalism** [nætʃərəlizm] 自然主義。 **269. stand by** 固守する。 **saying** [séiiŋ] 言うこと。 **argument** [á:gjumənt] 論証。 **offer** 提出する。 **convince...of** ...を納得させる。 270. **camel** [kǽməl] らくだ。 **caravan** [kǽrəvæn] 隊商。 271. **principle** [生活の] 主義。 **below the amount** 金額以下。 **anxiety** 不安。 **provide** 供給する。 **enterprise** [éntəpraiz] 事業。 **capital** 資本。 272. **absence** ないこと。 **contrary** [kɔ́ntrəri] 反対。 273. **ocean** [óuʃən] 大洋。 **constantly** [kɔ́nstəntli] たえず。 **moisture** [mɔ́istʃə] 湿気。 **vapor** [véipə] 水蒸気。 274. **violet** [váiəlit] すみれ。 **a good part** 大きな部分。

negative. They denounced it for *what they called* its cursing tone.

(32)

> Coal and iron made England **what she is.**

【訳】 英国の今日あるのは石炭と鉄との賜物である。

〖解説〗 この what も that which の意味であるが, **What one is** が「現在のその人」「その人の人物」などの意味をなすものである。上の例は直訳すれば,「石炭と鉄とが英国を現在の英国にした」である。類例:―

You have made me **what I am.**
(私の今日あるのはあなたのおかげです)
I am not **what I used to be.**
(私は昔の私ではない)
The Japan of to-day is not **what it was** ten years ago.
(今日の日本は10年前の日本ではない)

**276.** He is rich or poor according to *what he is*, not according to *what he has*. He is rich who values a good name above gold.

**277.** What men do makes them *what they are;* how they do what they do determines the quality of *what they are*.

(*H. Read*)

**278.** We can hardly leave Italy without a peep at Rome, its capital, a city famous for *what it was* rather than *what it is*.

---

**275. negative** 否定的、感心しない。 **denounce** [dináuns] 公然非難する。 **cursing** 人をそしる。

(32) **used** (*when followed by* to) [juːs, juːst]. **276. according to** ...によって。 **value** 価値をつける。 **above** [əbʌv] 上に。 **277. determine** [ditə́ːmin] 決定する。 **quality** 性質。 **278. Italy** [ítəli]. **peep** のぞき見。

Wherever we go we recall its ancient glory and power, when this city was the centre of the Roman Empire, which controlled nearly all the known world.

**279.** No matter where you go, no matter who your ancestors were, what school or college you have attended, or who helps you, your best opportunity is in yourself. The help you get from others is something outside of you, while it is *what you are*, *what you do yourself*, that counts.

**280.** More than half of my years have gone—perhaps two-thirds of them have gone. My brain is as good as ever it was, and will probably remain so for a very long time yet, but my energy is not and cannot be *what it was*, and it will gradually decline.

**281.** Man is the only animal that laughs and weeps; for he is the only animal that is struck with the difference between *what things are*, and *what they ought to be*.

**282.** We honour him not alone for *what he has done*, but for *what he is*.

---

( 33 )

He is handsome, clever, and **what is better** still, very rich.

---

**recall** [rikɔ́:l] 思い出す。 **ancient** 昔の。 **glory** 栄光。 **control** [kəntróul] 支配する。 279. **no matter** ...であろうとも。 **ancestor** [ǽnsistə] 祖先。 **attend** [əténd] 通学する。 **count** [kaunt] 重要である、価値を持つ。 280. **two-thirds** 3分の2。 **brain** 頭脳。 **probably** 多分。 **gradually** 徐々に。 **decline** [dikláin] 衰える。 281. **weep** 泣く。 **be struck with** ...に心を打たれる。 282. **honour** [ɔ́nə] 尊敬する。

(33) **handsome** [hǽnsəm] 美しい。

【訳】 彼は美男で、才子で、なおいいことには、非常な金持だ。

【解説】 この構文でも what=that which であるが、「何々なことには」など訳すべき挿入句となっているものである。類例:—

The rules should be few, and **what is more important,** comprehensive.

(規則は少数であるべく、そしてなお重要なことは、包括的であるべきことだ)

---

**283.** At sight of his visitor he sprang up from his chair and welcomed him with both hands and genuine feeling. For these two were old friends, old mates both at school and college, both thorough respecters of themselves and of each other, and, *what does not always follow*, men who thoroughly enjoyed each other's company.

**284.** Thus the young man of promise not only broke all the promise he had made to himself and others, but *what was worse than all*, the heart of his aged father.

**285.** The idle man does not know what it is to enjoy rest for he has not earned it. Hard work, moreover, tends not only to give us rest for the body, but, *what is even more important*, peace to the mind. If we have done our best to do, and to be, we can rest in peace.

**286.** *What is more*, if you are to make a success of writing, you will have to work. Many people who say they want to write mean only that they want to be writers. They want the

---

**comprehensive** [kəmprihénsiv] 包括的。 **283. sprang**＜spring とびあがる。 **genuine** [dʒénjuin] 真正の。 **mate** 仲間、相棒。 **thorough** [θʌ́rə] 十分な、徹底的。 **follow** 結果として当然そうなる。 **company** [kʌ́mpəni] 交際。 **284. of promise** 前途有望な。 **the promise** [誓った]望み。 **worse** [wəːs] よりわるい。 **the heart** は broke の目的語。 **aged** [éidʒid]=old. **285. earn** [əːn] 努力して得る。 **tend** …の傾きがある。 **286. make a success of** …で成功する。

status without the work.　　　　　　　　　　　　　(慶応大)

**287.** At the age of twenty-one, he was master of his trade; and, *what was more*, had laid up a vast amount of general and scientific information.

**288.** *What makes the matter worse* is, that we cannot help spoiling air ourselves by the very act of breathing.

---

( 34 )

( a ) This is **all** the money (that) I have.
( b ) I will give you **what** money I have.

【訳】（a） 所持金はこれだけ。

　　　（b）［たくさんはないが］ありったけの金を全部あげよう。

〖解 説〗（a） That is all. は「これで全部」「もうほかにはない」という意味である。例：—

**This is all** the money (that) I have.＝I have **no more** money.
（所持金はこれだけ＝ほかにはない）

**That's all** (that) I have to say.＝I have **nothing more** to say.
（言うことはこれだけ＝ほかに言うことはない）

I will do **all I can.**
（できるだけやってみましょう）

I will tell you **all I know.**
（知ってるだけのことは全部言います）

（b） 関係代名詞の形容詞用法としての what～ は、**that which；such～as；any～that** などの意味に解すべき場合もあるが、

　　**what～＝all the～that...**

---

status [stéitəs] 地位。　**287.** lay up 集積する。vast amount ばくだいな分量。scientific [sàiəntífik] 科学的。information [ìnfəméiʃən] 知識。**288.** breathe [bri:ð] 呼吸する。　cannot help せざるを得ない。　spoil 汚す。

　(34) money [mʌ́ni]。

と見るべき場合が多い。たとえば

    **what** money I have=**all the** money (**that**) I have
    (ありったけの金)

次に、what は little を伴なうことが多く、また little を伴なわなくても little の意味を含んでいる場合が多い。すなわち

    **what** money I have=**what little** money I have
    (少ないながらもありったけの金)

---

**289.** No longer able to satisfy every request that was made him, instead of money he gave promises. They were *all he had* to bestow, and he had not resolution enough to give any man pain by a denial.
(Goldsmith)

**290.** "Mr. Harris!" exclaimed Edward, and it was *all he could* say. For the remembrance of past favours bestowed on him by his benefactor, so filled his heart with gratitude, that farther utterance was denied.

**291.** The dear boy only slept a minute—just one little minute—at the post; I know *that was all*, for Bennie never dozed over a duty.

**292.** Those men of genius choose a particular profession not because they consider it the best, because it promises the most glory, money, or happiness, but because they cannot help it, and for the same reason they stick to it while life lasts. *All they*

---

**289. no longer** [lɔ́ŋgə] もうこれ以上...ない。**request** [rikwést] 依頼。**him** 間接目的。**bestow** [bistóu] 与える。**resolution** 決意、覚悟。**denial** [dináiəl] 拒絶、否定。 **290. Edward** [édwəd]. **favour** 恩恵。**benefactor** [bénifæktə, bènifǽktə] 恩人。**filled** 主語は remembrance. **gratitude** [grǽtitju:d] 感謝。**farther** それ以上の。**utterance** [Átərəns] 発言。 **291. post** 持ち場。**doze** [douz] 居眠りする。**over** しながら。 **292. men of genius** 天才たち。**profession** 職業。 **stick to** を固守する。

*know* is that they love what they are about, and they give their whole souls to it accordingly.

**293.** *What little* time I have been able to save has been necessarily employed in the examination of some points of law which admitted of no delay.

**294.** *What* money *we had* with us barely sufficed for our railway fare.

**295.** " I am a physician, madam," said he bowing respectfully; " your neighbours have informed me of your illness, and I am come to offer *what service* may be in my power."

**296.** Being at a distance from my papers, I will give you *what account I can* of them from my memory.  (*Franklin*)

**297.** I carried *what luggage* I immediately needed with me from my lodgings, and the rest was to be sent by the carrier.

(*Gaskell*)

**298.** *What curious books* I have, they are indeed but few, shall be at your disposal.

**299.** None of the boys who had caused the disaster followed to learn the fate of the wounded boy. There was one, however, who witnessed the accident from a distance, and went to render *what service* he could.

**300.** The daylight was a burden; it must be borne with *what*

---

about=doing, engaged in. 293. save さく、割愛する。 employ 使用する。 admit of ...を許す。 delay [diléi] 延引。 294. barely [béəli] 辛うじて。 suffice [səfáis] 足りる。 fare [fɛə] 賃金。 295. physician [fizíʃən] 内科医。 bow おじぎをする。 be in my power わたしにできる。 296. papers 書類。 give account of ...の話をする。 297. luggage 荷物。 immediately じきに。 lodgings 下宿屋。 298. curious [kjúəriəs] 珍しい。 be at one's disposal 自由に使える。 299. disaster [dizá:stə] 災難。 fate 運命。 witnesss [wítnis] 目撃する。 accident [ǽksidənt] 珍事。 render service 手助けをする。 300. burden 重荷、苦痛。 borne<bear がまんする。

*patience* she could summon. *(Gissing)*

**301.** The affectionate son used *what little* strength he had left to tie the medicine that he had received from the doctor around the dog's neck, and sent him home with it.

**302.** I discovered my limitations and it seemed to me that the only sensible thing was to aim at *what excellence* I could within them. *(Maugham)*

**303.** At the outset I had so mismanaged my affairs that, for a while, I found myself with some money owing me for work done, but no funds in hand. People who ask for money, however justifiably, have it remembered against them; so I made shift to manage on *what small cash* I had in pocket.

---

(35)

> Leaves **are to** the plant, **what** lungs **are to** the animal.

【訳】 葉の植物に対する関係は、肺の動物に対する関係と同じことだ。

〖解説〗 1. A : B = X : Y
2. A is to B as X is to Y.
3. A is to B what X is to Y.
4. As X is to Y, so is A to B.
5. What X is to Y, that is A to B.

　　=A の B に対するのは X の Y に対するのと同じ。

---

**summon** 奮い起こす。　**301. affectionate** [əfékʃənit] 愛情の深い。 **tie** 結びつける。 **medicine** [médisin] 薬。 **302. limitation** 限界。 **sensible** 賢明な。 **aim** ねらう。　I could の次に find とか acquire のような語を入れて解する。 **303. outset** [áutset] 手始め。 **mismanage** [mísmǽnidʒ] しそこなう。 **affairs** [əfɛ́əz] 事務。 **owing** [óuiŋ] 支払わるべき。 **justifiably** [dʒʌ́stifaiəbli] 正当に。 **remembered against them** 自分の不利益になるように覚えていられる。 **make shift** やりくりする。

おのおのの形を文法的に直訳して見れば、(2)「AはBに対してXがYに対するごとくである」。(4)はそれの順序を変えて、「XがYに対するごとく、そのようにAはBに対する」としたのである。(3)は「AはBに対してXがYに対するところのものである」で、what X is to Y は名詞節で、is の補語である。(5)は補語となる名詞節を先に出し、さらにそれと同格の that を加えたのである。この that ははぶいてもさしつかえない。(4)および(5)の後半にある主語と動詞との位置の転換に注意せよ。

類例:—

$$\begin{cases} 5 : 7 = 10 : 14 \\ \text{Five \textbf{is to} seven \textbf{what} ten \textbf{is to} fourteen.} \\ =5 と 7 との比は 10 と 14 との比に等しい。\end{cases}$$

Reading **is to** the mind **what** food **is to** the body.
(読書の精神におけるはあたかも食物の肉体におけるがごとし)

〖注　意〗　この形の be が他の動詞（たとえば stand など）に変わったり、to が他の前置詞に変わったりすることがある。例:—

A nurse **stands to** a patient **as** a mother **does to** a child.
(看護婦は患者に対して、母が子供に対すると同じ関係に立つ)

**What** the lion **is among** beasts, **that is** the eagle **among** birds.
(ししが獣類の中に占める地位は、わしが禽類の中に占める地位と同じである)

---

**304.** It is said the civility *is to* a man *what* beauty *is to* a woman: it creates an instantaneous impression in his behalf.

**305.** Few animals can see colours; apparently the world as seen even by most mammals is a black and white world, not a coloured world. On the other hand, we are much worse off than many other creatures—dogs, for instance, or some moths

---

(35) **among** [əmʌ́ŋ] …の中。　**304. civility** [sivíliti] 礼儀。　**create** [kriéit] 創造する、生む。　**instantaneous** [ìnstəntéinjəs] 即時の。　**behalf** [bihɑ́ːf] 利益。　**305. apparently** 外から見たところは。　**mammal** 哺(ニュウ)乳動物。**be worse off** 暮し向きがもっとわるい、劣っている。**moth** [mɔθ] 蛾(ガ)。

—in regard to smell. Our sense of smell *is to* a dog's *what* an eye capable of just distinguishing big moving objects *is to* our own eye.

**306.** *What* the horns *are to* the buffalo, *what* the paw *is to* the tiger, *what* the sting *is to* the bee, *what* beauty, according to the old Greek song, *is to* woman, deceit *is to* the Bengalee.

(*Macaulay*)

**307.** A bank *is to* a country *what* the heart *is to* the body. It must pump the money through the commercial arteries, causing the whole body to function effectively. As the body depends on the proper working of the heart, so the business of a country depends upon the proper working of the banks.

**308.** Love *does to* women *what* the sun *does to* flowers: it colours them, embellishes them, makes them look radiant and beautiful; but when it is too ardent it consumes and withers them.

(*Max O'Rell*)

**309.** Sociey is like a building, which stands firm when its foundations are strong and all its timbers are sound. The man who cannot be trusted *is to* society *what* a bit of rotten timber *is to* a house.

**310.** He surpassed the acknowledged masters in various fields of landscape work, and left matchless studies of natural

---

**sense of smell** 嗅覚(きゅうかく)。 **distinguish** 区別する。 306. **horn** つの。 **buffalo** [bʌ́fəlou] 水牛。 **paw** 足。 **sting** 針。 **deceit** [disíːt] 虚偽。 **Bengalee**＝**Bengali** [beŋɡɔ́ːli] Bengal 人。 307. **pump** ポンプの作用をする。 **artery** [áːtəri] 動脈。 **function** 機能をはたす。 **proper** 適正な。 308. **embellish** [imbéliʃ] 飾る。 **radiant** [réidiənt] 輝かしく。 **ardent** [áːdənt] 熱烈な。 **consume** [kənsjúːm] 消費する。 **wither** しぼませる。 309. **foundation** 土台。 **timber** [tímbə] 用材。 **trust** 信頼する。 **bit** 小片。 **rotten** [rɔ́tn] 腐った。 310. **surpass** [səːpáːs] 凌駕(りょうが)する。 **acknowledged** [əknɔ́lidʒd] 定評ある。 **field** 分野。 **matchless** 比類のない。

scenery in lines never before attempted. *What* Shakespeare *is in* literature, Turner *is in* his special field, the greatest name on record.

(36)

> As the lion is king of beasts, so is the eagle king of birds.

【訳】 ししは獣類の王、わしは鳥類の王。

〖解　説〗 **As A is B, so is X Y.** (A が B であるようにそのように X は Y である)。類例：—

 **As** fire tries gold, **so** does adversity try virtue.
  (火が黄金を試みるように不幸が徳を試みる＝熱火の試練によって黄金の真価を知るように、人も逆境に会ってその真価を発揮する)
 **As** the desert is like a sea, **so** is the camel like a ship.
  (沙漠が海なららくだは船だ)

〖注　意〗 so の次には主語と動詞と転換されることも、されないこともある。(問題 **311, 312, 315** など)。諺などにはこの形を省略したものが多い。

 例：— **As** you sow, **so** will you reap.
   (種をまけば、実を刈りとる。因果応報)
  **As** is the teacher, **so** is the pupil.
   (教師も教師なら生徒も生徒)

---

**311.** Our life is not short, but we make it so. *Just as* great wealth is scattered in a moment when it comes into the hands of a bad owner, while wealth however small, if it is entrusted

---

**scenery** [síːnəri] 風景。　**line** 方面。　**Shakespeare** [ʃéikspiə]。　**literature** [lítəritʃə] 文学。
(36) **lion** [láiən] しし。　**adversity** [ədvə́ːsiti] 逆境。　311. **scatter** [skǽtə] まき散らす。cf. **shatter** [ʃǽtə] 粉砕する。**in a moment** 一瞬にして。**entrust** [entrʌ́st] 委託する。

to a good keeper, increases by use, *so* our life is long enough for him who uses it properly.

**312.** *As* some men gaze with admiration at the colours of a tulip, or the wing of a butterfly, *so* I was by nature an admirer of happy human faces. *(Goldsmith)*

**313.** *As* storm following storm, and wave succeeding wave, give additional hardness to the shell that contains the pearl, *so* do the storms and waves of life add force to the character of man.

**314.** *As* the present is rooted in the past, and the lives and examples of our forefathers still to a great extent influence us, *so* are we by our daily acts contributing to form the condition and character of the future.

**315.** *As* daylight can be seen through very small holes, *so* little things will illuminate a person's character.

**316.** *As* you cannot have a sweet and wholesome abode unless you admit the air and sunshine freely into your rooms, *so* a strong body and a bright or happy countenance can only result from the free admittance into the mind of the thoughts of joy and good-will.

**317.** The blessings of health and fortune, *as* they have a beginning *so* they must also have an end. Everything rises but to fall, and increases but to decay.

---

311. **by use** うまく使って。 312. **gaze** 見つめる。 **tulip** [tjú:lip] チューリップ。 **by nature** 生まれつき。 313. **additional** [ədíʃənl] 追加の。 **hardness** 固さ。 **pearl** [pə:l] 真珠。 314. **is rooted** 根を下している。 **forefather** [fɔ́:fɑ̀:ðə] 先祖。 **to a great extent**＝largely. **influence** 影響を及ぼす。 **contribute** [kəntríbju:t] 貢献する。 315. **hole** 穴。 **illuminate** [iljú:mineit] 照らす。 316. **wholesome** [hóulsəm] 健康によい。 **abode** [əbóud] 住居。 **admit** 入れる。 **countenance** [káuntinəns] 顔つき。 **result from** ...から生まれてくる。 **of the thoughts** ...の of は admittance にかかる。 317. **blessing** めぐみ。 **decay** [dikéi] 衰える。

( 37 )

> **It is in** studying **as in** eating; he who does it gets the benefits, and not he who sees it done.

【訳】 学問をするのは食事をすると同様で利益を得るのはそれをする人で、人のするのを見ている人ではない。

〖解　説〗 It is $\begin{Bmatrix} \text{with} \\ \text{in} \end{Bmatrix}$ ... as $\begin{Bmatrix} \text{in} \\ \text{with} \end{Bmatrix}$ ~.

=As it is $\begin{Bmatrix} \text{in} \\ \text{with} \end{Bmatrix}$ ..., so it is $\begin{Bmatrix} \text{in} \\ \text{with} \end{Bmatrix}$ ~.

= ... is like ~.
= ...は~のごとし。

この場合の it は文法上別にさすものはなく、物の道理というほどの意味。with は in the case of で、in とたいてい似た意味である。

---

**318.**　*It is in* men *as in* soils, where sometimes there is a vein of gold which the owner knows not of.

**319.**　Bacon was accustomed to say that *it was in* business *as in* way—the nearest way was commonly the foulest, and that if a man would go the fairest way, he must go somewhat about.

**320.**　If bad manners are infectious, so also are good manners. There is no one who can be disagreeable with sunny people. *It is with* manners *as with* the weather. "Nothing clears up my spirits like a fine day," said Keats, and a cheerful person descends on even the gloomiest of us with something of

---

(37) **benefit** [bénifit] 利益。 318. **vein** [vein] 鉱脈。 **owner** 所有者。 319. **be accustomed to** ...する習わしである。 **foul** [faul] 悪い。 **would** 欲する。 **fair** きれいな、よい。 **about** まわって。　320. **infectious** [infékʃəs] 伝染性の。 **disagreeable** 不愉快な。 **sunny** 陽気な。 **descend** [disénd] 降りる。 **gloomiest** [glú:miist] もっとも陰気な、gloomy の最上級。

the blessing of a fine day.

**321.** *It is with* words *as with* sunbeams; the more they are condensed, the deeper they burn. (*Southey*)

**322.** *It is with* books *as with* nuggets of gold in alluvial diggings. The miner patiently washes a ton of dirt, well content if after his toil he should find single nugget of gold in his pan.

**323.** This *is as true of* a nation *as of* an individual. The nation in which the average individual economizes his energy and his money, or which means the same thing, spends them wisely, will always be a prosperous nation. (防衛大)

---

(38)

(a) He is **as** brave **as any** man alive.
(b) He is **as** brave a man **as ever** breathed.
(c) He is **the bravest** man **that ever** lived.

【訳】 (a) 彼は世にもまれな勇者である。
(b) 古今無双(むそう)の勇者だ。
(c) 古今未曾有の勇者だ。

〖解 説〗 (a) **as～as any...** は本来の意義からいえば、「いずれのとも同じくらい」であるが、一歩進んで「いずれのにも劣らず～」の意味に用いられる。したがって上の例 (a) は「彼はこの世に生きている何人にも劣らず勇敢=世にもまれなる勇者」となるのである。alive を in the

---

321. **condense** [kəndéns] 圧縮する。 322. **nugget** [nʌ́git] 天然金塊。 **alluvial** [əljúːviəl] 冲積(충적)層の。 **digging** 採掘。 **content** 満足して(形容詞)。 **toil** 骨折り。 323. **average** [ǽvəridʒ] 普通の。 **individual** [indivídʒuəl] 個人。 **economize** [i(ː)kɔ́nəmaiz] 節約する。 **which means the same thing** これは同じことになるのだが。 **prosperous** [prɔ́spərəs] 繁栄した。

world などとし、次のように言っても意味はまったく同じである。

He is **as** brave a man **as any** (man) *in the world.*

（b）　**as～as ever...** は (a) の変化であるが、(a) においては any の次に名詞（もっともはぶかれる場合もある）であったが、ever の次にはいつも過去動詞がくる。すなわち any は形容詞で、**ever** は副詞である。両者の関係は

**as～as ever...＝as～as** (any that) **ever...**

の any that をはぶいて、as を関係代名詞として用いたものと思えばよい。それで ever 以下の文句の名詞の性質でいろいろの変形がある。まずふつうの人間ならば

　...as ever *lived*
　...as ever *breathed*

などを用い、船ならば

She was **as** fine a ship **as ever** *walked the waters.*
　（かつて海原を渡ったいずれの 船にも 劣らず──古今無比のりっぱな船だった）

などいい、兵士ならば

He was **as** brave a soldier **as ever** *shouldered a rifle.*
　（彼は銃をかついだことのあるだれにも劣らず勇敢な兵士だった）

などいう。soldier を officer に代えたら as ever wore a sabre (剣をおびた) などとすればよいわけである。

（c）　「**the＋最上級＋that ever...**」は、(b) の前の方を最上級にし、that という関係代名詞で受けたまでである。that 以下は

　...that I ever saw
　...that I ever set my eyes on

などのほかに (b) に付いたと同じような文句が勝手につけられる。

〖**注　意 1**〗　**as～as ever** (before)「以前どおり」の意味に用いられることがある。これは

**more～than ever** (before) （前よりもいっそう）

───────────────
(38) **walked** [wɔːkt] 歩いた。　**shoulder** [ʃóuldə] になう。　**sabre** [séibə] 剣、サーベル。

に対するものである。例：—

He is **as** poor **as ever.**
(彼はあいかわらず貧乏だ)
He is **as** diligent **as ever.**
(彼はあいかわらず勤勉だ)
The wind blew **harder than ever.**
(風はいっそう激しくふいた)

〖注　意 2〗 **as...as ever** (いくら)
と訳すべき場合もある。例：—

Take **as** much **as ever** you like.
(いくらでも好きなだけお取りなさい)

---

**324.** You see in him, madam, *as* complete a villain *as ever* disgraced humanity. (*Goldsmith*)

**325.** For miles and miles around, the prospect extended over *as* fair a land *as ever* rejoiced the sight of man.

**326.** He now entered, handsomely dressed in his regimentals, and without vanity (for I am above it), he appeared *as* handsome a fellow *as ever* wore a military dress. (*Goldsmith*)

**327.** He [*i.e.* the dog] was *as* courageous an animal *as ever* scoured the woods. (*Irving*)

**328.** The entire career of " Old Ironsides " was that of what is called in the navy " a lucky ship." Perhaps this may be explained by the fact that she always had excellent commanders,

---

324. **villain** 悪者。**disgrace** [disgréis] 恥辱を与える。**humanity** [hju:mǽniti] 人類、人性、人道。　325. **prospect** [próspekt] 眺望。　**extend** 広がる。**rejoiced** [ridʒɔ́ist] 喜ばせた。　326. **handsomely** りっぱに。**regimentals** [rèdʒiméntlz] 軍服。**without vanity** 自慢なしに。**above it** 自慢を超越して。327. **courageous** [kəréidʒəs] 勇敢な。**scour** [skáuə] 走る。　328. **career** [kəríə] 経歴。**Old Ironsides** [áiənsaidz] 艦名。**be explained** 説明される。**excellent** [éksələnt] 優れた。**commander** 艦長。

and that she probably possessed *as* fine a ship's company *as ever* manned a frigate.

**329.** I was curious to know what the pink dust was. Suddenly the name of it occurred to me, though I had never heard of it before. It was fire! I was *as* certain of it *as* a person could be of anything in the world. *(Mark Twain)*

**330.** I have *as* much right *as any* one to contradict such an assurance.

**331.** Scrooge has *as* little of what is called fancy about him *as any* man in the city of London. *(Dickens)*

**332.** He was in his personal habits one of *the most* untidy men *that ever* drove a fellow lodger to distraction. *(Doyle)*

**333.** Dear little souls, they hate flattery, so they tell you; and, when you say, " Oh, darling, it isn't flattery in your case, it's plain, sober truth; you really are, without exaggeration, *the most* beautiful, *the most* good, *the most* charming, *the most* divine, *the most* perfect human creature *that ever trod this earth*," they will smile a quiet, approving smile, and leaning against your manly shoulder, murmur that you are a dear good fellow after all. *(Jerome K. Jerome)*

**334.** " I am a citizen, not of Athens or Greece, but of the world." These are the words of Socrates, the ancient Greek

---

**company** 乗組員。　**man** (船に)乗り組む。　**frigate** [fríɡit] 快速帆船。　329. **curious** 〜したがる。　**occur** 思いつく。　**could be** の次に certain を入れてみる。　330. **contradict** [kɔ̀ntrədíkt] 反駁(ばく)する。　**assurance** 断言。　332. **untidy** [ʌntáidi] だらしのない。　**fellow lodger** 同宿人。　**distraction** [distrǽkʃən] 狂気。　333. **hate** にくむ。　**flattery** おせじ。　**sober** まじめな、冷静な。　**exaggeration** [iɡzæ̀dʒəréiʃən] 誇張。　**divine** [diváin] 神のような。　**creature** [kríːtʃə] 生物、人。　**trod** < tread 踏む。　**approving** その通りですというような。　**murmur** ささやく。　334. **Athens** [ǽθinz]。　**Socrates** [sɔ́krətiːz] ソクラテス。

philosopher, and perhaps *the wisest man who ever lived.*

**335.** The whole world is engaged in searching for happiness, but judging by appearances, very few succeed in their search. Some expect to find it in money, some in fame, some in the gratification of their ambition, in the attainment of a certain position or object, but, when they get the thing that was going to make them happy, they find happiness just *as far as ever.*

---

(39)

(a) **Who in the world** are you?
(b) He **had not** a penny **in the world.**
(c) **The greatest** naval power **on earth.**

【訳】(a) 一体全体お前はだれだ。
　　　(b) 彼はびた一文もなかった。
　　　(c) 世界第一の海軍国。

〖解　説〗(a) **in the world**
　　　　　(b) **on earth**

この二つは疑問、打消し、最上級を強めるのに用いる。疑問には「一体全体」、打消しには「全然」、最上級には「世界第一」など、場合に応じて適宜に訳すべきである。

〖注　意 1〗 疑問を強めるために **in the name of God**; (in the name of) **the devil**; **the dickens**; **the deuce** などを who, what, where の疑問詞に付けることがある、いずれも「一体全体」など訳せばよい。例：—

---

335. **be engaged in** 熱中している。　**appearances** [əpíərənsiz] 外観、様子。**fame** 名声。　**gratification** [græ̀tifikéiʃən] 満足。　**attainment** [ətéinmənt] 達成。**position** 地位。
　(39) **dickens** [díkinz] 悪魔。　**deuce** [dju:s] 悪魔。

**What the deuce** is the matter?
（一体全体どうしたのだ）

〖注　意 2〗　最上級を強めるのには on earth にならって **on record** がある。前者は「地球上」、後者は「記録上」の意味である。比較：——

> the greatest man **on earth**
> （世界第一の偉人）
> the biggest earthquake **on record**
> （史上第一の大地震）

この二つをいっしょにすれば古今東西に類のないという意味となるわけである。この用法では earth には冠詞をつけない。実際に地球そのものをさすときはもちろん the earth という。

---

**336.** *What on earth* are you talking to him for?

**337.** *Who in the world* would have thought this!

**338.** Donald is *the most* practical man *on earth*.

**339.** It passed through his mind that there was *no one in the world* who cared what sort of memory he left behind him.

**340.** He is very easy to get on with. He is much liked. But he has no friends. He is an agreeable companion, but neither seeks intimacy nor gives it. There is *no one in the world* to whom he is not at heart indifferent. His happiness depends not on persons, but on himself.

**341.** Altogether he had not *the most* dignified aspect *in the world*, but the spectators gazed at him as if there was something superhuman and divine in his person. They even shaded their

---

**record** [rékɔːd] 記録。　**338. practical** 実際的な。　**339. care** 気にかける。**behind him** 死後に。　**340. get on with** いっしょにやって行く、交際する。**intimacy** [íntiməsi] 親密。　**indifferent** [indífrənt] 冷淡な。　**at heart** 心の中で。　**341. altogether** 全体として。　**dignified** [dígnifaid] 威厳ある。**aspect** すがた。**spectator** [spektéitə] 見物人。**superhuman** [sjùːpəhjúːmən] 超人的。**shade their eyes with their hands** 目に手をかざす。

eyes with their hands, as if they were dazzled by the glory of his countenance.

**342.** " My poor papa could give me nothing, and I had *but two* frocks *in all the world!* " (*Thackeray*)

**343.** " Why, Friend West," exclaimed the merchant, " what has possessed thee to cover thy walls with all these pictures? *Where on earth* didst thou get them? " (北海道大)

**344.** " This is terrible! " she exclaimed. " *How in the world* shall I ever be able to explain this to her? I should have known better than to give you that money in the first place, and I was a fool for listening to you . . . . "

**345.** He knew nothing could be so grateful to his poor sick mother as a good, sweet orange and yet he had *not a penny in the world*.

**346.** *How in the name of Heaven* had he found it out?

**347.** " *What, in God's name,*" said he, " is all this? "

**348.** I cannot tell *what the dickens* his name is. (*Shakespeare*)

**349.** " What! " he yelled, springing up. " You silly cuckoo! Why can't you be more careful what you're doing? *Why the deuce* don't you go and dress on the bank? You're not fit to be in a boat." (*Jerome K. Jerome*)

---

**dazzle** 目をくらます。 **countenance** [káuntinəns] 容貌。 **342. frock** 女の子の服。 **343. exclaim** 叫ぶ。 **possess** とりつく、心を捕える。 **to cover** 被うとは。 **344. explain** 説明する。 **should have known better than** ...のようなばかなことはすべきでなかった。 **345. grateful** ありがたがる。 **orange** [ɔ́rindʒ] みかん。 **349. yell** [jel] 叫ぶ。 **cuckoo** [kúku:] かっこう鳥、ばか者。

( **40** )

> He is **something of** a lawyer.

【訳】 彼は法律も少しは知っている。

〖解 説〗 something of...
anything of...
nothing of...
much of...
little of...

は、いずれも分量、度合をいうのに用いられる。類例:—

Is he **anything of** a scholar?
　(少しは学問があるのか)
He is **very much of** a scholar.
　(なかなか学者だ)
He is **more of** a scholar than a teacher.
　(教師というよりもむしろ学者という方だ)
He is **a bit of** everything.
　(彼は何でも少しずつかじっている)
He has **something of** the hero in him.
　(彼は少し英雄肌である)
He has **a great deal of** the diplomatist in him.
　(彼は大いに外交家肌だ)
Do you **see anything of** him lately?
　(近ごろちっとは彼に会うか)
I have **seen little of** him of late.
　(近ごろあまり会わない)

---

**350.** Reimer, though *something of a scholar*, was a mere compositor, knowing nothing of press work.　　　(*Franklin*)

(40) **scholar** [skɔ́lə] 学者。　**diplomatist** [diplóumətist] 外交官。　350. **compositor** [kəmpɔ́zitə] 植字工。　**press work** 印刷業。

**351.** He was also *a great deal of a politician*.

**352.** Haru had cause for jealousy; but she was *too much of a child* to guess the cause at once; and her servants too fond of her to suggest it. (*L. Hearn*)

**353.** I think she talked more willingly to her lodgers because her husband was a serious man and wasn't *much of one for a joke*. (*Maugham*)

**354.** Of course, the first thing to do with an adopted cat is to give it a name, and Jack Harmon, who was *a bit a wag* in his way, and a great admirer of the monster elephant which was just then making such a stir in New York, called his new pet "Jumbo."

**355.** In his definite prose-poems Turgenev was *much less of a poet* than in his sketches and novels, because self-consciousness destroys true poetry, which is the springing forth of mood and feeling almost in spite of itself. (*Galsworthy*)

**356.** My friend Sir Roger, amidst all his good qualities, was *something of a humorist*. (*Addison*)

**357.** The English politician is a little *too much of a debater;* the Indian politician a little *too much of an essayist*. (*Macaulay*)

**358.** Although not a strong boy, there was *nothing of the coward* about him, and at an early age he showed the spirit of

---

351. **politician** [pɔ̀litíʃən] 政治家。 352. **jealousy** [dʒéləsi] 嫉妬(しっと)。 **guess** 推測する。 **suggest** [sədʒést] 暗示する。 353. **lodger** 下宿人。 **for a joke** 冗談の好きな。 354. **adopt** [ədɔ́pt] 採用する、養子にする。 **wag** [wæg] おどけ者。 **admirer** [ədmáiərə] 嘆賞者。 **monster** [mɔ́nstə] 巨大な。 **make a stir** さわぎを起こす、評判となる。 **pet** 愛玩(あいがん)動物。 355. **definite** はっきりした。 **Turgenev** [tə:géinjev]. **self-consciousness** 自己意識。 **spring** ほとばしり出る。 **in spite of himself** われ知らず。 356. **amidst all** ...いろいろ〜があったが。 357. **debater** [dibéitə] 討論家。 **essayist** [éseiist] 随筆家。 358. **coward** [káuəd] 臆病者。

absolute fearlessness which in later years enabled him to do such great services for the nation.

**359.** The engagement made *something of a stir* in Florentine society and a number of parties were given for the young couple.

(*Maugham*)

---

### (41)

(a) You shall want for nothing **as long as** I live.
(b) Any book will do, **so long as** it is interesting.

【訳】（a）私の生きている間はお前たちに不自由はさせない。
　　　（b）おもしろくさえあればどんな本でもよろしい。

〖解　説〗（a）**as long as**...＝**while**...＝「する間は」すなわち内より外へ範囲を拡張しようとする心持ちである。

類例：—

　I shall keep your present **as long as** I live.
　　（くだされた物は生涯大事に取っておきます）

（b）**so long as**...＝**provided that**...＝**if**...＝「...するからには」「...さえすれば」

すなわち外から範囲を制限する心持ちである。類例：—

　**So long as** you are innocent, you need not fear.
　　（潔白であるからには何もおそれるには及ばない）

〖注　意〗　この二つを上述のように明瞭に区別することが困難な場合もあり、また往々(おうおう)混同して用いられた例もある。ついでに **as far as; so far as** の例も加えておく。

---

**absolute fearlessness** 絶対に物を怖れない心。　**service** 奉仕、功労。　**359. engagement** 婚約。　**stir** 大騒ぎ、センセーション。　**Florentine** [flɔ́rəntain] フロレンスの。
　（41）**do** 間に合う、目的にかなう。　**interesting** [íntəristiŋ] おもしろい。　**provided** [prəváidid] もし。　**innocent** [ínəsnt] 罪のない。

(a) **as far as**... $\begin{cases} 1. & \text{「...だけ」(程度)} \\ 2. & \text{「...まで」(距離)} \end{cases}$

例:—

1. I will try **as far as** I can.

   (できるだけのことをやってみよう)

2. I am going by train **as far as** Kobe, and then take ship for Shanghai.

   (神戸まで汽車で行ってそれから上海行きの船に乗るつもりだ)

(b) **so far as**...＝...の限りでは；...からいえば。例:—

**so far as** I know

(私の知っている限りでは)

**So far as it concerns** me, there is nothing wrong.

(私に関する限りでは——私だけは——何も故障はない)

**So far as** grammar **is concerned,** this composition leaves nothing to be desired.

(文法の点だけではこの作文は申し分がない)

---

**360.** A man can never be hindered from thinking whatever he chooses *so long as* he conceals what he thinks. The working of his mind is limited only by the bounds of his experience and the power of his imagination.

**361.** Lincoln went through life bearing the load of a people's sorrows with a smiling face. *As long as* he lived he was the guiding star of a whole brave nation, and when he died the little children cried in the street.

**362.** At any rate, America and Soviet Russia and Britain are telling one another again and again that they want nothing

---

360. **hinder** さまたげる。**conceal** かくす。**be limited** 限定される。**bounds** [baundz] 限度。　361. **Lincoln** [líŋkən] リンカーン。**go through life** 一生を通す。**bear** になう。**load** 荷物。**guiding** [gáidiŋ] 導きの。　362. **at any rate** とにかく。

more than to reach an agreement to end the testing of atomic weapons. At the same time, however, they declare that they cannot stop the tests *as long as* there is no such agreement.

(東北大、*Albert Schweitzer*)

**363.** If two liquids which do not readily mix are put into the same vessel, the lighter liquid floats on top of the heavier. It is perhaps possible to have the heavier liquid floating on top of the lighter, but this can only be possible *so long as* the liquids are entirely undisturbed.

**364.** *As far as* eye can reach, nothing is to be seen but sand.

**365.** Steamboats ply along the rivers, carrying people and merchandise to and fro, going sometimes *as far as* three thousand miles from their starting point.

**366.** The history of mankind is the history of man's activity, and *so long as* human nature and man's material conditions are what they are, so long must economic and industrial factors have a potent influence in the course of political and social life. (岡山大)

**367.** The simplest measure of time is the revolution of the earth round its axis, which *so far as* we know is uniform, perfectly regular, and has not varied in speed during any period of human observation.

---

**agreement** 協定。 **to end** 終らせるための。 **declare** 公言する。 **363. liquid** [líkwid] 液体。 **readily mix** すぐに混ざる。 **vessel** [vésl] 容器。 **float** 浮かぶ。 **be undisturbed** かき乱されない、そっとして置かれる。 **365. ply** [plai] 通う。 **merchandise** [mə́:tʃəndaiz] 商品。 **to and fro** あちらへ、またこちらへ。 **366. activity** 活動。 **condtion** 条件。 **what they are** 現状のまま。 **factor** 要因。 **potent** 有力な。 **in the course** 進行に。 **political** 政治的。 **367. measure** [méʒə] 尺度。 **revolution** [rèvəlúːʃən] 回転。 **axis** [ǽksis] 軸。 **uniform** 一定の、不変の。 **vary** [véəri] 変化する。 **observation** 観察。

**368.** I spend much of my spare time painting pictures. It gives me extraordinary pleasure; but I do not for that reason imagine that I am producing masterpieces. *So far as* the slightly talented individual *is concerned*, the nature of the excellence of his productions is essentially inferior to that of the excellence we find in the work of a great artist.

**369.** The happiest time of my boyhood was at that early period, little past the age of six, when I had my own pony to ride on, and was allowed to stay on his back just *as long* and go *as far* from home *as* I liked.

**370.** *So far as* his eyes *were concerned* the boy was already an old man, and needed a pair of spectacles almost as much as his own grandfather did. *(Hawthorne)*

**371.** *As far as* future professional men *are concerned*, Europeans are convinced that the traditional education in languages, literature, mathematics, and European history, comprises the best general education. *(J. Conant)*

**372.** There may be other beings in this vast universe endowed with reason, purpose, and aspiration; but we know nothing of them. *So far as* our knowledge goes, human mind and personality are unique, and constitute the highest product yet achieved by the cosmos.

---

368. **spare** 余分の。 **extraordinary** 異常な。 **for that reason** その理由で。 **masterpiece** [máːstəpiːs] 傑作。 **slightly talented** わずかな才能しかない。 **nature** 性質。 **essentially** 本質的に。 **be inferior to** ...に劣る。 369. **little past** すぎるかすぎない。 **pony** 小馬。 **be allowed** 許される。 370. **spectacles** [spéktəklz] 眼鏡。 371. **professional** 知的職業をもつ。 **be convinced** 確信している。 **traditional** 伝統的。 **comprise** [kəmpráiz] 含む、構成する。 372. **universe** 宇宙。 **endow** [indáu] 賦与(ふよ)する。 **reason** 理性。 **aspiration** [æ̀spəréiʃən] 向上心。 **personality** [pə̀ːsənǽliti] 人格。 **unique** [juːníːk] 無比の。 **constitute** 構成する。 **achieve** 成就(じょうじゅ)する。 **cosmos** [kɔ́zməs] 宇宙。

**373.** Coat, hat, boots, and gloves had evidently seen their best days, but *so far as* mending and brushing go, everything had been done apparently, to make them presentable. (一橋大)

---

### (42)

(a) I got up **so** early **as to** be in time for the express.
(b) I got up early **so as to** be in time for the express.

【訳】 (a) 私は早く起きたから急行に間に合った。
　　　(b) 私は急行に間に合うように早く起きた。

〖解　説〗 (a) so~as to... のように **so** と **as**(+不定詞)との間に副詞あるいは形容詞の挿まる構文は自然の結果を示す。

　I got up **so early as to** be in time.
　=I got up **so early** that I was in time.
　(間に合うくらい早く起きた＝早く起きたから間に合った)

類例：—
　She is **so young as to** look like a child.
　=She is **so young that** she looks like a child.
　(彼女はまだ若くてこどもみたいだ)

(b) **so as to...** とつづく形は「...するために」と目的を示す。ゆえに

　I got up early **so as to** be in time for the first train.
　=I got up early **so that I might** be in time for the first train.
　=I got up early **in order to** catch the first train.
　(一番列車に間に合うように早く起きた)

---

**373. have seen better days** 昔はよかった、今はひどくなっている。　**mending** つくろい。　**apparently** 見たところ。　**presentable** 人前に出せる。
(42) **express** [iksprés] 急行。

**374.** Almost always, however, the leaf is green: it is broad and flat, with a large expanded surface, and this surface is spread out horizontally, *so as to* catch as much as possible of the sunlight that falls upon it.

**375.** It is a popular belief that the aim of science is to explain things; as a matter of fact, the so-called explanations of science do not usually get much beyond describing the observed facts in the simplest possible terms *so as to* make their relations with one another clear and intelligible.

**376.** If ever you travel with a Scotchman from Edinburgh to London, you may observe that he does not take his eyes off the country the train goes through. He looks out of the window all the time, *so as not to* miss a penny worth of the money he has paid for his place. *(Max O'Rell)*

**377.** On the third day, the barometer fell *so* low *as to* induce the captain to believe that they should have a severe gale, and every preparation was made to meet it, should it come on.

**378.** How on earth is a novelist *so* to combine these incompatible traits *as to* make the plausible harmony that renders a character credible? *(Maugham)*

**379.** Our dressing and undressing, our eating and drinking,

---

374. **expanded** 広がった。 **surface** [sə́:fis] 表面。 **horizontally** 水平に。 375. **popular** 一般の人の。 **as a matter of fact** 実際のところ。 **so-called** いわゆる。 **describe** 記述する。 **term** [tə:m] 語。 **intelligible** [intélidʒəbl] わかりやすい。 376. **ever** は強意の用法。 **Edinburgh** [édinbərə] エディンバラ。 **London** [lʌ́ndən] ロンドン。 **take one's eyes off** ...から目を離す。 **miss** 見落として損をする。 **place** 座席。 377. **barometer** [bərɔ́mitə] 晴雨計。 **induce** [indjú:s] 誘う。 **gale** 大風。 **preparation** 準備。 **meet it** 大風に対処する。 **should it**=if it should. 378. **combine** 結合する。 **incompatible** [ìnkəmpǽtibl] 両立しない。 **trait** [trei, treit] 特性。 **plausible** [plɔ́:zəbl] もっともらしい。 **render**=make. **credible** なるほどと信用できる。 379. **undressing** 着物を脱ぐこと、ここでは dressing と対照になるから [ʌ́ndresiŋ] のように発音する。

our greetings and partings, even most of the forms of our common speech, are *so* fixed by repetition *as* almost *to* be classified as reflex actions.

(津田塾大)

---

### (43)

(a) I got up **so** early **that** I was in time for the express.

(b) I got up early (**so**) **that** I **might** be in time for the express.

【訳】(a) 早く起きた<u>から</u>急行に間に合った。

(b) 急行に間に合う<u>ように</u>早く起きた。

〚解説〛(a) so~that... の構文においては that の前後が<u>原因結果</u>の関係をなしている。

〚注意〛 so that が独立に therefore, accordingly などの意味の接続詞として用いられることがある。そんな場合には「だから」「したがって」などと訳すればよい。

(b) **so** (or **in order**) **that** one **may**... のように may が加わると「...するために」と<u>目的</u>をあらわす。類例：—

I work hard **that I may** succeed.
（私は成功したいために勉強する）

I work hard **that I may not** fail.
（私は失敗しないように勉強する）

〚注意〛(b) の構文では前後両節の主語が同一物をさすときは "(in order) to—" の構文に改めることができるが、前後の主語が異なる場合はそうはできない。例：—

**He** works hard **that he may** maintain his family.

---

**fix** 固定する。 **class** 分類する。 **repetition** 反復。 **reflex** [ríːfleks] 反射的。
(43) **maintain** [mentéin] 支える、養う。

=He works hard **in order to** maintain his family.
（彼は一家を支えるためにけんめいに働く）
He works hard **that his family may** live in comfort.
（彼は家族が安楽に暮し得るようにけんめいに働く）
過去になると may はもちろん might に変わる。例：—
He *worked* hard *that* he *might* maintain his family.

---

**380.** The land thereabout was *so* fertile *that* I decided to make a vegetable garden. In the tropics gardening would be a delightful occupation and it might easily prove *so* profitable *that* I should never again need to resume my old trade of journalism. (中央大)

**381.** This particular morning, an idea occurred to me, *so* simple, *so* reasonable, and *so* easily to be accomplished, *that* it filled me with surprise that such a plan had not presented itself before.

**382.** The boom was *so* high, and everything *so* ripe, *that* we saw that it would be a mistake not to strike now, right away, without waiting any longer. (*Mark Twain*)

**383.** *So* much did he amuse me, although without intending it, *that* I thought it would be only fair, in my turn, to do something for his entertainment.

**384.** Charity shown by the publication of an inferior article

---

**comfort** [kʌ́mfət] 安楽。　**380. thereabout** そのあたりの。　**fertile** [fə́ːtail] 肥沃(ひよく)な。　**decide** 決心する。　**tropics** 熱帯地方。　**gardening** 園芸。　**prove profitable** やって見ると利益があることがわかる。　**resume** [rizjúːm] ふたたび取り上げる。　**381. particular** ほかではないこの。　**reasonable** [ríːznəbl] 合理的な。　**accomplish** 達成する。　**present** [prizént] **itself**＝appear 現われる。　**382. boom** 人気。　**ripe** [機が]熟して。　**strike** ことを始める。　**right away** ただちに。　**383. amuse** 楽しませる。　**fair** 公平な。　**entertainment** [èntətéinmənt] もてなし。　**384. charity** 慈悲。　**publication** 発表。　**article** 記事、作品。

would be like the generosity of those highwaymen of old, who pitied the poor *so much that* they robbed the rich to have the means of relieving them. (東大)

**385.** But what made him remarkable *so that* people turned round in the streets to stare at him was that he had a thick head of hair, with a great wave in it, of deep rich red.

(*Maugham*)

**386.** The water was very shallow; *so that*, in the event of the ice giving way, there was nothing to fear beyond a slight ducking.

**387.** He kept an accurate journal of the days on which he worked and those on which his ill health prevented him from working, *so that* it would be possible to tell how many were idle days in any given year.

**388.** The role of wanderer is, to a large extent, imposed by necessity on most birds during the colder months. In winter food is much less abundant than at other seasons, *so that* a greater area of ground must be covered daily *in order that* sufficient *may* be obtained. (慶応大)

**389.** I mean to sit up every night and look at them (*i.e.* the stars) as long as I can keep awake; and I will impress those sparkling fields on my memory, *so that* by and by when they

---

**generosity** 気前よさ。 **highwayman** 追いはぎ。 **means** 資金。 **relieve** 救う。 385. **remarkable** 目立つような。 **turn round** ふりかえる。 **stare** じっと見る。 386. **shallow** 浅い。 **in the event of** ...の場合に。 **give way** (重さのため)破れる、おちこむ。 **ducking** ちょいと水にもぐること。 387. **accurate** 正確な。 **journal** [dʒə́:nl] 日誌。 **prevent...from** をさまたげる。 **given** 任意の。 388. **role** 役割。 **wanderer** [wɔ́ndərə] 放浪者。 **impose** [impóuz] 負わせる。 **abundant** 豊富な。 **area** [ɛ́əriə] 地域。 **cover** 踏破する。 **sufficient** 十分の食料。 **obtain** 獲得する。 389. **mean to...** するつもりだ。 **keep awake** 目を覚している。 **impress** 印象づける。 **sparkling** きらめいている。

are taken away I can by fancy restore those lovely myriads to the black sky and make them sparkle again, and double them by the blur of my tears. *(Mark Twain)*

**390.** He preferred fishing and other amusements to the work of the school. At last, however, he realized that his father, who had little means, was making great sacrifice *in order that* he *might* obtain an education.

**391.** Today the rich people who in the past ages donated their wealth for the building of a cathedral, construct vast laboratories where silent men do battle upon the hidden enemies of mankind and often sacrifice their lives *that* coming generations *may* enjoy greater happiness and health.

**392.** The good plan is to spend in proportion to what we gain, but never to spend all that we gain. We should lay by something, *so that*, in the event of our being unable to work from sickness or old age, we *may not* be in want.

**393.** The captain never so much as moved. He spoke to the sailor, as before, over his shoulder, and in the same tone of voice; rather high, *so that* all the room *might* hear, but perfectly calm and steady.

**394.** Mice and rabbits are being sacrificed daily by thousands *so that* men *may* learn how to live in this atomic age.

---

**by fancy** 想像力で。 **restore** とり戻す。 **myriads** [míriədz] 無数。 **double** 2倍にする。 **blur** [blə:] にじみ、かすみ。 390. **prefer** [prifə́:] 選ぶ。 **realize** 悟る。 **means** 財産。 **sacrifice** 犠牲。 **obtain** 得る。 391. **donate** [dounéit] 寄付する。 **cathedral** [kəθíːdrəl] 大聖堂、大寺院。 **construct** 建設する。 **laboratory** 実験所。 **battle upon** …と戦う。 **sacrifice** [sǽkrifais] 犠牲にする。 **coming generation** 未来の世代。 392. **in proportion to**… に釣り合って。 **lay by** 貯える。 **be in want** ものがなくて困る。 393. **never so much as**… さえしない。 **over his shoulder** 肩ごしに。 **calm** [kɑ:m] 落ち着いた。 394. **mice**<mouse はつかねずみ。

These experimental animals are being exposed to the deadly gamma rays that come from atomic explosion. (神戸外大)

**395.** All night we rode slowly onwards, keeping our horses' tail to the polestar. There were many tracks in the snow, and we kept to the line of those, *that* no one *might* remark that a body of cavalry had passed that way. These are the little precautions which mark the experienced officer.

**396.** As every climate has its peculiar produce, our natural wants bring on a mutual intercourse; *so that* by means of trade each distant part is supplied with the growth of every latitude.

**397.** The old gentleman elbowed the people aside, and forced his way through the midst of them, rolling his body hither and thither, *so that* he needed twice as much room as any other person there.

---

( 44 )

(a) I work hard (**for fear**) **lest** I **should** fail.
(b) I work hard **for fear** (**lest**) I **may** fail.

【訳】(a)(b) 私は失敗するといけないから勉強する。

〘解　説〙 lest は fear その他恐怖懸念などを意味する語の次に来て

experimental 実験用の。 be exposed to ...にさらされる。 explosion 爆発。 deadly [dédli] 致命の。　395. polestar [póulstɑ:] 北極星。 track 道。 keep to 沿って行く。 body 一隊。 cavalry [kǽvəlri] 騎兵。 precaution [prikɔ́:ʃən] 用心。　396. climate (一地方の)気候。 peculiar [pikjú:ljə] 特有の。 produce [prɔ́dju:s] 農産物。 mutual [mjú:tjuəl] 相互の。 intercourse [íntəkɔ:s] 交際。 by means of ...の手段によって。 growth 生じたもの。 latitude [lǽtitju:d] 緯度、地方。　397. elbow aside ひじで押しのける。 force one's way 無理に押しわけて進む。 roll 左右によろめく。 thither [ðíðə] あちらへ。 room 余地、場所。

that の意をあらわす接続詞である。例:—

There are some **fears lest** I should fail.
(私が失敗するかもしれないという心配がある)

囲みの中にかかげた (a)(b) の例も直訳すれば、「私は失敗するかもしれないという懸念があるから勉強する」となり、けっきょく前章に掲げた I work hard **that** I **may not** fail. (私は失敗しないように勉強する)と同じ意味になる。lest 以下は名詞節で fear という名詞の同格であるが、(a) では for fear がはぶかれ、(b) では lest がはぶかれることが多い。それから主文の動詞が過去になれば may は might に変わって I **worked** hard for fear I **might** fail. となるが、should は現在過去共通である。

類例:—

Take care **lest** you **should** fail.
=Take care **that** you **may not** fail.
(失敗しないように気をつけなさい)

Take an umbrella with you { [for fear] **lest** it **should** rain.
　　　　　　　　　　　　　　{ **for fear** [lest] it **may** rain.
(雨が降ると悪いから傘をお持ちなさい)

I trembled [for fear] **lest** I **should** be discovered.
(見つかりはしないかとふるえていた)

---

**398.** It was not that play, or time for it, was refused him. Though no holidays were allowed, *lest* the habit of work *should* be broken, and a taste for idleness acquired, he had time enough every day to amuse himself, and the need of physical activity was satisfied by walking.

**399.** The rush of waters at this spot was tremendous, and no one ventured to approach it, even in canoes, *lest* he *should*

---

**398. It was not that** ...というわけではなかった。**refuse** 拒否する。**acquired** この前に should be が略されている。 **amuse** 楽しませる。 **physical** [fízikəl] 肉体の。 **activity** [æktíviti] 活動。 **399. tremendous** [triméndəs] すさまじい、ひじょうな。 **venture** [véntʃə] 冒険する。 **canoe** [kənúː] 丸木舟。

be dashed to pieces.

**400.** In London he had only two or three acquaintances, and from them he held aloof, *lest* necessity or temptation *should* lead to his spending money which he could not spare. (*Gissing*)

**401.** I dared not speak to Mary, *for fear* he *might* see me, for his eyes were fixed on me every moment.

**402.** If I had been less cautious I might have been more wise, but I was half crazy with *fear lest* you *should* learn the truth. (*Conan Doyle*)

**403.** Mr. St. John Ervine, who opened the inquiry, accepted pocket-money as an established institution, not liable to question. His one concern was *lest* the institution *should* fall into abuse through parental laxity and injudicious generosity.

**404.** With light and cautious steps, *lest* we *might* be as unpleasantly surprised as we had been when we made our hasty retreat, we advanced, holding our torches before us.

**405.** Never allow your husband to frequent your dressing room and poke his nose into all your little jars and bottles, *for fear* he *should* discover the secret of your beauty and of your lovely complexion. (*Max O'Rell*)

**406.** I was almost ashamed, *lest* he *might* think I wanted to show off my superior knowledge.

---

**dash to pieces** ばらばらに打ちくだく。 **400. acquaintance** 知人。 **hold aloof** 遠ざかっている。 **temptation** 誘惑。 **spare** なしですませる。 **402. cautious** [kɔ́:ʃəs] 用心深い。 **crazy** [kréizi] 狂気の。 **403. inquiry** 問い合わせ。 **established** 既定の。 **institution** 制度、慣習。 **liable to question** 問題となりやすい。 **concern** 関心、心配。 **abuse** [əbjú:s] 濫用。 **parental** 親の。 **laxity** だらしなさ。 **injudicious** 無分別な。 **generosity** 寛大さ。 **404. hasty retreat** 急いだ退却。 **advance** 進む。 **torch** [tɔ:tʃ] たいまつ。 **405. frequent** [frikwént] しばしば訪問する。 **poke one's nose** 鼻をつっこむ、おせっかいする。 **complexion** [kəmplékʃən] 顔の色つや。 **406. show off** 見せびらかす。

**407.** She, affrighted at his earnest manner, and *fearful lest* in his lunacy he *should* do her a mischief, cried out. (*Lamb*)

**408.** His love for the wild flowers was almost a passion; he watched for their annual return, and knew where, for miles around, he should find their first blooming. In plucking wild flowers, he always refrained from taking many from one locality, *lest* he *should* injure the future growth.

**409.** When I was a rich man in this city, I *was afraid*, in the first place, *lest* somebody *should* break into my house, seize upon my money, or do me personal harm.

**410.** When travelers came into Kotgarh, Lispeth used to lock herself into her own room *for fear* they *might* take her away to Simla, or out into the unknown world. (*Kipling*)

**411.** I still was in great *fear lest* he *might* think it necessary to come and apologize in person for "bothering" me.

**412.** I presently discovered that the family treasury contained still another feature—a jewel of some sort, apparently—and that she was trying to get around speaking squarely about it, *lest* I get paralyzed again. (*Mark Twain*)

---

407. **affright** おどす、恐れさす。 **lunacy** [lú:nəsi] 狂気。 **do mischief** 危害を加える。 408. **watch for** 気をつけて待つ。 **annual return** 年々もどってくること。 **pluck** つみとる。 **refrain** [rifréin] 控える。 **locality** [lokǽliti] 地方。 **injure** [índʒə] そこなう。 409. **seize** [si:z] つかむ。 **personal** 身体の。 410. **lock oneself** 錠をかけて 部屋に自分を閉じこめる。 411. **apologize** [əpɔ́lədʒaiz] 詫(わ)びる。 **in person** 自分で。 **bother** なやます。 412. **presently** すぐに。 **treasury** 宝庫。 **feature** めぼしいもの。 **apparently** 明らかに。 **get around** 避ける。 **squarely** 正直に。 **paralyze** [pǽrəlaiz] 麻ひさせる。

## (45)

(a) He **had the kindness to** show me the way.
(b) He **was so kind as to** show me the way.

【訳】 (a)(b) 彼は親切にも道案内をしてくれた。

〖解説〗　have the＋抽象名詞＋不定詞
　　　　　＝be so＋形容詞＋as＋不定詞
　　　　　＝be＋形容詞＋enough＋不定詞
　　　　　＝副詞＋動詞

というような関係になる。そこで上の例はまた

　　　　　＝He was **kind enough to** show me the way.
　　　　　＝He **kindly** showed me the way.

となる。類例：—

⎰Will you **be so good as to**　　　⎱ lend me your knife?
⎱Will you **be good enough to**　⎰
Will you **kindly** lend me your knife?
（どうかナイフを貸してくださいませんか）

⎰I **was so fortunate as to**　　　⎱ succeed in my first attempt.
⎱I **had the good fortune to**　⎰
（ぼくは運よく最初から成功した）

⎰He **was so unfortunate as to**　⎱ lose both his parents in his
⎱He **had the misfortune to**　　⎰
infancy. （あわれにも彼は幼い時両親に死に別れた）

⎰I **was so foolish as to**　⎱ trust such a man.
⎱I **had the folly to**　　　⎰
（私はおろかにもあんな人間を信用した）

⎰He **was so insolent as to**　⎱ write me such a letter.
⎱He **had the insolence to**　⎰
（彼は無礼にもこんな手紙をよこした）

---

(45) misfortune 不幸。 insolence [ínsələns] 傲慢(ごうまん)。

〖注 意 1〗 (a) の形式で不定詞が動名詞にかわって「**have the**＋抽象名詞＋**of**＋動名詞」
の形を取ることがある。例:—

　　He **had the temerity of dashing** (=*temerariously dashed*) into the enemy's ranks with only ten men.
　　(彼は無鉄砲にもわずか 10 人を率いて敵陣に突入した)

〖注 意 2〗 (b) の **so~as to**... は (42) (a) に述べた自然の結果を示す **so~as to**... から転じたものと考えてよい。

〖注 意 3〗 単に「...する」というところを「...するの光栄を有する」などいうもったいぶった言い方をすることがある。例:—

　　I **had the honour of being** (=I was) elected.
　　(余は当選の光栄を得た)
　　I **have the honour to inform** (=I inform) you that...
　　(...の旨ご通知申し上げます)
　　Whom **have I the honour of** addressing?
　　(失礼ですがどなたでいらっしゃいますか)
　　May **I have the pleasure of seeing** you next Saturday?
　　(こんどの土曜にお目にかかれますでしょうか)

このほか **to have the satisfaction of** (満足する); **to have the consolation of** (なぐさめとなる)などもこの類に属する。

---

**413.** The fact that a book is famous is enough to scare off some people who, if they *had the courage to* open the pages, would find there delight and profit.　　　　　　　(立教大)

**414.** I would have made him Prime Minister had he *had the good fortune to* live in my epoch.　　(*Conan Doyle*)

**415.** But he *had the ill fortune to* be older by a couple of

---

**temerity** [timériti] 向う見ず、無鉄砲。　**whom...address** だれに言葉をかける。　**413. scare off** おどかして近づけない。　**profit** 利益。　**414. had he**＝if he had.　**Prime Minister** 総理大臣。　**epoch** [í:pɔk] 時期。　**415. by a couple** [kʌ́pl] 二つだけ。

years than most of his fellow-students.

**416.** In leaving his castle for any length of time, he *had the consolation to* reflect that this village afforded, on the slightest notice, a band of thirty stout men, which was more than sufficient for its defence.

**417.** Donald was not *so silly as to* fall into trap. (*Max O'Rell*)

**418.** I published some tracts upon the subject myself, which, as they never sold, I *have the consolation of thinking* were read only by the happy few. (*Goldsmith*)

**419.** Ah! my dear Donald, what good stories you told me in the few months that I *had the pleasure of passing* with you.

**420.** Let your company be always, where possible, better than yourself and when you *have the misfortune to* move amongst your inferiors, bear in mind this seriously, that if you do not seize the apt occasion to draw them up to your level—which requires wisdom as well as love—they will certainly not be slow to drag you down to theirs.

**421.** The original artist who counts on understanding and reward is a fool. He may *have the luck to* be found out by some wind of chance which blows a sympathetic critical talent in his direction.

**422.** My girls attempted to please him with topics they

---

416. castle [káːsl] 城。 consolation [kɔnsəléiʃən] なぐさめ。 to reflect 考えると。 afford 出すことができる。 on the slightest notice 少しでも知らせがあれば。 band 一団、一隊。 its defence 城の守護。 417. silly 愚かな。 trap わな。 418. tract [trækt] 論文。 were read 主語は which. 420. move amongst 交わる。 inferior [infíəriə] 劣った者、目下の者。 bear in mind 念頭におく。 seize [siːz] 捕える。 apt occasion 適当な機会。 drag down 引きおろす。 421. count 当てにする。 wind of chance 偶然という風。 sympathetic [simpəθétik] 同情のある。 critical 批評的な。 422. attempt 企てる、試みる。

thought most modern; while Moses, on the contrary, gave him a question or two from the ancients, for which he *had the satisfaction of being* laughed at. (*Goldsmith*)

**423.** My wife also hoped one day to *have the pleasure of returning* his kindness at her own house.

**424.** Before disputing the bill, they *had the precaution of sending* on their baggage-cart in charge of a Chinese lad who had accompanied them. (*General Gordon*)

**425.** Oates, going into partnership with the new informer, *had the audacity to accuse* the poor queen herself of high treason. (*Dickens*)

**426.** Your son was *fortunate enough to* meet me in the city, and informed me of the fact that the widow of one of my bravest officers was suffering from poverty and sickness, without any means of assistance.

( 46 )

(a) Do not trust **such** men **as** praise you to your face.

(b) He is **such** a fool **that** no one will keep company with him.

---

**modern** [mɔ́dən] 近代的。 **on the contrary** 反対に。 **question** [kwéstʃən] 質問。 **ancients** [éinʃənts] 古人、古代の作家。 **424. dispute** [dispjúːt] 論ずる。 **bill** 勘定書。 **precaution** 用心。 **send on** 先へ送る。 **in charge of** ...に託して。 **425. go into partnership with**... と共同する、ぐるになる。 **informer** 告発者。 **audacity** [ɔːdǽsiti] 大胆。 **accuse...of** について告発する。 **high treason** 大逆罪。 **426. inform of** について知らせる。 **poverty** [pɔ́vəti] 貧困。 **means of assistance** 救助の手段。

【訳】（a）面と向かって人をほめる<u>ような人</u>には油断がならないよ。
　　　（b）彼はあまりばか<u>だから</u>だれも交際する人がない。

〖解　説〗（a）
$$\text{such}\sim\text{as}=\begin{cases}\text{those}\sim\text{who} & （人）\\ \text{that}\sim\text{which} \\ \text{those}\sim\text{which}\end{cases}（物）$$

〔ただし　～＝名詞〕

すなわちこの場合の as は who, which などと同じく関係代名詞で、大体は上の式のように見てよろしいが、such～as の方には

　　**those sort of～which...**

　　　＝「...のような～」

の意味を含めて訳すべき場合が多い、しかし必ず常にそうだというのではない。比較：―

　　**those** men **who** praise you to your face
　　　（面前で人をほめる人）
　　**such** men **as** praise you to your face
　　　（面前で人をほめるような人）

類例：―

　　**Such** eloquence **as** his is rarely to be met with.
　　　（あの人のような雄弁はまれだ）[his＝his eloquence]
　　You should read only **such** books **as** you can understand easily.
　　　（たやすくわかるような本ばかり読むべきだ）
　　**Such** [people] **as**
　　**Those** [people] **who** ｝ have money will not want for friends.
　　　（金のある人は友だちにこと欠かない）

〖注　意〗 such as が名詞の次にくる場合は like の意味となる。「たとえば...のような」などと訳すべきである。例：―

　　Birds of prey, **such as** the eagle and the hawk, do not lay many eggs.
　　　（猛禽[肉食する鳥]――たとえば、わし、たかのごとき――は卵を多

---

(46) eloquence [éləkwəns] 雄弁．　be met with でっくわす．

（b）「**such**＋名詞＋**that**...」は (43) (a)「**so**＋形容詞または副詞＋**that**...」と等しく原因結果の関係をあらわす。もっとも such は形容詞だから名詞に付き（名詞に伴なわない such は代名詞である）、so は副詞だから形容詞や、他の副詞の前にくるところに相違がある。例：—

**Such** was his diligence **that** he made remarkable progress.
He was **so** diligent **that** he made remarkable progress.
（彼はひじょうに勉強したから進歩がいちじるしかった）

〖注 意〗(a) の as は関係代名詞、(b) の that は接続詞であるから、両者は文章の構造を異にすることはいうまでもない。比較：—

His eloquence is **such as** is rarely heard anywhere. [二番目の is の主語は as]
（彼の雄弁は天下まれに見るところだ）
His eloquence is **such that** it compels applause even from his opponents. [compels の主語は it]
（彼はひじょうに雄弁で反対者さえも喝采(かっさい)しなければならないほどだ）

The book is written in **such** easy English **as** I can read. [as が read の目的語]
（この本はぼくにも読めるようなやさしい英語で書いてある）
The book is written in **such** easy English **that** I can read it. [read の目的語は it]
（この本はやさしい英語で書いてあるからぼくにも読める）

---

**427.** I love *such* mirth *as* does not make friends ashamed to look upon one another the next morning.

**428.** The year was spent in moral or rural amusement; in visiting our rich neighbours, and relieving *such as* were poor.

**progres** [próugres] 進歩。 **compel** [kəmpél] 強いる。 **applause** [əplɔ́ːz] 喝采(かっさい)。 **427. mirth** [məːθ] 歓楽。 **make ashamed** はずかしいと思わせる。 **428. rural** [rúərəl] 田園の。 **relieve** 救済する。

**429.** Words are in a real sense living things. There is, indeed, a continual birth and death of words. As life marches on, language must march with it, taking in new words to express new ideas, and leaving behind *such* words *as* belong to thoughts and facts that have had their day.

**430.** As many of the terms of science are *such as* you cannot have met with, think it would be well to have a good dictionary at hand, to consult immediately when you meet with a word you do not comprehend the meaning of.

**431.** At that time, in fact, if any one desired knowledge beyond *such as* could be obtained by his own observation, or by common conversation, his first necessity was to learn the Latin language. (*T. Huxley*)

**432.** Habits are easily formed—especially *such as* are bad; and what to-day seems to be a small matter, will soon become a great one, and hold you with the strength of a cable.

**433.** That the object of education should be to fit the child for life is *such* a well-worn saying *that* people smile at its commonplaceness even while they agree with its obvious common sense. (奈良女子大)

**434.** Even what may seem minor matters, *such as* attention to the teeth, may make no small difference to the comfort of life.

---

429. language [lǽŋgwidʒ] 言語。 continual birth たえず生まれること。 take in とり入れる。 leave behind 後へ残こす。 have had their day 古くなった。 430. have at hand 手近におく。 consult 引く。 immediately [imíːdjətli] ただちに。 comprehend [kɔmprihénd] 理解する。 431. desire 求める。 be obtained 得られる。 observation 観察。 neccessity 必要なこと。 432. hold おさえておく。 cable [kéibl] 大綱、錨索。 433. fit 適合させる。 well-worn 使い古した。 commonplaceness 平凡さ。 obvious 明らかな。 434. minor [máinə] 重要でない。 no small 小さくない。 difference 相違。 comfort 安楽。

## (47)

> (a) He is **not so much** a scholar **as** a writer.
> (b) He can**not so much as** read his own name.

【訳】（a）彼は学者というよりも<u>むしろ</u>著述家だ。
　　　（b）彼は自分の名を読む<u>ことさえ</u>できない。

〖解　説〗（a）　**not so much A as B**
　　　　　　　=**less A than B**
　　　　　　　=**not A, but rather B**
　　　　　　　=**more B than A**
　　　　　　　=B ほど A でない
　　　　　　　=A よりもむしろ B である

故に　　　　He is **not so much** a scholar **as** a writer.
　　　　　　=He is **more** of a writer **than** a scholar.
　　　　　　=He is a writer **rather than** a scholar.

類例：—

The oceans do **not so much** divide the world **as** unite it.
（海洋は世界を分割しないでむしろこれを結合するのだ）

〖注　意〗この形式の so much が not と離れて as につき

**not A so much as B**

の形を取ることもあるが意味はまったく同じである。例：—

It is { **not so much** poverty **as** pretence / **not** poverty **so much as** pretence } that harasses a ruined man.

（零落[ﾚｲﾗｸ]した人を苦しめるのは貧乏そのものでなくて、むしろ貧乏をかくそうとする苦心である）

It is { **not so much** advice **as** approval / **not** advice **so much as** approval } that he seeks.

（彼の求めるのは意見でなくて賛成である）

---

(47) **pretence** [priténs] 体裁（をつくろうこと）。　**harass** [hǽrəs] 悩ます。 **advice** [ədváis] 助言。　**approval** [əprúːvəl] 是認、賛成。

(b)　**not so much as...＝not even...**
　　＝...というそれだけのことも(否)；...さえ(否)

すなわち so much as は副詞の用をなすものである。この not が without に変わり、付属副詞句となる場合も多い。類例：—

I don't know him; indeed I have **not so much as** heard his name.
（私はその人を知りません、いや、名前さえ聞いたことがありません）
He left the room **without so much as** saying good-by to me.
（さようならともいわずに室を出て行った）

〖注　意〗 so much as＝even を「すら」「さえ」など訳す場合に適宜にその言葉の置き場所を変えてさしつかえない。たとえば上の例では厳格にいえば「名前を聞いたことさえない」「一言を発することさえなく」というべきであるが、「名前さえ聞いたことがない」「一言も発せずに」と訳しても別にさしつかえないようなものである。

---

**435.** Insects are man's oldest and most constant enemies. Sabotage against the world's food supply is committed *not so much* by bad men *as* by harmful insects. Year after year, in peacetime and in wartime, insect pests have to be battled.

**436.** The great use of a school education is *not so much* to teach you things *as* to teach you the art of learning; so that you may apply that art in after life for yourselves, on any matter to which you choose to turn your mind.　　　　　(*Kingsley*)

**437.** The man who has lived most is *not so much* he who has numbered the most years *as* he who has had the keenest sense of life.

**438.** What Dr. Arnold said of boys is equally true of men

---

435. **constant** 不断の、不変の。**sabotage** [sǽbotɑːʒ] 破壊行為。**supply** 供給。**commit** 犯す、行なう。**insect pests** 害虫。　436. **art** 技術、方法。**apply** [əplái] 適用する。**in after life** 後になって。**for yourselves** 自分で。**turn one's mind to** 心を...に向ける。　437. **number** 数える。**keen** 鋭い。　438. **equally** [íːkwəli] 等しく。**be true of** ...について真実だ、あてはまる。

—that the difference between one boy and another consists *not so much* in talent *as* in energy.

**439.** After the introduction into Europe of cotton and linen rags as materials for paper-making, the use of other vegetable fibres was for many centuries entirely, or almost entirely, given up; *not so much*, however, on account of their unfitness, *as* because rags, besides being admirably adapted for the purposes, were cheaper than any other material.

**440.** Henry Ford has no pride in his riches and no use for them except to make still cheaper motorcars, have still more highly paid labour, and bring more miracles of mechanics to birth. He belongs to the common people, and is *not so much* indifferent to *as* unconscious of social distinction.

**441.** An Englishman has always been attached to his home, *not so much* owing to his affection for his family *as* to his dislike of interference from outsiders, and to his love of being alone and minding his own business.

**442.** They said no more, but sat on in the warm twilight, until at last they could scarcely distinguish each other's faces. They were *not so much* thinking, *as* lost in a smooth, still quiet of the mind. A bat flitted by.

**443.** It is *not* accident that helps a man in the world *so much*

---

**consist in** ...にある。 **439. introduction** 導入、輸入。これは of につづく。 **rags** ぼろきれ。 **material** [mətíəriəl] 材料。 **vegetable** [védʒitəbl] 植物の。 **fibre** [fáibə] 繊維(せんい)。 **be given up** やめられる。 **on account of** ...のために。 **adapted** [ədǽptid] 適して。 **440. highly paid labour** 労賃を高く払うこと。 **bring to birth** 生み出す。 **miracle** [mírəkl] 奇蹟。 **mechanics** [mikǽniks] 機械学。 **indifferent** 無関心な。 **distinction** [distíŋkʃən] 差別。 **441. be attached to** ...に愛着する。 **affection** 愛情。 **interference** [ìntəfíərəns] 干渉、容喙(ようかい)。 **outsider** [áutsáidə] 局外者。 **442. twilight** [twáilait] たそがれ。 **distinguish** [distíŋgwiʃ] 見わける。 **flit** とびまわる。

*as* purpose and persistent industry.

**444.** Law, in its true notion, is *not so much* the limitation *as* the direction of a free and intelligent man to his proper interest.
(東大)

**445.** The line of mountains gave the impression of a wall guarding vast wonders behind it. I was filled *not so much* with admiration of what I saw *as* with curiosity to see what there was behind that wall. My spirit was eagerly pressing on to things not yet revealed.

**446.** It is *not so much* professional education *as* the education provided prior to professional studies that varies from nation to nation.
(*J. Conant*)

**447.** There was something curious and touching in the fact that she had groped about in the darkness, until she found her own clothing, which she put on and departed *without* taking *so much as* a pin that belonged to us.

**448.** If you knew who I was, you would *not so much as* speak to me.
(*Stevenson*)

**449.** Indeed, I have never seen this person till this moment —I have *never so much as* set eyes upon him.
(*Stevenson*)

**450.** A man came up to me and asked me whether I were going towards a certain town of which he gave me the name, but as I had *not so much as* heard of this town, I told him I

---

**443. persistent** [pəsístənt] 根気強い。 **444. limitation** 制限。 **direction** 指導。 **intelligent** [intélidʒənt] 理解力ある。 **proper** [prɔ́pə] しかるべき、妥当な。 **445. guard** 守る。 **vast** [vɑːst] 巨大な。 **admiration** [æ̀dmərέiʃən] 感嘆。 **curiosity** [kjùəriɔ́siti] 好奇心。 **press on** 前進する。 **reveal** [riví:l] 明らかにする、あらわす。 **446. professional** 専門的。 **provided** 施される。 **prior** [práiə] **to** ...の前に。 **vary** 変化がある。 **447. touching** 感動的な。 **grope** [group] **about** 手さぐりで歩きまわる。

knew nothing of it. I had no map, for there was no good map of that district, and a bad map is worse than none.

**451.** He hurried after the princess even into her innermost apartment, *without so much as* waiting to remove his sandals.

(*L. Hearn*)

---

(48)

> (a) He is rather hot-tempered, and owns **as much.**
> (b) What takes you only three hours, takes me **as many** days.

【訳】(a) 彼は少々怒りっぽい方だ、そしてまた自分でも怒りっぽいといっている。

(b) あなたが3時間しかかからないことに私は3日かかる。

【解説】(a) **as much** は (1) 同量、同程度をあらわす場合と、(2)「同じこと」「そのとおり」などの意味に用いられる場合とある。例:—

(1) He was greatly respected, and his brother **as much** despised.
(彼はひじょうに敬われた、弟はまたひじょうに卑しまれた)
(2) I thought **as much.** [=I thought **so.**]
(そんなことだろうと思った)
(b) **as many=the same number of** (同じ数の)

類例:—

These are not all the books I have. There are **as many** more upstairs.

---

451. **princess** [prinsés, prínses] 王女。 **apartment** [əpáːtmənt] 部屋。 **remove** [rimúːv] 除く、脱ぐ。 **sandal** [sǽndl] サンダル。
(48) **respect** [rispékt] 尊敬する。 **despise** [dispáiz] 軽蔑する。 **upstairs** [ʌ́pstɛ́əz] 階上に。

(ぼくの持ってる本はこれだけじゃない、2階にはまだこのくらいある)

I found ten mistakes in **as many** pages.
(10 ページ読む中に間違いが 10 あった)

〖注　意 1〗　上の例は as much; as many が前を受けるのであるが、後を受ける場合は as をもう一つ置く。

（a）　**as much as**〜＝〜と同じ程度(あるいは分量)。例：—
　　It is **as much as** (＝all) I can do to keep out of debt.
　　(借金せずにいるのがせいぜいだ)
（b）　**as many as**〜＝〜と同じ数。例：—
　　There are **as many** minds **as** there are men.
　　(十人十色)

〖注　意 2〗　**as few** (as); **as little** (as) は二つのものを同様に打消す。例：—
　　He meant no harm and I meant **as little** (as he).
　　(彼は悪意でしたのではなかった、ぼくも同様悪意でしたのではない)
　　He has **as little** knowledge of the world **as** a new-born baby.
　　(彼は生まれたての赤ん坊同様世間知らずだ)

〖注　意 3〗　**as much as** には次のような用法がある。
　　He gave **as much as** (＝**no less than**) 1,000 yen.
　　(彼は千円も出してくれた)
　　He looked **as much as** (＝**as if**) to say, "Mind your own business."
　　(彼は「余計なお世話だ」といわんばかりの顔つきをした)

―――――

**452.**　I was not in the least surprised, for I had fully expected *as much*.

**453.**　Yes, marriage helps a doctor. It stamps him respectful, and many will not consult a doctor unless they know

---

452. **in the least** すこしも。　453. **stamp** 極印を押す。　**consult** かかる。

that he is a married man; but white hair will help him quite *as much*. (*Max O'Rell*)

**454.** The poor novelist of the bygone time with his long-winded preparation has about *as much* chance *as* an accordion in a storm of thunder. (東大)

**455.** On arriving at Liverpool, I made the acquaintance of a man who had been in America some years previously, and not having his hopes realized at that time, had returned desperate to England, gained fresh hopes, and was now making a second attempt with *as much* enthusiasm, if not more, *than* others in making their first.

**456.** Parties are good servants but bad masters; they should always be treated as means and never as ends themselves. Though *this much* is clear in general, it may not be easy in practice to determine how loose or tight the party rein should be kept; and the tightness of the rein has in fact varied greatly from time to time.

**457.** We worked at the oars for fifteen minutes; it seemed to me *as many* hours.

**458.** Although men are accused for not knowing their own weakness, yet perhaps *as few* know their own strength.

**459.** It sometimes happens that men are much better than they have credit for being, and *as often* men are much worse than they appear to be.

---

454. **bygone** すぎ去った。**long-winded** 長たらしい。**preparation** 本筋へはいるまでの文章。**thunder** 雷。 455. **acquaintance** [əkwéintəns] 知人、近づき。**previously** それ以前に。**realize** 実現する。**desperate** 絶望して。**enthusiasm** 熱意。 456. **party** 政党。**in practice** 実践にあたって。**loose or tight** ゆるくあるいはきつく。**rein** たづな。 458. **accuse** [əkjúːz] 非難する。 459. **credit** [krédit] 信用。**being** の次に good のような語を補ってみる。

( 49 )

> (a) Apples are sold at **so much** a piece.
> (b) Apples are sold at **so many** for a hundred yen.

【訳】 (a) りんごが一ついくらで売買される。
　　　(b) りんごが百円にいくつで売買される。

〖解　説〗 (a) **so much** （分量）
　　　　　(b) **so many** （数）

が「いくら」「いくつ」などと不定量あるいは不定数をあらわすことがある。類例:—

In Japan, we do not say that a room is **so many** feet long or wide, but that it has **so many** mats.
(日本では室の大きさをいうのに、長さいくフィート、幅いくフィートといわないで、何畳[じょう]敷きという)

───────────

**460.** Men spend fortunes to gain a few months or years of life, but who ever heard of any one cutting off years for *so much* a year?

**461.** Now men press buttons, turn wheels; don't make completed articles; work with monotony at the section of an article—*so many* hours of machine-driving a day, the total result of which is never a man's individual achievement.

*(Galsworthy)*

**462.** An Englishman gives his wife *so much* a month for housekeeping and *so much* for dressing and pocket-money.

*(Max O'Rell)*

───────────

(49) **sold** [sould] sell の過去および過去分詞。　**460. fortunes** ばく大なお金。**cut off** 切りとる、切り売りする。　**461. press** 押す。　**completed** 完成した。**monotony** [mɔnɔ́təni] 単調。　**section** 一部分。　**total** 総計の。　**462. housekeeping** 家計。　**pocket-money** [pɔ́kitmʌ́ni] 小使銭。

**463.** A picture is made up of *so many* square inches of painted canvas; but if you should look at these one at a time, covering the others, until you have seen all, you would still not have seen the picture.

---

(50)

> They worked hard **like so many** ants.

【訳】 彼らはさながらありのようにせっせと働いた。

〖解 説〗 同数、同量をあらわすに **as many, as much** を用いることは (48) に説いたが、その前に as もしくは like がくると、as を so にかえて、as so many, like so many などと言う習慣がある。

さて「彼はありのように働いた」という場合は主語が単数だから、He worked **like an ant.** でよいが、主語が they になると、もし5人ならば5匹のありのように、10人ならば10匹のありのように、つまり「同じ数だけのありのように」という意味で like so many ants というのである。しかし日本語では一々「それと同数の...」「それと同量の...」などと几帳面(きちょうめん)なことは言わないから、訳すときには単に like ants と見て「ありのように」としてもかまわない。しかし前に言ったとおり、5人ならばそのまま5匹のありのようにということだから「さながら」「まるで」などという語を添えて訳してもよい。もっともこれは単数のときでも言われる。つまり日本語では単数、複数の区別を立てることが困難だから次のような場合にはちょっと困る:―

1. The *lamp* shone **like a star.**
2. The *lamps* shone **like so many stars.**

この二つはどちらも

「ランプがさながら星のように輝いた」

---

463. **square** 平方。 **painted canvas** 描かれた画布。 **one at a time** いちどに1平方インチずつ。

と訳してさしつかえない。ぜひ単複の区別を立てる必要があったら
1. その灯火は星一つが輝くように見えた。
2. 数ある灯火がさながら星くずのように輝いた。
とでもいうような苦しいくふうをしなければならない。

数には many を用い、数えられない分量には much を用いる。例:—

He regards his children **as so many** encumbrances.
（彼は自分の子供をさながらやっかい物のように心得ている）
He looks upon any time not spent in study **as so much** lost time.
（彼は勉強に使わない時間はまるで損したもののように思う）
I look upon it **as so much** labour lost.
（私はそれだけの労力をまるで損したようなものと思う）

---

**464.** In an instant I felt above a hundred arrows discharged on my left hand, which pricked me *like so many* needles.

**465.** All our streets are lined with trees, and *like so many* stars among the leaves and branches, the street lamps shed their light. When we pass under them we notice how the light tinges the foliage that is nearest to it with a greenish ash-colour.

**466.** Liberty proved anything but a blessing to the people. They were so helpless *as so many* children turned loose upon the world. They had so long been accustomed to rely upon the rulers for defence as well as for government that they knew not how to set about either.

**467.** The climate proved more destructive than the service.

---

(50) **encumbrance** [inkʌ́mbrəns] やっかい物、係累(けいるい)。　464. **instant** [ínstənt] 瞬間。　**arrow** [ǽrou] 矢。　**discharge** [distʃɑ́:dʒ] 発射する。　**prick** ちくちく刺す。　465. **be lined with** …で列を作られている、並木になっている。　**shed** [ʃed] (光を)放つ。　**tinge** 染める。　**foliage** [fóuliidʒ] 群葉。　**ash-colour** 灰色。　466. **anything but** …どころではないもの。　**turned loose** 放り出された。　**be accustomed to** …に慣れている。　**rely** [rilái] 信頼する。　**government** [gʌ́vənmənt] 政治、統治。　**set about** とりかかる。　467. **destructive** 破壊的。　**service** 軍務。

Of two thousand men, above half were sick, and the rest *like so many* phantoms. (*Southey*)

**468.** The girl spread the table, set the children round the fire, and fed them *like so many* hungry birds. (*Alcott*)

**469.** He took a pride in servility to a beautiful woman; received Lady Vandeleur's commands *as so many* marks of favour. (*Stevenson*)

**470.** I stopped, for, I tell you, I was out of breath, and, to my wonder, not a man of them moved, but all sat staring at me *like as many* sheep. (*Stevenson*)

**471.** Having lived under the influence of no very clear or settled principles, religious or political, they speak of every one and everything, only *as so many* phenomena. (都立大)

( 51 )

It was very cold last evening—**so much so** that I could not stir out of doors.

【訳】 ゆうべはたいへん寒かった——戸外へ出られないほどだった。

〖解 説〗 同一の形容詞、副詞等の反復を避けるために so を用いることがある。上の例では、...so cold that I could not... というところを、cold の反復を避けて so とすれば so so that となって口調が悪いか

---

phantom [fǽntəm] 幽霊。　**468.** fed feed (養う)の過去。　**469.** servility [səːvíliti] 奴隷となること。command [kəmáːnd] 命令。　**470. out of breath** 息がきれて。**to my wonder** ふしぎなことに。　**471. settled** 確立した。**religious or political** 宗教上にせよ政治的にせよ。前の principles を修飾する。**phenomena** [finɔ́minə] 現象。phenomenon の複数。

(51) **stir** 動く、身動きする。

ら much を加えて so much so that とするのである。類例：—

It was very cold last year—**more so** (=colder) **than** it is this year.
(去年は寒かった——今年よりも寒かった)

It was very cold yesterday—**as much so** (=as cold) **as** it is today.
(きのうは寒かった—きょうに劣らず寒かった)

---

**472.** The rhinoceros is very fierce and savage—*so much so* that the natives dread it more than they do the lion.

**473.** As autumn came on, the caterpillar quite lost its appetite; *so much so* that even the tenderest and most juicy leaves could not tempt it to eat any more.

**474.** The body, as well as the head, was fearfully mutilated—the former *so much so* as scarcely to retain a semblance of humanity. *(Poe)*

**475.** Sometimes the cold was intense, *so much so* that raw eggs were frozen as hard as if boiled. *(General Gordon)*

**476.** I found myself an object of great interest; *so much so*, that the driver told me he had to keep our route secret, in order to avoid the press that would otherwise have awaited.

**477.** "I have heard Sir William Thornhill represented as one of the most generous, yet whimsical men in the kingdom; a man of consummate benevolence."—"Sometimes, perhaps,

---

**472. rhinoceros** [rainɔ́sərəs] さい。**fierce** [fiəs] 猛烈な。**savage** [sǽvidʒ] 獰猛(どうもう)な。**native** 土民。**dread** [dred] 恐れる。**473. caterpillar** [kǽtəpilə] 毛虫、芋虫。**appetite** [ǽpitait] 食欲。**tender** やわらかい。**juicy** [dʒúːsi] 液汁の多い。**tempt** さそう。**474. mutilate** [mjúːtileit] 切りきざむ。**retain** 留める。**semblance** [sémbləns] 見せかけ、類似。**humanity** [hjuːmǽniti] 人間。**475. intense** [inténs] はなはだしい。**raw** なまの。**476. object** 対象物。**keep secret** 秘密にしておく。**route** [ruːt] 路。**the press** 新聞記者(集合的に)。**otherwise** そうしないと。**477. represent** [rèprizént] 言いあらわす。**whimsical** [hwímzikəl] 気まぐれな。**consummate** [kənsʌ́mit] 完全な。**benevolence** 慈悲心。

*too much so;* at least, he carried benevolence to an excess when young." (*Goldsmith*)

---

( 52 )

---

(a) He is an Edokko, **if ever** there was one.
(b) He can do it, **if any** one can.
(c) **If** you do it **at all,** do it well.

---

【訳】（a）あれこそ本当の江戸っ子だ。
　　（b）彼にできなくてできるものがあろうか。
　　（c）いやしくもするからには、念を入れてやりなさい。

〖解　説〗（a）**if ever**
　　　　　（b）**if any**
　　　　　（c）**if at all**

この三つはいずれも言おうとすることを強くひびかせるためにもったいをつけていうのに用いる。いずれも裏面に打消しの観念を含めて、次のように解するのが便利である。

（a）江戸っ子なるものが古来絶対にないならばいざ知らず、いやしくもあるとすれば彼こそすなわちそれである。

　=If he is not an Edokko, there **never** was one.
　　（彼が江戸っ子でなければ、江戸っ子なんてものはいまだかつてないのだ）

（b）だれもなし得る人がないならばいざ知らず、いやしくもあるとすれば彼こそなし得る人である。

　=If he can't do it, **no** one can.
　　（彼にできないならば誰にもできない）

（c）まったくしないならばそれもよいがいやしくもするくらいならよくするがよい。

---

**excess** [iksés] 過度。

=If you do not do it well, do **not** do it **at all.**
　　　(よくしないくらいなら絶対にするな)
類例:—
　　**If ever** eyes spoke, hers did very plainly.
　　　(眼が物をいうものなら彼女の眼こそはっきり物をいった)
　　He is a scholar, **if anybody** is.
　　　(あの人が学者でなかったら天下に学者はない)
　　A rescue party should be sent, **if at all,** speedily.
　　　(救助隊を派遣するというなら敏速に派遣すべきだ)
〖注　意1〗 **if a...** の形を「ほんとうに」「たしかに」などいう副詞の意味に用いるのも同じりくつである. 例:—
　　He must be over fifty, **if** (he be) **a day.**
　　　(彼はたしかに 50 以上にちがいない [彼が 50 以上でないというなら生まれてまだ1日にもならないといってよい])
　　He stands six foot two, **if an inch.**
　　　(彼は身長まさに6フィート2インチある [6フィート2インチないというなら1インチないといってもよい])
　　I'll get you a hundred, **if I get you a penny.**
　　　(たとえ1ペニーでも取って売るなら、100ポンドには売ってあげる)
〖注　意2〗 **seldom, little, few** など打消しの語が加わって
　　**seldom, if ever** (=seldom or never)
　　**little, if any** (=little or no)
　　**few, if any** (=few or no)
　　**little, if at all** (=little or no)
など用いられた場合の if は「...ならば」の意でなくて「...とも」の意味である. 例:—
　　He **seldom, if ever,** goes to such places.
　　　(彼はそんなところへはたとえ行くことがあってもごくまれだ、まずない)
　　The book has **few, if any,** glaring mistakes.
　　　(ひどいまちがいはたとえあるとしても、ごくすくない)

---

(52) glaring [glέəriŋ] 明白な.

There is **little, if any,** fear of your failing.
(君が失敗する心配は、たとえあるとしても、ごくすくない＝失敗の心配はまずない)
He is **little, if at all,** better than a beggar.
(ほとんどこじきも同様だ)

---

**478.** All the small stones or pebbles, *if* there *ever* were *any*, seem to be imprisoned in pavements or quite melted away.

**479.** *If ever* there was a nation formed for living under a republic, it is the Scotch—serious, calm, wise, law-abiding, and ever ready to respect the opinion of others.  (*Max O'Rell*)

**480.** *If ever* man was mad with excess of happiness, it was myself at that moment.  (*Poe*)

**481.** *If any* language deserves to be so called, English may claim to be called the universal language.

**482.** There are few, *if any*, spots where Nature has been more generous in her gifts than the island of Ceylon. With very little labour the poorest can keep themselves sufficiently supplied. The sea abounds in fish, and the land yields so abundantly that curry and rice cannot run short.

**483.** If there were *ever* two people who seemed to dislike each other, Miss Abigail and Kitty Collins were those people. *If ever* two people really loved each other, Miss Abigail and Kitty Collins were those people also. They were always either

---

478. **imprison** [imprízn] 閉じこめる。 **pavement** 敷石、舗装。 **melt** 溶ける。
479. **formed** 形造られた。 **republic** [ripʌ́blik] 共和国。 **abide** [əbáid] 守る。
480. **excess** 過剰。 481. **deserve** 値する。 **claim** 承認を求める。 **universal** [jùːnivə́ːsəl] 普遍的、世界的。 482. **spot** 地点。 **generous** 寛大な。 **island** [áilənd] 島。 **be supplied** 食物を供給される。 **abound** [əbáund] 富む。 **yield** [jiːld] 作物ができる。 **abundantly** 豊富に。 **run short** 欠乏する。

skirmishing or having a cup of tea lovingly together.

(*T. B. Aldrich*)

**484.** *If anything* he looked rather less than his age, a result, perhaps, of having always lived with the young. (*Gissing*)

**485.** My first impressions of Leningrad: the center not much changed after twenty-three years; *if anything*, more dilapidated and run-down. (*Merle Fainsod*)

**486.** There are two virtues much needed in modern life, *if* it is *ever* to become sweet. These virtues are honesty, and simplicity of life, and it must be noted that the practice of either of these virtues will make the other easier to us.

**487.** He was *seldom, if ever*, provoked into treating any person with unkindness.

**488.** True greatness has *little, if anything*, to do with rank or power.

**489.** Though the French are *little, if at all*, inferior to the English either in boating or sailing, their taste for these two pursuits are extremely limited.

**490.** In the majority of cases it is right and proper that a grievously sick patient should realize that his time on this earth is likely to be short, *if* for no other reason than that he may be enabled to put his affairs in order. (慶大)

---

483. **skirmish** [skə́:miʃ] 小競合(ぜりあ)いをする、言い争う。　484. **less than**＝younger for.　**a result** 結果。この前に which was を入れて考える。　485. **dilapidated** 荒廃した。**run-down** 疲弊した。　486. **virtue** [vɔ́:tju:] 徳。**simplicty** [simplísiti] 簡易。　487. **provoke** 怒らせる。　488. **have to do with** …と関係がある。　**rank** 階級。　489. **pursuit** [pəsjú:t] 仕事。　**extremely** [ikstrí:mli] 極度に。　490. **majority** 多数。　**grievously** ひどく。**realize** さとる。　**put in order** 整理する。　**affairs** 身辺のこと。

(53)

> (a) He has **ever so** many children.
> (b) Home is home, be it **ever so** homely.

【訳】(a) 彼にはいくら子供がいるかしれないほどたくさんいる。

(b) どんなにみすぼらしくても家はやはり家——故郷にまさる所はない。

〖解 説〗(a) ever so=very 類例：—

There are **ever so many** English teachers.
(英語の教師なんかはいくらもある)
He has **ever so much** money.
(彼にはいくら金があるかしれない)
Thank you **ever so much.**
(お礼の申しようもありません)

(b) 譲歩をあらわす付属節 (**Concessive Clause**) 中にあっては、ever so...=however... と解する。(95) [注意 1] 参照。例：—

**However** rich a man may be (=be a man **ever so** rich), he ought not to be idle.
(いくら金があっても遊んでいるべきではない)

〖注 意〗この ever so は古文体の never so が転化したものである。

———

**491.** People will always be shy of receiving any man who comes from a place where the plague rages, let him look *ever so* healthy. (*Chesterfield*)

**492.** There is no living plant or animal, be it *never so* common, that will not repay study, and provide, if intelligently

---

491. **be shy of** 用心して避けたがる。　**plague** [pleig] 疫病、ペスト。　**rage** ひどくはやる。　492. **repay** [riːpéi] (労に)報いる。　**provide** 供給する。

observed, quite an interesting story. A spider and its habits will give us quite as much interest as strange animals in some far-distant land; and no more wonderful story has ever arisen out of the imagination of man than is daily enacted in the lives of ants and bees.

**493.** "I shall not touch it, I assure you," said she. "If I were *ever so* hungry, I should never think of eating such a miserable, dry pomegranate as that." (*Hawthorne*)

**494.** The honest man, *though e'er sae* poor,
   Is king o' men for a' that. (*Burns*)

**495.** Conviction, *never so* excellent, is worthless till it converts itself into conduct. (*Carlyle*)

**496.** How can two affianced people know each other, *even if* for years they try *ever so* hard? (*Max O'Rell*)

**497.** This characteristic of woman is probably, after all, what makes her *ever so* interesting to us. (*Max O'Rell*)

**498.** What would it avail us to have a hireling clergy, though *never so* learned? (*Milton*)

**499.** She may be *ever so* learned, she is never a pedant.

(*Max O'Rell*)

---

**arise** 現われる。**enact** [inǽkt] 演ずる。**493. assure** うけ合う。**pomegranate** [pɔ́məgrænit] ざくろ。 **494. e'er sae**=ever so. **o'**=of. **for a'** (=all) **that** それにもかかわらず。 **495. conviction** 信念。**excellent** すばらしい。**convert** [kənvə́:t] 変える。 **496. affianced** [əfáiənst] 婚約した。 **497. characteristic** [kæ̀riktərístik] 特色。 **498. avail** 役に立つ、益する。 **hireling** [háiəliŋ] 金で働く。**clergy** [klə́:dʒi] 牧師。 **499. pedant** [pédənt] 学者ぶる人、衒(げん)学者。

(54)

>  (a)　*A.*—You seem to be a physician.
> 　　　*B.*—**So** (*indeed*) **I am.**
>  (b)　*A.*—I am a physician.
> 　　　*B.*—**So** (*also*) **am I.**

【訳】　(a)　甲——あなたは医師のようですね。
　　　　　　乙——<u>おおせのとおり</u>医師です。
　　　(b)　甲——私は医師です。
　　　　　　乙——私<u>も</u>医師です。

〖解　説〗　主語と動詞の位置のちがいで上のような差異が起こる。
類例:—
　((*A*) He is clever, is he not?—(*B*) **So he is.**
　　　(彼は りこうじゃないか——そうだ りこうだ)
　((*A*) He is clever.—(*B*) **So is his brother.**
　　　(彼は りこうだね——彼の兄も りこうだ)
　I like apples.—**So do I.**
　　(ぼくはりんごが好きだ——ぼくも好きだ)
　I am fond of music.—**So am I.**
　　(私は音楽が好きです——私も好きです)
　I have a bicycle.—**So have I.**
　　(ぼくは自転車を持っている——ぼくも持っている)

〖注　意〗　打消しに伴なう場合は so を用いないで nor あるいは neither を用いる。
比較:—
　⎰I like beef.—⎱I like it, **too.**
　⎱　　　　　　⎰**So do I.**
　　＝ぼくは牛肉が好きだ——ぼくも好きだ。

---

(54)　**bicycle** [báisikl] 自転車。

I don't like pork.— 
- I don't like it, **either**.
- **Nor** do I.
- **Neither** do I.
- **Nor** I **either**.

＝私は豚肉は好かない――私も好かない。

My mother has gone to the play.—**So has mine**.
＝母は芝居へ行った――ぼくの母も。

My mother doesn't smoke.—
- My mother **dosen't** smoke, **either**.
- **Neither** does mine.

＝私の母はたばこをのまない――私の母も。

---

**500.** "Who has a woodsaw?" said Frank. "I have." "*So have I*," replied three of the boys.

**501.** Dirty walls, ceilings, and floor give the air musty, close smell; *so do* dirty clothes, muddy boots, cooking, and washing.

**502.** Rose bushes which we see in gardens are shrubs. *So also are* grapevines, honeysuckles, ivy, and all other creeping vines.

**503.** It is nearly half a century since Tolstoy wrote these words. Science has made notable advances in the intervening years—*so has* despotism　　　　　　　　　　（福島県立医大）

**504.** The first thing for a boy to learn, after obedience and morality, is a habit of observation—a habit of using his eyes. It matters little what you use them on, provided you do use

---

500. woodsaw [wudsɔ:] のこぎり。 501. musty [mʌ́sti] 黴(か)びた。 close むっとする。 muddy 泥でよごれた。 502. bush [buʃ], shrub 灌木、藪。 honeysuckle すいかずら。 ivy [áivi] きづた。 creeping はう、からみつく。 503. notable 注目に値いする。 advance 進歩。 intervene [intəvíːn] 間にはさまる。 despotism 独裁政治。 504. obedience [əbíːdjəns] 従順。 morality 徳行。 matter little 大して重要でない。 provided=if.

them. They say knowledge is power, and *so it is*—but only the knowledge which you get by observation.

**505.** It was thus with Franklin,—it can be thus with you. He strove for the prize, and he won it! *So may* you!

**506.** You may think that this was a very lonely home for the little lass. And *so it was*. She had no friends to play with except a kitten and a dog.

---

(55)

| I had waited an hour **before** he appeared. |

【訳】 1時間も待ってからようやく彼がやって来た。

〖解 説〗 こういう構文を尻から逆に「彼が来た前に長く待った」などの直訳するのはまずい。下の例に示すように「1時間も待ってからようやく…」というふうに訳し下すがよい。単に時間のみをいう場合は次の形を取る。

It was an hour **before** he appeared.
　　(1時間もたってからようやく彼はやって来た)
未来ならば

It will be some time **before** he appears.
　　(彼が来るにはまだしばらく間(ま)があるだろう)
距離についてもこの構文を利用することができる。例:—

I had gone some distance **before** I missed my watch.
　　(しばらく行ってからはじめて時計のないのに気がついた)

〖注 意 1〗 この構文の before が when に変わっていることが往々ある。

〖注 意 2〗 …before~ を「~しないうちに…」のように、逆に打

---

505. strove<strive 努力する。　**won** [wʌn]<win 得る。　506. **lonely** さびしい。　**lass** 小娘。

消しを入れて訳してよいこともある。例：―

It was dark **before** we got home.
(ぼくらは日が暮れてから家に着いた ＝ ぼくらが家に着かない中に日が暮れてしまった)

---

**507.** *It was a long time before* the English and Scotch could live together like brethren. *(Parley)*

**508.** Night was far advanced *before* they halted.

**509.** Presently he would begin to laugh *before* his tears were dry. *(Dickens)*

**510.** His reputation as a writer was built up slowly, and *a long time passed before* his merits were recognized. Even at the end of his life his books had gained only a limited popularity.

**511.** The poor fellow's health so gave way under this meagre diet, that he died *before* his course of study was finished. *(Max O'Rell)*

**512.** We are committing a folly in thoughtlessness. It must not happen that we do not pull ourselves together *before* it is too late. We must summon up the insight, the seriousness, and the courage to leave folly and to face reality. (東北大)

**513.** She stared at him with an ashen face, and gulped twice *before* she could speak. *(Doyle)*

**514.** The fierce brutes, swept along by the force of their

---

507. **brethren** [bréðrin] 同胞。 508. **advance** 進む、ふける。 **halt** [hɔːlt] 止まる。 509. **presently** [prézntli] ほどなく。 510. **reputation** 名声。 **merits** 功績。 **recognize** [rékəgnaiz] 認める。 **popularity** 人気。 511. **give way** くずれる、衰える。 **meagre** [míːgə] (栄養の)とぼしい。 **diet** 食事。 512. **commit** 犯す。 **pull oneself together** 立ちなおる。 **summon** ふるい起こす。 **insight** 洞察力。 **face** 直面する。 513. **stare** じっと見る。 **ashen** [ǽʃn] 灰色の。 **gulp** [gʌlp] ごくりと呑む。 514. **swept along** おし進められて。

running, were carried a long distance upon the ice *before* they could turn themselves.

**515.** When I paid for the books I was in a great hurry, fearing the boat would leave *before* I could reach it and did not examine the bill.

---

( 56 )

> I had **not** waited **long before** he appeared.

【訳】 長いこと待たないうちに彼がやって来た。

〖解 説〗 not～long before... は直訳すれば「...の前長くは～しなかった」であるが、「長いこと...しないうちに」とか、少し古い文体ならば、「...すること久しからずして～」と訳してよい。単に時間ばかりをいうときは、

It **was not long before** he appeared.
(まもなく彼がやって来た)

ということもできる。未来ならば

It **will not be long before** he appears.
(彼はまもなくやって来るだろう)

距離をいう場合には long のかわりに far をおく。また定まった時間、距離をおくこともある。例:—

I had **not** gone **far before** I met an old man.
(それほど行かないうちに ひとりの老人に会った)

I had **not** waited **an hour before** he appeared.
(1 時間も待たないうちに彼がやって来た)

They had **not** been married **a month before** they began to quarrel.
(結婚してから 1 ヵ月も立たないうちに夫婦げんかを始めた)

〖注 意〗 before が when に変わっていることが往々ある。

---

515. **be in a hurry** 急いでいる。 **bill** 勘定書。
(56) **married** [mǽrid] 結婚して。

**516.**　Immediately after breakfast the prisoners were sent on their way to Savannah, under the guard of a sergeant and a corporal, with eight men.　They *had not been gone long before* Jasper took leave of his brother, and set out on some pretended errand.

**517.**　*It was not long before* we again met by chance.　We came face to face at a street corner in my neighbourhood, and I was struck by a change in him.

**518.**　One day the gentleman went out to see what the elephant and the children were doing. . . . Old Soup was fishing too.　He was standing beside the children, holding a large bamboo fishing-rod with his trunk.　The gentleman *had not waited long before* the elephant had a bite.

**519.**　I had *not gone very far before* the wind brought to me the clanging of a bell, and somehow, I can scarcely tell why, my heart sank within me at the sound.

**520.**　We *had not gone half a mile when* I was astonished to see Peggoty burst from a hedge.　　　　　　　　　　(*Dickens*)

**521.**　We *had not much time* to reflect upon the poor animal's distress, *when* we perceived the dogs and horsemen come sweeping along, taking the very path it had taken.　　　(*Goldsmith*)

---

516. **breakfast** [brékfəst] 朝食。　**under the guard of** …の監視つきで。**sergeant** [sá:dʒənt] 軍曹。　**corporal** [kɔ́:pərəl] 伍長。　**men** 兵。　**take leave of** に別れをつげる。　**pretend** [priténd] 偽る、装う。　**errand** [érənd] 使い。　517. **by chance** 偶然に。　**strike** おどろかす。　518. **Soup** 象の名。**bamboo** 竹。　**trunk** 象の鼻。　**bite** 魚が餌にくいつくこと。　519. **clang** がんがんと鳴る。　**somehow** [sʌ́mhau] どういうわけだか。　520. **burst** 突然現われる。　521. **reflect** [riflékt] 考える。　**distress** [distrés] 窮状。**perceive** 認める。　**sweep** さっと通る。

(57)

> (a) We had **scarcely** got on shore **when** it began to blow hard.
> (b) We had **no sooner** got on shore **than** it began to blow hard.
> (c) **As soon as** we got on shore it began to blow hard.

【訳】（a）我々が上陸するかしないうちに風がひどく吹き出した。
（b）我々が上陸すると同時に風がひどく吹き出した。
（c）我々が上陸するやいなや風がひどく吹き出した。

〖解説〗 (a) $\begin{Bmatrix} \text{scarcely} \\ \text{hardly} \end{Bmatrix} \cdots \begin{Bmatrix} \text{when}\ldots \\ \text{before}\ldots \end{Bmatrix}$

= ...するかしないうちに...

scarcely や hardly はほとんど打消しに等しい副詞である。したがって前章の not long before... から推察すれば容易に解せられよう。比較:—

{ I had **not** waited an hour **before** he appeared.
{ I had **scarcely** waited an hour **when** he appeared.

(b) **no sooner...than**
(c) **as soon as...**

この二つも (a) とほとんど同じ意味と考えてよろしい。(a) と (b) とでは前が過去完了で、後が過去のことが多く、(c) は両方とも過去なのが普通。

〖注意1〗 (a)(b) で scarcely; no sooner を文頭に出すと主語と助動詞と位置の変わるのが通例である。

**Scarcely** had the trees been planted **when** they were all blown down by a storm.
（樹木は植付けが終わるか終わらないうちに みな暴風のため 吹き倒されてしまった）

〖注 意 2〗 directly という副詞、the moment, the instant など
いう名詞が、接続詞代用として as soon as の意にに用いられることがある。例:—

He ran off **the moment** he saw me.
（彼は私を見るやいなや逃げ去った）
I started **the instant** I heard the report.
（その報を聞くやいなや出発した）
**Directly** he saw me, he ran away.
（彼はぼくを見るやいなや逃げ去った）
**Directly** he comes, send him to me.
（彼が来たらすぐぼくの所へよこしてくれたまえ）

---

**522.** Up to the present, man has been, to a certain extent, the slave of machinery, and there is something tragic in the fact that *as soon as* man had invented a machine to do his work he began to starve.

**523.** A mean man is very anxious to receive a favour, but *as soon as* he has received it, he forgets his benefactor; a noble man hesitates to receive favours from others, but if so, he feels under obligations to return them.

**524.** No matter which is cause, then, and which effect, the increase of population in every part of the globe and rise of the industrial system,—together with the complex series of imperative needs that every nation necessarily feels *as soon as* it becomes thickly populated and is fairly well advanced on the

---

(57) **instant** [ínstənt] 瞬間。 **report** [ripɔ́ːt] 知らせ。 **522. up to** …まで。 **extent** 程度。 **machinery** [məʃíːnəri] 機械。 **tragic** [trǽdʒik] 悲劇の。 **523. mean** 卑しい。 **be anxious to** 切望する。 **favour** 恩恵。 **benefactor** 恩人。 **obligation** 義務。 **524. population** [pɔ̀pjuléiʃən] 人口。 **globe** 地球。 **rise** ぼっ興。 **complex** 複雑な。 **imperative** [impérətiv] 避けがたい。

road to industrialism,—are the primary causes of all modern wars.

**525.** *As soon as* I was out of that house I opened my envelope, and saw that it contained money! My opinion of those people changed, I can tell you! I lost not a moment, but shoved note and money into my vest pocket, and broke for the nearest cheap eating house. *(Mark Twain)*

**526.** The king was *no sooner* dead *than* all the plans and schemes he had laboured at so long, and lied so much for, crumbled away like a hollow heap of sand. *(Dickens)*

**527.** *No sooner* were the words spoken *than* I saw the delight they caused the hearer. He hesitated, murmured reluctance, but soon gratefully accepted my offer, and flushed with joy as he took the volume. (徳島大)

**528.** We were *no sooner* returned to the inn, *but* numbers of my parishioners, hearing of my success, came to congratulate me. *(Goldsmith)*

**529.** The boy took the paper, and *no sooner* had he glanced at its contents, *than* he uttered an exclamation of joyful surprise.

**530.** Nicholas was *scarcely* awake *when* he heard the wheels

---

**industrialism** [indʌ́striəlizm] 産業主義。 **primary** 主要な。 525. **contain** 中にもっている。 **lose not a moment** 一刻のゆうよもない。 **shove** [ʃʌv] 押しやる。**vest** チョッキ。**break for** 向かってかけ出す。 526. **scheme** [ski:m] 計画。**lie...for** そのためにうそを言う。 **crumble** [krʌ́mbl] くだける。**hollow** うつろな。 527. **caused the hearer** 聞き手に与えた。 **hesitate** 躊躇(ちゅうちょ)する。**murmur** つぶやく。**reluctance** [rilʌ́ktəns] 不本意。**gratefully** ありがたく。**flush** 顔を紅(あか)くする。**volume** [vɔ́ljum] 書物。 528. **parishioner** [pərɪ́ʃənə] 教区民。**congratulate** [kəngrǽtʃuleit] 祝う。 529. **glance** ちらっと見る。**contents** [kənténts, kɔ́ntents] 内容。**utter** [ʌ́tə] 発する。

of a chaise approching the house.

**531.** I had *scarcely* started *before* a man came up to me and asked me if he was right in thinking my name was so-and-so.

(*Maugham*)

**532.** But, one day, he heard of a spot he had never seen, nor had his armies conquered—this spot was Paradise. *No sooner*, however, did he hear of it *than* his resolution was taken: " I will subdue the country too."

**533.** *Scarcely* had I seated myself *before* a great brown animal, with black eyes, round and fierce, rose to the surface of the stream half a dozen yards from my feet; then quickly catching sight of me, it plunged noisily again under water, breaking the clear image reflected there.

**534.** *Scarcely* had the thought crossed his mind *than* the lane took a sudden turning; and he found himself hidden from his enemies. (*Stevenson*)

**535.** From this motive I had *scarcely* taken orders a year *before* I began to think seriously of matrimony. (*Goldsmith*)

**536.** " I wish the sausage was hanging from the end of your nose!"

He had *hardly* spoken the words *before* the sausage was hanging from the end of his wife's nose.

**537.** The president had *but just* seated himself at his morn-

---

530. chaise [ʃeiz] 馬車。approach 近づく。 531. so-and-so 誰々、某。 532. conquer 征服する。 Paradise [pǽrədais] 楽園。 resolution 決心。 subdue [səbdjúː] 征服する。 533. seat oneself 腰をおろす。 fierce どう猛な。 eyes の形容詞。 surface 表面。 catch sight of ...を認める。 plunge とびこむ、もぐる。 image reflected 映った影。 534. lane 小道。 535. motive [móutiv] 動機。 take orders 牧師の職につく。 seriously [síəriəsli] まじめに。 matrimony [mǽtriməni] 結婚。 536. sausage [sɔ́sidʒ] ソーセージ。

ing's task of looking over and signing important papers, *when* without one word of announcement, the door softly opened.

**538.** *Directly* the hawk saw the bird, it flew after it and quickly brought it to the ground.

**539.** She was hot and breathless by the time she reached the top of the hill, and came out upon a bare grassy ground. *The moment* she sat down there, she forgot her exhaustion, so attractive was the sight that lay before her.

**540.** The desire to tell her (*i.e.* his mother) the truth came up in his throat, but *the moment* he sought to express it in words it became untruth, and it was to save himself from falsehood that he remained silent.

**541.** Millions of tiny red ants carried away most of my seed, and if any happened to be overlooked by the ants, *the moment* they sent forth green shoots these were sheared off by land crabs. (中央大)

**542.** Why so many decent people get big-shot complex *the moment* they climb into the driver's seat is a mystery to me. It may be the only time they feel a real release from the curbs of everyday life, or it may satisfy a starved ego.

**543.** *The instant* the woman saw the young man, she exclaimed, " O sir, you will do something for me! Make them

---

537. **task** 仕事。**sign** 署名する。**important** [impɔ́:tənt] 重要な。**announcement** [ənáunsmənt] 予告。538. **hawk** 鷹(たか)。**flew**＜fly 飛ぶ。539. **breathless** [bréθlis] 息切れした。**bare** 木のはえていない。**exhaustion** [igzɔ́:stʃən] 疲労。**attractive** 美しい。540. **throat** のど。**sought** [sɔ:t] seek の過去および過去分詞。**falsehood** [fɔ́:lshud] 偽り。541. **seed** 種子。**overlook** 見のがす。**shoot** 芽。**shear** [ʃiə] はさみでつむ。**crab** かに。542. **decent** 行儀正しい、おとなしい。**big-shot complex** 気が大きくなること。**mystery** なぞ。**release** 解放。**curb** 拘束。**ego** [égou] 自我。

release me. My boy—my poor boy is drowning, and they will not let me go!"

## (58)

> I shall see him **before long**.

【訳】 私は<u>近いうちに</u>彼に会います。

〖解 説〗 **before long** は **before a long time has elapsed** の省略された形と見て **shortly ; soon**（近いうちに；まもなく；久しからず）などの意味の副詞として用いられるのである。これを (56) に説いた **not long before** の構文と混同してはならない。**ere long** は **before long** の古い形である。

**544.** Once he tried to jump across a brook, but it was so wide that little Try fell into the water. Still he did not cry. He made up his mind that, when he was a little older, he would make another trial; and *before long* he could jump over the brook in its widest place.

**545.** Owing to the increase of knowledge, it is possible for governments nowadays to achieve many more intended results than were possible in former times, and it is likely that *before very long* results which even now are impossible will become possible.

**546.** But directly he leaves his home and travels abroad, he begins to find out that there are a great many things in the

---

543. **release** [rilíːs] 放す。 **let go** はなす。 544. **brook** [bruk] 小川。 **make up one's mind** 決心する。 **trial** 試み。 545. **intended result** 意図した結果。 **former times** 以前の時。

world which he has not seen, and a good many, too, which he has never even heard of, and *before very long* he will stop talking about the wonders of his own home.

**547.** In a very short time, however, new sprouts spring up from the old root, and *ere long* the native has another cluster. So rapidly do they follow each other, that one cluster is scarcely consumed before another is ready to ripen.

---

( 59 )

People do **not** know the blessing of health **till** they lose it.

【訳】 健康を失って初めて健康のありがたさを知る。

〚解 説〛 （a） **not~till** (or **until**)…
　　　　＝…するまでは~しない；…のときはじめて~

この形の変化に

　（b） **it is not until…that~**

　（c） **~but not until…**

などがある。例：—

　**It was not until** he was actually dying that he said, " I can work no more."

　　（彼は死に瀕(ひん)するまで、「もう働けない」とは言わなかった）

　**It was not till** the next day **that** I learned the truth.

　　（翌日になってはじめてことの真相がわかった）

---

546. **wonder** [wʌ́ndə] ふしぎ。 547. **sprout** [spraut] 芽。 **cluster** (バナナなどの)ふさ。 **rapidly** [rǽpidli] 迅速に。 **consume** [kənsjúːm] 消費する。 **ripen** 熟する。

**548.** We do *not* know a nation *until* we know its pleasures of life, just as we do *not* know a man *until* we know how he spends his leisure. It is when a man ceases to do the things he has to do, and does the things he likes to do, that his character is revealed.

**549.** *Not until* the middle of the century did the tonnage of steamships upon the sea begin to overhaul that of sailing ships. After that the evolution in sea transport was rapid.

**550.** I no sooner breathed the free, wholesome air of desert, than I felt that a great burden which I had been scarcely conscious of bearing was lifted away from my mind. For nearly three weeks I had lived under peril of death; the peril ceased, and *not till* then did I know how much alarm and anxiety I had really been suffering.

**551.** *It was not*, however, *till* sunrise on the following morning *that* they saw land and then it was not the island they had expected to see; for they had been swept by a current some thirty miles in the wrong direction.

**552.** *Not until* he was secured would they let me get to him. I flung myself upon his poor insulted form and cried my grief out upon his breast, while my father and all my family scoffed at me and heaped threats and shameful epithets upon him.

*(Mark Twain)*

---

548. **pleasure** 娯楽、楽しみ。 **leisure** ひま。 **cease** [si:s] やめる。 **reveal** 示す、あらわす。 549. **tonnage** トン数。 **overhaul** [ouvəhɔ́:l] 追いつく。 **evolution** 発展。 **transport** [trǽnspɔ:t] 輸送。 550. **wholesome** 健康的な。 **burden** 重荷。 **lift away** 取りのける。 **peril** [péril] 危険。 **alarm** 恐慌。 **anxiety** [æŋzáiəti] 心配。 551. **current** [kʌ́rənt] 潮流。 **sweep** 押し流す。 **some**=about. 552. **secure** しっかりしめつける。 **flung**<fling 投げる。 **insult** [insʌ́lt] 侮辱する。 **scoff** 嘲(ぎょう)笑する。 **heap** 積み重ねる。 **threat** [θret] 脅迫の言葉。 **epithet** [épiθət] 形容辞。

**553.** Those on board the mother ship had no idea of what had occurred. They, of course, knew that submarine could not stay under water for longer than three hours, and *it was not until* this limit was approaching *that* suspicion began to be aroused that all was not well.

**554.** At the approach of evening he took leave; but *not till* he had requested permission to renew his visit, which, as he was our landlord, we most readily agreed to.

**555.** Well, then, by way of preamble I will ask you to note this fact in human history: that the merit of many a great artist has *never* been acknowledged *until* after he was starved and dead.                                                  (*Mark Twain*)

---

(60)

(a) **Persevere, and** you will succeed.
(b) **Persevere, or** you will fail.

【訳】(a) 忍耐せよ、そうすれば成功するだろう。
(b) 忍耐せよ、そうしなければ失敗するだろう。

〖解 説〗(a)「命令法+and...」の形では命令法は条件をあらわし、and 以下は自然の結果をあらわす。すなわち and=and then (そうすれば)で、

Persevere, and you will succeed.
=If you persevere, you will succeed.

---

553. **have no idea of** ぜんぜん見当がつかない。 **submarine** [sʌ́bməriːn] 潜水艦。 **approach** [əpróutʃ] 接近する。 **suspicion** 疑念。 554. **request** [rikwést] 乞う。 **renew** [rinjúː] 新たにする、くりかえす。 **readily** [rédili] 容易に、進んで。 555. **by way of** ...として、...のつもりで。 **preamble** [priːǽmbl] 前置き。 **merit** 功績。 **acknowledge** 認める。

(60) **persevere** [pəːsivíə] 忍耐する。

＝忍耐すれば成功する。

（b）「命令法＋or...」の形では裏から行って、条件とその結果をあらわすのである。すなわち or＝or else; otherwise（そうでなければ）で、

**Persevere, or** you will not succeed.

＝**If you do not persevere,** you will fail.

＝忍耐しなければ成功はしない。

類例：—

**Make haste, and** you will be in time.

（お急ぎなさい、そうすれば間に合います）

**Stop, or** you are a dead man.

（とまれ、とまらないと命がないぞ）

【注　意】 let を用いるいわゆる間接命令の場合も同様。

比較：—

**Work hard, and** you will succeed.
＝If you work hard, you will succeed.
**Let him work hard, and** he will succeed.
＝If he works hard, he will succeed.

---

**556.** *Give* him an inch, *and* he will take an ell.　　(*Proverb*)

**557.** *Take care* of the pence, *and* the pounds will take care of themselves.　　(*Proverb*)

**558.** *Be* what nature intended you for, *and* you will succeed; *be* anything else, *and* you will be ten thousand times worse than nothing.

**559.** If the simple reactions of animal bodies are tested, it will be found that they clearly serve certain ends. Lightly *touch* the foot of a sleeping child *and* it will withdraw it.

---

**otherwise** [ʌ́ðəwaiz] そうでなければ。　**556. ell** 長さの単位で45インチ。　**557. take care of** 大事にする。　**558. intend one for** 人を...にしようと思う。　**559. reaction** [riǽkʃən] 反応。　**serve certain ends** ある目的にかなう。　**withdraw** [wiðdrɔ́ː] 引込める。

*Tickle* the ear of a cat *and* it will shake it.

**560.** We only exist ourselves because the earth receives exactly the right amount of radiation from the sun; *upset* the balance in either direction, of excess or defect, *and* life must disappear from the earth. (滋賀大)

**561.** Transportation and production are inseparable. If there is a free flow of goods from the producers to the consumers, the greater the quantity of useful articles the producers can turn out, the better off everyone concerned will be. But *interfere* with this flow anywhere *and* everyone will suffer loss; *stop* it, *and* civilization will disintegrate.

**562.** And if you have ever been on a walking tour or a cycling tour you know that early rising is the key of the business. *Start early and* you are master of your programme and your fate.... *Start late and* you are the slave of the hours. You chase them with weary feet. (神戸商船大)

**563.** *Ask, and* it shall be given; *seek, and* ye shall find; *knock, and* it shall be opened unto you. (*Bible*)

**564.** It is surprising how man believes in words. If he is told he is a fool, for instance, he will suspect himself a fool and be sad; *call* him a clever fellow, *and* he will be delighted if you go off without paying him for the article you have bought from him.

**565.** Top-notch interpreters are so much at home in two

---

**tickle** くすぐる。 560. **amount** 分量。 **radiation** [reidiéiʃən] 輻(ふ)射熱。 **upset** ひっくり返す。 **balance** 均衡。 **excess** 過多。 **defect** 不足。 561. **inseparable** [insépərəbl] 分ちがたい。 **consumer** [kənsjúːmə] 消費者。 **turn out** 生産する。 **concerned** 関係のある。 **interfere with** ...をじゃまする。 **suffer loss** 損害をうける。 **disintegrate** [disíntigrèit] 徐々にくずれる。 562. **key** 秘訣(けつ)。 **fate** 運命。 **chase** [tʃeis] 追いかける。 **weary** 疲れた。 564. **suspect** [səspékt] そうかしらと思う。 565. **top-notch** 一流の。 **interpreter** [intə́ːpritə] 通訳。

cultures that they can, figuratively, soar above purely literal translation. *Let* a well-read Russian *cite* an animal story by Krylov *and* they will be ready with a similar fable from Aesop.

(*P. T. White*)

---

## (61)

| **One more effort, and** you will succeed. |

【訳】 もうひと奮発だ、そうすれば成功する。

【解 説】 この構文は前章に述べた「**命令法＋and**」の一種の変形と見ることができる。

　　[**Make**] one more effort, **and** you will succeed.
　　＝**If** you make one more effort, you will succeed.
類例：—
　　**One more such loss, and** we shall be ruined.
　　＝**Let** us make one more such loss, and we shall...
　　＝**If** we make one more such loss, we shall...
　　＝もういちどこんな損をすれば没落だ。

---

**566.** *A single misstep, a slip, or a fall, and* nothing remains but a horrible death by being dashed to pieces upon the jagged rocks below.

**567.** *A few days more and* this fine library will no longer exist! These books will pass into a thousand strange hands and quit his room where they have been guarded with such tender

---

**figuratively** 比喩的に。　**soar above** 以上に高く飛ぶ。　**literal** 文字どおりの。 **cite** [sait] 例としてあげる。　**similar** 同類の。
　(61) **effort** [éfət] 努力。　566. **be dashed to pieces** ばらばらに打ちくだかれる。　**jagged** [dʒǽgid] ぎざぎざの。　567. **library** [láibrəri] 図書館、蔵書。 **quit** [kwit] 去る。　**guard** 保護する。　**tender** 心やさしい。

care.

**568.** *The least movement in his sleep and* he must have rolled over and been dashed to pieces on the rocks below.

**569.** *Another moment and* I was swallowed completely in the dark, gray mass with nothing but the dancing needles on the instrument dials to guide me and tell me whether I was right-side-up or up-side-down. (茨城大)

**570.** The last tramp of footsteps, the last rumbling of the waggon-wheels died away in the distance. No renewal of firing from the position occupied by the enemy disturbed the silence that followed. The Germans knew that the French were in retreat. *A few minutes more and* they would take possession of the abandoned village; the tumult of their approach would become audible at the cottage. In the meantime the stillness was terrible. Even the wounded wretches who were left in the kitchen waited their fate in silence.

---

( 62 )

---

(a) I love you more than he **does.**

(b) He **does** work hard, but somehow he remains as poor as ever.

---

【訳】 (a) ぼくが君を愛するのは彼が君を愛する以上だ。

---

568. **roll over** ころげ落ちる。569. **swallow** [swóulou] のみこむ。**instrument dials** [dáiəlz] 計器盤。 **right-side-up** 上下が正しい位置にある。 **up-side-down** 上下さかさまの。570. **tramp** [træmp] 足音。**rumbling** [rʌ́mbliŋ] とどろき。 **renewal** 再開始。**retreat** [ritríːt] 退却。**abandoned** [əbǽndənd] 放棄された。**tumult** [tjúːmʌlt] 騒ぎ。**audible** 聞える。**in the meantime** それまでの間。**wretch** [retʃ] あわれなやつ。

(b) 彼はかせぐことはかせぐが、どういうものか相変わらず貧乏だ。

【解説】(a) 同一動詞の反復をさけるために do を用いることがある。いわば **Pro-verb**(代動詞)ともいうべきものである。類例:—

Use a book as a bee **does** (=*uses*) a flower.
(書物を利用することはちが花を利用するごとくにせよ)
Did you go?—Yes, I **did** (=*went*).
(君は行きましたか——ええ、行きました)

(b) 助動詞の **do** が打消しや疑問に用いられるのはふつうの規則であるが、打消しでも疑問でもない文の動詞に do の付いているのは強意のため、すなわち動詞の意味を強めるためであるから訳すのに手心が必要である。「実際…することはするが」「…するからには」「ぜひ…せよ」など、ときに応じて訳すがよい。類例:—

You did not go to see him?—I **did go,** but found him absent.
(君は彼の所へ行かなかったんだね——行ったことは行ったが不在だった)
Mother, **do take** me to the play.
(お母さん、お芝居へ連れて行ってくださいよう)
**Do take** some! (まあ一つ召し上がれ)
**Do come!** (ぜひいらっしゃい)

---

**571.** It is clearly evident to everyone that a big airplane requires more power to keep it going than *does* a little one; that there must be some limit to the total weight which can be supported and propelled by the power of a given engine. Certainly we cannot hope to carry an infinite weight with zero power—stones don't float in the air.

**572.** 'A good citizen' does not mean a high-tax payer, nor the shrewd politician, nor the learned man, nor does it mean

---

571. **keep~going** 飛行しつづけさせる。 **propel** [prəpél] 推進する。 **infinite** [ínfinit] 無限の。 572. **tax payer** 納税者。 **shrewd** [ʃru:d] 機敏な。

an excellent artist. It *does* mean a common man who does his duty conscientiously to his utmost.

**573.** He is generally very reserved, but if he *does* talk, he always speaks to the purpose.

**574.** Unless he *does* attempt to read analytically, it is doubtful whether any beneficial result can be had, no matter how many stories he reads or how many details of plot he can remember or how many characters he can name. (長崎大)

**575.** X-rays *do* provide us with a means of seeing into and learning a great deal about the interior of many articles without destroying or in any way harming them. Therein lies the immense value of the application of the science to industry.

**576.** As the soil and the rain and the dew cause the tree to put forth its tender shoots, so *do* books and study *feed* the mind and make its hidden powers unfold.

**577.** "I take the flowers to the people myself," she announced, with a friendly smile. "You were right; it *does* make them happy. And it makes me happy. The doctors don't know what is making me well—but I *do!* I have something to live for." (教育大)

---

**conscientiously** [kɔ̀nʃiénʃəsli] 良心的に。 **utmost** [ʌ́tmoust] 極度。 **573. reserved** [rizə́:vd] 遠慮がち。 **to the purpose** [pə́:pəs] 要領よく、適切に。 **574. analytically** [æ̀nəlítikəli] 分析的に。 **beneficial** [bènifíʃəl] 有益な。 **detail** 詳細。 **plot** 筋。 **name** 名を挙げる。 **575. provide** 供給する。 **see into** 調査する。 **interior** 内部。 **immense** 多大の。 **application** 応用。 **576. shoot** [ʃu:t] 若芽。 **feed** 養う。 **make...unfold** 開かせる。 **577. live for** 目あてとして生きる。

(63)

(a) He **goes** to school.
(b) He **will** *often* sit for hours together, absorbed in deep thoughts.
(c) I **used** to take the "Yomiuri," but not now.
(d) He **would** *often* come home drunk and beat his wife.

【訳】 (a) 彼は学校へ通っている。
(b) 彼は考えこんで何時間もつづけてすわっていることがよくある。
(c) もとは「読売」を取っていたが今は取らない。
(d) 彼はよく酔っぱらって帰って来ては細君を打ったものだ。

【解説】 (a) 現在の規則的習慣をあらわすには現在時制 (Present Tense) を用いる。たとえば

He **goes** to school.

は、彼は現に毎日学校へ通うということで、つまり、He is a student. ということになる。類例:—

He **rises** early.＝He is an early riser.
　（彼は早起きだ）

(b) 現在の不規則的習慣をあらわすには will を用いる。この場合には often, sometimes などの副詞を伴なうことが多い。「よく...する」「往往...することがある」など訳して当たる。類例:—

He **will often** come of a Sunday morning and stay all day.
（彼はよく日曜の朝などにやって来て一日遊んで行く）

---

(63) **together** [təgéðə] 共に、つづけて。　**absorbed** [əbsɔ́ːbd] 吸収されて、夢中になって。

He **will sometimes** sit up all night poring over a novel.

(彼は小説を耽読(たんどく)してよく夜あかしをすることがある)

【注 意】 この will を「何々しがち」など訳してよい場合がある。例:—

He spends all the money he has, **as students will.**

(学生はそうありがちだが、彼も金があればあるだけ使ってしまう)

She kept all the letters she received, **as girls will.**

(女の子にはありがちのことだが彼女は人から来た手紙を皆しまっておいた)

(c) 過去の規則的習慣をあらわすには used to を用いる。「もとは...していた」「いつも...していた」などと訳す。類例:—

I **used to** go there, but I go no longer.

(もとはそこへ行っていたが今は行かない)

{ I **take** the "Asahi."
(私は「朝日」を取っている)[現在]
I **used to take** the "Yomiuri."
(もとは「読売」を取っていた)[過去]

この過去の場合にただの過去時制 (Past Tense) を用いて I took とすれば1回の動作をあらわすことになる。比較:—

{ He **used to say** that...
(彼はいつもそう言っていた)[常習]
He **said** that...
(彼は...と言った)[1回の動作]

【注 意】 used to は過去の形ばかりであって use to という形はない。この used は ought などと等しく助動詞的の性質を有している。それからこの used to と次の章に述べる to be used to と混同してはならない。

(d) 過去の不規則的習慣をあらわすには (b) の will をそのまま過去にして would を用いる。比較:—

{ He **will** *often* come home drunk, and beat his wife.
He **would** *often* come home drunk, and beat his wife.

**578.** When whales are lying quietly on the surface of the water, you cannot see very much of their bodies; but *sometimes* they *will* jump out of water.

**579.** A man will throw away or part with a useless watch which does not keep time, but he *will often* be content with his mind although it be so sick that it cannot distinguish error from truth, though it has grown almost useless in its vanity, and perhaps has never told him what he himself is.

**580.** My brother and I *used to* put all the house in disorder *as children will.*

**581.** Earthquakes have attracted universal attention from the earliest times, and on account of their destructive power it is not surprising that they *used to* be regarded as supernatural phenomena.

**582.** He made it a rule to go out every day and *used to* say that as he never consulted the weather, he never had to consult the physicians.

**583.** With every passing day his health improved. "Ah," he *would* exclaim to me, " island life has charms not to be found elsewhere! Half the ills of mankind might be shaken off without doctor or medicine by mere residence in this lovely portion of the world."

**584.** As soon as I could speak so as to be understood I *used*

---

578. **quietly** [kwáiətli] 静かに。  579. **part with** 手ばなす。 **keep time** 時間を正確に示す。 **be content with ...** で満足している、がまんしている。 **it be sick**＝his mind is sick. **distinguish** 区別する。 **vanity** 虚栄。  580. **put in disorder** 乱雑にする。反対は put in order.  581. **universal** 一般の人の、万人の。 **on account of ...** のために。 **destructive** [distrÁktiv] 破壊的な。 **supernatural** 超自然の。 **phenomena** [finɔ́minə] 現象。phenomenon の複数形。  582. **consult** 相談する、忠告を求める。 **physician** 医者、内科医。  583. **medicine** [médisin] 薬。 **residence** [rézidəns] 居住。 **portion** 部分。

*to* be their waiter at breakfast and was sent to the butler to ask for whatever was wanted instead of ringing the bell. (兵庫農大)

**585.** The sea-wind, which *used to* begin gently, and then gradually increase to a pleasant breeze, came on suddenly, and with great violence; so that the waves curled and broke into a white sheet of foam as far as the eye could reach.

**586.** It sounded like the drone of airplane engines. Someone would say, "Hark!" Then we *would* listen, our hearts beating wildly. The sound *would* stop, and we *would* know that it had been only the general's snoring.

**587.** When you were very small, you *would often* laugh heartily when there was nothing to amuse you. That was because you had so much energy to spare that some of it bubbled up in laughter.

---

( 64 )

| I **am used to** hardships. |

【訳】 私はつらいことには慣れている。

〖解 説〗 be used to～＝be accustomed to～ ［～は名詞］
　　　＝～には慣れている(から平気)。

この場合の used は過去分詞で形容詞的性質をもっていて、前の章の used が過去助動詞的性質をもっていたのとは全然性質が違う。ただし「be accustomed＋不定詞」の過去形は前章の「used＋不定詞」に等しくなる。

比較：—

---

584. **butler** 召使頭。 585. **breeze** [briːz] 軟(なん)風。 **violence** 猛威。 **sheet of foam** 一面の泡。 586. **drone** うなる音。 **snore** いびきをかく。 587. **to spare** 余分の。 **bubble** [bʌbl] 泡立つ。 **laughter** [láːftə] 大笑い。

$\begin{cases} \text{I \quad used \qquad\qquad to work hard.} \\ \text{I was accustomed to work hard.} \end{cases}$ [work は動詞]
　=ぼくはもとは勉強したものだ。
$\begin{cases} \text{I was used \qquad\qquad to hard work.} \\ \text{I was accustomed to hard work.} \end{cases}$ [work は名詞]
　=ぼくは労苦には慣れていた。

---

**588.** I *am not used to* being called a liar.

**589.** If you have *been used to* wearing a great many clothes and to living in hot rooms, you will feel very cold if you suddenly try to wear much less and to keep the room cool. And if you are not careful you may catch a cold.

**590.** My time was my own after the afternoon board, Saturdays, and I *was accustomed to* put it in on a little sailboat on the bay.

**591.** Still, Ida was happy, for her father loved her dearly, and she had *become used to* living in the lighthouse.

---

( 65 )

---

(a) I **have a liking for** that man.
(b) I **have a dislike to** that man.
(c) He **has a genius for** poetry.

---

【訳】　(a) ぼくはあの人がどこやら好きだ。
　　　(b) ぼくはあの人はどこか虫が好かない。
　　　(c) 彼は詩の天才がある。
〖解　説〗　(a)　have a...for~ の形をもって嗜好(しこう)をあらわすこ

---

588. liar [láiə] 虚言者。　590. board「会合」、「取引」。　**put it in** 時間を使う。　591. Ida [áidə]. lighthouse [láithàus] 灯台。

とが多い。...のところは通例抽象名詞であるが、a certain liking (一種の好み)の意味で不定冠詞を付けるのである。

He **has a passion for** sporting.
（彼は猟が大好きだ）

He **has a partiality for** Maugham and Orwell.
（彼はモームとオーウェルがことに好きだ）

He **has an appetite for** novels.
（彼は小説が好きだ）

He **has an** unconquerable **love for** drink.
（酒が好きでとうていやめられない）

I **have a fancy for** your garden.＝I **have taken a fancy to** your garden.
（ぼくは君の家の庭園にほれこんだ）

(b) きらいなことをあらわす方には for のかわりに to を用いて **have a...to~** の形を取ることが多い、しかし for を用いる形もある。

He **has an aversion to** all sorts of work.
（彼は仕事と名のつくものは何でもきらいだ）

He **has a deep hatred for** Communists.
（彼はひどく共産党がきらいだ）

(c) 嗜好をあらわす **have a...for~** は、転じて「~の才がある」の意味にも用いられる。

He **has an eye for** the beautiful.
（彼は審美眼がある）

He **has an ear for** music.
（音楽の耳がある）

He **has an aptitude for** languages.
（語学の才がある）

He **has a head for** mathematics.
（彼は数学の頭がある）

---

(65) **sporting** 遊猟。 **partiality** [pàːʃiǽliti] 偏愛。 **appetite** [ǽpitait] (食)欲。 **unconquerable** [ʌnkɔ́ŋkərəbl] うち勝ちがたい。 **fancy** [fǽnsi] 好み。 **aversion** [əvə́ːʃən] 嫌悪(けんお)。 **hatred** [héitrid] 憎悪(ぞうお)。 **aptitude** [ǽptitjuːd] 素質、才。 **mathematics** [mæθimǽtiks] 数学。

**592.** My father's library consisted chiefly of novels, most of which I read and have since often regretted that, at a time when I *had* such *a thirst for* knowledge, more proper books had not fallen in my way, since it was now resolved I should not be a man of letters.

**593.** He was said to *have a great liking to* things Japanese. He was a great admirer of the Japanese family system, saying that such virtues peculiar to the Japanese as modesty and courtesy were the products of the family system.

**594.** We *have a liking*, and perhaps more than a liking, *for* the place where we were born and where our lives are passed. We should *have*, in the same way, *a love for* the whole of our country as opposed to all other countries, and ought to do everything that lies in our power to preserve it from harm.

**595.** He was a clever man; a pleasant companion; a careless student; *had a great propensity for* running into debt, and *a partiality for* the tavern. (*Thackeray*)

**596.** I feel sure you *have a very special aptitude for* Greek, and that if you will but direct your attention to that, you have a brilliant future before you. (*Max O'Rell*)

**597.** As we expected our landlord the next day, my wife went to make the venison pasty; my daughters seemed equally busy

---

592. **consist of** ...から成っている。 **regret** [rigrét] 遺憾とする。 **thirst** 渇望。 **proper** 適当な。 **fall in one's way** 偶然にその人の前に現われる。 **it was** ...の it は (that) I should ...を代表する。 **resolve** きめる。 593. **admirer** [ədmáiərə] 崇拝者。 **modesty** [mɔ́disti] 謙遜。 **courtesy** 礼儀。 594. **as opposed to** ...に対立しての。 **preserve ~ from** から...護る。 595. **companion** [kəmpǽnjən] 友。 **propensity** [prəpénsiti] 性癖。 **run into debt** [det] 借金をする。 **tavern** [tǽvən] 居酒屋。 596. **brilliant** [bríljənt] 輝かしい、はなばなしい。 597. **venison** [vénzn, vénizn] 鹿肉。 **pasty** [pǽsti] まんじゅうのようなパイ。

with the rest; and I observed them for a good while cooking something over the fire. I at first supposed they were assisting their mother; but little Dick informed me, in a whisper, that they were making a wash for the face. Washes of all kinds, I *had a natural antipathy to;* for I knew that, instead of mending the complexion, they spoilt it. I therefore approached my chair by slow degrees to the fire, and grasping the poker, as if it wanted mending, seemingly by accident overturned the whole composition, and it was too late to begin another. *(Goldsmith)*

**598.** Like all Frenchmen, Napoleon *had a passion for* stage-effect. *(Emerson)*

**599.** In less than another year we had another daughter, and now I was determined that Grissel should be her name; but a rich relation *taking a fancy to* stand godmother, the girl was, by her direction, called Sophia. *(Goldsmith)*

**600.** He patted me on the shoulder, told me I was a good boy, and he had *taken quite a fancy to* me. *(Stevenson)*

( 66 )

(a) He **took** me **by the hand.**
(b) He **struck** me **on the head.**
(c) He **looked** me **in the face.**

【訳】 (a) 彼は私の手を取った。

assist 助ける。 wash 化粧水。 antipathy [æntípəθi] 反感。 mend よくする。 complexion 顔の色つや。 spoil だいなしにする。 poker 火ばし。 overturn ひっくり返す。 composition 調合薬。 599. relation 親類。 stand godmother 名づけ親になる。 Sophia [sofáiə]. 600. pat 軽くたたく。 shoulder [ʃóuldə] 肩。

(b) 彼は私の頭を打った。

(c) 彼は私の顔を見た。

〖解 説〗 日本語で「私の手を取った」「私の頭を打った」「私の顔を見た」というところを英語ではまず「私を取った」「私を打った」「私を見た」と言って、あとからその場所を言うのがごくふつうの言い方である。こういう文句に出会ったら、日英文法の差異を心得ていて、おかしくないような訳し方をしなければならない。類例：—

I **seized** him **by the collar**.
　（あいつの胸ぐらを取った）
He **seized** her **by the hair**.
　（彼女の髪をつかんだ）
Some one **pulled** me **by the sleeve**.
　（だれかが私のそでを引いた）
I **patted** the dog **on the back**.
　（犬の背中をなでてやった）
I **chucked** the child **under the chin**.
　（子供のあごを軽くたたいてやった）
I **slapped** him **across the face**.
　（横面を張ってやった）
He was **shot through the heart**.
　（心臓を撃ちぬかれた）
He was **wounded in the leg**.
　（足に負傷した）

---

**601.** "O here's a perfectly lovely one! Do *take* him *by his little black head* and eat him quick!"

**602.** A soldier, stationed at the entrance of a picture gallery, had strict orders to allow no one to pass without first depositing his walking stick. A gentleman came in with his hands in his

---

602. **stationed** 配置された。　**gallery** [gǽləri] 美術館。　**strict order** 厳重な命令。**deposit** [dipɔ́zit] 預ける。

pockets. The soldier, *taking* him *by the arm*, said: "Stop, where is your stick?" "I have no stick." "Then you will have to go back and get one before I can allow you to pass."

**603.** Squeers left the room, and shortly afterward returned, *dragging* Smike *by the collar*. (*Dickens*)

**604.** Squeers, in a violent outbreak, spat at him, and *struck* him a blow *across the face*. (*Dickens*)

**605.** He *patted* me *on the head;* but somehow I didn't like him. (*Dickens*)

**606.** What was Franklin? A printer! once a subordinate in a printing office! Poverty *stared* him *in the face;* but her blank, hollow look could nothing daunt him. He struggled against a harder current than most are called to encounter; but he did not yield.

**607.** We need a working estimate of the disorders we have to face. Certain facts now *stare* us *in the face*. All war is not nationalist; abolish nationalist sovereignty and there would still be a social war on hand. (東工大)

**608.** It is the bounden duty of every man to *look* his affairs *in the face*, and to keep an account of his incomings and outgoings in money matters.

---

**603. drag** ひきずる。 **collar** [kɔ́lə] えり。 **604. violent** [váiələnt] 激しい。 **outbreak** [áutbreik] 怒りのばく発。 **spat** <spit つばを吐く。 **606. subordinate** [səbɔ́:dnit] 部下、下っぱ。 **her** Poverty を女性と見て。 **stare** じっと見る。 **hollow** うつろな。 **nothing**=not at all。 **daunt** [dɔ:nt] ひるませる。 **be called** 求められる。 **encounter** [inkáuntə] 遭遇する。 **yield** [ji:ld] 負ける。 **607. working** 実際的。 **estimate** 評価。 **disorder** 混乱。 **nationalist** 国家主義的。 **abolish** 廃止する。 **sovereignty** [sɔ́vrinti] 主権。 **608. bounden** [báundən] 必ずしなければならない。 **affairs** 財政状態。 **incomings** [ínkʌ̀miŋz] 収入。 **outgoings** [áutgòuiŋz] 支出。

( 67 )

> "I will **ease** you **of** your burden." So saying, the highwayman **robbed** the traveller **of** his money.

【訳】「荷物を軽くしてやろう」と言って追いはぎが旅人の金を奪った。

〖解 説〗 of は元来 from と等しく分離を示す前置詞であった。現在でも人から物を借りる、あるいは買うなどという場合には

**Of** (or **from**) whom did you buy this?
（だれから買ったか）
I borrowed it **from** (or **of**) Mr. Tanaka.
（田中君から借りた）

などと of, from のどちらを用いてもよい。

しかし奪取の類の動詞の次にこの of がくる場合は、日本語と英語とでは句法を異にするので、よく注意しないと往々まごつくことがある。

こっそり物を盗むのは to **steal** a thing **from** a person で、日本語と同じ語脈だから解しやすいが、rob (強奪する) という動詞になると to **rob** a person **of** his property という構文を取る。

そこで、He **robbed** me **of** my purse. を of=from として直訳すると、「彼は財布から私を奪った」というこっけいなことになる。しかし理屈はこれでもよいのである、人間を主として財布を従ときめておくから、こういうとおかしく聞えるが、もし人間も財布も対等と見れば「人から財布をとる」のも「財布から人をとる」のも同じことである。そんな理屈はさておき、of は何でもその前後にある二つのものを分離することを示すから、「動詞 + 人 (あるいは物、場所) + of + 物 (あるいは人)」の構文に出会ったならば「人から物を奪う」「人から負担を減じる」「場所からやっかい物を取り除く」というふうに解すればよい。

〖注 意〗 この構文が受身になってまごつかないよう注意が必要。
例：—

(67) **highwayman** [háiweimən] 追いはぎ。　　**property** [prɔ́pəti] 財産。

A highwayman **robbed** him **of** his purse.
=He **was robbed of** his purse by a highwayman.
  (彼は追いはぎに財布を奪われた)
この構文はどんな種類の動詞に用いられるかというと：—
(第一類)　負担を軽くする、苦しみを減じるなど軽減の動詞。
　The young should **ease** the old **of** their burden.
  (若者は老人の荷物を取って軽くしてやるべきだ)
　This medicine will **cure** you **of** your disease.
  (この薬を飲めば病気がなおる)
　This medicine will **relieve** you **of** your pain.
  (この薬を飲めば苦痛がなくなる)
　She has **been delivered of** a fine boy.
  (玉のような男子を生み落した)
**to be delivered of a child** (こどもを生む)は身持ちの人が身軽になるのである。

(第二類)　やっかい払いをする、盗賊などを退治するなど、いやなものを除去する動詞。
　What is the best way to **rid** a house **of** rats?
  (ねずみを退治するにはどうするのが一番いいか)
　I will **clear** the mountain **of** the robbers.
  (おれがこの山の賊を退治してやろう)
　I cannot **break** myself **of** the habit of late-rising.
  (朝寝のくせがどうしてもなおらない)
(第三類)　盗む、奪うなどの動詞。
　He **was robbed of** his money and **stripped of** his clothes
  (彼は金を奪われ着物まではがされた)
　Astonishment **deprived** me **of** my power of speech.
  (おどろいて口がきけなかった)

---

**deprive** うばう。　**rid** とりのぞく。　**clear** 追いだす。　**break** たち切る。

**609.** He does not care whom he *deprives of* enjoyment, so that he can obtain it.

**610.** If you are poor, have the courage to appear poor, and you *disarm* poverty *of* its sharpest sting. (*Irving*)

**611.** The patient was *deprived* at intervals *of* the use of reason.

**612.** My anxiety to *get rid of* him and have my library to myself was now so great that I could not wait a minute longer.

**613.** It was long before that she *disburdened* her heart *of* a secret which had weighed upon it. (*T. B. Aldrich*)

**614.** If I *rid* your town *of* rats, will you give me a thousand guilders? (*Browning*)

**615.** He who needlessly breaks an appointment, shows that he is as reckless of the waste of another's time as of his own. To the busy man, time is money, and the person who *robs* him *of* it does him as great an injury as if he had picked his pocket.

**616.** When you arrive at an English railway station, all the porters seem to say: "Here is a customer, let us treat him well." And it is who shall *relieve* you *of* your luggage, or answer any questions you may be pleased to ask.

**617.** His manners were then, as they continued ever afterwards, simple, manly and independent. He took his share in conversation but not more than belonged to him and listened with apparent attention and respect, on subjects where his want

---

610. **courage** [kʌ́ridʒ] 勇気。 **disarm** 武器をとりあげる。 **sting** 針。 611. **interval** [íntəvəl] 間隔。 **reason** 理性。 612. **anxiety** [æŋzáiəti] 切望。 **have to oneself** 独占する。 **library** 書斎。 613. **disburden** 荷をおろす。 **weigh** なやます。 614. **guilder** [gíldə] 金貨の名。 615. **reckless** 意に介さない。 **pick pocket** すりをする。 616. **porter** 赤帽。 **customer** お客。 **it is**=the question is. 617. **independent** [ìndipéndənt] 独立的。 **apparent attention** 見うけるところ注意[を払って]。 **subject** 話題。

of education *deprived* him *of* the means of information.

**618.** Mrs. Slocum, *bereft of* father, husband, and child, and *stripped of* all possessions but the house that sheltered her, could not leave the valley, for nine helpless children were yet in her household.

**619.** Let my experience supply your want of it, and *clear* your way in the progress of your youth *of those* thorns and briers which scratched and disfigured me in the course of mine.

*(Chesterfield)*

**620.** The room grew light; she got up, went to the little cracked mirror, and looked long at her face. If she had ever known that she was pretty, the life she led with her husband, sometimes ill-treated, always scantily clothed, and more or less in want, had *deprived* her *of* this knowledge.

**621.** Age-old fragments of misinformation still clutter our thinking, and there is a new accumulation ladled out by persons who have been in China very recently and very briefly. It will not be possible soon to *clear* our attics entirely *of* the residues of a century or so, but certain large and cumbersome myths might be thrown out for good and all.

*(Pearl Buck)*

**622.** However, when any one of our relations was found to be a person of a very bad character, a troublesome guest, or one

---

means [mi:nz] 手段。 **618. bereft of** ...をうばわれて、死なれて。 **possessions** [pəzéʃənz] 所有物。 **shelter** 雨つゆをしのがせる。 **valley** [væli] 谷。 **619. thorn** とげ。 **brier** [bráiə] 野ばら。 **scratch** ひっかく。 **disfigure** [disfígə] 外観を損ずる。 **620. cracked** ひびのはいった。 **scantily clothed** 衣服もろくに着せられない。 **in want** 不足している。 **this knowledge** むかし美しかったことを知っていたこと。 **621. fragment** 断片。 **misinformation** 誤報。 **clutter** 取りちらす。 **accumulation** 累積。 **ladle** [léidl] ひしゃくですくう。 **attic** 屋根裏部屋。 **residue** [rézidju:] 残余。 **cumbersome** やっかいな。 **myth** [miθ] 伝説。 **for good and all** 永久に。 **622. troublesome** やっかいな。

we desired to *get rid of*, upon his leaving my house I ever took care to lend him a riding coat, or a pair of boots, or sometimes a horse of small value, and I always had the satisfaction of finding he never came back to return them. By this the house *was cleared of* such as we did not like.　　　　　　　　　(*Goldsmith*)

## (68)

(a) I went to the station **to see** a friend off.
(b) He lived **to see** his son a great man.
(c) She wept **to see** her son in such a plight.

【訳】(a) 私は友人を見送りに停車場に行った。
　　(b) 彼は息子の偉くなるまで生きていた。
　　(c) 彼女は息子のあわれな様を見て泣いた。

〘解　説〙 (a) は不定詞が目的をあらわす例である。類例:—

　She ran **to meet** her mother.
　　(彼女は母を迎えるために駆け出した)
　I got up early in order **to catch** the first train.
　　(始発列車に乗るために早く起きた)

(b) の例は「息子の偉くなるのを見るために生きていた」のではない。人の寿命は天の定めで目的とならない。これは幸いに寿命があって子供の偉くなったのを見たということで、to see は目的でなく結果を示すので、例文を書きなおせば He lived **till he saw** his son a great man. となる。なお一例をあげれば、

　He awoke **to find** himself famous.

は「自らを有名に見いだすために眼ざめた」のではない、「眼ざめて見たらば有名になっていた」のであるから、

　He awoke **and found** himself famous.

---

**take care** 気をつける。

というのに等しいのである。類例:—

Few men live **to be** (=*till they are*) ninety years old.
(90まで生きる者は少ない)
He grew up **to be** (=*and became*) a strong youth.
(成長して丈夫な青年になった)

〖注　意〗 不定詞が only に伴なう場合は目的と結果とが混同するように見える、たとえば

I worked hard **only to fail.**
(失敗するために勉強したようなもの)〔目的〕

というのは、

I worked hard **but failed.**
(勉強したが、しかし失敗した)〔結果〕

ということである。要するに目的には意志があり、結果には意志がないという差はあるが、結果は一種の目的ともいえる。

結果を示す不定詞はまた never に伴なうことが多い。例:—

He sank beneath the waves, **never to rise again.**
(波間に沈んだまま再び浮び上がらなかった)
Byron left his native land, **never to return.**
(バイロンは故国を去って再び帰らなかった)

これは初めから帰るまいと思って去ったとは限らない。

（c） 不定詞の to hear, to see などが感情をあらわす**動詞**、形容詞の後に来る場合は原因をあらわす。たとえば例文 She wept to see... は「見るために泣いた」のではない、「見て泣いた」のである。

I am glad **to see you.**

は「あなたに会うことを喜ぶ」というのではなくて、「あなたに会ってうれしい」という意味である。この文句は主人が人を迎えるとき用いられるので「ようこそ」などに当る。類例:—

I could not help laughing **to see** such a strange sight.
(そんなおかしな光景を見て思わずふき出した)
I am sorry **to hear** of your illness.
(お病気の由、お気の毒に存じます)

**623.**　Mr. Acres was much *pleased to learn* of John's success, and felt hopeful that his boy would in time become a useful man, even if he was "without a genius."

**624.**　Some months later the clerk *was astonished to receive* another visit, doubly astonished because this time the woman was driving the car.　　　　　　　　　　　　　　　（教育大）

**625.**　For a moment or two Harmon was silent with surprise and mortification, *to think* that his father's apprentice whom he esteemed so far below him, should be possessed of knowledge equal to his.

**626.**　He who is not familiarized with the finest passages of the finest writers will one day be mortified *to observe* that his *best* thoughts are their indifferent ones.　　　　　　（鳥取大）

**627.**　When the Prince awoke in the morning from a deep sleep and looked around him, he *was* greatly *surprised to find* himself alone in a thatched shed.

**628.**　He embarked on a steamer as a third-class passenger, and landed in the United States in 1900, *to find* himself penniless, with little research opportunity waiting for an obscure young Japanese.　　　　　　　　　　　　　　　　　　（九州大）

**629.**　They were studying English and wanted to practice it. They asked my impressions of Leningrad. They *were disappointed to find* that I was not an engineer, and they parted

---

**623. in time** 時がくれば、いつかは。　**genius** 天才。　**624. doubly** [dʎbli] 二重に。　**625. mortification** [mɔ̀:tifikéiʃən] 煩悶(ﾓﾝ)。　**apprentice** 徒弟。**esteem** 考える、思う。　**be possessed of** ...をもっている。　**equal** [í:kwəl] 等しい。　**626. be familiarized** 親しんでいる。　**mortify** [mɔ́:tifai] 無念に思わせる。　**indifferent** よくもない悪くもない。　**627. thatched** [θætʃt] 草ぶきの。　**shed** [ʃed] 小屋。　**628. embark** 乗船する。　**land** 上陸する。　**research opportunity** 研究の機会。　**obscure** [əbskjúə] 無名の。　**629. impression** 印象。　**disappoint** 失望させる。

abruptly from me when I told them that I was a professor of government. (*Merle Fainsod*)

**630.** Human beings are always changing the nature of things, and always fancying that the things they have changed will still go on acting in exactly the same way as they did in the past, *only to be surprised* when new and unexpected things come out.

**631.** Is mankind going to rid itself of two of its three traditional scourges—war and pestilence—*only to be done* to death by the third scourge, famine? (*A. Toynbee*)

**632.** He *lived to have* his work rewarded with all the honours that a grateful world could bestow. He saw his ideas and investigations influence the thought and action of the whole world. If greatness be measured by the extent of the good done to one's fellow-men, his name will stand high for all time.

**633.** Spring is a season that approaches slowly with timid steps, although on occasion it dances forward joyously for one day *only to retire* again the next. There are bright, warm, sunny days in the depth of winter when Nature seems to awake from her sleep, and only the chill in the shadow and the bare branches remind us that the time of spring is still a long way off.

**634.** Last of all we visited the Traitor's Gate, through which many famous persons have passed *to return no more*.

**635.** A human being shut up in a room, of which every

---

**abruptly** 突然。 **government** 政治学。 **630. go on acting** 作用しつづける。 **unexpected** 予期しない。 **631. scourge** [skə:dʒ] 懲罰(罸)。 **pestilence** 疫病。 **be done to death** 死滅する。 **famine** [fǽmin] 飢餓。 **632. rewarded** 報いられる。 **honour** 名誉。 **bestow** [bistóu] 授ける。 **investigation** 調査、研究。 **measure** 測定する。 **fellow-men** [félounmen] 同胞。 **633. timid** おずおずした。 **joyously** [dʒɔ́iəsli] うれしげに。 **retire** 後退する。 **the depth of winter** 真冬。 **chill** 冷え。 **635. shut** ここでは過去分詞。

crack is closed, with a pan of burning charcoal, falls asleep, *never to wake* again.

---

(69)

> I **saw** him **enter** the room.

【訳】 私は彼が部屋へはいるのを見た。

〘解 説〙 すべて五感をあらわす動詞、see, hear, feel, watch, observe, perceive, notice, know など、いわゆる知覚動詞 (Verbs of Perception) は Root-Infinitive すなわち to を付けない不定詞を補語として「動詞＋目的語＋補語」の形を取る。

上の例文では him が目的語で、enter は Root-Infinitive で補語となっている。文法的に直訳すれば、「私は部屋にはいる彼を見た」となるが、日本語としては「私は彼が部屋にはいるのを見た」というように訳すのがよい。同様に " See the dog run." は文法的には「走る犬を見よ」で、dog は目的語であるが、日本語としては「犬が走るのをごらん」「犬の走るのを見よ」などとすべきである。類例:——

**Hear** the bird **sing.**
 (鳥の歌うのをお聞きなさい)
I **felt** the house **shake.**
 (家の揺れるのを感じた)
I **was watching** the crows **fly** home to roost.
 (烏がねぐらに帰って行くのを眺めていた)
I **observed** the mercury **fall** suddenly.
 (急に水銀が下るのを見た)
I did not **notice** any one **enter** the room.
 (だれも部屋へはいった様子もなかった)

〘注 意 1〙 以上の諸動詞が受身 (Passive) に用いられる場合には、to

---

crack すき間。close [klouz] 閉じる。pan さら状の器物。charcoal [tʃáːkoul] 木炭。
(69) roost [ruːst] ねぐらにつく。 mercury [mə́ːkjuri] 水銀。

の付いた不定詞を補語とする、比較:—

{ I **saw** a man **enter** the room.
{ A man **was seen to enter** the room.

〖注 意 2〗 hear がすぐに Root-Infinitive へつづいて hear say; hear tell; hear speak などなっていることがある。この場合は hear の次に people などという語が省略されているのである。比較:—

{ I **heard** *him* **say** so.
{ (彼がそういうのを聞いた)
{ I often **heard say** so.
{ (世間の人がそういうのをよく聞いた)

---

**636.** Nothing could be more interesting than to *hear him tell* of his travels, and of what he had seen.

**637.** It is pleasant to *watch the sun sink* behind a distant hill, to wander on and on in a huge forest with no thought of return, to stand upon the shore and gaze after a boat that goes to be hidden by far-off islands, to ponder on the journey of wild geese seen and lost among the clouds.

**638.** I often *heard tell* of the Leprechauns, and, to tell the truth downright, I never rightly believed in them. (*Quiller-Couch*)

**639.** Hamlet *observed* the king, his uncle, *change* colour at this expression.
(*Lamb*)

**640.** They fell into each other's arms and wept and laughed; and I had *heard say* they were happy ever after. (*Quiller-Couch*)

**641.** I therefore expect to *see* twentieth century Man *set* out

---

636. **interesting** [íntristiŋ] おもしろい。 637. **huge** 大きな。 **gaze** じっと見つめる。 **island** [áilənd] 島。 **ponder** [póndə] 案ずる。 **wild geese** がん、雁(がん)。 638. **Leprechaun** [léprikɔːn] 小天狗(こてんぐ)靴屋。 **to tell the truth** 正直のところ。 **downright** [dáunrait] あからさまに。 639. **colour** 顔色。 640. **laughed** [lɑːft] 笑った。 **ever after** ずっとその後。 641. **set out** 出発する。

on a quest for the recovery of religion.　I believe that he will recover it.

(*A. Toynbee*)

---

## (70)

>　(a)　I will **have** some one **come.**
>　(b)　I shall **have** some one **come.**

【訳】　(a)　だれかに<u>来させよう</u>；<u>来てもらおう</u>。
　　　　(b)　だれかに<u>来られるだろう</u>。

〖解　説〗　他動詞の have が Root-Infinitive [=to のない不定詞] を補語とする形，すなわち

　　**have＋目的語＋Root-Infinitive**

の形は、主語に意志の有る無しに従ってふた通りの解釈ができる。

　(a) は I will で I に意志があるから、自分の方から「命令して来させる」あるいは「頼んで来てもらう」ことになる。この場合には

　　**get＋目的語＋不定詞**

の形を代用することができる。すなわち

　　I will **have** some one **come.**
　　＝I will **get** some one **to come.**
　　＝だれかに来てもらいましょう。

類例:―

　　I will **have** him **go** with me.
　　＝I will **get** him **to go** with me.
　　　(彼にいっしょに行ってもらおう)

　　**Have** some one **carry** ⎱
　　**Get** some one **to carry** ⎰ my luggage to the station.
　　　(だれかに荷物を停車場へ持たせてやってください)

---

**quest** 探求。　**recovery** 回復。
　(70)　**luggage** [lʎgidʒ] 手荷物。アメリカでは baggage.

I will **have** my boy **show** you the way.
（こどもに道をご案内させましょう）

（b）の形は I shall で I に意志がないから、させるという Causative Meaning（使役の意味）はない、自然にそういうことになるのである。すなわち自分の方で人に来てもらいたいのではない、人が勝手に来るのである。この場合の have は一種の Passive すなわち「られる」意味である。

He **came** to see me yesterday.
＝He **visited** me yesterday.
（彼がきのう私を訪問した）
I **had** him **come** yesterday.
＝I **was visited** by him yesterday.
（きのう彼に来られた——訪問された）

類例：—

He **had** his wife **die**.
（彼は細君に死なれた＝細君が死んだ）
I don't like to **have** people **come** when I am busy.
（いそがしいとき人に来られるのは困る）
We **had** a fire **break out** in the neighbourhood last night.
（昨夜近所に火事があった——火事に出られた）
I **had** a curious thing **happen** this morning.
（私のところでけさふしぎなことがあった）

---

**642.** I am delighted to *have you play* football. I believe in rough, manly sports. But I do not believe in them if they become the sole end of any one's life. I do not want you to sacrifice standing well in your studies to any sport; and I need not tell you that character counts for a great deal more than either intellect or body in winning success in life.

---

**neighbourhood** [néibəhud] 近所。 **642. rough** 荒っぽい。 **believe in** よいと思う。 **sole** 唯一の。 **sacrifice** ~to...のために~を犠牲にする。 **stand well** 成績がよい。 **count** 重要である。

**643.** Soup was a very tall elephant, and sometimes the children would *have him stop* under a tree while they picked nuts or berries from the branches.

**644.** As we lived near the road, we often *had the traveller* or *stranger visit* us to taste our gooseberry-wine for which we had great reputation. *(Goldsmith)*

**645.** You will acquire skill better if you are active rather than if you are in a position to *have someone tell* you how to do it. Watching someone while he does what you want to do is a slight aid. You must do it.

**646.** I would *have* every student *come* to know, and the sooner the better, that there can be no thorough appreciation of the literature or culture without an exact knowledge of the language. (慶応大)

**647.** Try to do to others as you would *have them do* to you, and do not be discouraged if they fail sometimes.

**648.** I will *have the players play* something like the murder of my father. *(Shakespeare)*

**649.** Children always enjoy watching monkeys at their play, and, indeed, these little animals seem glad to *have people visit* them.

**650.** And if I am dismissed, Mrs. Jouett would never give me a letter of recommendation, either! What shall I do! What's to become of my career! After all I've tried to do for

---

644. **gooseberry** [gúzbəri] すぐり。 **reputation** 評判。 645. **active** 実際に行動する。 **watch** 傍観する。 **slight** [slait] わずかな。 646. **thorough** 徹底した。 **appreciation** 鑑賞。 **exact** 正確な。 647. **be discouraged** 落胆する。 648. **player** [pléiə] 役者。 **murder** [mə́:də] 殺害。 650. **dismiss** 解雇する。 **recommendation** 推薦(だ)。 **career** [kəríə] 生涯。 **after all I've tried ...** いろいろやった後で。

you, I can't bear to *have you do* this to me! (北海道大)

**651.** I would like to give you books, *have you attend* school, and do every thing to make you happy.

**652.** Malcolm did not like to *have his boy undertake* a journey of so much peril, as the snow was falling in heavy flakes, and it was growing very dark.

**653.** "A man brought her some wood to-day, and I heard her tell him that, unless she *got some one to saw* it to-night, she would not have anything to make a fire with in the morning."

**654.** "You told me to take my knife and fork off my plate when I passed it."—"I don't like to *have them fall off* and then pick them up for you."

**655.** "Well, you know I love you, Alice, and am delighted to *have you come*," said Mrs. Reed; "I am sure that were it in my power to do so, I would have you here all the time."

**656.** He led all the games, and when the children were tired of hunt the slipper, musical chairs, and family coach, he *got them to sit* down while he asked them riddles.

---

( 71 )

(a) I shall **have** my watch **stolen**.
(b) I will **have** my watch **mended**.

【訳】 (a) 時計を盗まれるだろう。

---

**bear** がまんする。 **651. attend** [əténd] 出席する。 **652. Malcolm** [mǽlkəm]. **undertake** 企てる。 **journey** [dʒə́ːni] 旅行。 **peril** [péril] 危険。 **flake** 雪片。 **653. saw** のこぎりで切ってこまかくする。 **654. plate** 皿。 **655. Mrs.** [mísiz] ...夫人。 **were it**=if it were. **be in one's power** その人にできる。 **656. led**<lead 先に立ってやる。 **riddle** [rídl] なぞ。

(b) 時計を<u>なおさせよう</u>。

〖解 説〗 他動詞の have が過去分詞を補語とする場合。すなわち

　　**have＋目的語＋過去分詞**

の形にもふた通りの解釈がある。

(a) は I に意志がない、何も時計を盗まれたいのではないが、そこらに置き放しにでもしておくと盗まれるというような受身の意味である。すなわち

　　I shall **have** my watch **stolen**.
　　＝My watch will **be stolen**.
　　　(時計を盗まれる＝時計が盗まれる)

類例:―

　　{I **had** my house **burnt down**} in the late fire.
　　{My house **was burnt down**}
　　　(私の家はこの間の火事に類焼した)
　　I **had** a gold watch **given** me.＝A gold watch **was given** me.
　　　(私は金時計をもらった)
　　I **had** a position **offered** (to) me.
　　　(就職口の申し出を受けた)

(b) は I に意志がある、「命じてさせる」あるいは「頼んでしてもらう」、使役の意味である。すなわち

　　I will **have** my watch **mended**.＝I will *cause* it *to be mended*.
　　　(時計をなおさせよう)

類例:―

　　I want to **have** my hair **cut**.
　　　(髪を刈ってもらいたい)
　　I went to **have** my photograph **taken**.
　　　(私は写真を写しに行った) [写させる]
　　I **had** this house **built** last year.
　　　(私は去年この家を建てさせた)

〖注 意 1〗 この構文でも I will とか I shall とかがついているわけではないから、主語の意志の有無は前後の関係で知らなくてはならない。た

---

(71) **photograph** [fóutəgræf] 写真。

とえば、

　　He **had** his head **cut off.**

は罪あって「首を切られた」のか、それとも切腹して人に「介錯(かいしゃく)させた」のかわからない、それは前後の関係によって解決しなくてはならない。

〘注　意 2〙　本構文の **have** を **get** に変えてもまったく同じ意味である。例：—

　　I **got** my house **burnt down** in the late fire.
　　　（この間の火事で家を焼かれた）
　　I must **get** a new house **built.**
　　　（新しい家を建てさせねばならない）

〘注　意 3〙　to **get** it **done** は人に「させる」という意味のほかに自分で「してしまう」という意味に用いられることがある。比較：—

　　I cannot **get** anything **done** to my satisfaction.
　　　（何事をさせても自分の気に入るように行かない）
　　I will **get** it **done** by evening.
　　　（晩までにはやってしまいます）

〘注　意 4〙　本章の過去分詞は前の章に述べた Root-Infinitive の受身になったものと考えることができる。比較：—

　　⎧ I shall **have** some one **steal** my watch.
　　⎪ 　[＝Some one will **steal** it.]
　　⎨ I shall **have** my watch **stolen** (by some one).
　　⎩ 　[＝My watch will **be stolen.**]
　　⎧ I will **have** the watch-maker **mend** my watch.
　　⎪ 　[＝He shall **mend** it.]
　　⎨ I will **have** my watch **mended** (by the watch-maker).
　　⎩ 　[＝It shall **be mended.**]

---

**657.**　When a man has made a happy effort, he is possessed with an absurd ambition to *have* it *thought* that it cost him

---

657.　**happy** よい結果をうむ。　**be possessed** とりつかれる。　**absurd** [əbsə́:d] ばかばかしい、不合理な。　**cost** 代償を払わせる。

nothing.

**658.** When a man's eyes have grown old with gazing at the ways of the world, it does not seem such a terrible misfortune to *have* them *bandaged*. (*Hawthorne*)

**659.** A man who wishes to understand a steam-engine can do so by going to an engineer and *having* each part *explained* to him; but if he wishes to know the history of steam-engine he must go back to the first one ever made and study each new improvement that arose.

**660.** One of his hind legs had been broken or otherwise injured, so that he limped along in a peculiar fashion; he had no tail, and his ears had been cut close to his head: altogether he was like an old soldier returned from the wars, where he had received many hard knocks, besides having *had* several parts of his body *shot* away. (鳥取大)

**661.** A mother took her daughter to a great artist to *have* her portrait *painted*, and when the work was at length finished they went to see it. The artist put it before them and the mother looked at it, her face expressing displeasure, and said not one word. Nor did the artist open his lips. And at last the girl, to break the uncomfortable silence, said, "Where shall we hang it, mother?" and the lady replied, "Just where you like, my dear, so long as you hang it with the face to the wall."

**662.** There beats not a heart, however debased by sin, or darkened by sorrow, that *has not* its noblest impulse *aroused*, in

---

658. **misfortune** 不幸。 **bandage** [bǽndidʒ] 包(眼)帯する。 660. **hind** 後の。 **otherwise** ほかのしかたで。 **limp** びっこをひく。 **knock** 打撃。 661. **portrait** [pɔ́:trit] 肖像。 **displeasure** [displéʒə] 不愉快、立腹。 **uncomfortable** 不愉快な。 **so long as** ...するかぎり。 662. **beat** 鼓動する。 **debase** [dibéis] 悪くする。 **impulse** [ímpʌls] 衝動。 **arouse** 喚起する。

view of a generous and kindly action.

**663.** At night it was worse still—for then the men could hardly keep on deck without *having* their hands or feet *frost-bitten*.

**664.** The Emperor commanded one of his orderlies to find out all about Ornano's death.... The orderly, to make sure, *had* the body *taken* up again, and found to his astonishment that it was still warm, and the general alive. He *had* him *covered* with warm rugs and *taken* off to headquarters.

**665.** Hitler's promise was that through him the Germans, being the best and noblest and most deeply wronged of nations, should be put in authority over the rest of the world, and *have* all the lower races such as Jews and Slavs and coloured peoples *trodden* underfoot. (*G. Murray*)

---

(72)

> **To tell the truth,** I am tired of teaching.

【訳】 実をいうと私は教えることはもうあきたのだ。

〖解説〗 ここにあげた不定詞の形は条件、譲歩などをあらわす句の省略されたもので、文中他の部分に関係がないように見えるから独立不定詞 (Absolute Infinitive) と称せられるものである。類例：—

**To tell the truth** (=*if I am to tell the truth*), he is not much of a scholar.

（実をいえば彼は大した学者でもない——条件）

---

663. **deck** 甲板. **frost-bitten** 凍傷にかかる。 664. **orderly** [ɔ́:dəli] 看護兵。 **astonishment** [əstɔ́niʃmənt] おどろき。 **rug** 毛布。 **headquarters** [hédkwɔ:təz] 本営。 665. **wronged** しいたげられた。 **be put in authority** 権威者の地位につけられる。 **trodden**＜tread ふみつける。

**To do my best** (=*though I did my best*), I could not understand the meaning.

（どんなに一生懸命になってもその意味がわからなかった——譲歩）

**To be frank** (or **plain**) **with you,** I do not like him.

（露骨に言えばぼくはあの人は好かない）

**To return** (to my subject)

（それはさておき、閑話休題）

**To go on** (with my story)

（話はもとに戻って）

〖注　意 1〗　この独立不定詞が形容詞、副詞を伴なうことがある。例：―

**Strange to say** (=*though it is strange to say*), the owl cannot see in the light as in the dark.

（ふしぎな話だが、ふくろうは明かるい所では暗い所ほどよく眼が見えない）

He is, **so to speak** (=*if I am allowed so to speak*), a wise fool.

（いわば——そんなことが言えるとすれば——彼は賢いばか者だ）

〖注　意 2〗　同じく独立不定詞であるが、**moreover**（その上）の意味で文の初めにおかれるものがある。「その上...のことには」などと訳してたいてい当たる。例：―

**To make matters worse,** it began to snow.

（かてて加えて［さらに悪いことには］雪さえ降りはじめた）

**To crown his misery,** he lost his wife.

（重なる不幸のあげくのはてに細君に死なれた）

---

**666.** *To do her justice,* she was a good-natured notable woman.

**667.** *To cut a long story short,* in May 1952, Iceland moved the limits of its fisheries outward to a perimeter four miles from

---

(72) **understand** [Àndəstǽnd] 了解する。 **subject** [sʌ́bdʒikt] 主題。 **moreover** [mɔːróuvə] その上。　**misery** [mízəri] 不幸。　**666. do her justice** 彼女を正しく判断する。**notable** [nóutəbl] 著名な；家政の上手な。**667. fishery** [fíʃəri] 漁場。 **perimeter** [pərímitə] 周囲。

the lines drawn between its longest promontories and between islets and rocks ashore, thus enclosing rich fishing grounds previously open.

**668.** *To express it in one word,* I valued myself upon being strict monogamist.

**669.** Poverty is a great evil in any state of life; but poverty is never felt so severely as by those who have, *to use a common phrase,* "seen better days."

**670.** *To make matters worse,* so some parents have said, a new type of examination is employed—so-called psychological tests —that has no apparent relation to school work! *(J. Conant)*

**671.** Concerning the influence of forests on climate, it may be said that large bodies of timber tend to make the climate more moderate. In the summer it is always cooler in the forest than outside in the open field, and, *strange to say*, it is warmer in the forest in the winter-time than in the open spaces.

**672.** *To return:* I continued thus employed in my father's business for two years, that is, till I was twelve years old.

*(Franklin)*

**673.** *To be plain with you*, sir, I do not like your looks or your conduct, and I fear you have some bad design in thus introducing yourself to my family.

**674.** It was a cozy place, with its comfortable chairs, its

---

**promontory** 岬。  **islet** [áilit] 小島。  **enclose** とりかこむ。  **previously** [príːvjəsli] 以前には。 668. **value myself upon** ...を誇りとする。 **monogamist** [mɔnɔ́gəmist] 一夫一婦主義者。  669. **evil** [íːvl, íːvil] わざわい。 **severely** ひどく。 670. **type** 型。 **psychological** [sàikəlɔ́dʒikəl] 心理学的。 **apparent** [əpǽrənt] 明白な、外見上の。  671. **concerning** ...に関して。 **climate** 気候。 **timber** [tímbə] 樹木。  **tend** 傾きがある。 672. **continue** [kəntínjuː] つづける。 **employed in** ...に従事して。 673. **design** たくらみ。 674. **cozy** こじんまりした居心地よい。

cheerful lamps, and its friendly open fire of seasoned olivewood. *To make everything perfect*, there was the muffled booming of the surf outside.

**675.** *To complete the sum of our miseries*, the night was at hand.
(*Aldrich*)

**676.** To establish the fact that someone has seen a ghost requires, *to start with*, the same sort of evidence as that required to verify any other occasional happening. (神戸商大)

**677.** The door of heaven, *so to speak*, can be opened only from within.

**678.** *Strange to say*, my coming to London was not to meet people, but for more solitude. For I had become so well known in the little town where I had lived that I could not step outside the house without being engaged in conversation almost immediately.

**679.** If it weren't for letters, how difficult it would be to order merchandise, pay bills, borrow money, join a club, accept invitations or apply for a job—*to name* just a few of the things that are part of the routine of living.

---

**seasoned** よく枯れた。 **muffled** 物でおおったような。 **booming** ぶーんと鳴る音。 **surf** よせ波。 675. **complete** [kəmplí:t] 完全にする。 **sum** 総計。 676. **establish** 確証する。 **evidence** 証拠。 **as that** の that は evidence で次に which is を入れて考える。 **verify** 立証する。 678. **solitude** [sɔ́litju:d] 孤独。 **be engaged in** ...に従事する。 **immediately** 即座に。 679. **order** 注文する。 **merchandise** [mɔ́:tʃəndaiz] 商品。 **bill** 勘定書。 **apply for** 申しこむ。 **part** 一部。 **routine** [ru:tí:n] 日常の仕事。

(**73**)

> (a) He knows German and French, **to say nothing of** English.
> (b) He does **not** know English, **to say nothing of** German or French.

【訳】 (a) 英語はもとよりドイツ語、フランス語も知っている。
　　　(b) ドイツ語、フランス語はおろか、英語すら知らない。

〖解　説〗 **to say nothing of...**
　　　　　**not to mention...**
　　　　　**not to speak of...**

この三つはいずれも
　One need not say anything of...
　　＝...はいうに及ばず
の意味であるが、肯定の場合と否定の場合とで訳し方を異にしなければならない。

(a) 肯定に伴なう場合
　**X to say nothing of Y**
　＝**X as well as Y**
　＝**not only Y but also X**
　＝Y は言うに及ばず X も
　＝Y と同様に X も
　＝Y のみならず X も

というような関係で、「X さえしかり、いわんや Y をや」と両方を肯定する。

(b) 否定に伴なう場合は
　**not X, to say nothing of Y**
　＝**not X, much less Y**
　＝Y は言うに及ばず X も(否)

＝X だに(否)、いわんや Y をや

と両方を否定する。類例：—

He has experience, **to say nothing of** (＝*as well as*) scholarship. (学問はもちろんのこと経験もある)

He has **no** scholarship, **to say nothing of** (＝*much less*) experience. (学問も無い、経験はなおさら無い)

He can**not** afford the ordinary comforts of life, **not to speak of** luxuries.

(ぜいたくはおろか、あたりまえの暮しさえできない)

〚注　意〛　形がこれに似て、しかも意味のちがうのに **not to say** がある。例：—

He is very frugal, **not to say** stingy. [＝*One might almost say stingy.*]

(彼はけちといわないまでもひじょうな倹約家だ[＝彼はけちといってもいいくらい倹約家だ])

―――――――

**680.**　"Alas, how my head aches!" she said wearily—"*to say nothing of* my poor heart."　　　　　　　　　　　(*Stevenson*)

**681.**　From this it would have been impossible for any one to reach the window itself, *to say nothing of* entering it.　(*Poe*)

**682.**　*Not to mention* riches and honours, even food and raiment are not to be come at without the toil of the hands and sweat of the brows.　　　　　　　　　　　　　(*Addison*)

**683.**　It is hard for a Scotchman, or an Irishman to disguise his nationality, *not to speak of* Londoner.

―――――――

(73)　**afford** [əfɔ́:d] もつことを(財政が)許す。**comforts** [kʌ́mfəts] 安楽を与えるもの。　**luxuries** [lʌ́kʃuriz] ぜいたく品。**frugal** [frú:gəl] 倹約な。**stingy** [stíndʒi] けちな。　680. **ache** [eik] 痛む。　681. **from this** ここから。　682. **mention** 話に出す。　**raiment** [réimənt] 衣類。　**be come at**＝be obtained 手に入れられる。　**toil** 労役。　**sweat** [swet] 汗。　**brow** [brau] ひたい。　683. **disguise** [disgáiz] 変装する、隠す。　　**nationality** 国籍、生国。　**Londoner** [lʌ́ndənə] ロンドン人。

**684.** As a matter of fact, all great discoverers worthy of the name have at one time or another been regarded as dreamers, *not to say* mad.

**685.** "The facts are singular, *not to say* grotesque," said Holmes. (*Doyle*)

---

(74)

(a) **There is no staying** at home in this fine weather.
(b) It is **no use crying.**

【訳】(a) こんないい天気に<u>とても</u>家に閉じこもっちゃ<u>いられない</u>。
(b) 泣いたって<u>だめだ</u>。

〖解 説〗 (a) **There is no —ing.**
=It is impossible to....
=We cannot....

類例:—

There is no $\begin{Bmatrix} \text{knowing} \\ \text{saying} \end{Bmatrix}$ what may happen.

(何事が起こるかしれたもんじゃない)

**There is no accounting** for tastes.

(趣味は人様々のものでとうてい説明はできない——たで食う虫も好きずき)

**There is no contending** against such odds.

(このように多勢に無勢ではかなわない——衆寡(しゅうか)敵しがたし)

---

684. **worthy of** ...に値する。 **be regarded as** ...と見なされる。 685. **singular** ふしぎな。 **grotesque** [grotésk] 奇怪な。 **Holmes** [houmz]。
(74) **contend** [kənténd] 争う。 **odds** 優劣の差、勝ち目。

**There is no denying** the fact.
(この事実を拒むことはできない——争われない事実だ)
 (b) **It is no use —ing.**
の形は元来

 It is $\begin{Bmatrix} \text{of no use} \\ \text{useless} \end{Bmatrix}$ to try.

 There is no use in trying.

の二つの形が混同して

 It is no use trying.

となったものである。だからいつもそのつもりで解釈するがよい。It is は略されることが多い。また no use のかわりに no good とすることも多い。類例:—

 $\left. \begin{array}{l} \textbf{It is no use trying} \\ \textbf{No good trying} \end{array} \right\}$ to excuse yourself.

 (言いわけをしようとしてもだめだ)
 **It is no use crying** over spilt milk.
 (こぼれた乳を悲しんで泣いたとて何の役にも立たない——覆水(ふくすい)盆にかえらず)

---

**686.**　Plants show no sign of interesting themselves in human affairs.　We shall never get a rose to understand that five times seven are thirty-five, and *there is no use in talking* to an oak about rise and fall in the price of rice.

**687.**　There is a danger that some people are, so to speak, getting too used to the present critical situation.　They read of it daily in the newspapers, find it all very complicated, but feel that, somehow, sooner or later, things will all come right again.

---

**deny** [dinái] 否定する。　**excuse** [ikskjú:z] 言いわけする; [ikskjú:s] 言いわけ。**686. sign** しるし。**interest** 関心を起こさせる。　**687. get used to** ...に慣れる。**critical** 危機的な。**complicated** こみ入っている。**come right** ちゃんとする、よくなる。

*It is no use waiting* for that doubtful thing—a good time coming.

**688.** The discipline should not be excessive—we do not want prohibition for prohibition's sake; and it must not be capricious—*it is no use forbidding* a thing one day and allowing it the next.

**689.** It seemed an obvious question to ask how animals inherit the result of their parents' experience, and enormous amounts of time and energy have been spent on trying to give an answer to it. It is, however, *no good asking* the question, for the simple reason that no such inheritance of acquired characters exists.

(福島県立医大)

**690.** *There was no contending* against the pen of Hastings.

(*Macaulay*)

**691.** *There is no satisfying* spoiled children. If they see the moon reflected in a pail of water, they must have it.

**692.** If he did not withdraw the accusation, *there was no knowing* what his wife might do.

---

( 75 )

---

(a) He **is possessed of** great wealth.
(b) I saw on every side faces **expressive of** anxiety.

---

【訳】(a) 彼はひじょうな金持ちだ。
(b) どっちを見ても心配そうな顔ばかりであった。

---

688. **discipline** [dísiplin] しつけ。 **excessive** 過度の。 **prohibition** 禁止。 **capricious** [kəpríʃəs] 気まぐれな。 689. **inherit** [inhérit] 遺伝する。 **enormous** [inɔ́:məs] 莫大(黙)な。 **acquired** 習得した。 **character** 性格。 690. **Hastings** [héistiŋz]. 691. **satisfy** [sǽtisfai] 満足させる。 **spoiled** 甘やかされた。 **reflected** うつった。 692. **withdraw** 引っこめる。 **accusation** [ækjuzéiʃən] 告訴、非難。

(75) **anxiety** [æŋzáiəti] 心配。

〖解説〗 （a） **be＋形容詞＋of＝動詞**
の形式に従うものが多い、たとえば

**be fond of**＝like
**be afraid of**＝fear

などは初学者でも知っている。

**be possessed of**＝possess

となるなどはおかしく思われるけれども、possessed は possess の形容詞化されたものと見ればこの形式に当てはまるもので、ふしぎはない。こういう形はたくさんあるから、そういうものに出会ったら、形容詞のままに訳そうとしないで動詞の意味に引きなおして見るがよい。類例：──

I **am fond of** (＝*like*) apples.
（私はりんごが好きだ）

I **am not afraid of** (＝*don't fear*) the dog.
（あの犬がこわくはない）

I **am doubtful of** success (＝I *doubt* if I shall succeed).
（成功おぼつかない）

I should **be glad of** (＝*like*) your company on the way.
（ご同行下されば喜ばしい）

I **was ignorant of** (＝*did not know*) the fact.
（私はそのことを知らなかった）

He blushes, because he **is conscious of** his guilt.＝He blushes, because he *feels* himself guilty.
（罪を犯した覚えがあるから顔を赤らめるのだ）

The enemy **was desirous of** (＝*desired*) peace.
（敵は和を願った）

（b） 語尾に -ive のついた形容詞には「形容詞＋of＝現在分詞」すなわち **—ive of＝—ing** の関係になるのが多い。類例：──

I used no word **expressive of** (＝*expressing*) contempt.
（軽べつの意味をあらわすような文句は使わなかった）

There are many stories **illustrative of** (＝*illustrating*) the love

---

**ignorant** [íɡnərənt] 無知の。　**conscious** [kɔ́nʃəs] 自覚して。　**guilt** [ɡilt] 罪。
**desirous** [dizáiərəs] 希望して。　**contempt** [kəntémt, kəntémpt] けいべつ。
**illustrative** [íləstreitiv, ilʌ́strətiv] 例証的。

of the Arab for his horse.
(アラビア人が馬を愛することを例証する話はたくさんある)

I owe you 5,000 yen, **exclusive of** (=*excluding*) the interest.
(利息は別にして5千円君に借りがある)

The whole amounts to 600 yen, **inclusive of** (=*including*) the expenses.
(費用も含めて総額6百円になる)

〖注　意〗 " —ive of " の形でもその前に **be** あるいはその類の動詞があると (a) の形式に属する。

**be —ive of**＝動詞

と見なければならない。例:—

The age **was productive of** (=*produced*) great men.
(その時代には偉人が輩出した)

He **seems** (to be) **apprehensive of** (=*seems to apprehend*) failure.
(彼は失敗をおそれているらしい)

---

**693.**　I *was* naturally *fond of* books and a great reader.

**694.**　I have often thought it would be a blessing if each human being were stricken blind and deaf for a few days at some time during his early life.　Darkness would make him more *appreciative of* sight; silence would teach him the joys of sound.

(東大)

**695.**　The vulgar and men of sense agree in admiring others for having what they themselves would rather *be possessed of:* the wise man applauds him whom he thinks most virtuous; the rest of the world, him who is most wealthy.

**696.**　His face *was* striking in outline, the mouth and chin *in-*

---

apprehend [æprihénd] 心配する。　**694. blessing** [blésiŋ] 幸い、めぐみ。 **be stricken blind** めくらになる。　**appreciative** 真価を知る。　**695. the vulgar** [vʌ́lgə] 俗人。　**sense** 分別。　**applaud** [əplɔ́ːd] 賞賛する。　**696. striking** きわだっている。　**outline** [áutlain] 輪郭。　**indicative of** ...を示す。

*dicative of* an iron will.

**697.** Nelson had less responsibility here than at Bastica, and was acting with a man after his own heart, who *was* never *sparing of* himself. (*Southey*)

**698.** I *was tired of* reading, and sleepy.

**699.** She learned from him some account of our misfortunes, but *was still kept ignorant of* young Mr. Thornhill being the cause. (*Goldsmith*)

**700.** Death, from want and exposure, was the best that could be expected from the prolonged wandering of so helpless a creature through a country *of* which he *was ignorant*. (*Dickens*)

**701.** Experience with this group left me with a question which I have not found easy to resolve: was this simply youthful nonconformity, or *was* it *symptomatic of* something more deep-seated? (*Merle Fainsod*)

**702.** When a man has *been guilty of* any vice or folly, I think the best atonement he can make for it is to warn others not to fall into the like.

**703.** Bonaparte often talked a great deal, and sometimes a little too much; but no one could tell a story in a more agreeable and interesting way. He *was* so *fond of* argument, that in the warmth of discussion it was easy to draw from him secrets which he was most anxious to keep.

---

697. **responsibility** [rispɔ̀nsibíliti] 責任。 **after his own heart** 自分の心にかなった。 **sparing** [spέəriŋ] *adj.* (努力を)惜しむ。 700. **exposure** 風雨にさらされること。 **the best** よくいってそれくらいなこと。 **prolong** [prəlɔ́ŋ] 長びかす。 701. **resolve** [rizɔ́lv] 解く。 **nonconformity** 非協力。 **symptomatic** [sìmptəmǽtik] 徴候となる。 **deep-seated** 根の深い。 702. **atonement** つぐない。 **warn** 警告する。 **the like** 同類のこと。 703. **argument** [á:gjumənt] 議論。 **warmth** [wɔ:mθ] 熱中。 **discussion** [diskʌ́ʃən] 討論。 **draw** 引き出す。

**704.** A self-conscious man is sometimes one who *is aware of* his worth; a conceited man is generally one who *is not aware of* his unworthiness.

(*Max O'Rell*)

---

(**76**)

> The watch I lost was **of** great **value**.

【訳】 私が紛失した時計はなかなか高価なものだった。

〖解説〗 「**of**＋抽象名詞＝形容詞」の形が補語として用いられることが多い。例：—

| | |
|---|---|
| of value＝valuable | of service＝serviceable |
| of use＝useful | of importance＝important |
| of no use＝useless | of moment＝momentous |

「**of**＋抽象名詞」の形を用いればその間に形容詞をおくことができるから重宝(ちょうほう)である。また「of＋名詞」の形に応ずる形容詞の無い場合もある。

---

**705.** Consider before you speak, especially when the business is *of moment;* weigh the sense of the expressions you intend to use, that they may be significant, pertinent, and inoffensive.

**706.** Of the various forms of activity engaged in by man, those which employ the use of the greatest number of muscles are obviously *of greater importance* from the point of view of general physical development.

**707.** Success in any kind of practical life is not dependent

---

704. **conceited** [kənsíːtid] うぬぼれの。 **unworthiness** 無価値、無能。
 (76) **moment** [móumənt] 重要。 **momentous** [mouméntəs] 重要な。 705. **weigh** 軽重をはかる。 **significant** [signífikənt] 意味深い。 **pertinent** [pə́ː-tinənt] 適切な。 **inoffensive** [ìnəfénsiv] 人の気にさわらない、害にならない。 706. **muscle** [mʌ́sl] 筋肉。 **point of view** 見地。

solely, or indeed chiefly, upon knowledge. Even in the learned professions, knowledge alone is *of less consequence* than people are apt to suppose.

**708.** But he said that wasn't any matter; he was quite willing to let the trifle stand over till another time. I said I might not be in his neighborhood again for a good while; but he said it was *of no consequence,* he could wait. (*Mark Twain*)

**709.** When in reading we meet with any maxim that may be *of use*, we should take it for our own, and make an immediate application of it, as we would of the advice of a friend whom we have purposely consulted.

**710.** From his father he derived little except a quick temper, but from his mother the artistic faculty which proved *of great service* to him.

**711.** The literature of the past is only *of value* in so far as it has significance to-day, just as history is only *of use* if it can throw a light upon the contemporary scene.

**712.** In the same way, we shall not be able to save ourselves from dying out, because our intellect has become too bulky for our small spirituality and morality. Perhaps this estimate is correct; if this is so, then all our outcries are vain and our appeals to mankind to become wiser and more humane are *of no*

---

707. **learned profession** 学問的職業。**consequence**＝importance。**be apt to ...** しがちである。709. **trifle** 些細なもの(お金)。**stand over** 延期する。**a good while** 長い間。708. **maxim** [mǽksim] 格言。**application** 応用。**advice** [ədváis] 助言。**purposely** [pə́:pəsli] 故意に。710. **derive** うけつぐ。**quick temper** 短気。**artistic** [ɑ:tístik] 芸術的。**faculty** [fǽkəlti] 才能。711. **contemporary** [kəntémpərəri] 現代の。**significance** 意義。**scene** [si:n] 舞台。712. **bulky** [bʌ́lki] かさばった。**spirituality** 霊性。**estimate** 見込み。**vain** むだな。**humane** [hju:méin] 人情のある。

*avail* and will not prevent the annihilation of so ill-balanced a species.

**713.** So close is the relation between the life of the artist and the life of his art that the stages of his decline are clearly marked in the record of his work. It is *of the highest importance*, therefore, that a man should keep himself in the most highly vitalized condition for the sake of productiveness.

**714.** The laws of heredity and evolution have made the world of life what it now is, and determine what it may yet be. Of recent years we have learned to understand these laws better, and our knowledge of them has become both *of deep theoretic interest*, and *of great practical importance*.

**715.** Riches do not consistute any claim to distinction. Some of the most wealthy men living are mere nobodies. Many of them are comparably ignorant. They are *of no moral* or *social account*.

(77)

(a) This pheasant is **of my own shooting**.
(b) I sent him a pheasant **of my own shooting**.

【訳】(a) このきじは私が自分でうったのです。
(b) 私は自分でうったきじを彼に贈った。

---

avail [əvéil]=use. annihilation [ənàiəléiʃən] 絶滅。ill-balanced 釣合いのとれない。species 種族。 713. close 密接な。 stage 段階。decline 衰退。vitalize [váitəlaiz] 活気を与える。 for the sake of ...のために。 productiveness [proudʌ́ktivnis] 製作力。714. heredity 遺伝。evolution [ìːvəlúːʃən] 進化。 theoretic 理論的な。 715. claim to distinction 名声を得る権利。nobody [nóubədi] 物の数にはいらない人。 comparatively 比較的に。

〖解　説〗 **of one's own —ing**
　＝自ら――した

類例:―

　Is this a picture **of your own drawing**?
　　(この絵は君が自身で描いたのか)
　This sweater is **of her own knitting**.
　　(このスエターは彼女が自分で編んだのだ)

〖注　意〗 ―ing という動名詞のかわりに抽象名詞を用いることがある。例:―

　The poems **of his own composing** (=of his own composition)
　(彼が自ら作った詩)

---

**716.** The walls on the inside were nicely whitewashed, and my daughters undertook to adorn them with pictures *of their own designing*.

**717.** These were the first pictures that Ben had ever seen, except *of his own drawing*.　　　　　　　　　　　(*Hawthorne*)

**718.** It was proposed that we should each of us, at our next meeting, produce a piece *of our own composing*, in order to improve by our mutual observations, criticisms, and correction.　　　　　　　　　　　　　　　　　　　　　(*Franklin*)

**719.** Usually that which a man calls fate is a web *of his own weaving*, from threads *of his own spinning*.

**720.** The words have been largely *of your own choosing*, but the sentences have seldom been *of your own making*.　You have

---

(77) **sweater** [swétə] スエター。**compose** [kəmpóuz] 作る。**composition** [kɔ̀mpəzíʃən] 作文、作詩。　716. **whitewash** のろ[塗料]で塗る。**adorn** 飾る。**design** 考案する。　718. **propose** 提案する。　**produce** [prədjúːs] 提出する。**mutual** 相互の。**criticism** 批評。719. **fate** 運命。**web** 織物、網。**weave** 織る。**thread** [θred] 糸。720. **seldom** めったに～ない。

inherited them from the immediate, the distant, and the long-distant past. (東京学芸大)

**721.** I believe in a heaven, but not in a hell, in the next world; but I firmly believe in the existence of both in this world; and the earthly heaven and hell are *of our own manufacture*. (*Max O'Rell*)

---

## (78)

| I will **make** a man **of** you. |

【訳】 私がお前を一人前にしてやろう。

〖解 説〗 **make～ [out] of...**
は元来「...を材料として～を作る」意味で

 We **make** many things **out of** paper.
 ＝We **make** paper **into** many things.
　(紙でいろいろなものを作る＝紙をいろいろなものに作る)

のように用いる。I will **make** a man (**out**) **of** you. は、「未製品であるお前を材料にして一個の人間を作りあげてやる」という意味である。

 比較:—
 (a) I will **make you a teacher** of my school.
　　(君を私の学校の教師にする)
 (b) I will **make a teacher of you.**
　　(お前を教師に仕込んでやる)

すなわち (a) は単に教師に採用すること。(b) は you というものを材料にして teacher というものを作り上げるような心持。

 この形は多くの成句を作る。例:—
 Do not **make an ass of yourself.**
　(ばかなまねをするな)

---

inherit 承け継ぐ。 immediate [imíːdjət] すぐの。 721. existence 存在。 earthly [ə́ːθli] 地上の、現世の。 manufacture [mæ̀njufǽktʃə] 製造。

Film stars are **made so much of** now.
(映画スターは今とてももてはやされる)
He **makes nothing** (or **little**) **of** working ten hours a day.
(1日10時間ぐらい働くのを何とも思わない——平気だ)
I **make a point of** siding with the weaker party.
(ぼくは弱者にくみする主義だ)
You must **make the most of** your time.
(時間をよく利用しなくてはいけない——時間を生かして使え)
I can **make nothing of** what he says.
(彼の言う事は何のことだかちっともわからない)
You **make fun of** everything I do or say.
(君はぼくのする事、言う事何でもひやかす)

---

**722.** Although cheerfulness of disposition is very much a matter of inborn temperament, it is also capable of being trained and cultivated like any other habit. We may *make the best of* life, or we may *make the worst of* it, and it depends very much upon ourselves whether we extract joy or misery from it.

**723.** The gentleman is just as well as firm. He does well what ought to be done well. He forgives or resents duly, but is never revengeful. He is ready to imitate Socrates in this respect. Some one said to the sage, "May I die, unless I am revenged upon you;" to which his answer was, "May I die, if I do not *make a friend of* you."

**724.** The Forty-seven Faithfuls—*of whom so much is made* in our popular eductaion—are known in common parlance as the

---

(78) **most** [moust] 最大。 **722. disposition** [dìspəzíʃən] 性質。 **inborn** [ínbɔːn] 生まれつきの。 **temperament** [témpərəmənt] 気質。 **cultivate** 涵養(かんよう)する。 **extract** 引き出す。 **723. forgive** 許す。 **resent** [rizént] 怒る。 **duly** [djúːli] 適当に、然るべく。 **revengeful** [rivéndʒfəl] 執念深い。 **imitate** [ímiteit] 模倣する。 **Socrates** [sɔ́krətiːz]。 **sage** 哲人。 **May ...** 願望をあらわす用法。 **724. parlance** [páːləns] 語法。

Forty-seven Gishi. (*Nitobe*)

**725.** I hope you haven't been only *making a cat's paw of me?* 'Pon my soul, I hate being *made a cat's paw of*, sir!

(*Warren*)

**726.** By justice is meant fair play, equality before the law, and opportunity for each man and woman to *make the most of* life. This is essentially the ideal of democracy towards which the bright minds of Japan are persistently turning.

**727.** My fortune is no inheritance—all my own acquisition. I can *make ducks and drakes of it*. (*MacKenzie*)

**728.** The Japanese care but little for some flowers which to Europeans commend themselves as the fairest, and they *make much of* others which Europeans would scarcely notice.

**729.** We often think and talk of those days when we had such a good time of it and *made light of* all our troubles.

**730.** Men had made up their minds to submit to what they could not help, and to *make the best of* a bad bargain. (*Freeman*)

**731.** The conference line—and very sensible too—is that we are all imperfect creatures, so how do we *make the most of* ourselves.

(*J. B. Priestley*)

**732.** He asked me my name, and then he looked at the paper and read it all over to me, but I *could't make anything of* it.

(*Warren*)

---

725. **make a cat's paw of** ...を手先に使う。 **'Pon my soul** 誓って、本当に、'pon=upon。 726. **fair play** 公明な行動。 **equality** [ikwóliti] 平等。 **democracy** [dimókrəsi] 民主々義。 **persistently** 根気強く。 727. **inheritance** [inhéritəns] 遺産。 **acquisition** [æ̀kwizíʃən] 取得物。 **make ducks and drakes of** ...を浪費する。 728. **commend** 気に入らせる。 **notice** 気にとめる。 730. **submit** [səbmít] 従う。 **bargain** [bá:gin] 取引、買い物。 731. **conference line** 会議の方針、態度。 **sensible** 賢明な。 **creature** [krí:tʃə] 生きもの、人間。

**733.** You did say some queer things, ma'am, and I couldn't *make head or tail of* what you said.  (*Mrs. Oliphant*)

---

( 79 )

(a) **Writing** something on a card, he gave it to me.
(b) **Written** in an easy style, the book is adapted for beginners.

【訳】 (a) 名刺に何か書いてそれを私にくれた。
(b) 平易な文体で書いてあるからこう本は初学者に適する。

〚解 説〛 ここではいわゆる分詞構文 (Participial Construction) の解釈法を述べる。こういう構文に用いられた場合には

　　分詞＝定形動詞 (**Finite Verb**) [有主格動詞]＋接続詞

の関係であるから、訳すときはその心持で適当に考える。

類例:—

**Writing** something on a card, he gave it to me.
=He **wrote** something on a card, **and** gave it to me.
（名刺に何か書いて、それを私にくれた）
**Seeing** the policeman, he ran off.
=He **saw** the policeman, **and** ran off.
（彼は警官を見て逃げ出した）
**Living** so remote from towns, I rarely have visitors.
=I **live** so remote from towns, **so** I rarely have visitors.
=**As** I **live** so remote from towns, I rarely have visitors.
=私は片いなかに住んでいるものだからめったに訪ねて来る人もない。

以上3例を見ると、

---

733. queer [kwiə] 奇妙な。
(79) **remote** [rimóut] 遠方の。

**writing**＝wrote＋and
**seeing**＝saw＋and
**living** $\begin{cases} \text{live＋so} \\ \text{as＋live} \end{cases}$

のようにいずれも分詞は本動詞と接続詞とを兼ねたもので
　(イ)　「...して」
　(ロ)　「...だから」
など訳すべきである。

　以上はいずれも現在分詞であるが、(b) の例は written という**過去分詞**が文頭に出ている、しかしこれは being written という受身の形の省略されたものである。そこで、これも前述の3例と同様に、

　**(Being) written** in an easy style, the book is adapted for beginners.＝**As** the book **is written** in...

となって、Being written＝as＋is written ということになる。

　以上4つの例のように現在分詞を「動詞＋接続詞」になおす場合、動詞の時制は主節の時制と一致させる。ところが完了形の分詞すなわち " having written " のような形を言い換える場合には動詞の時制を完了の時制にするか、主節の時制より一段進めなくてはならない。例：—

　**Having written** my exercise, I **have** nothing else to do.
　＝As I **have written** my exercise, I **have**...
　＝(練習問題を書いてしまったから ほかに何もすることがない)
　**Having lived** in England, he **was** proficient in English.
　＝As he **had lived** in England, he **was**...
　＝(彼は英国にいたことがあったから英語に堪能(たんのう)であった)

【**注　意 1**】　過去分詞が文の初めに出ている場合はその前に **Being** あるいは **Having been** が略されているのであるから、言い換えるとき注意を要する。例：—

　**(Being) written** in English, the book has many readers.
　＝As it **is written** in English, the book has...
　＝(英語で書いてあるからこの本は読者が多い)

---

**proficient** [prəfíʃiənt] 熟達した。

(**Having been**) **written** in haste, the book has many faults.
 =As it **was written** in haste, the book has ...
 =(急いで書かれたのだからこの本には欠点が多い)

〘注 意 2〙 以上諸例において見るように

分詞＝$\begin{cases} 動詞＋\textbf{and} & (\ldots して\ldots) \\ \textbf{As}＋動詞 & (\ldots だから\ldots) \end{cases}$

が多かったがこのほかにまた

分詞＝$\begin{cases} \textbf{If}＋動詞 & (\ldots すれば\ldots) \\ \textbf{Though}＋動詞 & (\ldots だが\ldots) \\ \textbf{When}＋動詞 & (\ldots すると\ldots) \end{cases}$

などの場合もある。例：——

**Turning** (=*if you turn*) to the right, you will find the house you want.

(右へ曲るとおたずねの家があります)

〘注 意 3〙 以上の諸例では分詞の意味上の主語はいずれも主節の主語と同一であったが、同一でない場合は、次のようになる。例：——

*The moon* **having risen,** *we* put out the light.
 (月が出たから灯火を消した)

*He* **being** absent, *I* did not know what to do.
 (彼が不在だったから私はどうしていいかわからなかった)

*The weather* **being** fine, *I* kept the windows open.
 (天気がよかったから窓を明けはなしておいた)

---

**734.** *Sitting* on the ground in the shade of a large tree, I began to hear a confused noise as of a coming tempest of wind mixed with shrill calls and cries. (同志社大)

**735.** The birds were all busily searching for and pursuing the insects, and in a very few minutes they had finished examining the trees near me, and were gone; but *not satisfied* with

---

734. **confused** [kənfjúːzd] 混乱した。**tempest** あらし。**shrill** 金切りごえの。
735. **pursue** [pəsjúː] 追いかける。**insects** 昆虫。**satisfy** 満足する。

what I had witnessed, I jumped up and rushed after the flock to keep it in sight. (同志社大)

**736.** *Born* in a land of Liberty, and *having* early *learned* its value, my sympathetic feelings are irresistibly attracted, whensoever in any country I see an oppressed nation unfurl the banner of freedom.

**737.** *Referring* to the outbreak of two world wars in one lifetime and the invention and employment of the most destructive bomb in human experience, he is compelled to add.... (慶応大)

**738.** *Refreshed and rested*, Ali was able to satisfy his hunger on some ripe dates from the palm tree, while Meek-eye began to feed upon the grass and leaves around.

**739.** *Left* after he was twenty to his own guidance, he pursued his studies in Belgium and France with the idea of establishing himself as an engineer.

**740.** One sometimes hears it said that the characteristic feature of American education is the proportion of the nation's youth attending a university. *So phrased*, this is a completely misleading statement. What is characteristic is the very large proportion of American youth from 18 to 20 years of age who are engaged in full-time studies. (*J. Conant*)

**741.** And at last a multitude of birds of many kinds, but

---

**witness** 目撃する。 **rush** かけ出す。 **flock** 群。 **keep in sight** 見失なわない。 736. **sympathetic** [sìmpəθétik] 同情ある。 **irresistibly** [ìrizístibli] 抵抗しがたく。 **attract** 引きつける。 **oppressed** 圧迫された。 **unfurl** [ʌnfə́:l] 広げる。 **banner** 旗。 737. **refer** [rifə́:] 言及する。 **outbreak** ぼっ発。 **bomb** [bɔm] 爆弾。 **compel** よぎなくさせる。 738. **refresh** 元気づける。 **date** なつめやしの実。 **palm** [pɑ:m] やし。 739. **left to guidance** 指図にまかせられて。 **pursue** 従事する。 **Belgium** [béldʒəm] ベルギー。 **establish** [istǽbliʃ] 立てる。 740. **feature** [fí:tʃə] 特色。 **proportion** 割合い。 **misleading** 誤解させる。 **be engaged in** ～に従事する。 **full-time** 全時間をそれに使う。 *cf.* part-time 741. **multitude** [mʌ́ltitju:d] 多数。

mostly small, appeared in sight swarming through the trees, *some running* on the trunks and large branches, *others keeping* on the wing.　　　　　　　　　　　　　　　　　(同志社大)

**742.** The rat and mouse cannot be considered as domestic animals, but they have been transported by man to many parts of the world, and now they have a far wider range than any other rodent, *living* free under the cold climate in the north and south, and on many islands in the torrid zones.

---

(**80**)

---

(a) **Written, as it is,** in an easy style, the book is adapted for beginners.
(b) **Living, as I do,** so remote from towns, I rarely have visitors.

---

【訳】　(a) この本はこのとおり平易な文体で書いてあるから初
　　　　　学者に適している。
　　　(b) 私はこのとおり片いなかに住んでいるからめったに
　　　　　訪ねてくる人もない。

〖解　説〗　理由を示すには **as** を用いるか、あるいは過去または現在分詞を用いるだけでよろしい(前章参照)。例:―

(a) **Written** in an easy style,...
　　＝**As it is written** in an easy style,...
(b) **Living** so remote from towns,...
　　＝**As I live** so remote from towns,...

ところで分詞を用いた上なお文意を強めるために as... の形を挿入句と

---

swarm [swɔːm] 群がる。trunk 幹。742. domestic [dəméstik] 飼いならした。transport はこぶ。range 棲息(せいそく)範囲。rodent [róudənt] 齧歯(げっし)類。**torrid** [tɔ́rid] 焼けるように暑い。

して加え、上に掲げた文例のようにすることがある。すなわち (a) の as it is, (b) の as I do は意味を強めるにすぎないもので、まったく無くても文意に変わりはない、場合に応じ「あのように」「このとおり」「実際」などの文句を入れて訳せばよい。類例：—

**Living, as he does,** ⎫ so much among foreigners, he ought to be
*As he lives* ⎭ at home in English.

（あのように外国人に交わっているのだから英語が達者なはずだ）

**Used, as they are,** ⎫ to all sorts of dangers, they are not to be
*As they are used* ⎭ daunted by anything.

（実際あらゆる危険に慣れているから何事にもびくともしない）

〖注　意〗 過去分詞の次をコンマで切らずにすぐ as... へつづけると、前後の文勢で意味がふた通りに取れる。例：—

**Written as it is...** = ⎰(1) **As** it is written...
⎱(2) **Though** it is written...

この (2) の形は (82) (d) に説くところのものである。

---

**743.** *Governed as we are* entirely by public opinion, the utmost care should be taken to preserve the purity of the public mind.

*(Irving)*

**744.** The use of 'the' before comparatives and superlatives is so little related to its other uses, *qualifying, as it does*, adjectives and adverbs and not nouns, that we might very properly consider it a different word altogether, and class it as an adverb.

**745.** *Opening* too, *as we do*, an asylum for strangers from every portion of the earth, we should receive all with impartiality.

*(Irving)*

---

(80) **daunt** [dɔ:nt] ひるませる。　**743. govern** 支配する。　**preserve** 維持する。　**744. comparative** [kəmpǽrətiv] 比較級。　**superlative** [sjupə́:lətiv] 最上級。**qualify** [kwɔ́lifai] 修飾する。**class** 分類する。　**745. asylum** [əsáiləm] 避難所、救済所。**portion**=part. **impartiality** [ímpɑ:ʃiǽliti] 公平。

**746.** *Possessing*, then, *as England does*, the fountainhead whence the literature of the language flows, how completely is it in her power, and how truly is it her duty, to make it the medium of amiable, and magnanimous feeling! (*Irving*)

**747.** *Working as he did* rather for the love of his art than for the acquirement of wealth, he refused to associate himself with any investigation which did not tend towards the unusual, and even the fantastic. (*Doyle*)

**748.** *Coming as it did* at a period of exceptional dullness it attracted perhaps rather more attention than it deserved.

(*Doyle*)

---

( 81 )

> **Generally speaking,** girls make better linguists than boys.

【訳】 概していえば女の子が男の子より語学が得意だ。

〖解 説〗 不定詞に独立不定詞があるように分詞にも独立分詞がある。すなわち分詞の意味上の主語が省略され、したがって他に関係なく独立の観を呈する場合がある。

独立分詞は (a) 副詞；(b) 前置詞；(c) 接続詞として用いられるが、解釈法としては一々分類する必要もあるまいから、ただ例だけを列挙しよう：——

**Properly speaking,** you have no right to interfere in the matter.
(本当を言えば君はこの件に干渉する権利はないのだ)

---

746. **fountainhead** [fáuntinhed] 源泉。 **whence**=from which. **medium** 媒介物、手段。 **amiable** 温雅な。 **magnanimous** [mægnǽnimǝs] 雅量ある。
747. **associate** [ǝsóuʃieit] 連合する、たずさわる。 **investigation** 調査。 **fantastic** [fæntǽstik] 奇異な。 748. **exceptional** 異例の。 **dullness** 不活発、沈滞。 **deserve** 当然うける。
(81) **linguist** [líŋgwist] 語学者。 **interfere** [ìntǝfíǝ] 干渉する。

**Strictly speaking,** there is no history before that period.
（厳密に言えばその期以前には歴史はないのだ）
**Judging from** reports, he seems to be an able man.
（評判でみると彼は才幹があるらしい）
He speaks Japanese very well, **considering** that he is a foreigner.
（彼は外国人の割には——外国人であることを思えば——日本語がじょうずだ）
**Talking of** automobiles, I have bought a used one.
（自動車のことをいえば——自動車の話で思い出したが——ぼくは中古車を買ったよ）
**Granting** that he was drunk, that is no excuse for his conduct.
（酩酊(めいてい)していたということは認めても、それはあの行為の言いわけとはならない——酒の上とは言えあんなことをしては申しわけが立たない）
We make allowances, **seeing** that he is young.
（彼はまだ若いのだから斟酌(しんしゃく)してやる）

---

**749.** The distance of the Sun from the Earth, is, *roughly speaking*, ninety-three millions of miles. If it were possible to travel to the Sun in a railway train, night and day without stopping, at the uniform rate of forty miles an hour, it would require no less than two hundred and sixty-five years to reach its destination.

**750.** In fact, *relatively speaking*, the unexplored regions of the brain are greater by far than the still unexplored region of the earth, or, for that matter, of the solar system. （横浜市立大）

**751.** *Speaking simply from self-observation*, I find that in my

---

**consider** [kənsídə] 考える。 **allowance** [əláuəns] 酌量(しゃくりょう)。 **749. uniform** 一定の。 **require** 要する。 **destination** [dèstinéiʃən] 目的地。 **750. relatively** 相対的に、物の比例で。 **unexplored** 未調査の。 **by far** はるかに。 **for that matter** そのことなら。 **solar system** 太陽系。 **751. self-observation** 自己観察。

own case tea and coffee are far more perilous than tobacco.

(*Hamerton*)

**752.** Of twenty-four arrows shot in succession, ten were fixed in the target, and the others ranged so near it that, *considering the distance of the mark*, it was thought to be good archery.

**753.** *Strictly speaking*, the actor is but one of the media of dramatic art. Being a live medium, he occupies what is, *speaking strictly*, a false position; the history of the drama in all its rises and declines is the history of the dramatist's sure eclipse by the actor.

---

( 82 )

---

**Brave as he was,** a tremour passed through him.

【訳】 さすが勇敢な彼もわなわなと身ぶるいした。

〖解説〗 (a) 名　　詞  
(b) 形　容　詞  
(c) 副　　詞  
(d) 過去分詞  
 ｝＋as＋主語＋動詞

の形式においてはたいていの場合 **as=though** と解してよろしい。ゆえに：—

　Brave as he was,...  
　＝Though he was brave...

類例：—

---

**coffee** [kɔ́fi] コーヒー。 **perilous** [périlǝs] 危険な。 **tobacco** [tǝbǽkou] たばこ。　752. **in succession** 次ぎ次ぎに。　**target** まと。　**range** 矢がとどく。 **archery** [ɑ́:tʃǝri] 弓術。　753. **media** [mí:diǝ] medium の複数。　**live** [laiv] 生きた。　**false position** 誤解を招くような立場、迷惑な立場。 **decline** [dikláin] 衰微。 **eclipse** [iklíps] 光を失うこと。
　(82) **tremour** [trémǝ] 身ぶるい。

(a) **Woman as I am,** I may be of help in time of need.
　　(女ながらもまさかの時には助けになりましょう)
(b) **Poor as he is,** he is honest.
　　(貧乏はしているが正直だ)
(c) **Gallantly as they stormed** the position, they were at last repulsed.
　　(勇敢にその陣地を襲撃したけれど とうとう撃退された)
(d) **Burdened as he was,** he walked too quick for me.
　　(荷物を負うていたにかかわらず、彼は私がいっしょについて行けないほど早く歩いた)

〖注　意 1〗　名詞をこの構文に用いるとき冠詞をはぶくことに注意せよ。

　**Hero** as he is, ...
　=Though he is **a** hero ...
　**Woman** as I am, ...
　=Though I am **a** woman ...

〖注　意 2〗　(d) は (80) の (a) と同形であるからその区別は前後の関係で知らなければならない。

---

**754.** *Young as he was*, he was not unequal to the task.

**755.** Not a day passed by, that the world was not the better because this man, *humble as he was*, had lived.

**756.** He most kindly corrected the literary faults which abounded in my scientific paper, *short as it was*.　　(日本歯科大)

**757.** I found it a little difficult to keep pace with my guides, *burdened as they were*.

**758.** *Unacquainted as I am* with what has passed in the

---

(82) **gallantly** [gǽləntli] 勇敢に。**repulse** [ripʌ́ls] 撃退する。**754. unequal** [ʌníːkwəl] 堪えない。　**755. humble** 身分のいやしい。　**756. literary** 文章上の。**abound** たくさんある。**paper** 研究論文。**757. keep pace with** 歩調を合わせて進む。**758. unacquainted with** ...を知っていない。

world for these last ten years, I cannot be so imposed upon as to believe so foolish a tale; but I see you have a mind to sport with my ignorance.

**759.** *Little as I like* the deduction, I cannot but accept it; and this is that the work of art must be judged by its fruits, and if these are not good it is valueless.

**760.** No doubt, *much as worthy friends add* to the happiness and value of life, we must in the main depend on ourselves, and every one is his own best friend or worst enemy.

**761.** It is not every one who can see a landscape as writers like Ruskin or Tyndall did. Their beautiful descriptions of mountain scenery depend less on their mastery of the English language, *great as that is*, than on their power of seeing what is before them.

**762.** They made light of his popularity, *considerable as it was*. But when it was grown to such a height that it was scarce possible to ruin it, they found out, when it was too late, that no beginnings of things, however small, are to be neglected.

**763.** The Greeks, *eminent as they were* in almost every department of human activity, did surprisingly little for the creation of science.

**764.** *Poor as he was*, he was above selling his honour at any price.

**765.** A great man said to us the other day: "This age will be known in history as the age of invention. The king of today

---

**be imposed upon** だまされる。 759. **deduction** 推論。 **fruit** 成果。 760. **worthy** [wə́ːði] 価値ある。 **in the main** 主として。 761. **not every one** 部分否定の用法。 **description** 描写。 762. **considerable** [kənsídərəbl] かなり大きな。 **scarce**=scarcely, hardly. **ruin** うちこわす。 **be neglected** おろそかにされる。 763. **surprisingly** [səpráiziŋli] おどろくほど。 **creation** 創造.

is the engineer. *Wonderful as are the machines* now in existence, they will be surpassed by machines such as nobody has dreamed of yet."

**766.** *Exhausted as the world was*, events still compelled states, great and small, to maintain large standing forces and even in the face of bankruptcy to contemplate costly additions to the armaments of peace.

**767.** It may at first sight seem strange that society, while constantly moving forward with eager speed, should be constantly looking backward with tender regret. But these propensities, *inconsistent as they may appear*, can easily be resolved into the same principle. Both spring from our impatience of the state in which we actually are.

( 83 )

(a) He **may well** be proud of his son.
(b) He is proud of his son, and **well he may.**

【訳】(a) 彼がむすこ自慢なのももっともだ。
(b) 彼は子供が自慢だ、また自慢するのも無理はない。

〖解説〗 この二つは may well を中へ挿入するのと、別に後から付け加えるのとちがうだけで、意味はまったく同じく、well=justly と見てよろしい。

---

765. **in existence** 存在している。**surpass** しのぐ、まさる。 766. **exhausted** [igzɔ́:stid] 疲弊して。**maintain** 維持する。**standing forces** 常備軍。**bankruptcy** [bǽŋkrʌptsi] 破産。**contemplate** [kɔ́ntempleit] 企てる。**armaments** [ɑ́:məmənts] 軍備。 767. **at first sight** ちょっと見たところ。**constantly** たえず。**tender** なつかしがる。**regret** 惜しむ心。**propensity** 傾向。**inconsistent** 相反する。**be resolved into** 解消して...となる。**spring** 出てくる。

(a) He **may well** be proud of his son.
   =He **has good reason to** be proud of his son.
   (彼がむすこを自慢するのにはりっぱな理由がある;無理はない;もっともだ)

(b) He is proud of his son, and **well he may**.
   =He is proud of his son, and **with good reason**.
   (彼は子供が自慢だ、しかもそれはりっぱな理由があってのこと;無理はない;もっともだ)

〖注 意〗 この場合の may は過去になると might に変わる。例:—
He **was** proud of his son, and **well he might**.
(彼は子供が自慢であった、またそれももっともであった)

---

**768.** *Well may* poets look to the falling snowflake for their image of purity and innocence, ere it receives the stain of earth.

**769.** The good lady was in an ecstasy of delight. And *well might she be proud* of her boy; for there were touches in his picture, which old artists, who had spent a lifetime in the business, need not have been ashamed of.  (*Hawthorne*)

**770.** Science sets as many problems as it solves. It lays its discoveries on our doorstep, and the responsibility is ours for the use we make of them. The argument here is not, as *it well might be*, concerned with H-bombs but with inventions nearer at home.  (大阪大)

**771.** Mr. Harding *may well* be said to have been a fortunate man, for he was not born to wealth, and he is now director of a railway company; but nevertheless he has his cares.

---

768. look to... for を見て...を求める。 innocence 純潔、潔白。 ere=before. stain よごれ。 769. ecstasy [ékstəsi] 有頂天。 touch 筆致、てぎわ。 be ashamed of ...を恥じる。 770. set 提起する。 argument 論。 concerned 関して。 invention 発明品。 771. director 取締役。 care 心配ごと。

**772.** The beginnings of the work were beset with difficulties, which *might well* have defeated any ordinary man. But to one who had fought his way to learning and culture from a childhood of slavery, they were just some more obstacles to be overcome—and overcome them he did.

**773.** The lecture itself followed a very familiar orthodox line —indeed, the same lecture *might well* have been delivered under Stalin.

---

(84)

---

(a) You **may as well** call a cat a little tiger **as** call a tiger a big cat.
(b) You **might as well** call a horse a fish **as** call a whale one.

---

【訳】 (a) 虎を大きな猫というように猫を小さな虎といっても よい。

(b) 馬を魚ということができないようにくじらを魚と いうこともできない。

〖解 説〗 may と might とちがうだけであるが、

(a) **may as well...as** 〜の方は「〜してよろしいと同じく...してもよろしい」と両方とも許される場合に用いる。

類例:—

You **may** go just **as well as** not, if you wish to do so.
(行きたいなら行ってもいい＝どちらでもかまわない)

---

772. **beset** [bisét] (四方八方から)取り囲む、(道などを)ふさぐ、なやます。 **defeat** うち負かす。 **slavery** [sléivəri] 奴隷の身。 **obstacle** 障害物。 **overcome** [ouvəkám] うち勝つ。 773. **orthodox** [ɔ́:θədɔks] 正統派の。 **deliver** [dilívə] 述べる。

(b) **might as well**...**as** ~は「~してよいなら...してもよい」「~することのできないのは...することのできないと同様だ」となる、すなわち~を強く否定するために...という否定できることの明らかなものを引合いに出したものである。「~するのは...するようなものだ」などと訳して当たる場合もある。類例:—

You **might as well** reason with the wolf **as** try to persuade that man.

(あの人間を説きつけようとするのはおおかみに説法するようなものだ)

〖注 意 1〗 この構文では may, might とも現在に関することをいうので、けっして may が現在のことをいい、might が過去のことをいうのではない。

〖注 意 2〗 may を用いたのと might を用いたのとでは大体上に述べたような差別はあるが、往々 might を用いるべき場合に may を用いた例があるから、解釈の場合には必ずしも上の区別に拘泥(ﾆｳ)しないで、前後の関係により適当な判断を下すべきである。

〖注 意 3〗 またこの構文で引合いに出された部分 might as well...ばかり文面にあらわれて、主眼として打消すべき as~ が省略されている場合が多い、もっとも前後の関係で何を打消すべきかはたやすくわかる。

例:—

You **might as well** go to a tree for fish.

(そんなことをしようとするのは木によって魚を求むるようなものだ)

You **might as well** expect the river to flow back.

(そんなことを期待するのは河がさかさに流れるのを期待するようなものだ)

〖注 意 4〗 may as well...as~
　　　　　=had better...(than)
　　　　　=(~するより)...する方がよい。

と解してよいことが往々ある。

---

(84) persuade [pəswéid] 説得する。

例:—

> One **may as well** not know a thing at all, **as** know it but imperfectly.
> (中途半端に物を知るくらいなら いっそうまったく知らない方がましだ)
> You **may** just **as well** stay at home (**as not**).
> (お前は家にいた方がいい)
> I **might as well** kill myself.
> (それくらいならいっそ死んだ方がましだ)
> I **may as well** tell it at once.
> (どうせ話すならすぐ話してしまった方がいい)

---

**774.** One *may as well* expect to make a great patriot—a Bruce or a Wallace—of a fencing master, *as* to make a great thinker out of a mere logician. (*Blackie*)

**775.** You *might as well* take the black spots out of the moon *as* try to get at that nest. (*Thomas Hughes*)

**776.** There was not long ago a tendency in some quarters to say that, because scientific discovery had been put to destructive and terrible uses—poison gas, bombing aeroplanes, submarines and so on—civilization might have fared better with no science at all. But this is plainly a hasty and superficial judgment. One *might as well* say that, because coal gas is used for suicides, and the radio for broadcasting jazz music, it would be better to prohibit both.

**777.** " Pray, what is coal but a kind of stone; and is not

---

**imperfectly** [impɔ́:fiktli] 不完全に。 **774. patriot** [péitriət] 愛国者。 **logician** [lo(u)dʒíʃən] 論理学者。 **776. quarter** [kwɔ́:tə] 方面。 **be put to use** 使用に供される。 **poison** 毒。 **fare better** よりよくことが運ぶ。 **superficial** [sjupəfíʃəl] 皮相な。 **suicide** [sjúisaid] 自殺。 **broadcasting** [brɔ́:dkɑ:stiŋ] 放送。 **prohibit** [prəhíbit] 禁ずる。 **777. Pray** ここでは一種の間投詞のようなもの。「ねえ」「では」など。 **but** でなくて。

butter, grease; and wheat, seed; and leather, skins; and silk, the web of a kind of caterpillar; and *may* we not *as well* call a cat an animal of the tiger kind, *as* a tiger an animal of the cat kind?"

**778.** You *might as well* advise me to give up my fortune, *as* my argument.

**779.** You *might as well* let him eat your dinner *as* 'do your sums' for you.

**780.** He who cannot say something in sympathy with, or in aid of the great movements of humanity, *might as well* hold his peace.

**781.** *As well might* the glowworm match himself against the lightning.

**782.** Many young people continue to practise bad manners simply because they were not born with natural grace. We *might as well* refuse to go to school because we were not fitted for college when we were born.

**783.** To make matters clear, I *may as well* explain at once what had happened.

---

( 85 )

(a) Accidents **will** happen.
(b) This cork **will not** come out.

---

grease 油脂。 caterpillar 毛虫。 778. advise [ədváiz] すすめる。 argument [áːgjumənt] 議論。 779. do your sums 君の算術をやってもらう。 780. hold one's peace だまっている。 781. glowworm つちぼたる。 782. natural grace 生れつきの優雅さ。 college [kɔ́lidʒ] (単科)大学。

【訳】（a）事故はどうしてもあるものだ。
　　　（b）この栓はどうしても抜けない。

【解説】　元来意志のないものを意志があるように取り扱って will, will not を用い、

（a）**will**—*insistence*（主張）

（b）**will not**—*refusal*（拒絶）

を示すことがよくある。しかし主語は必ずしも無生物に限らない。

　　　Accidents **will** happen.　[=Accidents *insist on* happening.]

すなわち事故というものに心があって、"I *will* happen."（どうしても私は起こる）と主張してやまないような心持である。

　　　This cork **will not** come out.　[=This cork *refuses to* come out.]

すなわち栓(せん)が "I *will not* come out."（私は抜けるのはいやだ）と拒むような心持。類例：―

　　　Boys **will** be boys.

　　　　（子供はどこまでも子供だ）

　　　This wood **will not** burn.

　　　　（このたきぎはなかなか燃えない）

　　　This door **will not** open.

　　　　（この戸のやつどうしても開かない）

過去のことをいう場合にはそのまま would, would not に変わる。

　　　I pulled and pulled very hard, but the cork **would not** come out.

　　　　（一生けんめいひっぱっても栓はどうしても抜けなかった）

---

**784.**　Nature *will* be obeyed.

**785.**　It was not many years ago that the first bold attempts were made at flying. Bold, because no one then knew how to fly; because, also, the engines were bad and *would not* work smoothly; and because the wings and all other parts of the machine were not strong enough and wrongly shaped. And

---

785.　**bold attempt** 大胆な試み。　**work smoothly** 滑らかに回る。

when flights were made they generally were only short hops close to the ground and in the deadest calm.

**786.** Rasselas was desirous to go, but *neither* his sister *nor* Imlac *would* consent. (*Johnson*)

**787.** He is a man who pays prompt cash, but *will* have the value of his money.

**788.** What the world wants to-day is young men who *will not* offer " English woolens " manufactured in American mills; who *will not* sell " Irish linen " made in New York.

**789.** Man does not live by bread alone, but neither does he live by taking thought alone. I love to think, and talk, and feel, but I cannot forget that I have hands which clamour to be put to use, arms which *will not* hang idle.

**790.** She now found that the key of the closet was stained with blood, and tried two or three times to wipe it; but the blood *would not* come off. In vain did she wash it, and even scrub it with soap and sand; the blood still remained.

(*Quiller-Couch*)

(86)

(a) **You shall** live.
(b) **He shall** die.

【訳】 (a) 貴様は助けてやる。

hop ぴょんと飛ぶこと。 deadest calm [kɑ:m] 最も静かな無風状態。 **786.** desirous [dizáiərəs] 願って。 consent 同意する。 **787.** prompt cash 即座の現金。 **788.** woolens [wúlnz, wúlənz] 毛織物。 mill 工場。 linen [línin] リンネル。 **789.** clamour [klǽmə] わいわいさわぐ。 hang idle ただぶらりと下っている。 **790.** stain 汚れる。 in vain むだに。 scrub ごしごしこする。

(b) あいつは殺してしまう。

〖解 説〗 you shall＝I will let (or make) you
he shall＝I will let (or make) him

第二人称および第三人称に shall を用いるのは、第一人称の意志、すなわち "I will" を裏面から述べるものである。こういう構文は日本語には無いから訳すときにはそのまま直訳はできない、第一人称になおすか、あるいは何とかほかに工夫しなければならない。

(a) **He shall** live. $\begin{cases} I \text{ will let him live.} \\ I \text{ will spare him.} \end{cases}$

(b) **He shall** die. $\begin{cases} I \text{ will make him die.} \\ I \text{ will kill him.} \end{cases}$

(a) と (b) との異なる点は前者は好意の約束、後者は悪意の脅迫となるところにある。(a) は I will **let** で、(b) は I will **make** で言いかえる。

比較：―

**You shall go** (＝*I will let you go*), *if* you wish to.
 （行きたいなら行かせてやる）
**He shall go** (＝*I will make him go*), whether he will or not.
 （いやでも応でも彼を行かせる）

比較：―

**You shall have** (＝*I will give you*) this watch.
 （お前にこの時計をやる）

**Your father shall know** (＝*I will tell him*) what you have been doing.
 （お前の行状をおとうさんに知らせてやる）

**You shall hear** (＝*I will tell you*) my story after dinner.
 （ご飯がすんでから私の身の上話をして聞かせよう）

**He shall be** (＝*I will make him*) the companion of my travels.
 （彼を旅の道づれにしよう）

打消しを伴なう場合も容易に解することができよう。

**He shall not** die.＝*I will not* let him die.
 （見殺しにしない）

**He shall not** live.＝*I will not* allow him to live.
 （生かしちゃおかない）

類例:—

**You shall not** want for anything while I live.
（私の生きてる間はお前たちに不自由はさせない）
**My children shall not** disturb you again.
（もう子供におじゃまをいたさせません）

〚注　意 1〛　意味を強めるために shall not と must not とを重ねて用いることがよくある。例:—

**He must not, shall not** die.
（彼が死ぬようなことがあってはならない、私が死なせはしない、どうしても助ける）

〚注　意 2〛　この shall が命令文などに用いられると立法者の意志をあらわす。例:—

The association **shall** be called the Eiyu-kai.
（本会を英友会と称する）

〚注　意 3〛　現代英語、特にアメリカ英語では、あらゆる意義用法を通じて shall は will に統一される傾向がある。

---

**791.**　*Thou shalt* want ere I shall.

**792.**　If you have lost your way, *you shall* be willingly supplied with such conveniences as this cavern will afford.　　*(Johnson)*

**793.**　Select from my store any ten books you choose, *which*, in addition to the two you had before, *shall* be a present to you.

**794.**　*He shall* know that I am not to be trifled with.

**795.**　" My noble Edward! " said the old gentleman. "And you needed a friend. Well, *you shall* have one."

**796.**　The blood of my master *shall not* be spilt, while I have

---

(86)　**disturb** [distə́:b] 乱す、さまたげる。　**association** [əsòuʃiéiʃən] 協会。
**791. want** 不自由する。　**ere**＝before.　**792. convenience** [kənví:njəns] 便宜。　**cavern** [kǽvən] 洞窟(ぅ)。　**afford** 与え得る。　**793. in addition to** ...に加えて。　**present** [préznt] 贈り物。　**794. trifle** [tráifl] **with** ...をもてあそぶ。　**796. spilt**＜spill こぼす、流す。

a drop felt in my veins. *(Scott)*

**797.** Unless they can teach without resorting to such a fundamental error as flogging, *my boy shall never* go to school.

*(Marryat)*

**798.** " I myself will stand at the lattice," said Rebecca, " and describe to you as I can what passes without."—" *You must not, you shall not*," exclaimed Ivanhoe; " each lattice, each aperture will soon be a mark for the archers." *(Scott)*

**799.** The development of popular education since the beginning of the century has been rapid. People have gradually begun to realize the value of a good education. Almost all parents of to-day are anxious that *their children shall* have as good an education as possible.

---

( 87 )

## Why should I not succeed?

【訳】 私が成功して<u>何が悪かろう</u>、成功した<u>っていいじゃないか</u>。

〖解 説〗 Why should I not...?

$=\begin{Bmatrix} \text{I see no reason} \\ \text{There is no reason} \end{Bmatrix}$ why I should not...

=...してはいけないという理由がない。

すなわち上の例を言い換えると

*I see no reason why I should not* succeed.

---

vein 血管。 797. resort [rizɔ́:t] 頼る。 fundamental [fʌndəméntəl] 基礎的な。 flog むち打つ。 798. lattice [lǽtis] 格子。 without 外で。 aperture [ǽpətjuə] 隙間。 archer [á:tʃə] 弓の射手。 799. devolopment [divéləpmənt] 発達。 anxious 切望して。

(ぼくだって成功して悪いというはずはあるまい＝ぼくにだって成功できないはずはない)

**Why should I not own** a motorcar?

(私だって自動車があってどこが悪いか)

〖注　意〗 この構文には否定文が多いが、肯定文も往々ある。例：―

**Why should I** dwell any longer on the story?

(もうこの話はくわしく述べ立てる必要はあるまい)

---

**800.** There is no character more contemptible than a man that is a fortune-hunter; and *I can see no reason why* fortune-hunting women *should not be* contemptible, too.

**801.** The poor live pleasantly without our help; *why* then *should not we learn* to live without theirs?

**802.** "Your father intends to make a milkman of you?"— "*Why not?*"

**803.** *There can be no reason why* the spectres *should* haunt the pyramids more than any other places. (*Johnson*)

**804.** The Chancellor Oxenstiern was afraid that the young queen would burst out a laughing at the first sight of these queer ambassadors, or else that she would be frightened by their unusual aspect.

"*Why should I be frightened?*" said the little queen. "And do you suppose that I have no better manners than to laugh?"

(*Hawthorne*)

---

(87) **dwell on** くわしく述べる。800. **contemptible** [kəntémptəbl] いやしむべき。**fortune-hunter** 財産目的の嫁さがしをする男。803. **spectre** [spéktə] 幽霊。**haunt** 出る。**pyramid** [pírəmid] 三角塔。804. **chancellor** [tʃɑ́:nsələ] (ドイツの)首相。**ambassador** 大使、使節。**aspect** [ǽspekt] 様子。

## (88)

(a) **What a pity** that things **should** have come to this!
(b) **I am surprised** that you **should** say so!
(c) **Who** are you that you **should** speak thus to me?

【訳】(a) 事ここに至る<u>とは</u>なんという<u>遺憾なこと</u>であろう。
(b) 君がそういう<u>とは</u>意外だ。
(c) そんな失敬なことをいう<u>とは</u>いったい貴様は<u>何者だ</u>。

〖解説〗(a) it is a pity; it is to be regretted; I am sorry など遺憾の意味をあらわす文句に従う節は通例 should を含む。

(b) I am surprised; it is strange; it is surprising のような驚き、いぶかしさをあらわす文句に従う節もまた通例 should を含む。

これらの文句は全然省略されて that...should 以下だけ残る場合が多い。例:—

**That** a brother **should** be so perfidious!
(兄弟にしてこのように不信であるとは!)

比較:—

O that it **would** be so!
(ああ、そうであれかし——願い)
Alas! that it **should** be so!
(ああ、そんなことになるとは——嘆き)

(c) **should** はまた疑問詞に伴なって驚きをあらわすことがよくある。例:—

**What** has he done that you **should** resort to violence?
(彼はどんなことをしたからといって君はそんな手荒なことをするのか)

---

(88) perfidious [pəfídiəs] 不信な。  resort to violence [váiələns] 暴力に訴える。

**Who** are you that you **should** speak thus to me?
(何者なればわしに対してかく無礼を言うぞ)

---

**805.** "How beautiful she looks!" said Ben to himself. "*What a pity it is* that such a pretty smile *should* not last forever!"

**806.** *Oh that* men *should* put an enemy into their mouth to steal away their brains! (*Shakespeare*)

**807.** "Indeed," said she, "you do not need to go to the hippopotamus for sensation. Look at a pig! There is something dire in the face of a pig. *To think* the same power *should have created* it that created a *star*!" (千葉大)

**808.** *What* is man *that* he *should* fight against nature?
(*Burke*)

**809.** Oh, the widows! Now, *what have they done that* they *should* be the butts for the jokes that are made at their expense?
(*Max O'Rell*)

**810.** "Ralph, my dear lad, it was very wrong of you to play against your father's orders," said Sir Henry Allerby, when they were on their way to Ralph's home; "you are a good boy, and *I am surprised* that you *should* have done it. I must tell you kindly, as a true friend, that obedience to parents is one of a boy's first duties."

---

805. **last** つづく。　**forever** [fərévə] 永久に。　806. **enemy** ここは酒のこと。807. **hippopotamus** [hìpəpɔ́təməs] かば。　**for sensation** センセーションを求めて。　**dire** [daiə] おそるべき。　809. **butt** [bʌt] (弓の)的、(笑いの)種。　**at one's expense** その人を犠牲にして。　810. **wrong** まちがって。　**against** ...にそむいて。　**obedience** 従順。

(89)

> (a) One **should obey** the dictates of one's conscience.
>
> (b) You **should have obeyed** your father.

【訳】（a）人は良心の命ずることに従うべきものである。

（b）お前はおとうさんのいうことを聞くべきだった [聞かなかったのが悪い]。

〖解説〗（a）**should** は義務、本分をあらわし、「...すべきもの」と解する。打消しに伴ない、**should not**... となれば「...すべからざるもの」の意味。

類例:—

We **should** prefer duty to pleasure.

（われわれは快楽よりも義務を先にすべきものである）

Brothers **should not** quarrel.

（兄弟は争うべきものでない）

（b）この should が完了形に伴なって、

**should have**＋過去分詞

となると、「...すべきはずであったのにそうしなかったのが悪い」という意味になる。すなわち、

You **should have obeyed** him.＝You have done wrong in not obeying him.

（君は彼のいうことを聞かなかったのが悪い）

打消しに伴なって、

**should not have**＋過去分詞

は「...すべからざるはずであったのにそうしたのが悪い」となる。例:—

You **should not have concealed** the matter from me.＝You have done wrong in concealing it from me.

（お前はそれを私に隠したのが悪い）

---

(89) **prefer** [prifə́:] えらぶ。

転じて次のような意味となることがある。

It was a fine sight. **You should have** seen it.
(実に壮観だった。君に見せたかった)

これは「君は見るべきであった——見なかったのは残念だ」という意味である。

---

**811.** One *should* always be prepared for death. (*Johnson*)

**812.** The average man necessarily spends the greater part of his waking life in earning his living. A man's work *should* be his chief pleasure and from it he *should* derive a large part of his enjoyment of life.

**813.** The aim of fine manhood *should* be not to make life easy but to make it so strong that it can stand the utmost strain. The magnitude of a man is measured by the magnitude of his motive.

**814.** Most fitting, indeed, is it, that while riches are power, and to grow as rich as possible the universal object of ambition, the path to its attainment *should* be open to all, without favour or partiality.

**815.** Charity begins at home, but *should not* end there.

(*Proverb*)

**816.** One *should* endeavor to utilize all his spare time in either work or amusement, as time simply idled away is an

---

812. **average** ふつうの。 **necessarily** [nésisərili] 必ず。 **waking** 目をさましている。 **living** [líviŋ] 生計(の資)。 **derive** 引き出す。 813. **manhood** 男子たること、男らしさ。 **stand** 耐える。 **strain** 緊張。 **magnitude** [mǽgnitjuːd] 大きさ。 **motive** [móutiv] 動機。 814. **fitting** [fítiŋ] 適当な。 **attainment** 達成。 **favour** [féivə] えこひいき。 **partiality** [pɑ̀ːʃiǽliti] 不公平。 815. **charity** [tʃǽriti] 慈善。 816. **endeavor** [indévə] 努力する。 **utilize** [júːtilaiz] 利用する。 **idled away** 何もしないで過ごされた。

absolute loss to both oneself and the public.  One *should not* even understand the expression "to kill time."

**817.**  During these hours the child *should not* be surrounded by valuable but fragile objects which he must not touch.  The walls *should not* be so exquisitely coloured that on no account must dirty finger marks appear upon them. (日本大)

---

### (90)

**It is right that** one **should** speak well of the absent.

【訳】 いない人のことはよく言う<u>べきものだ</u>。

〖解 説〗 it is good, right, wrong, proper, improper, necessary, natural などの次に来る名詞節には should がはいることが多い。これは前の (89) の should と同じものと見てよい。類例:—

> You **should** know this.
> **It is well** that you **should** know this.
> =君はこのことを知っておくべきだ。

> Children **should not** sit up late.
> **It is not good that children should** sit up late.
> =子供が夜ふかしをするのはよくない。

---

**818.**  But Ben *considered it* more *necessary that* he *should* have paintbrushes than *that* puss *should* be warm.

**819.**  *It is perhaps as well* that the facts *should* now come to light, for I have reasons to know there are wide-spread rumours

---

**absolute** まったくの。 **public** [pʌ́blik] 公衆、社会。 **kill** つぶす。 **817. surround** とり囲む。 **fragile** [frǽdʒail] こわれやすい。 **exquisitely** [ékskwizitli] ひじょうに美しく。 **on no account** どんなことがあっても…しない。 **818. paintbrush** 絵筆。 **puss** [pus] ねこ。 **819. come to light** 明るみに出る。 **wide-spread** 広く伝わった。 **rumour** うわさ。

as to the death of her stepfather which tend to make the matter even more terrible than the truth. (静岡薬大)

**820.** A state of health is necessary, not only to the comfort and activity of the body, but also to the comfort and activity of the mind. *It is* therefore *of the greatest importance that* we *should* take every means in our power to promote bodily health.

**821.** *It is desirable that* a storyteller and a story reader *should* establish a mutual understanding as soon as possible. (*Dickens*)

**822.** *It is right that* every man *should* love his country.

---

### (91)

(a) I **would rather** die than live in dishonour.
(b) You **had better** go to the seaside.

【訳】(a) 生き恥をかくより死んだ方がましだ。
　　　(b) 君は海岸へ行く方がいい。

〖解説〗 would rather と had better とは元来同じものであったのが今日の英語では区別ができて、

(a) **would rather...** は「むしろ...した方がまし」と選択の意味をあらわし、

(b) **had better...; had best...** は「...する方が得策」「...するのが一番よい」と忠告の意味をあらわすことが多い。したがって would rather は I に伴ない、had better は you に伴なって I would rather; you had better という形が多いけれど、また he had better, I had better という形も少なくはない、そのときももちろん得策とするという意味である。例：—

The doctor says that **I had better go** to the seaside, but I

---

as to ...に関して。tend 役立つ。 820. activity 活動。promote [prəmóut] 増進する。 821. establish [istǽbliʃ] 確立する。 mutual [mjú:tuəl] 相互の。

would rather **go** to the mountain.
(医者は私に海岸へ行くがよいというけれど、私はむしろ山へ行きたい)

〖注意 1〗 would rather も had better もいずれも現在のことをいうので、けっして過去のことをいうのではない。比較:—

You **had better do** so.
(君はそうする方がいい——現在)
You **had better have done** so.
(君はそうした方がよかったのだ——過去)

〖注意 2〗 would rather にはいろいろの変化がある。

I would { **rather** die **than** yield.
**sooner** die **than** yield.
**as soon** die **as** yield.
**as lief** die **as** yield. }

＝降参するくらいなら死んだ方がましだ。

---

**823.** No doubt, to the primitive hunter hunting was just as much work as his business is now to the city man. He *would rather* have caught his prey without any trouble; and the modern practice of killing domestic animals in the slaughterhouse would have seemed to him a solution of the whole problem of life.

**824.** If we read with care and sympathy, taking pains to understand and appreciate, we shall soon find out the books which nourish our mind, and agree with Macaulay when he said that he *would rather* live in a garret with a library than in a palace without one.

---

**lief** よろこんで。 **823. primitive** 原始時代の。 **prey** 獲物。 **trouble** 苦労、めんどう。 **slaughter** [slɔ́:tə] 屠殺(ほう)。 **solution** 解決。 **824. take pains** 努力をする。 **appreciate** [əprí:ʃieit] 鑑賞する。 **nourish** [nʌ́riʃ] 養う。 **garret** [gǽrət] 屋根裏部屋。 **palace** [pǽlis] 宮殿。

**825.** I know men who say they *would rather* read any book in a library copy than in one from their own shelf. To me that is unintelligible. For one thing, I know my books individually by their own scent, and I have but to put my nose between pages to be reminded of all sorts of things. (宮崎大)

**826.** You *had better* be alone than in mean company. Let your companions be such as yourself or superior; for the worth of a man will always be ruled by that of his company.

**827.** It's time he came to call me to dinner. What can be making him so late? Something must have happened. I think perhaps I *had better* go and find out what is the matter.

**828.** One of our number remarked that we *had best* take a short cut.

**829.** I *would as soon* live at the galley *as* live with Madam Gambourge. (*Thackeray*)

**830.** You *had better* go home, and say nothing about it; for every effort to recover your money will only expose your folly.

**831.** If the customers or guests are to be dunned, all the burthen lies upon my back; he'*d as lief* eat that glass *as* budge after them himself. (*Goldsmith*)

**832.** "Many can't go there [*i.e.* to the workhouse]; and many *would rather* die."—"If they *would rather* die," said Scrooge, "they *had better* do it, and decrease the surplus popula-

---

825. **shelf** 本棚。 **unintelligible** わけのわからない。 **scent** におい。 **individually** 個々に。 **but**=only. 826. **mean** いやしい。 **superior** [sjuːpíəriə] 優越者。 827. **can be** は is を強めた言い方。 828. **short cut** 近道。 829. **galley** [gǽli] ガレー船(奴隷のこぐ船)。 830. **recover** 取りもどす。 **expose** ばくろする。 831. **dun** [dʌn] 催促する。 **burthen** 重荷。 **budge after** 追って身動きする、つまり、催促する。 832. **workhouse** 救貧院。 **decrease** [diːkríːs] 減ずる。 **surplus** [sə́ːpləs] 余剰の。

tion."　　　　　　　　　　　　　　　　　　(*Dickens*)

**833.**　The bat has very long and thin fingers on its forelegs, or arms, as *we had better* call them.

**834.**　I *had rather* be a doorkeeper in the house of the Lord, than dwell in the tents of wickedness.　　　　　(*Psalms*)

---

### (92)

(a) If you **would** be happy, be virtuous.
(b) **Would** that I were young again!

【訳】（a）心楽しくなろうと欲するならば徳を行え。
　　　（b）もういちど若くなりたいものだ。

〖解　説〗（a）**would**＝**wish to.**　類例：—

He who **would** (＝*wishes to*) search for pearls, must dive deep.
　（真珠を求めようと欲するものは深く潜らなければならない——虎穴に入らずんば虎児を得ず）

I **would** not (＝*do not wish to*) have people know this.
　（このことは世間に知られたくない）

What **would** you have me do?
　（ぼくにどうしてもらいたいというのか）

(b)　**would**＝**I wish.**　類例：—

**Would that** it were so !＝I *wish* it were so !
　（そうならばいいが）

**Would to Heaven** I had never seen him !
　（彼に会わなければよかったのに＝彼に会ったのは悪運だ）

---

834. wickedness [wíkidnis] 悪。　**Psalms** [sɑːmz] 聖書の詩篇。

**835.** This King is believed to have been the first English ruler to build a considerable fleet and it is said that he left to his successor the maxim that he who *would* be secure on land must be supreme at sea.

**836.** He who *would* catch fish, must not mind getting wet.
*(Proverb)*

**837.** If we *would* study with profit the history of our ancestors, we must never forget that the country of which we read was a different country from that in which we live. *(Macaulay)*

**838.** Perseverance and tact are the two great qualities most valuable for all men who *would* mount, especially for those who have to step out of the crowd.

**839.** *Would to God* we had died by the hand of the Lord in the land of Egypt.
*(Bible)*

**840.** *Would to heaven* that all my servants *were* like you!

---

( 93 )

(a) **Whatever** the matter **may be,** do your best.
(b) **No matter what** the matter **may be,** do your best.
(c) **Let** the matter **be what it may** (or **will**), do your best.
(d) **Be** the matter **what it may** (or **will**), do your best.

---

835. considerable かなり大きな。 fleet 艦隊。 successor [səksésə] 後継者。 maxim 金言、処世訓。 secure 安全な。 supreme [sju:príːm] 最高の地位の。 837. with profit 利益を得て。 838. perseverance [pə̀ːsivíərəns] 忍耐。 tact [tækt] 如才ないこと。 mount 高い地位に上る。 839. Egypt [íːdʒipt].

【訳】 たとえ何事であろうとも全力を尽せ。

〖解 説〗「たとえ...であろうとも」という語法は通例

(a) **whatever (whoever, whenever, wherever, however) may...**

(b) **no matter what (who, when, where, how) may...**

の形であらわすが、また、

(c) **let** を文頭におく間接命令の形を取り、またあるいは

(d) 動詞を文頭におく古い命令法の形を取ることもある。日本語で、「よし...ならば...なれ」「たとえ...にもせよ」などと命令法で言うのに相当する。類例:—

> **Whoever may** say so, it is not true.
> **No matter who may** say so, it is not true.
> **Let** any one **who will** say so, it is not true.
> **Say** so **who will**, it is not true.
> ＝言いたい人は勝手にそう言え、だれがそう言おうと、それはほんとうじゃない。

> **Come what may** (or **will**), I am prepared for it.
> **Whatever may** happen, I am prepared for it.
> ＝何事でも来るなら来い、私は覚悟をしている。

> **Wherever you may** go, you cannot succeed without perseverance.
> **Go where you will,**...
> ＝どこへでも好きな所へ行け、どこへ行ったって忍耐がなくては成功はできない。

> **No matter when you may** call, you will find him at his books.
> **Call when you will,**...
> ＝いつでも好きなとき訪ねてごらん、いつ訪ねてもきっと彼は勉強している。

〖注 意 1〗 **however** は通例つぎに形容詞、副詞等を伴なう(もっともはぶかれることもある)。これを言い換えるには **as~as; ever so~** などを用いる。

例:―

$\left\{\begin{array}{l}\textbf{However (hard) you may try,}\\ \textbf{Try as hard as you will,}\\ \textbf{Try as you may,}\end{array}\right\}$ you will not succeed so easily.

=いくら一生けんめいやってもそうたやすく成功するものじゃない。

$\left\{\begin{array}{l}\textbf{However rich a man may be,}\\ \textbf{Let a man be ever so rich,}\\ \textbf{Be a man as rich as he will,}\end{array}\right\}$ he ought not to be idle.

=いくら金があったってなまけているべきものではない。

区別:―

(1) **Whatever** the matter may be, always speak the truth.

　　=**No matter what** the matter may be, ...

　　=その事は何事であろうとも常に真実を語れ。

(2) **However** that may be, I will do my duty all the same.

　　=**No matter how** that may be, ...

　　=**Be that as it may**, ...

　　=**At all events**, ...

　　=それはどうあろうとぼくはやはり尽すだけのことは尽す。

上例の (1) は事の何たるを問わないことを言い、(2) は事態のいかんを問わないことをいう。

〖注　意 2〗　may を伴なわない場合は

　**whatever**=anything that　（何事でも）

　**whoever**=any one who　（誰でも）

　**whichever**=any or either that　（どちらでも）

比較:―

(i) **Whatever** (=anything that) he undertakes, succeeds with him.

　　（彼のすることは何でも成功する）

(ii) **Whatever** he **may** (=no matter what he may) undertake, **it** succeeds with him.

　　（何をしようときっとあの人は成功する）

(i) の Whatever he undertakes は名詞節で succeeds の主語となって

いる。(ii) の Whatever he may undertake は副詞節で、succeeds には別に it という主語がある。

〖**注 意**〗 (ii) の場合に may の省略されることが往々ある。

---

**841.** *Be the motive what it may*, it is always well to be on the side of caution.

**842.** Never does a plain, *however beautiful it may be*, seem so in my eyes. I need torrents, rocks, firs, dark woods, mountains, steep roads to climb or descend, abysses beside me to make me afraid. (都立大)

**843.** Brain work in moderation is unquestionably healthy, but brain work in excess is the very reverse. All who work their brains too much—*be they* mathematicians, philosophers, lawyers, authors, or men of business—do so at the expense of physical health.

**844.** Possessing, as the island does, a climate that allows the cultivation of almost every vegetable product, it might be excepted that agriculture in the island would be both easy and profitable. Such, however, is not the case; *whatever the real cause may be*, certain it is that the farmer, in general, reaps but little for his labour.

**845.** *No matter what road is chosen*, the travelers who started from different valleys will all meet on the top of the mountain, provided they keep on ascending. (早大)

---

841. **motive** [móutiv] 動機。 **caution** 用心。 842. **torrent** 急流。 **fir** もみの木。 **abyss** [əbís] 深淵。 843. **moderation** 適度。 **unquestionably** [ʌnkwéstʃənəbli] もちろん。 **excess** 過度。 **reverse** 逆、反対。 **mathematician** [mæθimətíʃən] 数学者。 **at the expense of** ...を犠牲にして。 844. **cultivation** 栽培。 **the case** 実情。 **reap** 刈り取る、収穫する。 845. **valley** 谷、低地。 **provided**=if; on the condition that. **ascend** [əsénd] 登る。

**846.** We should never despise any person, *however humble his condition may be.*

**847.** *No matter how* healthy or strong or fortunate you *may be*, every one of you must expect to endure a great deal of pain, and it is worth while for you to ask yourselves whether you can not put it to good use. For pain has a very great value to the mind that knows how to utilize it.

**848.** My companion could not help laughing at the accident, *do what he could.*

**849.** The man who would know one thing well must have the courage to be ignorant of a thousand other things, *however attracting and inviting.*

**850.** A man's life is to be measured by what he does in it, and what he thinks and feels in it. The more useful work the man does, and the more he thinks and feels, the more really he lives. The idle, useless man, *no matter to what* extent his life *may be* prolonged, is merely a vegetable.

**851.** *However well* any article *may* be written, and *however well* any speech *may* be reported, there is a charm in the spoken word, in the utterance of the living man, which no beauty of style can imitate, and no arrangement of words can equal.

**852.** The manners of a child are of more or less importance, according to his station in life; his moral cannot be attended to too early, *let* his station *be what it may.*

**853.** Be content with a small salary at the beginning, and

---

847. **worth while** …する価値がある。**put to good use** 利用する。**utilize** [júːtilàiz] 利用する。 849. **attractive and inviting** おもしろそうで、したくなる。 850. **extent** 程度、限度。**prolong** 長くする。 851. **article** [áːtikl] 論文。**utterance** 発言。**style** 文体。**arrangement** [əréindʒmənt] 配列。**equal** [íːkwəl] 匹敵する。 852. **station** 地位。**be attended to** 注意が払われる。

then you will appreciate every little addition that is made to it. But *no matter how small it is*, determine never to live above it.

**854.** Thank Heaven, *whatever it was*, it was over now. I reasoned with myself, and recovered my firmness. I became convinced that I had only been dreaming more vividly than usual.
(立命館大)

**855.** The free nations of the world in planning for their youth, as in many other matters, must be in constant communication, for *however diverse their methods* their fundamental aims remain the same: the preservation and extension of personal freedom.
(*J. Conant*)

**856.** The subject of diet—he prefers to call it diet—is apparently one of unlimited interest to the Englishman, *meet him when you will*, he is ever ready to discuss, first, the weather, and then the things—that is to say, the kind of food—that agree with him.

**857.** If you ride to and from work, *however noisy* or *crowded* your surroundings, close your eyes to rest them and allow yourself that interlude for silence and meditation.

**858.** All books have essential points somewhere. Men who are skilled in grasping these points and comprehending useful information at first sight, can truly be called good readers. *However busy* or *poor men may be*, they can find time and get books to read.

---

853. **appreciate** ありがたみが解る。 **above it** 給料以上に。 854. **reason** 理を説く。 **convinced** 確信して。 **vividly** ありありと。 855. **communication** 連絡、伝達。 **diverse** 異なる。 **preservation** 保存。 **extension** 拡大。 856. **diet** 食物。 **apparently** 見たところ...らしい。 857. **surroundings** 周囲。 **rest** 休ませる。 **interlude** [íntəljuːd] 合間。 **meditation** 黙想。 858. **grasp** 把握する。 **comprehend** 理解する。

**859.** *Let the world without go as it may; let kingdoms rise or fall,* so long as he has the wherewithal to pay his bill, he is for the time being the very monarch of all he surveys.　　　(*Irving*)

---

### (94)

| |
|---|
| (a)　**If** I **were** a bird, I **would** fly to you. |
| (b)　I **wish** (that) I **had** wings, and **could** fly to you. |

【訳】（a）鳥ならばあなたの所へ飛んで行くのだが。
　　　（b）つばさがあってあなたの所へ飛んで行かれるのだといいがなあ。

〖解　説〗（a）　現在の事実に反対の仮想をあらわすにはいわゆる**仮定法過去**の形 (to be は人称にかかわらず常に were) を用い、その条件を受ける本文には should (would, could, might) do などの形を用いる。
類例：—
　I have no money. If I **had** any, I **would** lend it to you.
　　（ぼくは金は無い。もしあれば貸してあげるんだが）
　If I **knew** it, I **would** tell you.
　　（知っていれば話すのだが、知らないから話せない）
過去の事実の裏をいうには仮定法過去完了の形を用い、これを受けるには should (would, could, might) have done の形を用いる。類例：—
　If I **had been** there, I **should have been** killed.
　＝I *was not* there at that time, so was not killed.
　　（もしそこにいたら殺されたのだが、いなかったから助かった）
　If the doctor **had come** earlier, the man **might have been** saved.
　　（医者が早く来たらばその人は助かるのであった、医者がおそかったので助からなかった）

---

859. **without** 外の。world を修飾する。　　**wherewithal** [hwéəwiðɔːl] 資力。**for the time being** 当分は。**monarch** [mɔ́nək] 帝王。**survey** [səːvéi] 見渡す。

(b) **I wish** (that) の次に上記の形を用いれば現在、過去、未来のことに関するかないがたい願いをあらわす。

類例：—

**I wish I were** rich.＝I am sorry I *am not* rich.
（金持ならばさぞよかろうに——現在）
**I wish I had been** there.＝I am sorry I *was not* there.
（あの時あそこへ行っていればよかったのに——過去）
**I wish he would** come.
（彼が来ればよいが——未来）

〚注　意 1〛　**O that** を I wish (that) に代用することがある。例：—

**O that** (＝I wish) **it were** so!
（そうならいいが）
**O that he would** succeed.
（彼に成功させたいものだが）

〚注　意 2〛　I wish の意味を **oh, if; ah, if** などであらわすことがある、これは I should be glad などがはぶかれたものと見るべきである。類例：—

**Oh, if I could only see** him once more.
（ああもういちど彼に会いたいものだ、会えたらうれしかろうに）

---

**860.** We allow a man three strikes in baseball to see what he can do with those three. *If* we *allowed* him a dozen no man *would* care to play the game; too many opportunities spoil the sport.

**861.** *If* art *were* merely a record of the appearances of nature, the closest imitation *would* be the most satisfactory work of art, and the time *would* be fast approaching when photography should replace painting.

(熊本大)

**862.** Whether he *could* ever *have taken* high rank as a novelist

---

860. **spoil** だめにする、損う。　861. **appearance** 外観。　**imitation** 模倣。
**approach** 近づく。　**replace** とって代わる。　862. **novelist** [nɔ́vəlist] 小説家。

*if* he *had thrown* himself completely into the profession may be doubted, for his defects were such as industry and practice would hardly have lessened.

**863.** Indeed, *if* one *were to* attempt to write a book on any branch of science in which all discoveries made by youthful workers were left out, there *would* be very little left to write about. (神戸大)

**864.** *If I were* a boy again, I *would* school myself into a habit of attention; I *would* let nothing come between me and the subject in hand; I *would* remember that an expert on the ice never tries to skate in two directions.

**865.** A star player once said to me; " I *wish I knew* how to get off the team. It isn't that I want to quit playing football. I like it, but I'm sick of playing it as if my life depended on it. It's too serious. There's no fun." (高知大)

**866.** On most men his clothes *would have looked* terribly shabby, but there was something about this man that prevented one from criticizing his garments, and the details I have mentioned were only recalled afterwards. (一橋大)

---

### ( 95 )

(a) The child talks **as if** it were a man.
(b) He talks **as though** he knew everything.

---

throw oneself into …に一身をささげる。 defect 欠点。 lessen 減少させる。 863. attempt 試みる。 leave out 除外する。 864. school 訓練する。 let… させる。 in hand 考究中の。 expert [ékspəːt] 専門家。 865. get off 離れる。 quit やめる。 be sick of つくづくいやになる。 866. shabby 見すぼらしい。 prevent 妨げる、…させない。 criticize 批評する、わるく言う。 garments 衣裳。 details 詳細。 mention 言及する。 recall 思いださせる。

【訳】（a）あの子は大人みたいな話しぶりをする。

（b）彼は何でも知らないことはないようにしゃべる。

〘解 説〙 as if あるいは as though に仮定法過去、あるいは仮定法過去完了の付いた節は「あたかも...かのように」の意味である。この節は一種の省略文で、次のように補って見ることができる：—

The child talks as (he would talk) if he were a man.

（あの子はもしおとなだったら、そうも言うだろうと思われるようにものを言う）

He talks as (he would not talk) though he knew everything.

（彼はたとえ何でも知っていてもそうは言うまいと思われるようにものを言う）

〘注 意1〙 if, though に率いられる節中の主語も動詞も共に省略されて、ただちに不定詞、前置詞、分詞などへつづくことがある。例：—

She opened her lips as if [she were going] to speak.

（何か物を言いそうに唇を開いた）

His eyes were restless as if [it were] from fear.

（彼は物をおそれるかのように不安な眼つきであった）

Her hands were white and delicate as though [they were] carved in ivory.

（彼女の手は象牙できざんだように白くきゃしゃであった）

He said in a low voice as though [he were] speaking of himself.

（彼はひとり言のように小さい声でいった）

〘注 意2〙 as it were は as if it were actually so などの省略と見てよく、すこし無理なことをいう場合に言いわけのために添える文句で、公式 (72) 中に述べた so to speak と同じく in a sense（ある意味では、いわば）の意味である。

He is, as it were, a walking dictionary.

（彼はいわば生き字引だ）

He is, as it were, trusting to a broken reed.

（彼はいわば折れた葦(あし)にすがっているようなものだ）

---

(95) delicate [délikit] 繊(せん)細な。　ivory [áivəri] 象牙。

**867.** I dare say I need not tell you how rude it is to take the best place in a room, or to seize immediately upon what you like at table, without offering first to help others *as if* you *considered* nobody but yourself.

**868.** Football isn't played for pleasure; it is played as a desperately serious business, and the players have to give hours of attention to it daily *as if* the next game *were* the sole interest in life. (高知大)

**869.** The sun seemed unwilling to go, but some invisible power was pulling it down behind the horizon; however, *as if* eager to exhaust its glory before it disappeared, it sent out long, golden-red rays of living fire that turned the earth into fairyland.

**870.** The workman who drops his tools at the stroke of twelve, *as* suddenly *as if* he *had been struck* by lightning may be doing his duty,—he is doing nothing more. No man has made a great success of his life by doing merely his duty. He must do that,—and more. If he puts love into his work, the " more " will be easy.

**871.** And if we've been under the strain of worry or anger, or fear, our exhaustion is just as real *as if* we *had been* busy chopping trees. If this fatigue is not removed by sufficient sleep, its effect upon our behaviour is undeniable. (西京大)

---

867. **I dare say** おそらく。**rude** 不作法な。**seize upon** つかみかかる。**offer** 申し出る。**help** とってやる。 868. **desperately** ひどく。**sole** 唯一の。 869. **unwilling** [ʌnwíliŋ] 気が進まない。**invisible** [invízəbl] 目に見えない。**horizon** [horáizn] 地平線、水平線。**exhaust** [igzɔ́:st] 使いつくす。**fairyland** [féərilænd] よう精の国。 870. **at the stroke** 打つとすぐに。**merely** [míəli] 単に。 871. **strain** 緊張。**exhaustion** [igzɔ́:stʃən] 極度の疲労。**chop** 切る。**fatigue** [fətí:g] 疲労。**effect** 影響。**undeniable** [ʌndináiəbl] 否定できない。

**872.** The blaze from the burning ship was so fiercely bright that the sea was lighted up clear to the horizon, and objects became *as* distinctly visible *as though* it *had been* broad daylight.

**873.** When we gaze at the white clouds floating in the sky above, or at the flaming colour of the varied flowers at our feet, we feel *as though* we *were* suddenly flung into the bosom of heaven and earth.

**874.** It seems *as if* the present age *had found* a form of tyranny more difficult to tackle than any that has gone before. The old tyranny was simple by comparison. There was very little pretence that the tyrant ruled his people for their good.

**875.** A strange-looking lame dog suddenly appeared on the scene, *as if* it *had dropped* from the clouds, and limping briskly after the astonished and frightened sheep, drove them straight home and into the fold.　　　　　　　　　　　　　　(鳥取大)

**876.** In spite of himself, his eyes turned again and again, *as if fascinated*, to the gun over the mantel.

**877.** Then she waved her hand *as though* to keep some dreadful thing off, and fell back dead!

**878.** It goes almost without saying that inspiration is not peculiar to religion. An inspiration is an idea which seems to enter the mind suddenly, and, *as it were*, from without.

---

872. **blaze** 火焰。 **object** 物体。 **broad daylight** 真昼。　873. **flaming** かがやかしい。 **varied** [véərid] いろいろな。 **flung**＜fling 投げる。 **bosom** [búzəm] ふところ。　874. **tyranny** [tírəni] 専制、虐政。 **tackle** とりくむ。 **pretence** 見せかけ。　875. **lame** びっこの。 **limp** びっこを引く。 **briskly** 元気よく。 **fold** 囲い。　876. **fascinate** [fǽsineit] 魅する。 **mantel** [mǽntl] 炉棚。　877. **keep off** 払いのける。　878. **go without saying** 言うまでもない。 **inspiration** [ìnspəréiʃən] 霊感。

( 96 )

> **Should I fail** this time, I would try again.

【訳】 私は万一こんど失敗したらまたやってみる。

〚解 説〛 条件の節は if で導くのが通常であるが、それを省略すると、その省略された場所,すなわち主語の前へ仮定法の助動詞を出すのである。すなわち上文は **If I should fail** this time,... の if をはぶいたから、should をその位置に進めたのである。類例:—

**Were it not** (=*if it were not*) for his idleness, he would be a good student.

（怠惰でさえなければ彼はいい生徒だが）

**Had it not been** (=*if it had not been*) for your care, I should have died.

（あなたが介抱してくださらなかったら私は死ぬのであった）

---

**879.** Newspapers *could* not be sold so cheaply *were it not* for the immense income derived from advertising. Some firms spend thousands of pounds every year in advertising their products in the daily papers.

**880.** *Were I called* upon to express in a word the reason for so many failures among those who started out in life with high hopes, I *should say* unhesitatingly, they lacked will power.

**881.** To ambition he owed both his greatness and his ruin. With all his failings, he possessed great and admirable qualities; and, *had he kept* himself within due bounds, he *would have lived and died* without an equal.

---

879. **advertise** [ǽdvətàiz] 広告する。 **firm** [fə:m] 会社。 **product** [prɔ́dəkt] 製品。 880. **be called upon** 求められる。 **unhesitatingly** [ʌnhéziteitiŋli] 躊躇(ちゅうちょ)せずに。 881. **owe to** ...におかげをこうむる。 **admirable** [ǽdmərəbl] りっぱな。 **due bounds** 適当な限度。 **equal** [í:kwəl] 匹敵者。

**882.** *Were it not* for much rain, Japan *would be* one of the most comfortable countries to live in.

**883.** *Had I known* whom I was to have the pleasure of meeting, wings *could not have conveyed* me swiftly enough.

(横浜国立大)

**884.** I am certain I *could have performed* twice the labour, both better and with greater ease to myself, *had I known* so much of the laws of health and life at twenty-one, as I do now.

**885.** Before Nelson could rise again, the savage beast was upon him, with his terrible paw raised ready to strike. *Had that blow fallen*, the whole history of Europe *might have been changed*.

**886.** It *would have done* him much good, *had he had* spare time to go out into the country.

**887.** The impression which he always left upon me was *had he been born* in a less exalted sphere he *would have acquitted* himself equally well in any branch of public life.

**888.** The natives of Africa are very fond of ostrich eggs, using them for food. In taking the eggs, they exercise great caution; for *should the birds discover* them, they *would break* all the eggs and leave the nest.

**889.** To impose a new civilization on an ancient culture is naturally a gigantic undertaking; and Japan can only be admired for attempting it, and having so well succeeded in accom-

---

883. **convey** [kənvéi] 運ぶ。 884. **perform** なしとげる。 885. **savage** どう猛な。 **be upon** 襲いかかる。 **paw** 足。 887. **exalted** [igzɔ́:ltid] 高い。 **sphere** 地位、階級。 **acquit oneself well** りっぱなことをする。 **branch** [brɑ:ntʃ] 部門。 888. **Africa** [ǽfrikə]. **ostrich** [ɔ́stritʃ] だちょう。 **exercise** [éksəsaiz] 働かす。 889. **impose** [impóuz] 負わせる。 **undertaking** [ʌ̀ndətéikiŋ] 事業。

plishing it. *Could the achievement have been realized* without losing some of the virtues of either civilization, it *would be* nothing short of a miracle.

---

( 97 )

> He worked very hard, **otherwise** he would have failed.

【訳】 彼は非常に勉強した、さもなければ失敗したのだ。

〖解 説〗「さもなければ」「もしそうでなかったら」などという条件が otherwise という一語にちぢめられていることがある。類例：—

 I am ill, **otherwise** (=**or else**) I would go.
  (ぼくは病気だ、さもなければ行くのだが)

この例には would go という形が用いてあるから otherwise は**仮定法過去**のちぢまったものであることがわかる。すなわち上文は

 *If I were not ill*, I would go.

というのに等しい。囲いの中の例では would have failed という形が用いてあるから otherwise は**仮定法過去完了**のちぢまったものである。すなわち

 *If he had not worked hard*, he would have failed.

というのに等しい。こういう otherwise が文の中間にはまっている場合はちょっと訳をつけにくいから大いに注意を要する。例：—

 The light, which would **otherwise** have disturbed the invalid, was excluded from his chamber by means of shutters.
  (光線は、そうしないと病人にさわるので、雨戸をしめて室内にはいらないようにしてあった)

---

achievement [ətʃíːvmənt] 成就、大事業。 realize 実現する。 short of a miracle [mírəkl] 奇蹟には達しない。
(97) otherwise [ʎðəwaiz] さもなければ。 disturb 安静を乱す。 invalid [ínvəliːd] 病人。 exclude 閉め出す。 chamber [tʃéimbə] 室。

この文は下のように2文にわけて見れば解しやすい：—

The light was excluded from his chamber by means of shutters. **Otherwise** it would have disturbed him.
　　（光線は雨戸をしめて室内へはいらないようにしてあった。そうしなかったら光線が病人の安静を乱したであろう）

〖注　意 1〗 otherwise に応ずる動詞が事実の反対を想定するものでないこともある。例：—

Seize the chance, **otherwise** you *will* regret it.
　　（機会をとらえよ、さもないと後で悔いるだろう）
You must work hard, **otherwise** you *will* fail.
　　（勉強せよ、さもないと失敗するぞ）

これについては公式 (**60**) を参照せよ。

〖注　意 2〗 otherwise にはこのほかに次のような二つの用法があるから混同しないよう注意を要する。

　(1)　otherwise＝in a different way; not so
　　　　　（それとちがったふうに；そうでなく）例：—
　I think **otherwise** (＝I do *not* think *so*).
　　（私の考えはちがう、私はそうは思わない）
　I could not have acted **otherwise.**
　　（そうするよりほかはなかったのだ）
　(2)　otherwise＝in other respects
　　　　　（その他の点においては）例：—
　He is unruly, but not **otherwise** blameworthy.
　　（彼は乱暴だがそのほかには別に非難すべきところはない）
　The rent is high, but **otherwise** the house is satisfactory.
　　（家賃は高い、けれどもほかは、その家は申し分がない）

---

**890.**　As the peninsula has such a long coast line, the climate is milder than it would *otherwise* be.

---

**blameworthy** [bléimwə̀:ði] 非難すべき。　890.　**peninsula** [pinínsjulə] 半島。**mild** 温和な。

**891.** You know business men seldom lend money without adequate security; *otherwise* they might soon be reduced to poverty.

**892.** The tea plant is not allowed to grow to a height of more than six feet; *otherwise* the leaf could not easily be reached. The plant will grow to the height of a tall tree, if it is allowed; and it is said that in some part of China monkeys are trained to climb up the tree and pick the leaves.

**893.** His punctuality was one of the most carefully cultivated of his habits; *otherwise* it had not been possible for him to get through so huge an amount of literary labour. He made it a rule to answer every letter received by him on the same day, except in case where inquiry and careful consideration were required.

**894.** Riches and ease, it is perfectly clear, are not necessary for man's highest culture, *else* had not the world been so largely indebted in all times to those who have sprung from the humbler ranks.

**895.** If a man writes a diary which he feels sure that nobody will ever see except himself, he is probably perfectly truthful. There is no motive for being *otherwise*.

**896.** The taxation necessary to support the army and navy compels every man and woman to work at least an hour a day more than they *otherwise* need.

---

891. **adequate** [ǽdikwit] 十分な。 **security** [sikjúəriti] 担保物。 **be reduced to ...**になる。 892. **train** しこむ、訓練する。 893. **punctuality** [pʌ̀ŋktjuǽliti] 時間厳守。 **get through** 仕遂げる。 **huge** 巨大な。 **literary** [lítərəri] 文学の。 **inquiry** 調査。 **consideration** 考慮。 894. **indebted** [indétid] おかげをこうむって。 **sprung**＜spring 身を起こす。 **rank** 階級。 895. **diary** [dáiəri] 日記。 **truthful** 正直に書く。 896. **taxation** [tækséiʃən] 徴税。

**897.** The French are more luxurious in their food than are the Anglo-Saxons, but their inclination to self-indulgence in this respect is counterbalanced by the satisfaction with more inadequate dwellings than would *otherwise* content them. (東大)

**898.** Into these missiles can be fitted the nuclear cargo which on arriving will completely destroy the societies of the humans and shatter the delicate conditions which alone make life possible. This is the unhappy meaning of what *might otherwise be* the greatest triumph of the human mind in the story of man.

(一橋大)

**899.** Fortunate it was that they were so near, *else* the mother would have jumped in after her child, and both be lost.

**900.** You did what was right and nothing more. If you had acted *otherwise*, you would have been dishonest.

**901.** The sweet things of the world have to be patiently waited for, and do not usually come *otherwise* than drop by drop.

**902.** He was much bruised and had his ankle dislocated, but was not *otherwise* hurt.

---

897. **luxurious** ぜいたくな。**inclination** 傾き。**self-indulgence** 放縦。**respect** 点。**counterbalance** 埋め合わせをする。**inadequate** [inǽdikwit] 不十分な。**content** 満足させる。 898. **missile** [mísail] 誘導弾。**nuclear cargo** 核弾頭。**shatter** 粉砕する。**triumph** 勝利、がいせん。 899. **be lost** の前に would を入れてみる。 正確には would have been lost となるところ。 901. **patiently** [péiʃəntli] 気長に。**drop by drop** 一滴ずつ、少量ずつ。 902. **bruise** [bru:z] 傷つける。**ankle** [ǽŋkl] くるぶし。**dislocate** [dísləkeit] 関節をはずす。

( 98 )

> (a) **I might have been** a rich man.
> (b) **A wise man would** not do such a thing.
> (c) **Without water,** nothing **could** live.
> (d) **To hear him speak English,** one **would** take him for an Englishman.

【訳】（a）私は金持になろうと思えばなれたのに〔残念なことをした〕。
　　　（b）りこうな人ならそんなことはしない。
　　　（c）水が無ければ何物も生きることはできない。
　　　（d）彼が英語を話すのを聞いたらイギリス人と思うね。

〘解　説〙 条件の文句 (Conditional Clause) が全然省略されていたり、前置詞、不定詞、名詞などの中にかくれている場合がある。上の例は、

(a) I **might\* have been** a rich man, **if I had wanted to.**
(b) **If he were a wise man,** he **would** not do such a thing.
(c) **If there were no water,** nothing **could** live.
(d) **If one were to hear him speak English,** one **would** take him for an Englishman.

の省略された形である。条件を示す should, would, might, could などがあって、それに対する条件が文中に見えない場合には、上のように補ってみなければならない。類例:——

He **might\*** at least **have come** to say good-bye.
　（いとま乞いぐらいには来ようと思えば来られたろうに、いとま乞いにも来なかったとはひどいやつだ）
You have done better than I **could have done.**
　（ぼくがやったって君のようにうまくはできなかったんだ）
You **could have done** no better.
　（君はこれよりうまくやろうたってできはしなかったのだ＝君はきわめてうまくやった）

One or two **would not be missed**; there are so many.

(一つや二つ盗んだってわかりはしまい、こんなにたくさんあるのだから)

I **should** be happy **to be** (=if I could be) of service to you.

(お役に立てば しあわせですが)

**With your assistance** (=if I had your assistance), I **should** certainly succeed.

(ご援助があればきっと成功するのですが)

〘注 意〙 \*印を付けた might は could easily の意味。

---

**903.** When the " impossible " deed was accomplished, others saw that it *might have been done* long before.

**904.** His look seems to say;—" Come, my fine fellow, listen to me a minute; you have money, and I have none; you *might give* me a penny." (*Max O'Rell*)

**905.** There was in his nature a trait which some people *might have called* laziness, though it was not quite that. (新潟大)

**906.** She *would* fain *have removed* the body to her home, but she could not.

**907.** One or two of them *would never have been missed*, and I *might* easily *have enriched* myself without fear of detection.

**908.** Flowers and insects are fitted to one another as glove to hand; in many cases the flowers *would* probably *disappear without* their visitors and the insects *without* their flowers.

**909.** A few stars are known which are hardly bigger than the earth, but the majority are so large that hundreds of thou-

---

(98) **miss** ないのに気がつく。 **904. come** 相手を促す場合の言葉、「さあ」、「ねえ」など。 **905. trait** [trei, treit] 特質。 **906. fain** [fein]=willingly. **remove** [rimúːv] 移す。 **907. enrich** 豊富にする。 **detection** 発覚。 **908. be fitted** しっくり適合している。 **glove** [glʌv] 手袋。 **disappear** [dìsəpíə] 無くなる。 **909. majority** 大多数。

sands of earths *could be packed* inside each and leave room to spare; here and there we come upon a giant star large enough to contain millions of millions of earths.

## (99)

(a) I **cannot but** laugh to hear such a story.
(b) I **cannot help** laughing to hear such a story.

【訳】 (a) そんな話を聞いては笑わざるを得ない。
(b) そんな話を聞いては笑いを禁ずることはできない。

〚解 説〛 (a) **cannot but**+原形不定詞 (**to** のない不定詞)
(b) **cannot help**+動名詞

この二つはまったく同じ意味に用いられる。(a) は cannot の次に **choose** という動詞がはぶかれているので、「...するほかに選ぶべき道がない」という意味である。(b) の help は **avoid, forbear** などに代えることができるので「...するを禁ずるわけにいかない」などの意味である。

〚注 意〛 疑問をもって打消しに代える場合があるが、それは次の式を見たらすぐ解されよう。

　We **cannot but** pity her.
　=**No** one **can but** pity her.
　=**Who can but** pity her?
　=だれが彼女をあわれまざるを得よう。
　=何人といえども彼女をあわれまざるを得ない。

次に help の代りに **keep, refrain** などを用いれば from を加える、すなわち:—

　I **cannot** (choose) **but laugh**.
　I **cannot do otherwise than** (to) **laugh**.

---

pack 詰めこむ。　room to spare もっと容れる余地。　come upon 出会う。
(99) forbear [fɔːbέə] 忍ぶ、堪える。

$$\text{I cannot} \begin{cases} \text{help} \\ \text{avoid} \\ \text{forbear} \end{cases} \text{laughing.}$$

$$\text{I cannot} \begin{cases} \text{keep} \\ \text{refrain} \\ \text{abstain} \end{cases} \text{from} \begin{cases} \text{laughing.} \\ \text{laughter.} \end{cases}$$

などはいずれも同じ意味に用いられるのである。なおまた

How can I help laughing?

How can I (choose) but laugh?

など疑問にしても同じことになる。

---

**910.** I *could not but* smile to hear her talk in this lofty strains but I was never much displeased with those harmless delusions that tend to make us happy.

**911.** I was taking a walk in this place last night between the hours of nine and ten, and *could not but* fancy it one of the most proper scenes in the world for a ghost to appear in.

**912.** The mother had never been further from home than the next village, and she *could not help* being a little frightened at the thought of her husband taking such a long journey.

**913.** There was almost a violent contrast between the beauty of the Metro and the drab clothes of the riders. One *could not help* being impressed by the Metro as a remarkable technical achievements.
(M. Fainsod)

**914.** *No one can help* influencing others, however little he may wish to do so or is conscious of what he is doing. None

---

abstain [əbstéin] 控える。910. lofty strain 高慢な調子。delusion [diljú:ʒən] 幻想。tend 役立つ。911. proper 適当な。912. frighten [fráitn] びっくりさせる。at the thought 考えると。913. violent ひどい。Metro 地下鉄。drab さえない。technical 技術的。914. influence 影響を与える。is conscious of ...を意識する。

can be neutral; if he is not doing good, he will in some sense be doing harm.

**915.** Whatever he might choose to say, his auditors *had no choice but* to believe him. (*Hawthorne*)

**916.** Honesty and truth, even in children, *cannot fail to* exert an influence for good upon those around them.

**917.** He *could not fail to* be touched by the admirable self-helping spirit which they had displayed.

**918.** The prettiest anecdote, in Dean Ramsay's Reminiscences, relates to whisky, and I *cannot refrain from* quoting it.

(*Max O'Rell*)

---

### (100)

(a) **No one but** a fool would do such a thing.
(b) He is **nothing but** a student.

【訳】 (a) ばかでなくてはそんなことはしまい。
(b) 彼はただの学生にすぎない。

〖解 説〗 この場合の but はもちろん except の意味で、
(a) **no one** (or **none**) **but**〜＝〜のほかはだれも (打消し)
(b) **nothing but**〜＝〜のほかは何も (打消し)
の意味であるから別にむずかしいことはない。ただそれが文の主語になる場合、目的語になる場合、補語になる場合などで、いくぶん訳しぐあいがちがう。場合に応じて **only, the only, alone** などを用いて言い換えることができる。三、四の例を挙げておこう:—

---

**neutral** [njúːtrəl] どっちつかずの。 **915. auditor** [ɔ́ːditə]＝listener. **choice** 選択の余地。choose の名詞。 **916. exert** 及ぼす。 **917. touch** [tʌtʃ] 感動させる。 **display** [displéi] 示す。**918. anecdote** [ǽnikdòut] 逸話。 **reminiscences** [rèminísnsiz] 回想録。 **relate** 関する。 **quote** [kwout] 引用する。

**None but** the brave deserve the fair.＝The brave *alone* deserve the fair.

（勇士のみ美人を得るにふさわしい）

**No man** is truly free **but** the beggar.＝The beggar is *the only* free man in the world.

（世の中で本当に自由な者は乞食ばかりだ）

Write **nothing but** (＝*only*) the address on this side.

（この表面には住所姓名のみ書くこと）

He has **nothing but** (＝*only*) his salary to live on.

（彼はほかに収入がなくて給料だけで食っている）

〖注　意 1〗　**but** の次に来るものは名詞や代名詞に限ってはいない。

例：—

She **does nothing but cry** all day.

（彼女は一日中ただ泣くばかりだった）

**There is nothing for it but to** wait for an opportunity.

（機会を持つよりほかはない）

〖注　意 2〗　この形式でも、前の章の場合と等しく疑問をもって打消しに代えても同じことである。すなわち

　　What...but～？＝nothing but～

　　Who...but～？＝no one but～

のような関係となる。例：—

**What** is coal **but** a kind of stone?＝Coal is **nothing but** a kind of stone.

（石炭は石の一種でなく何か＝石の一種にほかならない）

**Who but** a fool would do such a thing?＝**No one but** a fool...

（ばかでなくては だれがそんなことをしよう）

**Whose** fault is it **but** your own?＝It is **no one's** fault **but** your own.

（だれの落ち度でもない、お前自身の落ち度だ）

**What** would one take him for **but** what he is?＝One would **not** take him for **anything but** what he is.

---

(100)　address [ədrés, ǽdres] あて名。

(あれだけの人間とほか何と人が見よう＝たれが見てもあれはあれだけの人間だ)

〖注 意 3〗 none は not one; not any の意味であるから単数複数いずれにも用いられる。しかし単複どちらでもいいような場合には複数として取り扱うのが今日の通例である。例：—

　**None** of my brothers **are** here.

したがって none but の場合にも

　**None** but the brave **deserve** the fair.

とするのが今日ふつうの用法である。ただし古いところなどにはもちろん単数に取り扱われた例もある。

〖注 意 4〗 but を only の意味の副詞として用いるのは、その前に否定詞が略されたものと見ることができる。

　There is **but** one God.＝There is **no** God **but** one.
　　(神はただ一人だけである)
　She is **but** a child.＝She is **nothing but** a child.
　　(彼女はほんのこどもだ)

---

**919.** So she moved again, in order that her son might see *none but* scholars and men of learning.

**920.** Pedagogues knew *no* way of imparting knowledge *but* by beating their pupils. Husbands, of decent station, were not ashamed to beat their wives.

**921.** Not a soul was in sight, and there was no time to go all the way to the village and give the alarm; *no one but* the little boy could avert the coming danger.

**922.** It is true that the ship itself was in a sense *nothing but* a floating bit of land, on which we could lead a life not sur-

---

919. **man of learning** 学問のある人。 920. **pedagogue** [pédəgɔ̀g] 児童教育者。**impart** 伝える。**decent** [díːsnt] ちゃんとした、上流の。**station** 地位。 921. **soul** 人間。 **alarm** 警報。 **avert** [əvə́ːt] そらす。 922. **floating bit** 浮かんでいる一塊。 **lead a life** 生活をする。

prisingly different from our customary one.

**923.** *Nothing but* a suicidal recklessness lies behind the slaughter. National Safety Council figures show that 75 percent of the fatal smashups occur on open, straightway roads.

**924.** *Nothing* comes out of the sack *but* what was in it.

**925.** One morning, Will, a thoughtless boy,
  Who could care for *naught but* play,
 Went out into the pleasant fields
  To pass an idle day.

**926.** The more carefully nature has been studied, the more widely has order been found to prevail, while what seemed disorder has proved to be *nothing but* complexity.

**927.** He must beg his way and he could do that *nowhere but* on the public road.

**928.** Out upon merry Christmas! *What*'s Christmas time to you *but* a time for paying bills without money; a time for finding yourself a year older, and not an hour richer? (*Dickens*)

**929.** *What* would one take him for *but* what he is? *What but* ruin can be the result of such a course of conduct?

**930.** On the topic of duty the entire people has *but* one mind. Any schoolboy will say to you, if questioned about this subject: "The duty which everybody must do is to help to make our country strong and wealthy, and to help to defend and

---

**customary** [kÁstəməri] 平常の。 **923. suicidal** [sjuisáidəl] 自殺的。 **recklessness** 無謀。 **slaughter** 殺人。 **figure** 統計などの数字。 **fatal** [féitl] 致命的。 **smashup** [smǽʃʌp] 大衝突。 **925. naught** [nɔːt]=nothing. **926. prevail** [privéil] 行きわたる。 **disorder** [disɔ́ːdə] 無秩序。 **prove** 結果としてわかる。 **complexity** [kəmpléksiti] 複雑。 **927. beg one's way** こじきをしながら行く。 **928. Out upon** まっぴらだ！ **Christmas** [krísməs] クリスマス。 **929. ruin** 破滅、没落。 **course of conduct** 行動の過程。 **930. topic** [tɔ́pik] 題目。 **defend** 防衛する。

preserve our national independence."

**931.** "Ours is *but* humble fare," said Duddlestone; "for, sir, I can offer you only roast beef and plum pudding."

**932.** Once or twice, some one of the party fancied that he saw in the distance the top of a palm tree; but no, it turned out to be *but* a little cloud upon the horizon.

**933.** In short, man was made for action, and life is a mere scene for the exercise of the mind. The most important occupations are, in a sense, *but* graver species of amusement, and so long as we take pleasure in the pursuit of an object, it matters *but* little that we attain it not, or that it fades when acquired.

**934.** A tool is *but* the extension of a man's hand, and a machine is *but* a complex tool. And he that invents a machine augments the power of a man and the well-being of mankind.

---

( 101 )

**Who should** come in **but** the man we were talking of?

【訳】 だれがはいってくるかと思えば うわさしていたその人だった。

〚解 説〛 Who...but?＝none but
What...but?＝nothing but

であることは前の節に説いたが、これにおどろきをあらわす should の伴なった場合には訳し方に手加減が必要である。すなわち

---

**preserve** 維持する。 **independence** [ìndipéndəns] 独立。 931. **fare** 食事。 932. **horizon** [həráizn] 水平線。 933. **in short** 要するに。 **exercise** 行使。 **grave** まじめな。 **pursuit** 追求。 **fade** 消えうせる。 934. **extension** [iksténʃən] 延長。 **augment** [ɔːgmént] 増加する。 **well-being** 福利。

「だれかと思えば…」
などと意外の意をあらわすがよい。もっとも none but, nothing but の意味はもちろん含まれている。類例:—

**What tax should** I pay **but** a million?
(いくら税金を出すと思う、百万円だからおどろくじゃないか＝おどろくなかれ税金百万円だ)

**Who should** break the law first of all **but** the lawmaker himself?
(だれが真っ先に法律を破るかと思えばほかならぬ法律をこしらえたそのご当人だ)

**What should** I see **but** the thing I was looking for?
(何が見えるかと思えば自分がさがしていたものだ)

〖注　意〗 should と would とで次のような差異が起こる:—

**Who should** do such a thing **but** himself?
(だれがそんなことをするかと思えば、ご当人だ)

**Who would** do such a thing **but** a fool?
(ばかでなくてだれがそんなことをするものか)

---

**935.**　Confusion on confusion, *who should* enter the room *but* our two great acquaintances from town?　　　(*Goldsmith*)

**936.**　*Who should* come posting to bring the news, *but* John himself?　　　(*Scott*)

**937.**　I was gazing after him with bitter thoughts in my mind, when *who should* touch me on the elbow *but* the little priest whom I have mentioned?　　　(*Doyle*)

**938.**　Passing through one of the principal streets, *whom should* I meet *but* our cousin to whom you first recommended me?

---

935. **confusion** [kənfjúːʒən] 混乱、狼狽(ばい)。　**acquaintance** 知人。　936. **post** [poust] 急ぐ。　937. **elbow** ひじ。**priest** [priːst] 僧。　938. **principal** 主要な。**cousin** [kʌ́zn] いとこ。**recommend** [rèkəménd] 推薦する。

( **102** )

(a) He is **anything but** a scholar.
(b) He is **all but** dead.

【訳】(a) 彼が学者なものか＝学者どころの話じゃない。
(b) 彼はもう死んだものといってもいいくらいだ。

〖解 説〗(a) **anything but**～

＝～のほかは何でもよいが～ばかりはいけない。

と強く～を打消す。たとえば I will do **anything but** that. と言えば、「ほかのことは何でもするがその事ばかりは まっぴら 御免をこうむる」という意味、すなわち I will *never* do that. を強く言ったものにすぎない。同様に He is **anything but** a scholar. は「豪傑とでも、善人とでも、何とでも言えようが、学者とばかりはとても言えない」ということで、次のように書きなおしてみることもできよう：—

=He is *not* a scholar, *whatever else* he *may* be.

=He is *no* scholar *at all*.

=He is *far from* being a scholar.

すなわち anything but は強い打消しということがわかる。類例：—

Though diligent, he is **anything but** prudent.

(彼は勉強家ではあるが、とても思慮深い人とは言えない)

He looked **anything but** sorry at the idea of leaving school.

(学校をさがるのだと聞いてもとんと悲しそうではなかった)

He will do **anything but** work.

(彼は働くということはどうしてもしない)

He will blame **anyone but** himself.

(彼は自分が悪いとはどうしてもいわない)

(b) 「**all but**＋形容詞(または動詞)」の結合では **all but**＝**almost** という副詞の働きをするものと見て「ほとんど～」「～といってもいいくらい」「～とはいわぬばかり」など訳して当たる。

---

(102) **prudent** [prúːdənt] 用心深い。

anything but~ では but の力が強くて「何でもいいが~ばかりはいけない」と取り除けに重きを置くに反し、all but~ では all の力が強く「~のほかは皆」あるいは「~はいけないがそのほかなら何でもよい」という心持ちになる。すなわち He is all but dead. は「dead といわれぬばかりでそのほかはすべての条件を具備している」という心持である。類例:—

He **all but** did it.

（彼はほとんどそれをせんばかりであった）

He is **all but** ruined.

（彼は破滅したといってもよいくらいだ）

He hated cruelty with a hatred **all but** cruel.

（彼は残酷といわぬばかりの憎しみをもって残酷を憎んだ）

〖注　意〗「**all but**＋名詞または代名詞」の結合では「~のほかはすべて」とふつうに訳してよい。but の次にくる代名詞は目的格でも主格でもよろしい。例:—

They are **all** wrong **but** *he* (or him).

（彼のほかは皆まちがっている）

---

**939.** The Bakers loved nothing so much as being surrounded by relatives and friends. It was not that they had plenty of money; they were *anything but* rich, and Mrs. Baker's little purse must have been emptied of its last sixpence many a time to provide such hospitality as they offered.

**940.** There are people who are ready to attend to *anybody's* business *but* their own.

**941.** He lays his poverty at *any one's* door *but* his own.

**942.** They are too tired to care for *anything but* bed.

**943.** Rev. Wibird Hawkin's sermons are *none of the shortest*,

939. **surround** 取り囲む。**relative** [rélətiv] 親類。**be emptied of ...** を出してからになる。**provide** 用意する。**hospitality** 歓待。 940. **ready** [rédi] よろこんで。**attend to** 勤める。 941. **lay at the door of ...** のせいにする。 943. **Rev.** (=Reverend) [révərənd] 尊敬すべき、これは僧侶の尊称。

*whatever else they may be.* (*T. B. Aldrich*)

**944.** The flames seem a long way off at first; but they come nearer and nearer, until the poor elephants see fires on *all* sides of them *but* one.

**945.** Just now I stand on *anything but* good terms with my father, who keeps me short of cash.

**946.** Cromwell was king in *all but* name, and indeed had more power than any king since Henry VIII.

**947.** In England this kind of teaching is *all but* unknown.

**948.** I remember I *all but* worshipped him with his easy swagger and lordly air. (*Dickens*)

**949.** It was kept quiet at the time, and is forgotten now by *all but* a few old fellows like me.

**950.** The boy stood on the burning deck,
Whence *all but* he had fled. (*Mrs. Hemans*)

---

### (103)

> There is **no** rule **but** has exceptions.

【訳】 例外の無い規則はない。

〖解　説〗 上の例の **but** は一種の関係代名詞であって

$$\text{but} = \begin{cases} \text{who+not} \\ \text{that+not} \\ \text{which+not} \end{cases}$$

として解することができる。すなわち

There is **no** rule **but** has exceptions.
＝**Every** rule has exceptions.

---

945. **terms** [tə:mz] 間がら。**short of** ...が不足して。 948. **worship** [wə́:ʃip] 崇拝する。 **swagger** [swǽgə] 大いばり。 **air** 様子、態度。

＝どんな規則でも例外はある。

**Nobody but** has his faults.
＝There is **nobody who** has **not** his faults.
＝**Nobody** is **without** his faults.
＝**Everybody** has his faults.
＝欠点のない人はない、どんな人にも欠点はある。

〖注　意 1〗 but が関係代名詞として用いられる場合はその先行詞に必ず打消しが伴なっているが、その打消しは往々疑問に変わる。例：―

**Who** [is there] **but** [he] knows it?
＝[There is] **No** one **but** [he] knows it.
＝**Everybody** knows it.
＝それを知らない者はない。

〖注　意 2〗 but 以下が別に主語を備えている場合の but は関係代名詞ではなくて接続詞であるが、この場合にも **but＝that＋not** と見てたいてい解釈がつく、しかしこの場合の that は関係代名詞ではない。例：―

**Who** knows **but** it may come true?
＝**No** one knows **that** it may **not** come true.
＝それが本当にならないとだれが知ろう、本当になるかもしれないじゃないか。

---

**951.**　There is*n't* a thing beneath our feet, *but* teaches some lesson short and sweet.

**952.**　There was *not* a soul within the fort *but* was prepared for the worst.

**953.**　In London there is *not* even a cobbler *but* has a piano in his back parlour.　　　　　　　　　　　　　　(*Max O'Rell*)

**954.**　There is *no* law *but* has a hole in it if one could find it out.　　　　　　　　　　　　　　　　　　　　　(*Proverb*)

**955.**　There is *no* profession, however low in the opinion of

---

952. **fort** とりで。　**worst** [wə:st] 最悪のこと。　953. **cobbler** [kɔ́blə] 靴なおし。　**parlour** [pάːlə] 居間。これはイギリスの用法。

the world, *but* has been honoured with earth's greatest and worthiest.

**956.** To men at the end of the fifteenth century there was *scarcely* a year *but* brought another bit of received and recognized thinking to the scrap-heap; *scarcely* a year *but* some new discovery found itself surpassed and in its turn discarded, or lessened in significance by something still more new. (名古屋大)

---

( 104 )

> There is **nothing so** difficult **but** it becomes easy by practice.

【訳】 どんなむずかしいことでも慣れればやさしくなる。

〖解 説〗 **not so...but** の形式においても **but=that+not** として解することができる。しかし **however...may** の形になおして見るといっそうわかりやすい、すなわち上の例は次のように書きなおすことができる。

There is **nothing so** difficult **that** it does **not** become easy by practice.
**However** difficult a thing **may** be, it becomes easy by practice.
=練習によってたやすくならないほどむずかしいことはない、どんなにむずかしくとも練習によってたやすくなる。

類例:—

**No** one **is so** old **but** he may learn.
**No** one **is so** old **that** he may **not** learn.
**However** old a man **may** be, he may learn.
=もう学問はできないというほどの老人はない、どんな老人でも学問はできる。

---

955. **be honoured** 名誉を与えられる。 956. **received and recognized** 認められて通用していた。 **scrap-heap** ごみため。 **surpass** ...よりまさる。 **in its turn** こんどはそれの番で。 **discard** 捨てる。 **significance** 意義。

【注 意】 前の章の but=that+not の that は関係代名詞で、that 以下は先行詞を修飾する形容詞節であるが、本章の but=that+not の that は接続詞で、that 以下は so を修飾する副詞節である。

---

**957.** *No* man is *so* old, *but* thinks he may yet live another year. *(Proverb)*

**958.** *No* beast *so* fierce *but* has some touch of pity.

*(Shakespeare)*

**959.** As a form of literature a newspaper lacks, it is true, the element of permanence; but the ideas with which it seeks to inspire its readers produce an effect that is lasting. It is the only kind of a reading that is almost universal. *No* one is *so* occupied with the business of his calling *but* he finds time to read the newspaper.

**960.** *Hardly* shall you find any one *so* bad *but* he desires the credit of being thought good.

**961.** There is *no* act, however trivial, *but* has its train of consequences, as there is *no* hair *so* small *but* casts its shadow.

**962.** Life is *not so* short *but that* there is always time enough for courtesy.

---

**(105)**

{ I **never** see you **but** I think of my brother.
{ I **never** see you **without** thinking of my brother.

---

958. **touch** [tʌtʃ] 少量。  959. **permanence** [pə́:mənəns] 永続性。 **inspire** [inspáiə] 吹き込む。  **universal** 普遍的な。 **be occupied** 心を占領されている。 **calling** [kɔ́:liŋ] 天職。  960. **credit** 信望。  961. **trivial** [tríviəl] つまらぬ。 **train of consequences** 尾をひく結果。  962. **courtesy** [kə́:tisi] 礼節。

【訳】 ぼくは君を見るときっと弟のことを思い出す。

〖解　説〗　never...but～
　　　　　　＝never...without～ing
　　　　　　＝when...always～
　　　　　　＝...すれば必ず～

ゆえに上の例文は次のように言い換えることができる。

　　*When* I see you, I *always* think of my brother.

なお **(99)** と比較せよ：―

- I **cannot but laugh** to hear such a story.
- I **cannot help laughing** to hear such a story.
- ＝そんな話を聞いて笑わずにはいられない。

- I **never hear** such a story **but** I **laugh.**
- I **never hear** such a story **without laughing.**
- ＝そんな話を聞けばきっと笑う。

〖注　意 1〗 never の場所に他の打消し、cannot, seldom などのくる場合もある。例：―

　　I *seldom* went out *but* I met him.

　　(外へ出て彼に会わないことはめったになかった――外へ出るとたいてい彼に会った)

〖注　意 2〗 without の次に名詞の来た場合も同じように解釈ができる。

---

**963.** It *never* rains *but* it pours. 　　　　　　　　(*Proverb*)

**964.** I was a passionate, headstrong boy; and *never* did this frame of temper come upon me, *but* I seemed to see her mild, tearful eyes full upon me, just as she used to look in life.

**965.** I can *never* hear certain airs of Mozart and Handel *without* seeming to catch an echo of that sweet voice in which

---

963. **pour** [pɔː] そそぐ。　964. **passionate** [pǽʃənit] 熱情的、怒りやすい。**headstrong** [hédstrɔŋ] わがままな。**frame** 心の状態。**in life** 生存中。　965. **air** 曲。**echo** [ékou] 反響。

I first learnt to love them. (東大)

**966.** I *never* heard or saw the introductory words, "Without vanity I may say," &c., *but* some vain thing immediately followed.

**967.** It is an extraordinary thing, but I *never* knew a doctor called into any case yet, *but what* it transpired that another day's delay would have rendered cure hopeless.

**968.** The smallest bird *cannot* light upon the greatest tree *without* sending a shock to its most distant fibre; every mind is at times no less sensitive to the most trifling words.

**969.** He had grown a great boy and had gained wisdom by experience; for it was one of his peculiarities that *no* incident ever happened to him *without* teaching him some valuable lesson. Thus he generally profited more by his misfortunes than many people do by the most favorable events that could befall.

**970.** It is surely *not* to be observed *without* indignation that men may be found of minds mean enough to be satisfied with this treatment.

**971.** *No one* can read the heroic deeds of brave men grappling with danger and death, *without* a feeling of respect and admiration; but the heroic deeds are always the fruit of toil and self-sacrifice.

---

966. **introductory** [intrədʌ́ktəri] 前置きの。 **vanity** うぬぼれ、自慢。 967. **but what**=but. **transpire** [trænspáiə] 起こる。 **delay** [diléi] 遅延。 **render cure hopeless** 治療を絶望ならしめる。 968. **light** とまる。 **fibre** [fáibə] 繊維、末梢。 969. **peculiarity** [pikjù:liǽriti] 特長。 **incident** [ínsidənt] 出来事。 **profit by** ...で益する。 **misfortune** [misfɔ́:tʃən] 不幸。 **favorable** 好都合な。 **befall** [bifɔ́:l] (事が)起こる。 970. **indignation** [ìndignéiʃən] 憤慨。 **of minds** は men にかかる「心をもった人」となる。 **mean** いやしい、minds の修飾。 971. **heroic** [hiróuik] 英雄的。 **grapple with** ...と組み討ちする。 **fruit** [fru:t] 結果。 **toil** 労苦。 **sacrifice** [sǽkrifais] 犠牲。

**972.**　One *cannot* look at Emerson's picture *without* feeling that he was not only wise but good.　Look at the face thoughtfully.　It is a face to love and trust.　You will want to count this man among your friends.

**973.**　Emerson said: "Happiness is perfume you *cannot* pour on others *without* getting a few drops on your self."

(お茶の水女子大)

**974.**　Its [*i.e.* the jaguar's] roar produces terror and confusion among them and causes them to flee in every direction.　It is *never* heard by the natives *without* a feeling of fear, and no wonder; for a year does *not* pass *without* a number of these people falling victims to its ferocity.

**975.**　*No* man *can* work long at any trade *without* being brought to consider much whether that which he is daily doing tends to evil or to good.

(一橋大)

---

( 106 )

> There is **no** rule that has **not** exceptions.

【訳】　例外のない規則はない＝どんな規則にも例外はある。

〚解　説〛　打消しが二つ重なると相殺(そうさい)して肯定の意になることはいうまでもない。すなわち

　　There is **no** rule that **has not** exceptions.

　　＝**Every** rule **has** exceptions.

である。ここにはこういう類の文を集めてみた。

---

972. picture [píktʃə] 肖像画。　　thoughtfully [θɔ́:tfuli] 注意深く。　　973. perfume [pə́:fju:m] 香水。　　974. jaguar [dʒǽgwɑ:] アメリカとら。　roar うなりごえ。　fall a victim to ...の犠牲となる。　ferocity [fərɔ́siti] 猛悪。　975. be brought to ...するように仕向けられる。

〖注 意〗 以下に掲げる例題中 that...no, who...not はたいてい公式 (103) に述べた but に還元することができる。

---

**976.** It is well known that time once past never returns, and that the moment which is lost is lost for ever. Time therefore ought, above all other kinds of property, to be free from invasion; and yet there is *no man who does not* claim the power of wasting that time which is the right of others.

**977.** We are in a world where work is the condition of life. *Not* a meal can be had by any man *that* someone has *not* worked to produce. Those who work deserve to eat; those who do not work deserve to starve. There are but three ways of living: by working, by stealing, or by begging.

**978.** *No man ever* entered Mr. Pitt's closet *who did not* feel himself a braver man when he came out.

**979.** Just as good fortune is not necessarily all gain, so ill fortune is not necessarily all loss. Rome conquered Greece, but Greek civilisation overcame Roman civilisation and, as a great writer said, "*nothing* moves today in Europe which is *not* Greek in origin."

**980.** Facility comes by labour. *Nothing* seems easy, not even walking, *that was not* difficult at first.

**981.** But *no man* has ever made his mark on the world *who*

---

976. once past ひとたび過ぎ去った、time を修飾する。 invasion [invéiʒən] 侵犯。 claim 主張する。 977. deserve [dizə́:v] 値する。 starve [stɑ:v] 飢える。 978. closet [klɔ́zit] 面会室。 979. gain [gein] 獲得。 Rome [roum] ローマ。 Greece [gri:s] ギリシア。 Roman [róumən] ローマの。 Greek [gri:k] ギリシアの。 in origin 起源が。 980. facility [fəsíliti] 容易。 981. make one's mark 印をつける、足跡を残す。

*was not* possessed by some master passion.

**982.** There is *scarcely* a page of the history or lighter literature of the seventeenth century which *does not* contain some proof that our ancestors were less humane than their posterity.

**983.** So much are men enamoured of their miserable lives, that there is *no* condition so wretched to which they are *not* willing to submit, provided they may live. (*Montaigne*)

( 107 )

(a) **But for** his idleness, he would be a good student.
(b) **But that** he prevented me, I would have replied.

【訳】（a）なまけさえしなければいい生徒だが。
　　（b）彼がとめなければ答えたのであったのに。

〖解　説〗（a）but for～
　　　　　　＝ { if it were not for～
　　　　　　　　if it had not been for～
　　　　（b）but that...
　　　　　　＝but for the fact that...

この二つは共に仮定法過去または過去完了の代用である。主節がwould be, should be のような形になるときの but for; but that は仮定法過去の代用で、「...によらなければ...なのに」と現在に訳し、主節が would have been; should have been のような形のときの but for; but that は仮定法過去完了の代用で、「...によらなかったなら...であったものを」と過去に訳す。類例：—

---

**be possessed by** ...にとりつかれる。**master** 支配的な。**982. proof** 証拠。**humane** [hju:méin] 人情のある。**posterity** 子孫。**983. enamour** [inǽmə] 心を奪う。**wretched** [rétʃid] あわれな。**submit** [səbmít] 服従する、甘受する。**provided**＝if.
　(107) **prevent** [privént] さまたげる。

> **But for** your aid, I should have failed.
> =**If it had not been for** your aid, ...
> **But that you aided me,** I should have failed.
> =**If you had not aided me,** ...
> =君が助けてくれなかったら、ぼくは失敗するのだった。

I should have started **but that** the weather was so bad.
（天気がそんなに悪くなけりゃ出発したのだが）

---

**984.** *But for* his cheerfulness, he *could* never, with so delicate a frame, *have got* through so vast an amount of self-imposed work.

**985.** The combination of frugality, industry and genius *would* soon *have made* him successful *but for* the wretched health which repeatedly disabled him for work while it multiplied his expenses.

**986.** Thirty or forty feet of its tail was lying on the ground, like a fallen tree, and she thought she could climb it, but she was mistaken; when she got to the steep place it was too slick and down she came, and *would have hurt* herself *but for* me.

(Mark Twain)

**987.** The only two specimens of bird so far found were so unlike any ordinary bird in their construction that, if *it were not for* the lucky accident of their having been embedded in such fine mud that the imprint of their feathers is still preserved to us, we *should have been* in doubt as to whether they were birds at all.

(Julian S. Huxley)

---

984. **delicate** かよわい。 **frame** 体格。 **get through** やりとげる。 **self-imposed** 自分で課した。 985. **frugality** [fruːgǽliti] 倹約。 **disable** 無能力にする。 **multiply** 増す。 986. **slick** すべすべした。 **hurt oneself** けがをする。 987. **specimen** [spésimin] 標本。 **embed** [imbéd] 埋める。 **mud** 泥土。 **imprint** こん跡。 **preserve** 保存する。 **as to** ...について。

**988.** On account of his lameness he had to allow himself plenty of time for the walk to the station; and all *would have been* well, *but that*, just as he was about to start, in stepped a friend, who came to have a talk with him.

**989.** It *would* soon *die* of hunger *but for* the stores which it had laid up in the previous autumn.

**990.** Life *would be* short, *but that* hope prolongs it.

**991.** She *would have sent* away Miss Sharp, *but that* she was bound to her under a forfeit. (*Thackeray*)

---

### (108)

> I *do not deny* **but that** I know him.

【訳】 私は彼を知らないとはいわない。

〖解 説〗 doubt, deny などの打消し、(あるいは疑問)につづく場合の but; but that; but what は単に that に等しい。類例:—

    I **do not deny but that** he is diligent.
      (彼が勤勉であるということを否認はしない)
    **Nothing shall hinder but that** I will accomplish my purpose.
    =Nothing shall hinder me from accomplishing my purpose.
      (万難を排しても目的を遂げる)

〖注 意〗 **no fear but (that)** の形はここに説くものと似ているが、その **but (that)** は that...not と見るべきものである。比較:—

    There is **no fear but that** he will succeed.
      (彼が成功しないという心配はない——きっと彼は成功する)
    I do **not doubt but that** he will succeed.
      (ぼくは彼が成功するということを疑わない)

---

988. **lameness** [léimnis] 跛(ちんば)。 **allow oneself** 余裕を見ておく。 989. **die of hunger** 飢え死にする。of は原因を示す。 991. **be bound to** ...にしばりつけられる。 **under a forfeit** [fɔ́:fit] (違約すれば)罰金を払う条件で。

**992.** As he directed his looks and conversation to Olivia, it was *no longer doubted but that* she was the object that induced him to be our visitor.

**993.** Be that as it may, there was *little doubt but that* the panther would have made a leap, as soon as the intervening fire had burned down.

**994.** In the closing months of 1909 there was a sudden development in Tokyo and Yokohama of the use of solid rubber tyres for jinrikisha and there was *little doubt but that* the fashion would spread to nearly all the large towns in the provinces.

**995.** I have heard much of you of late: and I *cannot doubt but* you have also heard of me. I am Major O'Rooke. (*Stevenson*)

**996.** His [*i.e.* Newton's] old grandmother, I suppose, was never weary of talking about him. "He'll make a capital workman one of these days," she would probably say. "*No fear but what* Isaac will do well in the world and be a rich man before he dies."
(*Hawthorne*)

**997.** Better still, let a man walk for an hour before bed, or have a pleasant chat with a chum, and then there can be *no fear but that* nature, left to herself, will find, without artifice, the measure of rest that she requires.
(*Brackie*)

---

(108) **hinder** さまたげる。 992. **direct** 向ける。 **object** もの、対象物。**induce** 誘って...する。 993. **panther** [pǽnθə] ひょう。 **leap** 飛びかかること。 **intervene** [ìntəvíːn] 間に立つ。 994. **solid** 中がうつろでない。 **rubber** [rʌ́bə] ゴム。 **tyre** [táiə] タイヤ。 995. **major** [méidʒə] 陸軍少佐。 996. **weary** [wíəri] あきる。 **make** なる。 **capital** りっぱな。 **Isaac** [áizək]. **do well** 出世する。 997. **Better still** もっとよいことに。 **chum** [tʃʌm] 仲よし。**left to herself** 放任されていると。 **artifice** [ɑ́ːtifis] 技巧。 **measure** [méʒə] 程度。 **require** [rikwáiə] 要する。

## (109)

> **It is true** its flower is beautiful, **but** it bears no fruit.

【訳】 なるほどその花は美しいが、実を持たない。

〖解説〗 (it is) true ┐
　　　　 indeed　　 │　　┌ but...
　　　　 to be sure ├ ...┤
　　　　 I admit　　 ┘　　└ and yet

＝なるほど...であるがしかし...。

it is true のかわりに **no doubt** を用い、to be sure の意味で **certainly** を用い、また I admit の意味で **yes** を用いることなどもある。

類例:—

　**Indeed** he is old, **but** he is still strong.
　　(なるほど年は取っているが、まだ丈夫だ)
　**It is true** he is young, **but** he is prudent for his age.
　　(なるほど年は若いがそのわりに思慮が深い)

---

**998.** *It is true* that a sense of duty may at times render it necessary for you to do that which is displeasing to your companions. *But* if it be seen that you have a kind spirit, that you are above selfishness, that you are willing to make sacrifices of your own personal convenience to promote the happiness of your associates, you will never be in want of friends.

**999.** Without that knowledge or in the belief that two and two may in a certain environment make five, you may *indeed* upset a government, *but* you will never make an engine, nor, if

---

998. render=make.　displeasing [displí:ziŋ] 不愉快な。　**above selfishness** [sélfiʃnis] 利己主義を超越して。**convenience** 便宜。**associate** [əsóuʃieit] 仲間。**be in want of** ...に不自由する。　999. **in the belief that** ...ということを信じていても。**environment** [inváiərənmənt] 情況。**upset** 転覆する。

you were in possession of a ship, could you bring it into any port in the world. (九州大)

**1000.** *True*, there has been but one Napoleon; *but*, on the other hand, the Alps that oppose the progress of the average American youth are not as high or dangerous as the summits crossed by the Corsican.

**1001.** For my part, I really like the wet season. It keeps us within, *to be sure*, rather more than is quite agreeable; *but* then we are at least awake and alive there, and the world out of doors is so much the pleasanter when we can get abroad.

**1002.** A man who is careless and untidy about his clothes and personal appearance is often careless about other things. Great men, *it is true*, are sometimes very careless about their appearance; *but* they are great in spite of this and not in consequence of it.

**1003.** Every man has within himself a gold mine whose riches are limited only by his own industry. *It is true*, it sometimes happens that industry does not avail, if a man lacks that something which, for want of a better name, we call luck.

**1004.** What is a great love of books? It is something like a personal introduction to the great and good men of all past time. Books, *it is true*, are silent as you see them on their shelves; *but* silent as they are, when I enter a library I feel

---

**port** 港。 **1000. Napoleon** [nəpóuljən]。 **oppose the progress** 前進に立ち向う。 **average** [ǽvəridʒ] 平均の、ふつうの。 **summit** 頂上。 **cross** 越える。 **Corsican** [kɔ́:sikən] コルシカ人。 **1001. alive** [əláiv] 生き生きして(いる)。 **get abroad** [əbrɔ́:d] 外に出る。 **1002. untidy** [ʌntáidi] だらしない。 **in consequence of ...** の結果として。 **1003. mine** 鉱山。 **avail** [əvéil] 効果がある。 **for want of ...** がないため。 **1004. introduction** [ìntrədʌ́kʃən] 紹介。 **shelves** [ʃelvz] shelf (棚)の複数。

almost as if the dead were present, and I know if I put questions to these books they will answer me.

---

( 110 )

(a) He has **both** experience **and** scholarship.
(b) He has experience **as well as** scholarship.
(c) He has **not only** scholarship, **but also** experience.

【訳】(a) 彼は経験と学問とふたつながら持っている。
(b) 彼は学問もあるが、また等しく経験もある。
(c) 彼は学問があるばかりでなく経験もある。

〖解 説〗 二つの語句を結ぶにはただ and だけをもって **A and B** として足りるのであるが、「両方とも」と強くいうときには both, alike, at once などを加えて

(a) **both A and B**=A と B とふたつながら
　　**alike A and B**=A と B と一様に
　　**at once A and B**=同時に A と B と

などといい、また両者の間に軽重を付けて、A を少し重く見るときは

(b) **A as well as B**=B と等しく A も

といい、なおいっそう A を強くいうときには

(c) **not** $\begin{Bmatrix} \text{merely} \\ \text{only} \end{Bmatrix}$ **B but** $\begin{Bmatrix} \text{likewise} \\ \text{also} \end{Bmatrix}$ **A**=B のみならず A もまた

とする。(b) と (c) とにおいて軽重の順序が転倒することに注意を要する。しかし (b) においては (c) におけるほど軽重がいちじるしくない。

類例:—

---

**the dead** 死んだ人々。
(110) **experience** [ikspíəriəns] 経験。**scholarship** [skɔ́ləʃip] 学識、学問。**merely** [míəli] 単に。**likewise** [láikwaiz] 同じく。

This book is $\begin{cases} \text{both} \\ \text{alike} \\ \text{at once} \end{cases}$ interesting **and** instructive.

This book is instructive **as well as** interesting.
This book is **not only** interesting **but also** instructive.
＝この本はおもしろくてしかもまたためになる。
Games give moral **as well as** physical health.
(遊戯は肉体の健康のみならず精神の健全をも与える)

---

**1005.** In every sphere of art and knowledge, *as well as* in practical business, how often we find men wasting their energies, and spending powers that in the right lines would produce great result for themselves and the world.

**1006.** The man who does not work, and thinks himself above it is to be pitied *as well as* condemned. Nothing can be more terrible than ignorance and luxury.

**1007.** In the first place, he made out a scheme of his travels; he procured maps, read books, and after mature deliberation, adopted a certain route, as most likely to afford him pleasure *as well as* instruction.

**1008.** In the middle of the day when the sun is hottest the sand dazzles the eyes of the traveller, as if another sun were beneath the sand *as well as* one above.

**1009.** No food of any kind should be taken within two hours after a meal and the interval between regular meals should be

---

moral [mɔ́rəl] 精神的。　physical [fízikəl] 身体上の。　1005. sphere 領域。 in the right lines 正しい方面に使えば。　1006. above it 働くほど身分がいやしくない。condemn [kəndém] 非難する。　luxury [lʌ́kʃuri] ぜいたく。　1007. scheme [ski:m] 案。　procure [prəkjúə] 手に入れる。　mature [mətʃúə] 慎重な。　deliberation 熟慮。adopt 採用する、選ぶ。　route [ru:t] 道筋。　afford 与える。　1008. dazzle [dǽzl] 目をくらます。　1009. interval [íntəvəl] 間隔。

four hours at least. Supper should be taken two hours before going to sleep, that the stomach, *as well as* the other parts of the body, may have rest while we are asleep.

**1010.** I believe that plain living is a Christian duty, *as well as* a patriotic duty. The French understand the art of living much better than we do, and they avoid waste almost instinctively.

**1011.** The requisites of health are plain enough: regular habits, daily exercise, cleanliness, and moderation in all things, —in eating *as well as* in drinking—would keep most people well.

**1012.** Immense capacities for good *as well as* for bad are found in his nature. It rests with circumstances to develop either the one or the other.

**1013.** A brilliant career was opened up for the boys, who had inherited all their father's brave *as well as* their mother's gentle nature.

**1014.** So far as people who have no ear for music are concerned, it would be a waste of time and money, *as well as* a source of continual irritation to themselves, and to others, for them to try to learn music. (埼大)

**1015.** It is easy to say that servants should be treated well *not only* because humanity requires it, *but* because they will otherwise be unpleasant and dishonest servants. (慶応大)

---

stomach [stʌ́mək] 胃。 1010. plain 簡素な。 patriotic 愛国的な。 waste 浪費。 instinctively 本能的に。  1011. requisite [rékwizit] 必要なもの。 cleanliness [klénlinis] 清潔。 moderation [mɔ̀dəréiʃən] 適度。 well 健康に。 1012. immense [iméns] 莫大な。 capacity [kəpǽsiti] 能力。 rest with ...の いかんによる、...次第だ。 1013. career 前途。 inherit 承け継ぐ。 1014. it は for them to try ...を代表する。 irritation [ìritéiʃən] いらだち。 1015. treat 待遇する。 humanity 慈愛。

**1016.** For my own part, I have always gained the most profit, and the most pleasure also, from the books which have made me think the most; and when the difficulties have once been overcome, these are the books which have struck the deepest root, *not only* in my memory and understanding, *but likewise* in my affection.

**1017.** I attended a number of classes, and I was *both* impressed *and* depressed by the strong discipline which seemed to regulate the life of the school. (*Merle Fainsod*)

**1018.** It was above all on account of its freedom that England became so famous in the eighteenth century. Continental observers found in it *both* the model of a free state *and* the home of personal and individual liberty.

**1019.** Whether you are rich or poor, never allow yourself to owe any man anything. What you cannot afford to buy, do without. This is entirely a matter of habit, and those who fail to form the habit *not only* injure others, *but* lay up a store of unhappiness for themselves.

**1020.** The stranger's conversation, which was *at once* pleasing *and* instructive, induced me to wish for continuance of it; but it was now high time to retire and take refreshment against the fatigues of the following day.

---

**1016. struck** < strike [根を]おろす。 **affection** [əfékʃən] 愛情。 **1017. depress** ゆううつにする。 **discipline** 規律。 **regulate** 規則でしばる。 **1018. continental** 大陸の。 **observer** 観察者。 **1019. allow** [əláu] 放任する。 **owe** 借りる。 **afford** 余裕がある。 **injure** [índʒə] 害する。 **lay up** 蓄積する。 **1020. stranger** [stréindʒə] 見知らぬ人。 **induce** 勧誘する。 **continuance** [kəntínjuəns] 継続。 **high time** とっくに...すべき時間。 **retire**=go to bed. **refreshment** 休息。 **against** 備えて。 **fatigue** [fətí:g] 疲労。

## (111)

(a) **Not that** I dislike the task, **but that** I am unequal to it.
(b) The mountain is **not** valuable **because** it is high.

【訳】 (a) 仕事がいや<u>というわけではない</u>、その仕事に耐えない<u>から</u>です。
　　　(b) 山は高い<u>から</u>と言ってとうといのではない。

〖解説〗 (a) **not that...but that** (or **because**)...
　　　　　　=...のゆえでなく...のゆえである。
この形式では **that=because** である。

〖注意1〗 例文 not that の前に it is を補ってみよ。この that が because の意になるのは次の経路による:—

*How is it that* you wish to resign?
　(君が辞職したいというのはどういうわけか)
*Is it that* you have anything to complain of?
　(何か不平でもあるからか)
*It is not that* I am dissatisfied, *but that* I have my own business to attend to.
　(不平があるわけではない、しなければならない自分の仕事があるからだ)

〖注意2〗 not that は but that などを伴わずに独立に用いられることがある。それは it is not to be inferred, however, that と説明される。すなわち、「けれども...というわけではない」となる。

(b) **because...** が (1) 主節全体にかかる場合は「...なるがゆえに...」と解すればよろしい。しかし (2) **because...** が全文にかかるのではなくある一語にかかり、主節に打消しのある場合には「...からと

---

(111) **resign** [rizáin] 辞職する。 **business** [bíznis] 仕事。 **infer** 推論する。

いって...ではない」というふうに訳さねばならない。比較：—

> The mountain is valuable **because** it has trees.
> (山は木があるがゆえにとうとい)
> The mountain is **not** valuable **because** it is high.
> (山は高いからといってとうといのではない)

> People despised him, **because** he is poorly dressed.
> (彼の身なりが見すぼらしいから人が軽蔑する)
> I do **not** despise him **because** he is poorly dressed.
> (彼の身なりが悪いからといって私は彼を軽蔑しない)

〖注意〗 主節に打消しがあっても必ずしも (2) の意味でないことがある。たとえば、

I did **not** go, **because** I was ill.
(病気だったから行かなかった)

こういう場合にはたいてい because の前がコンマで切れている。

---

**1021.** *Not that* I loved Cæsar less, *but that* I loved Rome more. (*Shakespeare*)

**1022.** I played all the principal parts myself—*not that* I was a finer actor than the other boys, *but because* I owned the establishment.

**1023.** He said he hoped he *wasn't* afraid to trust as rich a gentleman as I was, merely *because* I was of a merry disposition, and chose to play larks on the public in the matter of dress. (*Mark Twain*)

**1024.** Men love and honour these heroes *not because* they were perfect in their character and life, *but because* they were brave, unselfish, and were able to do splendid deeds.

---

1021. **Cæsar** [síːzə]. 1022. **part** 役。**own** 所有する。**establishment** [istǽbliʃmənt] 建造物。 1023. **disposition** 気質。**play larks on** ...をからかう。 1024. **hero** [híərou] 英雄。**unselfish** [ʌnsélfiʃ] 非利己的。

**1025.** *Because* a lad does not happen to be strong, it does *not* necessarily follow that a sea life would not suit him. A sea life may be the very thing required to make a strong man of him.

**1026.** Birds are naturally the most joyous creatures in the world. *Not that* when you see or hear them they always give you pleasure, *but that* they feel joy more than any other animal. The other animals commonly look serious and grave; and many of them even appear melancholy. But birds for the most part show themselves extremely joyous by their movements and by their aspect.

**1027.** In some senses the balance of the world is about to be altered. It is not *merely that* distance, as measured by units of time, will be drastically diminished, or *that* backwoods towns may find themselves on a busy traffic lane, or *that* the equivalent of lighthouses will have to be maintained far out in the midst of the greatest oceans as outposts of Empire.

**1028.** We not longer live in obedience to a guidebook, but have made a new map of the place for ourselves in which many sights that the guidebook exalts are left out and many things not mentioned in the guidebook stand out as prominently as museums and cathedrals. *Not that* I would speak ill of guidebooks.

(鳥取大)

---

1025. **it does not follow that** …ということにはならない。 **suit** 適する。 **required** 必要とする。thing の修飾。 1026. **naturally** [nǽtʃrəli] 生まれつき。 **melancholy** [mélənkəli] ものがなしい、陰気な。 **for the most part** たいがい。 **extremely** 極度に。 1027. **unit** 単位。 **drastically** 極端に。 **backwoods** 奥地の。 **equivalent** [ikwívələnt] 同等の物。 **be maintained** 維持される。 **outpost** 前哨(ｼｮｳ)。 1028. **exalt** [igzɔ́:lt] 激賞する。 **be left out** とりのけられる。 **prominently** きわだった。 **museum** [mju:zíəm] 博物館。 **cathedral** [kəθí:drəl] 大聖堂。

## (112)

> It is an ill wind that blows nobody good.

【訳】 甲の損は乙の得。

【解説】 原文は直訳すれば、「だれにも益を吹き送らない風は悪い風である」となるが、言外に、「そういう悪い風はない、どんな悪い風でも必ずだれかに益を与えるものだ」という意味を含む。出船の逆風は入船の順風、病気がはやれば医者が繁昌し、大火事があればトタン屋や材木屋がもうかるといった工合に、どんなわざわいでも必ずだれかに利益を与えるものだということを教えるのがこの諺である。諺にはこの形式を取るものが多いが、いつも言外の意味を主とするのである。たとえば、It is a wise man that never makes mistakes. (けっして間違いをしないのは賢い人である) というのは、「そんな賢い人はない、どんな賢い人にも千慮の一失はまぬかれない」というのが主意である。類例:—

It is a skilful workman that never blunders.
(弘法にも筆の誤り)

It is a long lane that has no turning.
(どんな長い道でも必ず曲がることがある——人事にも曲折がある、不幸ばかりつづくものではない)

It is a wise father that knows his own child.
(どんな賢い父でも自分の子供は見誤るものだ——親の慾目、親ばか)

It is a good divine that follows his own instructions.
(どんな名僧でも自分が人に教えるとおりを身に行ないはしないものだ——ぼうずの不身持)

It is a wise physician that follows his own directions.
(医者の不養生)

It is a bad action (that) success cannot justify.
(どんな悪い行ないでも成功すれば正しいことになる——勝てば官軍負ければ賊)

---

(112) **blunder** 大失敗。 **lane** 小路。 **divine** [diváin] 神学者。 **directions** さしず。 **justify** [dʒʌ́stifai] 正当とする。

**1029.**　The night is long that never finds the day.

*(Shakespeare)*

**1030.**　It is a good horse that never stumbles and a good wife that never grumbles.　　　　*(Proverb)*

**1031.**　If money comes in slowly at first, do not be discouraged; it is a long lane which has no turning; and if it happens that money at first comes easily, do not spend it all, but lay up some for a rainy day, remembering that good lanes have their turnings as well as bad ones; and that as time goes on you will probably have more and more demands on your purse. Many a man in business has been ruined by being too fortunate at first.

---

1030. **stumble** つまずく。 **grumble** [grʌ́mbl] 不平をいう。 1031. **discourage** [diskʌ́ridʒ] 失望させる。 **lay up** 貯える。 **fortunate** [fɔ́ːtjunit] 幸運で。

# 新々英文解釈研究

## 解 答 篇

### ( 1 )

**1.** 世界を支配する者は刻苦勉励骨身をおしまぬ人たちである。すぐれた政治家で勤勉家でない者はいまだかつてないのである。

〖注〗 **a statesman of eminence**=an eminent statesman. **not...but** 公式 (103) 参照。 **a man of industry**=an industrious man.

**2.** 感情の強い熱情的な人にとって、清純を守る唯一の方法は、凡俗なものとの個人的接触をたえず本能的に避けることである。

〖注〗 **shrink from...**「...を避ける」「...をはばかる」。 **what**=that which (30) 参照。

**3.** 真の天才とは、何にでも適する大きな才能を、たまたまある特定の方向に注いだ人のことである。

**4.** 彼は貧困になるにつれ前後の考えがなくなって、口には分別のあるような事を言いながら、なすことは ばか者のすることであった。

〖注〗 **sense** は「常識」「分別」など、類例:—He has *good sense*. (彼は分別がある=物がわかっている) He lacks *common sense*. (彼は常識がない) **those of...**=the actions of... (27) 参照。

**5.** いかなる科学者も、もし彼が宗教の熱心に匹敵する熱心をもって自分の仕事をするのでなければ、また真理のみちびくところへはどこへでもついて行く覚悟がなければ、なんら偉大なことはおそらくなしとげられない。しかし熱心も知性の厳しい統制を欠いては、科学者に何の効果ももたらさないだろう。

〖注〗 **a man of science**=a scientist. **be likely to...**「...しそう」、類例:—He *is likely to* succeed. (彼は成功しそうだ=成功の見込みがある) **comparable with...**「...に比すべき」「...に匹敵する」。 **get him nowhere**「彼になんの結果もおさめさせない」。

**6.** その時計はけっして安くはなかった、ことに私のような財政の余裕

[ 289 ]

のない者にはあまりぜいたくすぎた。それでもその言い値では安かったのだ、というわけは、正確なことにかけてはその時計に匹敵するものがなかったのだから。

〖注〗 **low-priced** は代価が巨額でないのを言い、**cheap** は物の価値にくらべて代価の安いのをいう。**a person of my limited means**「私のような財産に限りある人」。**it defied all comparison**「それとくらべるべきものがなかった」、to defy は「...を無視する」という意味から「...をむなしうする」などの意味となる、例:—speed that *defies* pursuit. (とても追いつけない速力)

---

## ( 2 )

**7.** ジャック・ハーマンはこれより先、ねこを下[の船室]に閉じこめておいた、がかわいそうに、ねこはどうしてか抜け出した[ものらしい]、出しぬけに鋭い叫び声が聞えた、と見ると、ジャムボー[ねこの名]は手すりにすがりついて、その上に大山のような波がまともに落ちかかっていた。

〖注〗 **somehow**=by some means「どうにかして」。**for**... は escaped somehow を説明する、「...をもって見ればどうにかして逃げ出したのだ」という意。

**8.** 子供のような船長。

船長のむすこ。船長付の給仕。

**9.** それは前にも言ったように迷宮みたいな古い家です。

〖注〗 **labyrinth**「迷路」「迷園」など、道が錯綜(纟)して判別しがたい所をいう。ここは家の中があっちへもこっちへもつづいて錯雑していることをいったのである。

**10.** まあ、かわいいジェインちゃん。ほんとにご親切ね、ショールを持ってきてくださるなんて。

〖注〗 **how kind in you to...!**=it is very kind of you to...「...してくださるとはご親切かたじけない」。

**11.** 汽車の事故はまれである、おどろくべきほどまれである、見ただけでも頭がぐらぐらしようという、あのくもの巣みたいな鉄道網を思えば。

〖注〗 **enough to make one's head swim**「人の頭をぐらぐらさせるに足る=目まいさせるような」。

**12.** 彼女は姿のいい女であった。それで、若いときには確かに美人だったと思えた。

〖注〗 in youth は when young と書き換えられる。

**13.** これまでは、すくなくとも 20 もベッドの並んでいる完全に兵舎のような寄宿舎に彼はいたのだった。

〖注〗 **hitherto**=up till then. **dormitory** の dormi- は sleep の意味。

**14.** 先日、台風 11 号が関東地方を襲ったときにはひどい目にあった、窓は二つ吹きこわされるし、雨もれは五、六カ所もできて。

〖注〗 **a devil of time**「悪魔のようなとき」ということ。**what with ... and** (29) 参照。

**15.** 彼はさけんだ、「ねえ、おくさん、あなたのところのあのとんまな女中は、2 本の足にはくのに片一方の絹のくつ下しか包みに入れなかったんですよ。」

〖注〗 **Look here.** は相手の注意を呼ぶときの言い方。**pack**「荷作りする」。**stocking** は「長いくつ下」で、むかしは男性も着用した。

---

( 3 )

**16.** しろうとはこの第二の産業革命(オートメーション革命)は自分らの生活様式を作り変えてしまうという話をきいた。しかし、「ボタン操作の工場」が出来るといううわさで自分の職業の将来を心配している。

〖注〗 **the man on the street** は「街頭の人」、つまり、「市井(しせい)の人」「ふつうの人」で、専門家とか学者などでない人のこと。**industrial revolution** の第一のものは 18 世紀から 19 世紀にかけて、英国を中心に起こった産業革命。**push-botton** ボタンを押せば機械が運転すること。**worry about**「〜を心配する」。

**17.** 子供のときに精神上または肉体上の不健康の種子をまくと、おとなになってにがい収穫を刈り取ることになる。

**18.** 約束した以上は約束の表面のみならず、履行しようと約束した精神を遂行せよ。

〖注〗 **not only ... but ...** (110) 参照。

**19.** 人間関係のつまらなさを悟ってしまえば小説家の素質は死んでしまうのだ。

〖注〗 **human affairs**「人間関係の諸事」。

**20.** 私は怠情を一種の自殺とみなす。なんとなれば獣的欲望は残存す

るかもしれないが人間性は滅びたも同然だからである。

〖注〗 **look upon~as...**=regard~as...「~を...と考える」。**effectually**=in effect「実際に(...も同然)」。

21. 「なにフィラデルフィアですって」、といって子を思う親心で、涙が両眼にあふれた。「もしあなた、フィラデルフィアにお住まいなら私どものペンをご存じでしょうね」。

〖注〗 **all the mother**=all her maternal affection. **suffused her eyes** [with tears] として見よ,すなわち「子を思う親心が彼女の眼を涙でいっぱいにした」となる。

22. 力あるあわれみの言葉と、慈悲を求める強い訴えによって、彼はあわれみの情と同情の念とを呼び起こされ、人間としての情、父としての情が盛んに起こり、裁判官たるの職責を打ち忘れていすから立ち上がった。

〖注〗 **forget~in...** は「...に~を忘れる」、類例:—He *forgot* his own comfort *in* the cause of the public. (彼は公共の事に寝食を忘れた)

23. このような危機に際して、彼の性質中にはこじき根性が一番高く頭を上げ、天才肌は面くらって頭をかくしてしまった。

〖注〗 **in him**=in his composition. 人の性質はいろいろな要素から成り立っているから composition (調合物)というのである。

24. 読書はぜひ必要であり、実際的な本は助けになる。けれども諸君の心に作家の萌芽(ほうが)、物を書こうという不撓(とう)の意志がないならば、なんの成功も収められない。

〖注〗 **unbreakable will**「破ることのできない意志、何ものにも屈しない意志」。これは前の germ と同格で、内容を説明したもの。**get nowhere** (1) の 5.「注」参照。

25. マリンソンにはまだ少年の素直さが十分残っていたので、目上の者のぶっきらぼうな命令にもはいはいと応じた。もっとも、自制がよくできいことは明らかに見られたが。

〖注〗 **enough...to** とつづく、「するに十分」となる。**respond to**=obey. **curt**=rudely brief. **was in poor control of himself**=was not able to control himself properly. **obviously**=evidently.

( 4 )

26. 現代文明に直面する多数の問題の中で、老齢者の運命というものがたしかにまっ先きに一般人の心にうかぶ問題のひとつである。これは新聞、

雑誌に載せられる、この問題に関する記事の数から判断してみてである。
　〖注〗 facing「...に直面する、...に解決を求める」。the foremost「まっ先きに来るもの」。the aged=old people. judging by「...によって判断すると」。this subject「この老人の問題」。carried「掲載される」。過去分詞で形容詞の役。

**27.** たしかに悪くいうだけのことがあると信ずる場合のほかはけっして眼の前にいない人、いな、だれをでも悪くいうものではない。(また悪くいうだけのことはあるにせよ) 悪くいうのが先方の改悛(かいしゅん)に必要がないなら悪くいうものではない。
　〖注〗 speak ill of...「...のことを悪くいう」、類例:—to speak well of. ...(よくいう) to speak highly of...(ほめる)

**28.** 全体主義国家においては、こういう問題は全教育過程の統制に直結する。すなわち、有能な者が選抜されて、国家の必要に応じてそれぞれの職業に適するように教育されるしくみになっている。
　〖注〗 lead to~「~につながる」。the capable「才能のある青年たち」。are to「定められている」。sort out=arrange in groups. need for these professions「これらの職業に対する需要」。

**29.** あらゆる時代を通じて詩は、とくに、教育ある人、知性の高い人、感受性の強い人、の関心事であった、もっとも、いっそう単純な形では、無教育の人々や子供たちにもまた愛好されたけれども。
　〖注〗 appeal to=interest (v.t.); be liked by. 例:—Do these paintings appeal to you (=do you like them; are you interested in them)?

**30.** 新しい立法が達成しようとした目的の一つは貧しい人々の子弟に対して機会を広げてやることであった。
　〖注〗 objective「得ようとねらう目標」で、ただ object と言えば「目標」であり、「対象」でもある。the less well-to-do 前に言った者「より暮しのよくない人々」。well-to-do=fairly rich; financially prosperous「暮しむきの楽な人々」。

**31.** 道徳の力によって私たちは幾千年をも通じて幾十億もの人々の心をゆり動かすことができる。偉大にして善良な人々が今までにしてきたし、今後もするであろうように。
　〖注〗 thousands of millions「幾百万の幾千倍」「何十億(というほどの多数)」。

**32.** 活動的な人は自分のしなくてはならぬ仕事以上のことをなし、怠惰な人はそれより以下のことをする〔自分のしなくてはならないことも十分にはしない〕。

〚注〛 **they are bound to do**「ぜひしなくてはならない」。

**33.** 実は、岡の中腹から見たときあんな絵のように美しく見えたその小さい村の貧乏人の中にはいって、自分の仕事をしている間に、彼女はひじょうに多くのいたましいことを発見したのだった。

〚注〛 **The truth was that...**「事実は...であった＝実は...だった」、類例：—*The truth is that* I forgot all about it. (実はすっかり忘れてしまったのだ) **a great many**「ひじょうに多くの」。**in the course of her work**「彼女の仕事の進行中に」、類例：—*in the course of* discussion. (討議中に)

**34.** 青年は不可能なるもの(理想)を追求する、そして理想に触れることさえできないため、失望落胆しがちである。しかし、それにもかかわらず、彼の全生活は、そういう追求のために一段と快いのだ。

〚注〛 **strive after**＝make great efforts to get to. **apt**＝likely; have a tendency. 類例：—*Idle children are apt to* get into mischief. (何もしないでいる子供たちはとかくいたずらを始めたがるものだ) **it**＝the impossible. **the sweeter for** については (17) 参照。

**35.** 彼は往々ご都合主義のために正義を捨てることがあった。

〚注〛 **would often** (63) 参照。

---

( 5 )

**36.** [い合わせた]士官たちはフリッツがおとうさんの手を取って一部始終を物語るのをひじょうに注意して聞いていた。

**37.** 頭のてっぺんから足のつま先まで総身歓楽の固まりだ。

〚注〛 **crown**「頭のてっぺん」。

**38.** たぶん私は、彼女はたいへん若い、ほんの子供だということを思い、斟酌(しんしゃく)してやるべきです。彼女は物に対する興味と熱心と活発の固まりで、彼女にとってはこの世界は魅力、驚異、神秘そして歓喜そのものであるのだ。

〚注〛 **make allowances**「手心を加える、酌量(しゃくりょう)する」。**vivacity**＝liveliness; sprightliness.

**39.** ちょうどそのとき、マリーとピエールとが、遠足で上きげんになり、ぺちゃくちゃしゃべり、笑いながら工場にはいってきた。

〚注〛 **very** 公式 (12) 参照。

**40.** ぼくは子供のときに、こんな老紳士を知っていた、この人は、宿の

おかみさんを陰でものすごく悪く言うが、おかみさんがへやにはいってくるやいなや急ににこにこ、ぺこぺこするのだった。

〖注〗 **used to**「することをつねとした」(63) 参照。**behind one's back**「いない所で」「陰で」。**obeisance**「おじぎ、えしゃく」。**as soon as**「するやいなや」。(57) 参照。

**41.** 私が親切に彼に話しかけると彼はたちまちにこにこした。

**42.** 今のところ私はお前の舌には用はない。お前は体じゅう目と耳ばかりにしておってもよい、(目や耳が)たくさんならたくさんなほど結構だ。

〖注〗 **I have got** は I have の口語体で、意味の上からは got はまったくないも同じ。**that tongue of yours**「お前のその舌」。**the more, the better** 公式 (16) 参照。

**43.** 彼女が全身を神経にしてベルの鳴るのを今か今かと待っていると、突然彼が目の前に立った。

**44.** ワシントンは口をきくのにひじょうに慎み深かった、議論をするのにも、相手の隙に乗ずるとか、一時の勝を求めるようなことはけっしてしなかった。

〖注〗 **to take advantage of** は他の弱点、すきなどに乗じてみずから利するのをいう、「つけこむ」「あげ足を取る」など。**short-lived**「短命の」「長もちのしない」。

**45.** 先祖伝来のひじかけいすにすわって、太陽系の中心のようにあたりを見まわしながら、温情と喜びとを人々の心に与えている老郷士は、まことに歓待（たい）というものの権化かと思われた。

〖注〗 **beam warmth and gladness to every heart**「目もとから光と熱とを放って人々の心をあたたかくうれしく感じさせる」。

**46.** 強大なる野心と薄弱なる信念とを一身に体現していたフランシス一世は 20 歳にしてフランスの主権者となった。

**47.** 姑（しゅうとめ）という者は始終男の人の冷評の的になっている。継母という者はなんでも卑劣なことを一身に集めたもののように思われている。

**48.** スコットランド人はイングランドの人よりもなおいっそう常識に富んでいる。

〖注〗 **personified** は「擬人された」という意味。

**49.** フォークランドとケーレブ・ウィリアムズとはとどまるところを知らない名誉心と、禁じがたい好奇心との奴隷である。

〖注〗 **impersonation**＝personification「権化」。

**50.** 生活のあらゆる関係において 彼は 非難すべき点がなかったばかりでなく、それ以上だった。(すなわち)彼は他人に対する行動において模範的であった、これはそうあるべきことでありながらめったにできないことである。

〚注〛 not only は but also と対応するのがふつうであるが、この場合 much more がその代用をしている。 above reproach 「非の打ち所がない」。 a model of what men ought to be, yet seldom are 「実際にはめったにそうでないが、そうあるべきものの模範」。

───────────────

( 6 )

**51.** 何事も他人がそれをするからするので、そのこと自体が良いこと、親切なこと、あるいは正直なことであるから(するの)ではない、ということは、自分自身に対する道徳的抑制を全然放棄し、大急ぎで大多数の者と共にどんどん堕落していくことである。

〚注〛 in great haste 「大急ぎで」。 go to the devil 「悪魔のところへ行く」「地獄へ落ちる」「滅亡する」「堕落する」。 majority 「多数」に対し「少数」は minority である。

**52.** りっぱな礼儀というものはそれだけで一つの財産である。 行儀作法の正しい人々は財産はなくともりっぱにやって行ける。というのはそのような人々はどこへ行っても通行券を持っているようなものだから。

〚注〛 the good mannered=good mannered people. (4) 参照。 can do without 「なくてすまし得る=なくて間に合う」。

**53.** 馬車が止まった、するとスクィーヤズ夫人がだれに飲ませるのだか[気付けの]しょうちゅうを一杯持って来いと命じる声が聞えた。 このことだけでも何か異常なことが起こったということは明らかであった。

〚注〛 spirits 焼酎(しょうちゅう)(この意味には通例複数)。 a sufficient sign 「十分な証拠」。

**54.** 農業は労働のうち最も骨の折れる種類の一つで、そしてそのもの本来はけっして精神的発達を促進するものではない。農業が世界の歴史において文化的役割を演じたということは、富を創造することによって農業が人類の一部を鋤(すき)の労働から解放したという事実によるにすぎない。

〚注〛 free~from...「~に...を免れさせる」、類例:―This money will *free* me *from* debts. (この金で借金がきれいになくなる)

**55.** それは「ただ一つのこと、簡単な一つのことにすぎない、すなわち

幾億かの男女が悪いことはしないで、よいことをしようときめ、そこからのろいでなく、祝福を刈りとろうと決意するだけのことだ」。われわれの必要とするものが本当にそれだけで十分だとすれば、われわれはそういう決意をもっている、ほとんどもっていると言ってよいからだ。しかし、残念ながら、そのものそれだけではけっして十分でないのだ。

〚注〛 **set oneself to do**「するつもりになる」。**instead of**「のかわりに」「でなくて」。

**56.** われわれの社会はマルクス主義者のいう冷たい、血のない「経済人」の上に建てられているのでなく、人間それ自体を目的とする人間そのものへの信頼に土台をおくものだ。

〚注〛 **is founded upon~**「~の土台の上に建てられる」。find の過去、過去分詞の found と混同しないこと。**Marxist** の発音は [máːksist] だから注意。**faith in man** は belief in man などと同類。**end** は手段に対する「目的」。

---

### ( 7 )

**57.**「ジョージにいさん、ぼくはこれからはひとりで別にご飯をたべようと思います」と弟のハリーが言った。

兄が答えて言うには、「そうもゆくまいよ」。

「そんならご飯の時にみんなが私をしかるのをよしてもらいたいものです」。

**58.** ある朝のこと、彼は小舟に乗って食物と油とを取りに陸に行かなければならなかった。彼は娘をひとりで置いて行くことを欲しなかったが、海はないでいたから、きっとじきに帰れると思った。

〚注〛 **be back**＝return. 類例：—I shall *be back* in a few days. (2、3日たてば帰ります)

**59.** しばしば、天気がおだやかなときには、ぼくは晩さんをすませるとさっそくひとりでボートにとび乗って、湖水のまん中へこいで行った。

**60.** この陸はそれだけでは百姓と地主との種族をつくり出したことであろう、しかし海が想像力と冒険精神をつけ加えることによって、彼らを船乗り、貿易商、冒険家、征服者、植民地開拓者、帝国建設者とした。そして彼らの小さい島を、この同じ海によって結合されている大英帝国の母国にしてしまった。

〖注〗 **has made~of them**「彼らを~にした」(78) 参照。**the Empire** はここでは British Empire「大英帝国」のことである。

**61.** 私、何か家の仕事を責任を持ってさせていただきたいのです。あなたがどの仕事か私にすっかり任せてくださることができると思えば、どんなにうれしいでしょう。

**62.** 近代人はその魂の中の精神的真空をどうして埋めるつもりであるか。この真空は近代化学の勃興(ぼっこう)によって作られた。科学は伝統的形態の宗教を放逐した、しかし、科学はそれだけではこの空虚を満たすことはできないのだ。

〖注〗 **in its traditional forms**「その従来の形態をとっている」、前の religion を修飾する句。

**63.** 文字そのものは本来言葉ではなくて、言葉が組織される音声をあらわすのに用いられる記号にすぎない。書かれた記号にはそれだけでは生命もなく意味もなくて、それ(書かれた記号)はそれがあらわしている音声に、いわば、翻訳されてから初めて言葉ともなり、意味をもつことができるのである。

〖注〗 **in themselves**—(6) 参照。**of which language is composed**「(それから)言葉が構成されているところの」。**for which they** (=written symbols) **stand**「(それを)彼らが表象するところの」。**as it were**「いわば」(95) 参照。

──────────

( 8 )

**64.** 彼はひじょうに器用な少年であったから、自分ひとりで絵筆をこしらえようと決心した。

**65.** [他人の助けを借りずに]自らそれをなした少年は向上の道に一歩をふみ出したのである、そしてなおよいことには、他のいっそういい幾段もの進歩をなす力を得たことである。

〖注〗 **ones**=strides.

**66.** もうおかあさんに相談する暇がなかった。おかあさんはその時はすこし離れた所にいた。彼は生まれてから初めて自分一個の考えで、何とか処理しなくてはならなかった。

〖注〗 **in his life** は打消し、あるいは for the first time などに伴ない、「生

まれてから」と訳して当たる。類例—I have seen many great men in my time, but I *never* saw his like *in my life*. (私は偉い人もずいぶん見たが、彼のような人は生まれてからまだ見たことがない)

**67.** こどもたちは自分らの生活にしっかりしたわく組を必要としている。彼らは、自分の立場はどこにあるのか、おとなたちは自分らに何を期待しているのか、それを知りたいのだ。そして一から十までなんでも自分できめたいとは思わない。

〚注〛 **where they are**「社会生活の中で自分がいるところ」。 **expected of** の of は from と同じ意味。類例:—People *expected* great things *of* him. (人々は彼が将来偉いことをなすであろうと大いに嘱目(しょくもく)していた)

**68.** 私のした決定は私のものであり、しかも私だけのものであることを知っていただきたい。これは私がまったく独力で判断しなければならないことがらだったのです。

**69.** もっともよい援助とは他人のためにその労苦を負担してやることではなくて、その人々がみずから自己の荷物を負い、そして勇敢に人生の困難に立ち向かうように勇気と精力とを鼓吹してやることである。

〚注〛 **inspire** の用法:—
{ to *inspire* him *with* hope
{ to *inspire* hope *into* his heart
(彼に希望を与える、彼の心に希望を吹き込む)

**70.** { a. 人事を尽して天命を待つ。
     { b. 親知らず、子知らず。

〚注〛 このことわざには少しちがった二つの解釈がある。一つは (a) Let each man *do the best he can for himself*, and trust God to do the rest. (各自全力を尽してあとは神に任す)と解し、また一つは (b) Let every person *look out for himself*, and God will look out for us all. (人はみな自分のことだけ気をつけていればいい、神様が皆のことをしてくれるから)の意味で、「我がち」「てんでんこ」などと解す。

**71.** レーニン、トロッツキー、スターリンなどロシアのもろもろの独裁者たちは相互同志いがみ合っていたとしても、いずれも、自分のため、およびロシアのためには、同じ主張をしたのだった。

〚注〛 ここの might はただ may の過去で、譲歩的な言いまわし。事実に反する想定を示すのではない。 **to be at war with** の類例:—The two nations *were at war with* each other. (両国は交戦中であった) The spirit *is at war with* the flesh. (霊と肉とが相争う)

**72.** ラーキン君は踊り進んで、捨てられた櫂(かい)をつかんだ。「ボートの

底に寝ろ」とその男に言って、[それからこんどは私に向かって]「それから船長さん、あなた、そっちの櫂をおとりなさい、私たち自分でこがなけりゃだめです」と言った。

**73.** ラーキン君はみずから実見するために私の手から望遠鏡を取っていた。

**74.** 生徒が受動的に他人の思想感情に黙従するのでなく、みずから考えみずから感ずることを奨励するには、教育を行なう精神を全然変更することが必要である。

〚注〛 acquiesce in... 「...に甘んじて従う」。

**75.** もしわれわれが自分の考えをきちんと正確に忠実に表現する言葉を自分で見つけないで、他の作家の語句を借りて使うにすぎないならば、それはちょうど服を1着求めるのに、りっぱな洋服屋にぴったり寸法を合わせて作らせないで、出来合い服屋へ行く人のようなものだ。出来合いの服というものはだれにも合うが、またどれにも合わないものだ。

**76.** 君は独力で成功への道を開いた。 目的に達しようと思うなら辛抱しなければならない。さもないと初めが花々しいほど終りがいっそう暗くなると思いたまえ。

〚注〛 be assured that... 「...と確信せよ」。 the more splendid～, the darker～ (16) 参照。

**77.** 動物の中には卵を産み放しにして、あとの心配などはちっともしないものもあるが、中にはその卵をかえして、かえった子供がひとり立ちのできるまで育てるものもある。

〚注〛 as chance directs them 「運の彼らを指導するままに＝運に任せて」。 think of them no farther 「もはや、それ以上卵のことなどは思わない」。 tend the birth 「生まれたものを世話する」。

**78.** 年上の方のこどもたちは父の生存中にりっぱな教育を受けたが、父が死んでからは、年下のこどもたちは自活しなくてはならなかった。

〚注〛 younger members [of the family] と補ってみよ。

**79.** ほんとうにボートの好きなものは、ただボートをこぐのがおもしろいばかりでそれをやる。ちょうどそれは読書好きな者が、学位を得るためにのみ読書するのでないのと同じことである。

〚注〛 follows it は boating をやること。 for itself (=for its own sake) は運動のためなどにするのではない、boating そのものが愉快だからという意味。

**80.** 簡単に言えば、彼は正直のため[他に求むるところなく]正直を行なうどころか、利己的の見地から見ても正直は最良の政策なりということすら知らなかったのである。

〚注〛 **so far from~ing**「~するどころではなく」。

**81.** 彼は自分の小僧の腕前を自分のために利用しようと思った。

**82.** アイスランドの漁民は、その資源にさらに大きな圧迫を受けたので、これらの漁場をできるだけ多くわがものとしておきたいという希望をますます強く示した。

〚注〛 **pressure** については次のような用法を覚える。the *pressure* of a crowd (群衆のひしめき). the *pressure* of the times (不景気). *pressure* for money (金づまり). **as much...as possible** できるだけ多く. **keep for oneself** と似た表現に keep...to oneself (独占する)がある。(**10**) 参照。

---

( 9 )

**83.** おばあさんはテーブルの上にひきうすを置いて静かにいった。

ひけよ、ひきうす、ひけよひけ!

ねじれたパンをひいて出せ、お願いだぞよ後生(ごしょう)だぞ!
するとひきうすがひとりでぐるぐる回りはじめて、たちまち焼きたてのほやほやの巻パンをひき出した。

〚注〛 **away** は「休まず」「しきりに」「どしどし」などの意味、類例:—to work away (せっせと働く). to sing away (しきりに歌う). to smoke away (しきりにたばこを吹かす). **hot from the oven**「かまから出たての熱い」。類例:—fresh from school (学校から出たてのほやほや). wet from the press (印刷機から取り出したばかりのしめっているような)

**84.** われわれが幸、不幸ということにあまり心を使わず、厳密にかつ骨身をおしまず義務を遂行することに専心すれば、幸福はひとりでにくるものだ。

〚注〛 **to devote oneself to**...「...に身をささげる」。類例:—He *devoted* his whole life *to* literary work. (彼は一生を文学上の仕事にささげた)

**85.** アリ・ババは臆(おく)することなく洞窟(どうくつ)の中へはいって行き、袋にあった金貨を自分の3匹のろばが運べると思っただけかき集めた。ろばに袋を積み終わったとき、彼はそれを見られないようにその上にたきぎを置いた。思う存分何度も出はいりし終わったとき、彼はとびらの前に立った、

そして「閉じよ、ごま」と言うととびらはひとりでに閉まった。

〖注〗 **Ali Baba** はアラビアン・ナイト物語の中に出てくる人物。**as much of the gold coin as...**「...だけ(たくさん)の金貨」(48) 参照。**loaded them with bags**「彼らに袋を積んだ」、類例：—to *load* a wagon *with* coal (車に石炭を積む) **in such a manner that...**「...のようなふうに」。**on his pronouncing**=as soon as he pronounced. **Shut, Sesame!** これは洞窟のとびらを閉じるときの呪文(じゅもん)である。

**86.** 科学者は類似をさがすことによって自然界の事象の中に秩序を求める。というのは、秩序というものは、おのずと現われるものではない、見ればすぐそこにあるというものではないからだ。

〖注〗 **explore** は本来 travel into or through little-known parts (of land or sea) in order to learn more という意味。**display** は「すぐ見えるように示す」。**for the mere looking**「ただ見さえすれば(得られる)」、類例：— It's yours *for the asking*. (=It's yours if you ask for it.) (くれと言えば君のものだ)

**87.** ご存じでしょうが はつかねずみのような かっこうをした玩具(がんぐ)があります、あの玩具はある箇所に触れると、自分の勝手でするように駆けだします、生きてでもいるように。

〖注〗 **apparently** は「見たところ...らしい」の意味、ここでは自分の意志で走り出すように見えるという意。

**88.** フランス人は必要に迫られるとしぶしぶながらそれをする、(それなのに)イギリス人は自ら進んで古い絆(きずな)を絶ち、新生涯(しょうがい)を始めるだけの勇気がある。

**89.** びっくりしたのがすぎてしまったら、その動物は自分から帰ってくるだろうと思った者もあった。

**90.** 彼はだれかにそそのかされてそんなことをしたにちがいない、自分の考えでそんなことをするような男ではないから。

〖注〗 **at somebody's instigation**「だれかの扇動で」。

---

( 10 )

**91.**「まあ、なんてきれいな顔してるんだろう」とベンがひとりごとを言った。

**92.**「なんと鉄のような民族であろう、このスコットランド人は。だれ

がよく彼らとはりあうことができるだろうか」と私はしばしばひとり叫んだことがある。

**93.** そこ [病院] で私は、将校なみに1室を独占していた、で気持のいい日当りのへやに横たわって、自分さえうめかなければうめき声も聞こえないのはほとんど天国にいる感じであった。

〖注〗 **as each officer had**「各士官は 1 室を占領していたがそのように」。**hear no groans but my own** 他の患者と同室でないから人のうめき声は聞えないのである。

**94.** 私はいつか座敷へはいりこんで何時間だか知らんがうちのお客さんをひとりで占領していた。

〖注〗 **drift into** 漂然とはいりこむ。**for...** は for three hours とか for four hours とかいうべきところを何時間だかわからないから、そのかわりに don't know how many hours をつけたのである。類例:—He has gone I don't know where. (彼はどこかへ行ってしまった——どこだか知らないが)

**95.** ぼくはその件に関することをすっかり知っていたけれど、自分の胸だけにおさめておいた。

〖注〗 **the knowledge**「その知っている事がら」。

**96.** ひとりで勝手にさせておいたら、彼はまったく太平楽に生涯をうそぶき暮したであろう。

〖注〗 **whistle one's life away**「うそぶいて一生を過ごす」、類例:—to *dream* one's life *away*. (一生を夢みて暮す)

---

### (11)

**97.** 火事がすさまじい勢いで森の中を燃え進んだ、天さえもためにおどろくかと思われた。

〖注〗 **On went the fire** は The fire went on を強く言うために語の順序を変えたのである。**rush** は「突進する」、**crash** は「音を立てて物を破壊する」、rushing and crashing で「すさまじい勢いで」と訳した。

**98.** サー・ウィリアム・ソーンヒルは、自分はすこしで満足して、あとは自分の甥(おい)に自由にさせておく。

**99.** さてりんごはもちろん無生物である、したがってその物自体では動くことはできない。

**100.** そうだ、彼はりんご自体の外(そと)に何か力のあることを発見したのだ。

**101.** どんな一片の知識でも生徒が自分で修得したものなら、またどんな問題でも生徒が自分で解決したものなら、自分でやったおかげで、自分でやらなかった場合よりはるかに完全に自分のものとなる。

〚注〛 **by virtue of...**「...のおかげで」、類例:—He has succeeded *by virtue of* industry.（勤勉のおかげで成功した）**than it could else be**「そうしなかった場合に自分のものとなるよりは」。

---

( 12 )

**102.** 国民的感情の真の土台は過去に対する尊敬である。なぜなら1国民の最上の所有物は彼らが共有するもろもろの記憶であるから。これらの記憶は、各個人が自分の持っている他の何物よりとうといと考えるべき神聖な宝をなしている。

〚注〛 **have in common**「共有している」、類例:—to *have* nothing *in common* with each other.（すこしも似た点がない）

**103.** 多くの人々がぐちをこぼすような境遇は、われわれがちょうどそれを使って仕事をすべき道具そのもの、われわれがそれによって登るべき踏み石とも、みなされるべきものである。このような境遇は人生の航路における風と潮であって、熟練した船乗りはたいていこれを利用するか、あるいはこれに打ち勝つのである。

〚注〛 **many**=many people.

**104.** ああ、これです、私のさがしていたものは。どうぞそちらのものは脱ぎすててください、火にくべてしまってください、このシャツとこのお洋服をお着せ申しましょう。これです。これこそおあつらえです――ごてごてしなくて、しかもはなやかで、つつましやかで、しかもお殿様向きにスマートでございます。

〚注〛 **be after**=look for. 類例:—What *are* you *after*? (=What are you trying to get or do?) **Do me the favor to...**「私に～の恩恵を施してください」が文字の意味。しかしこれは物を頼むていねいな言い方。**ducally** は duke から出た語で、「公爵のように」がもとの意味。**nobby**=smart; stylish.

**105.** 彼の性格の長所がかえって彼を戦争の指揮に不適当ならしめた。

彼は実は平和の使徒であって、恐慌と熱狂——彼はこれにごくわずかしかあずからなかった——によってやむなく戦争へ押しやられたのである。

〖注〗 **unfitted him for...**「彼を...に不適当にした」、類例：—The weakness of his constitution *unfits him for* rough work. (からだが弱いので荒い仕事ができない) **Peace Minister**「平和の使徒」。minister は仕える者の意味から、大臣、公使、宣教師などとなる。

**106.** 女は、おごそかな姿をして、人もなげにごうまんに突っ立っていた。その眼はあたかも相手の心の底までも読もうとするようなふうに、彼の眼をじっと見つめて。

〖注〗 **defiant** は相手を軽蔑する態度。**a queenly figure**「女王のような威厳ある姿で」。**his**=his eyes.

**107.** 老人にせよ若者にせよ、自己以外の者となろうとする者は人生をしくじる、しかもそういうことをする者が多いのである。

〖注〗 **That person who tries to**=those (people) who try to. **make a failure of life**「人生から失敗を作る、人生に失敗する」。

**108.** もう幾年も前のことである——しかしそれだからなおのことこの話は、すっかり忘れられてしまわないうちに聞いておく価値があるのだ。

**109.** 彼らの性格の差異がかえって琴瑟(きんしつ)和合をうむこととなった。

**110.** われわれは数学をとおして、そもそもの初めにおいて、こういう教訓を学ぶ、すなわち、あまねくこれが知られかつ適用されるなら、世人が被りやすい害悪の大半は防止できると思われる教訓である。

〖注〗 **if universally known**=if it were universally known. **the world is liable to** この前に which が略されたと考える。be liable to の類例：— All men *are liable to* make mistakes. (人間はだれでも誤りはおかしやすいものだ) He *is liable to* malaria. (彼はマラリヤにかかりやすい)

**111.** ホレスが憎むべきものとみなしたその物が、実に、彼の友の不断の楽しみの源泉となったのである。

---

( 13 )

**112.** 「どんなに弱い生き物でも」とカーライルは言う、「ただひとつの目的に力を集中することによって、何物かをなし遂げることができる。反対に、どんなに強い生き物でも力を多くの目的の上に分散させれば何物を

もなし遂げ得ないことがある。水滴はたえず落下してどんな堅い岩にも通路を穿(うが)つ。せっかちな急流はおそろしい音をたてて岩の上を突進し、後になんのこん跡も残さない」。

〘注〙 **by dispersing his over many**=by dispersing his powers over many objects.　**fail to~**=be unsuccessful in ~ing.

**113.**　(世の中には)いろいろ事情というものがあって、その事情のもとではよくよくのいくじなしの人間でも活気、決断のある振舞いをするようになり、またもっとも用心深い人が思慮を忘れて向う見ずの決心をいだくようなことがある。

〘注〙 **in** (*or* **under**) **which**「その事情のもとにあっては」。**the least energetic of mankind**「人間中もっとも気力のすくない者」。**learn to ...**「...するようになる」。

**114.**　詩というものは言語そのものと同じほど普遍的であり、ほとんど同じくらい古くからある。もっとも原始的民族でも詩を用い、もっとも文明の人々もこれを養い育てる。

〘注〙 **as ancient** の次に as language を補ってみればよい。

**115.**　世界中で一番重要な思想でさえ数セントで印刷にして販売され得る。そしてもしあなたが(それから)その思想を得た場合、それはちょうどりっぱな紙に印刷し、絹でとじた高価な書物から得た場合と、まったく同様にあなたに役立つのである。

〘注〙 **in the world** は the most を強める、(39) 参照。**for a few cents** は printed and sold 全体にかける。

**116.**　世界一りっぱな大学の最上の教師でさえ学生に教育を授けることはできない。教師にできるのは、教育というものが掘り出せる鉱山まで学生をみちびいて行き、適当な道具を授け、その使い方を教えることだ。教師は学生が落胆したとき、はげまし、またいっそう奮闘するように激励することはできる、けれども、学生が自分で掘り出した貴金属だけしか学生のものにはならないのだ。

〘注〙 **it can be dug** の it は education を指す。もちろん鉱石にたとえている。**provide** の用法例：—I *am* already *provided with* everything I need. (私は必要なものはもうみんなもっている)　He had to *provide for* his large family. (大ぜいのこどもを養わねばならなかった)　**for himself** (8) 参照。

( 14 )

**117.** セント・ヴィンセント卿(きょう)はむかしの元気が少しも衰えなかったし、けっして自分の権威を無視されて黙っているような人ではなかった。

〖注〗 **suffer to be...**「...されて黙っている」、類例：—I'll not *suffer* myself *to be* ill-treated.(虐待されて黙ってはいない)　*Suffer* yourself *to be* bound.(神妙にしばられよ、尋常になわにかかれ)　**nought** or **naught**＝nothing.

**118.** ヘイスチングズは[ほかの物に事欠くことがあっても]口実に窮するようなことはけっしてなさそうであった。

**119.** この家で私は、ラプランドの辺地でだれしもこんなものを見ようとは思わないもの、すなわちピアノを見た。

〖注〗 **in the heart of ...** は「まん中」の意から「奥へひっこんだ所、へんぴの土地」の意味になる、類例：—*in the heart of* the city (市の中央に)　*in the heart of* the country. (片いなかに)

**120.** 周知のように、自己の健康に注意すること、言いかえれば、自己の肉体を合理的に取り扱うことこそ、実はこの人々がけっして真剣に考えようとはしないことだ。

〖注〗 **what is the same thing**「同じことであるが」。前に述べたものと次に述べることの内容は同じだということ。**very** は (12) を参照。

**121.** 夢にも会おうとは思っていなかったところへ突然彼が現われたので、私はまったくびっくりしてしまった。

〖注〗 **suddenness** という抽象名詞が文の主語で、それに対する述語が took である。**under heaven** は in the world などと同様に強意の用法。**take a person by surprise**＝act towards him in an unexpected way「思いがけないことをしてびっくりさせる」。

---

( 15 )

**122.** 世に常識ほどありふれていないものはない。(常識はじつにめずらしいものだ。)

〖注〗「ふつうありふれている」という意の **common** を commonsense の common と対照させたしゃれである。

**123.** この世の中で目的のないことほど希望のないものはない。人その

人がどうであるとか、その人の環境がどんなに有利であるとか、などは問題ではない。目的を持たない人は不幸になる運命にあるのだ。

〘注〙 **It matters not**＝it is not important. **the individual** は a man, the man, one よりもいっそう「1人1人の人間」「個々の人」の意味を強く持つ。**be destined to〜**「〜に運命づけられている」。

**124.** 人望を求める人ほど憎むべきものはない。

**125.** 粉屋ワングは生まれつきどん欲であった。だれだってこの男ほど金銭をほしがる者はなかったし、またこの男ほどに金持を尊敬する者もなかった。

〘注〙 **those that had it**「金を持っていた人々」、it は money をさす。

**126.** 何が美しいといって、若葉という春の衣を着た林や森や、畑や小道に沿った長い生垣ほど美しいものはない。果樹園ではなしや桜の木が青空を背景にして白と淡紅の雲のように見える。

〘注〙 **clumps of trees**「林」。**clad in...** 類例：—The hills are *clad in* verdure. (山が緑の衣を着ている) **spring garment of freshly opened leaves**「若葉という春の衣」、この of は同格関係をあらわす、類例：—the virtue *of* temperance (節制という徳) the month *of* July (7月の月)

**127.** 諸君は後になって悔いるような時間の費し方をしてはならない。およそ世に「時すでにおそし」というのと「ああもあったろうものを」という考えほど悲しいものはない。時間は預かり物である、1分1秒たりとも使途を明瞭にしなければなるまい。睡眠は節約すべし、飲食は節約すべし、そして時はもっとも節約すべきである。

〘注〙 **so...that** とかかる。**reproach yourself**「みずからを非難する」。**it might have been** すべて「might have＋過去分詞」の形は「...しようと思えばできたものを、しなくて残念なことをした」というような場合に用いられる、(98)参照。類例：—*I might have been* a rich man, if I had wanted to. (金持になろうと思えばなれたものをおしいことをした)

**128.** この両国の危機の基をなす原因ほど正反対のものはない。アメリカでは供給が実際の需要をはるかに上回っているが、ロシヤでは需要が利用し得る供給よりはるかに大きい。

〘注〙 **in excess of**＝over.

**129.** 優越の態度をとる人間に会うことほど不愉快なことはない。個人の関係において真実であることは、国際的な集りの場合においてはさらにいっそう真実である、そこでは伝統、感情、習慣を異にする国々から大勢

の人々が集まるのであるから。

〖注〗 **What is true**=that which is true. (**30**) 参照。**even**「さらに」。

**130.** 自己の労力によって得たパンほど食ってうまいパンはないということはたしかなことである。

〖注〗 **Certain it is** は It is certain の強意的表現法。

**131.** できる場合には、嘆賞するということは人間の心の真の喜びである。ほんのわずかの瞬間でも、真の嘆賞ほど人間をそのあらゆるいやしい束縛から高揚させるものはない。

〖注〗 **the very joy** (**12**) 参照。**where he can**=if he can. **were it but for moments**=even if it were only for moments.

**132.** ワシントンと同時代の人で、米国のまさに陥ろうとしている未来の危険を彼ほど明らかに予見し、あるいは、この危険をいかにして避くべきかを、彼ほど明白に力強く説き示した者はなかった。

〖注〗 **his day** の his は後にいう Washington をさす。**to which America would be exposed**「その危険にアメリカがさらされる——会うだろう」。

**133.** 観念連合の微妙な作用の効力のうちで、まったくとるに足らぬような事情が特定の人間をわれわれの記憶によびもどすその仕方ほど普遍的で、しかも奇妙なものはない。

〖注〗 **effect** 結果、効果。 **association of ideas** これはよく心理学で使われる用語。たとえば、モーツァルトのある曲を聞くと、必ず、その曲を初めて奏してくれた人の面影を連想するというようなこと。**trivial**「とるに足らぬ」、名詞に trifle がある。 **recall**=call back to mind. 知事のリコールなどというときの recall は cancel すなわち、「取り消しする」ことである。

**134.** いよいよせねばならないとなれば、彼ほど懸命に仕事をする人はなかったし、彼ほどりっぱに責任をになうことのできる者は少なかった。しかし彼がやたらに活動を好むものでなく、また責任などをすこしもよろこんで引き受けるものでないという事実は、依然として動かなかった。

〖注〗 **it had to be done** の it は work をさす。和文では能動態にして考える。前半の文ではもちろん than he がかくされている。**the facts remained that**... この that-Clause は facts と同格の名詞節。remain は自動詞。

## (16)

**135.** 人の品性が善良であれば（あるほど）、それだけ容易にその人はさらに善良になるし、不良であれば（あるほど）、それだけ容易にその人はまったくだめになるであろう。

〚注〛 **be ruined**「破滅する、だめになる」。

**136.** われわれは[病気でもないのに]病気だろうなどと神経を起こすことや、またちょっとした身体の工合の悪いことなどくよくよすることが少なければ少ないほど、[かえって]自己の健康を保存することができるらしく思われる。

〚注〛 **fancy** は「そうでないことをそうと思う」意味、類例：—She *fancies* herself beautiful.（自分では美人のつもりでいる）

**137.** 人は多くのものに興味を持てば持つほど、幸福の機会が多く、運命に翻弄(ほんろう)されることが少ない、なぜならひとつのものを失っても他のものに頼ることができるから。

〚注〛 **is interested in…**「…に興味を持つ」。**is at the mercy of fate**「運命にもてあそばれる」、類例：—The ship *is at the mercy of* the wind and waves.（船は風波のまにまにただよっている）**fall back upon~**「~にたよる、~を予備とする」。

**138.** しかし、過去の年代記を研究すればするほどわれわれはますます、われわれが慈悲深い時代に生きていることをうれしく思う。すなわち、この時代は、残酷はいみきらわれ、当然受けるべき苦痛でもこれを与えるものは不承不承に、そして義務の観念からこれを与えるのである（けっして、心よく、進んでひどい目に合わせるようなことはしない）。

〚注〛 **even when deserved** は even when the pain is deserved. 不当な処罰でなく、「当然の処罰」ということ。**inflict**（苦痛などを）「与える」。

**139.** 音楽は、最高の意味においては、新奇さをそれほど必要としない。古ければ古いほど、そして私たちがそれになじんでいればいるほど、音楽の私たちに与える効果はますます大きい。

〚注〛 **stands less in need of…**「比較的…を必要としない」。stand in need of=need (*v.t.*) である。**the greater** の次には述語動詞 is が略されている。**the effect** の次には which を補ってみよ。

**140.** 賢明に生活する方法について2つの相反する考えがある。ひとつ

の説によれば,文明とは欲望とこれを満足させる手段とを増すことである。他の1説によれば、満足して、なしに済ませるものの数が多ければ多いほど、われわれは楽に暮せるのである。

〚注〛 **consists in~**「~に存する、~にある」、類例:—Happiness *consists in* contentment. (幸福は満足にある) **be better off**「暮し向きが一段とよろしい」、類例:—*to be well off* (安楽に暮している), *to be badly off* (困っている)

141. 学問をする者はともすると睡眠を短かくすることによって知識を得ることができると考えがちである。彼らをしてそう考えさせるのは知識の足らないところがあるからである。健康な、夢のない眠りであれば、われわれは眠れば眠るほど、それだけよく、起きてから働くことができるのである。

〚注〛 **are apt to...**「とかく...しがちである」、類例:—People *are apt to* think so. (とかく世間ではそう考える) Glass utensils *are apt to* break. (ガラスの器はこわれやすい) **It is defective knowledge that allows them to think so.**「彼らにそう考えることを許すのは不完全な知識である」。

142. 政治というものが国民の手に帰し、観念上、人民のための、人民による、人民自身の政治となるこの傾向が強くなればなるほど、国家に対する忠誠を要求し、義務と献身の感情に訴えることがますますやさしくなった。こういう義務と献身の感情は(むかしの)暴君などはまったく要求できなかったのであった。

〚注〛 **in idea** とは in practice (実践上は)と対照になる。 the government of the people, by the people, for the people は有名な文句、また問題の文句でもある。 **was it able** の it は the government. **have call on~**,「~を要求する」、類例:—He *has* many *calls on* his income. (彼はいろいろなことのために収入をとられる)

---

( 17 )

143. もはや五官の感覚は(外国旅行の)楽しみの最高の手段ではなくなり、情の働きが使われるのだ、そして身辺の種々な事物は、親しみのあるものであるゆえに一段と好ましくなる。

〚注〛 **enjoyment** ここでは外国を旅行してその風物を「楽しむこと」を言っている。**affections** ここでは senses と対照されているから「情緒」といった意味になる。

**144.** 「お前たちはいくら小ざっぱりしていてもよろしい、そうすればなおさら私はお前たちをかわいがってやる、けれども、これは小ざっぱりじゃない、おめかしだよ」と私が口をはさんだ。

**145.** あなたの方がりっぱな教育を受けているし、またいっそうよい境遇にいたのだから、あなたがばかなことをしたり、事を疎略にすると［それだけ］ますます罪が重いわけになります。

〚注〛 **on your part** は抽象名詞の次にきて単に「君の...」「君が...すること」などいう意味をあらわす、類例：—Apology *on my part* is out of the question. (私がわびるなどとはもってのほか)　**culpable**「とがむべき」「罪ある」。

**146.** ゆえに、われわれは暗黒時代に出た大なる想像力の作品［文学上の著作］を嘆賞するけれども、それが暗黒時代に出たゆえをもって ことさらに嘆賞するのではない。

**147.** われわれは生活の各方面をいそがしく機械化してはいるけれども、いやむしろ、そういう機械化をしていればこそ、われわれの生活の機構の中に小鳥のいる場所を取っておくべき根拠がますます多くあるのだ。

〚注〛 **if we be** if we are の方が今日ではふつうの用法。be の方は形式ばっている。　**reserve** [rizə́:v]「取っておく」。reserve rooms at a hotel と言えば、「ホテルの部屋を予約する」意味。

**148.** 君たちはなお友人がある、すなわち君たちが以前ほどりっぱでない家に住むからと言って、それがために すこしも 君たちを 軽視しない真情(まごころ)のある友人がある。

**149.** 現代の生活において神経の疲労を免れるということはひじょうに困難である。労働時間中ぶっ通しに、なおその職場と家庭の間の往復ですごされる時間にも、都会の勤労者は騒音にさらされている。なるほどその大部分は意識的には聞かないようになりはするが、しかしそれでも勤労者をすっかり疲労させてしまう。

〚注〛 **all through**=throughout.　**spent** は spend の過去分詞で、which is spent と補ってみよ。　**is exposed to...**「...にさらされる」。　**it is true ..., but...** は (109) 参照。　**learns to...**「...するようになる」、類例：— You will *learn* to love music. (今に音楽が好きになる)

**150.** しばしば私は、ボートを風と波にまかせて 漂わせ 白日の 夢にふけったが、その夢はばかばかしくあったけれども、それでもやっぱり楽しいものだった。

〖注〗 **abandon oneself to**=give oneself up completely to「〜に身をまかせる、〜にふける」。もうひとつの意味は、「自制を失う」。**daydream**=idle thoughts of plesant things（楽しい空想）

**151.** よい話は二度したからといって悪くはない（何度でもけっこう）。

**152.** 青年は陛下にじっと見つめられて幾分か気恥ずかしいために落ち着かないところもあったが、優雅なところはすこしも平生と異ならなかった。

〖注〗 **underwent...not the less gracefully**「[凝視を]より少なくない優雅さでうけた」。 **that**=become. **〜was mingled with**...「〜は...とまざっていた」。

**153.** ある人が真に何を賛美するかがわかれば、その人がどんな人であるか、あるいは少なくともどんな人間になりそうであるかに関して何かしら推測を下すことができよう。 もちろんこれは徳性にしか当てはまらない。なぜなら、たとえば、（それを）持っていないためになおさらのこと ひじょうに醜い人は美を賛美し、弱い人は強さを賛美することもあるから。

〖注〗 **If we knew** は現在の事実に反対の仮定であるから knew と過去になり、これを受けて we might となっている。(94) 参照。 **as to** ...「...に関して」。 **what sort of a man**「どういう種類の人」。 **applies to**「当てはまる」。 **for not possessing it**「それを持たないことのために」。 it は beauty と strength を両方受けている。

**154.** 旅そのものでも同じだが、旅の話をするにも、私はとめどを知らない。なつかしい母のもとに近づくにつれて、私の心臓は高鳴った、けれどもそのために別に足を早めることはしなかった。

〖注〗 **throb**「どきどきする」。類例:—His heart ceased to *throb*. (彼はこと切れた) My heart gave a *throb*. (心臓がどきんとした)

---

( 18 )

**155.** 絶対の正義は絶対の真理と同様に達し得べきものではない。しかし真理を欲求する念で誠実な人と不誠実な人とを見分け得るように、正義を欲求する念で正しい人と不正の人との見分けがつく。

〖注〗 **the false** 次に man が略されたもの。

**156.** 人は無礼を働く権利のないと等しく無礼な言葉を発する権利はない。[また] 他人を打ち倒す権利のないと等しく他人に粗暴なる言葉を吐く権利はない。

**157.** 知識に関して言えば、骨を折らずに人間の心にこれを植えつけることができないのは、ちょうどあらかじめ犂(すき)を用うることなしには畑1枚の小麦も生産することができないと同様である。

〚注〛 **as for**「に関して言えば」。 **a field of wheat**「畑1枚の小麦」。

**158.** もし太陽が消滅することになるとすれば、1日か2日で全地球はひじょうにおそろしい氷にかたく閉ざされてしまって、あらゆる動植物は滅亡してしまうだろう。われわれは熱湯の中に生きていられないと同様にそのような氷の中に生きていられないのである。

**159.** ばか者に自分がばか者であることをどうして悟らせることができましょう。そういうお方はご自分の耳が見えないと同じようにご自分のばかなことに気がつきはしません。

**160.** 人が一生を送るに当って前方を見ないわけに行かないのは、ちょうどボートを走らせる場合と同様である。どちらの場合にもその方向は、前方に横たわっているものに関するその人の考え、希望する事物に関するその人の確信、によって決定される。

〚注〛 **avoid** help に置きかえてみよ。 **...than he can...** 次に avoid looking ahead を補ってみる。 **in one case as in the other** (case).「ひとつの場合においてももうひとつの場合のように」「前者の場合も後者の場合も」、(24) 参照。

**161.** その象は、それだけ離れていて、おだやかに(草を)食べていたから、め牛同様すこしも危険には見えなかった。

**162.** 人は一生をジャズ気分ですごすことができないと同様、教育をジャズ気分で通りすぎることはできない、ということは今もなお真理である。学問は常に厳格な知性の訓練、すなわち困難に堪えることと、むずかしい仕事を喜んで引き受けることとを含んでいなければならない。

〚注〛 **remains** is に置きかえてよい。 **jazz through**「ジャズを踊るようにして通り抜ける、ふざけてやっていく」。

**163.** 仕事が人生の目的ではないことはもちろんで、それはちょうど遊びが人生の目的でないと同様である。両者は共に同一の目的に達する手段である。

**164.** 彼は、さながら物音ひとつない沙漠の中に立っているように[周囲の]雑踏(ざっとう)に気づかないようであった。彼は深く思いに沈んでいたのである。

【注】「沙漠の静けさが 彼の周囲にあったかのようにその雑踏に 気がつかなかった」という意味であるけれども、He did not notice the bustle as if the silence of a desert had been around him. といわないで本文のようにいうのが英語の慣用である。**was wrapt in his own thoughts**「自分の思いに包まれていた」、wrapt のかわりに sunk, absorbed など用いても同じこと、類例:—He was *absorbed in* study. (勉強に夢中になっていた) He was *sunk in* deep thoughts. (深い物思いに沈んでいた)

**165.** ブラントがこの発見を どうしてよいか わからないことは こども同様であった。

**166.** 賢人は死をおそれない。また彼は自分に苦しみを与える人々に対し怒りを感じないが、それは母親がそのために自分の命をも投げ出すところの子供に対して、子供が自分に苦しみを与えたときでさえも怒りを感じないのと同様である。

【注】**lay down one's life for** ...「...のために命を捨てる」。**it has imposed** の it は the child をさす。

**167.** けれども、いつも運が悪いなどというのはとんでもない話だ。いつも運がよいということがないと同様に、いつも運が悪いということもないものだ。

**168.** エジプトの墓やローマやポンペーにも、岩石や草木を写実風に表現しているゆえに風景画として分類され得る壁画はある、けれども、それらは、たとえば中国の壁紙と同様、われわれの風景画の概念には一致しない。

【注】tomb は「納骨所」などと言って、建造物を考えてよいが grave はもっと一般に「死者を埋める所」の意味。churchyard は教会に所属する「墓所」、cemetery は「共同墓地」。**conform**=obey; be in agreement with what is generally accepted or required. 類例:—You must *conform* to the rules. (規則に従わねばならない) **this type of painting**「この型の絵画」、ここでは風景画のこと。

**169.** 女神ダイアナにもましてソファイヤ・ワクルズは身の振舞いにやかましいですよ、本当に。

【注】**Diana**=the moon goddess (月の女神). **I can tell you** が文の冒頭あるいは末尾にあると「...ですよ」「...だぜ」「...だわ」などの気持。類例:— It is hard work, *I can tell you*. (骨が折れるぜ)

( 19 )

**170.** どんなに電話をけなそうと、よろこんで電話なしにすましうるものはすくない。自宅に電話を持つことに慣れている人にとっては、電話をはずしてしまえと命ずることくらいつらい克己(の種類)は すくないであろう。

〘注〙 **Whatever may be said**=whatever people may say「なんと言おうとも」。**in dispraise of**「けなして」、類例：—to write poems *in praise of* the blossoms（花を賞して歌をよむ）　**be without**=do without「なしにすます」。

**171.** 心にだいじに抱いている信念の源を調べるような労をとるものはすくない、いやむしろ、そうすることに自然に憎しみの情をもつのだ。

〘注〙 **take pains**=work with great care. つまり複数形の pains は effort の意味になる。**cherish**=keep in the mind, memory or heart. 希望や思い出や憎しみなどを「心にいだく」意。**repugnance**=strong dislike or distaste. 形容詞は repugnant で、「に対する嫌悪(けんお)」の「に対する」は towards, against など。

**172.** 自分の前にも後にもあらゆることを未完成のままで、幾多の苦労もなめ幾多の偉業もなしたあげくに、彼は眠りについた。彼ほど疲れて墓へはいったものは少ない、しかしまた彼ほどおそれることなく墓へはいったものもない。彼は安心立命するに足るだけりっぱに仕事をしたのである。

〘注〙 **ever** は few を強調する。ただし日本語には訳しにくい。打消しのときは never となることを記憶すること。

**173.** スターリングラードの戦いほどに、「世界の大決戦」のひとつと称されるに値するものは史上にもあまりない。1945 年の春、ソ連軍によってヒットラーの軍隊がこうむった大敗北ほど完全な圧倒的敗北は史上にすくない。

〘注〙 **a better title** は **to rank among** とつづく、「仲に列するのによりよい資格」となる、類例：—He has *a title to* a place among the great poets.（彼は大詩人に列する資格をもっている）本問題では to の次に動詞がきている。**that which**=the military defeat which. **overtake** は catch up with すなわち「追いつく」意味で、ここの箇所の意味は、the military defeat inflicted upon Hitler's forces by the hands of the Soviet armies と書き換えればいっそうわかりよいだろう。

**174.** 音楽の最大の美は他の芸術とはちがってひとつの国際語であるという点である、というのは音楽は情緒の言語であり、情緒は世界中どこへ行ってもあまり変わらず、西ヨーロッパではほとんど変化のないものだからである。

〖注〗 **as against**...「...と対抗して、...と対比して、...とは違って」。as は *as* yet (=yet) の場合と同じくほとんど意味はない。**hardly at all** は little に対して「ほとんど...でない」という意味が強い。at all については **172** の few に対する ever を参照せよ。

**175.** その場所については、破壊と暴力の光景であり、初めてこれを見る者は「わが思いは我を悩ました」と言っても無理からぬところであった、と、こう言う以外は、今日は述べる必要はほとんどない所であった。

〖注〗 **one might be excused**...**for saying**〜 は仮定法で、if one said〜, he might be excused となおしてみればよくわかるだろう。すなわち、「何々と言っても、ゆるされるだろう、とがめられることはあるまい」ということである。"My thoughts troubled me." の出所は不明であるが、「いろいろと思いにふけって心が悩んだ」という意味になる。

**176.** われわれの人生における滞在は短いけれども、人生こそはその中において各人が各人の存在の大目的を全力を尽して仕遂げなければならないところの定められた世界である。そしてそれを仕遂げてしまえば、肉体上に起こるいろいろの出来事はわれわれが最後に身につけるところの永生不死にはほとんど影響しない。

〖注〗 **to the best of his power**=as best as he can.

**177.** 彼らの幾千という人は世に知られずに滅び、少数のものが偉人の名を得る。彼らは自分自身に対しても他人に対しても同様に敏感であり、思いやりがあって、しかもさしでがましくなく、彼らの勇気はから威張りではなく、耐えしのぶ力であり、また彼らはじょうだんを解するのである。

〖注〗 **in obscurity**「無名のまま」「世に知られずに」。obscure は「暗い」「不明瞭な」の意味。**sensitive** は「感じやすい」で、これと共に sensible (ものわかりがよい), sensuous (感覚的), sensual (官能的) など区別をよくわきまえておくこと。**considerate** は形容詞で、その動詞は consider. また、consider は別に considerable (少なからず) という形容詞も作る。

**178.** 科学上の大発見の中には、偶然になされたものがすくなくない。ある一定の目的に達しようと出発して、研究者は途中で自分の目的には

いっていなかった法則や元素にぶつかるのである。

〚注〛 **by accident**=accidentally.　**in his way**=on his way「途中で」。

**179.**　君が良い学者になることは私の望むところだが、心の美しいりっぱな人になることの方がもっと望ましい。君が健全な良心を身につけて卒業するならば、フランス語が少しぐらいまずくても私はそんなに気にしない。

〚注〛 **clean** 潔癖な。　**sound** 正しい。

**180.**　われわれは時々いなかで、すこし手を入れればすっかりちゃんとするだろうと思われるのに、門はちょうつがいがはずれ、垣($\frac{ヵキ}{ね}$)はこわれ、庭は草だらけになったままの家の前を通ることがある。われわれは、ここに住んでいる人はあまり物事をのんきに考えすぎているのだと思う。

〚注〛 **where the gates...weeds** は house を修飾する。**a little labor** は「もし少しの労力を加えれば」という条件文を省略した形であるから would をもって受けたのである。**takes things too easily**「物事をのんきに考えすぎる」。類例：—*Take it easy!* (のんきにしろ)

**181.**　私たちの傷はすくなからず痛んだ、そして、もういちど時間をかけて傷を洗ったけれど、傷口がひじょうにこわばってきて、そのために進むのに骨が折れまたおそくなった。

**182.**　航海士はようやくのことで、風下の方へ流れ去る氷塊をさし示した。

〚注〛 **with no little difficulty**=with great difficulty「けっしてすくなからざる困難をもって」、no little は「すくないどころかひじょうな(困難)」などの意味。

**183.**　彼がそれまでに学び知ったところは、ただ彼に、自分の知るところは、将来学び知らねばならないことの多いのに比すれば、いかに少ないかということを悟らせるにすぎなかった。

〚注〛 **in comparison to...**=as compared with...「...と比較すれば」。**what remained to be known**「これから知らねばならないこと」、「まだ知らないこと」、類例：—Much *remains yet to be done*. (まだしないことがたくさんある)

**184.**　ジョンは妻が持ってきてくれた財産のほかには生活の資はきわめてすこししか得られまい、ということを私は知っていた。

〚注〛 I knew John would have very little to live upon. と書きなおしてみよ。**to live upon**=upon which to live「それで生計を立てるべき」。類

例:—He has nothing but his salary to *live upon*. (給料だけで生計を立てている)

**185.** 彼はそれがどんな重大な結果を生じるだろうかということは想像もしなかったのである。

**186.** 彼らは、それが、ぼろ着物で家に置いてきたシンデレラだとはすこしも気がつかなかった。

**187.** あなたはどういう人といっしょに行進を始めるのかということをすこしも知らないのだ。

〚注〛 **in what company**=with whom と見てよい。

**188.** 彼らは都会に住む人が夢想だもしないような蛮勇(ばんゆう)をもって事業にとり組むのである。

**189.** 彼は自分のためにはきわめてすこししか費さなかったが、公益のためには惜しげなく費した。

〚注〛 **spend on**...「...に金を使う」、類例:—He *spends* much money *on* books. (彼は書物にたくさん金を使う) **his hand was open** とはいわゆる握りやの反対で、「惜しまず金を出したということ」。

---

( 20 )

**190.** お互いの様を見かわすと、二人とも妙な姿をしているので、笑っていいのやら、こわがっていいのやら わからないくらいであった。

**191.** ペリクリーズ時代の ギリシア国民はほとんど 皆役職についたり、業務を果たしたりする資格が一様にある人々であった。それで公職の大多数は抽せんによって定めるという規定があったが、これがために才幹なき無能な人を選択するようなことはきわめてまれであった。

**192.** 夜、星を見ていると、星はじっとして動かないように見えるから、そのとき星が今まで人間の出した最高速度をはるかに越える速度で走っているとはほとんど信じられない。

〚注〛 **velocity far exceeding any that man has ever accomplished**「人間が今までに出したどんな速さをもはるかに越えた速さ」。

**193.** 原子物理学全体がまだ発達の初期にあって、その理論的および実際的進歩の方面で当然予想しうることは、ほとんど無限である。

〚注〛 **what** (=that which)...**expected**「当然予想されること」。

**194.** 自然の活動のどの部門でも、人が行なうどの有用な技術でも、その中に化学の法則と原理が含まれていないものはほとんどないということが、時が進むにつれて、ますます明白になりつつある。

**195.** 彼は召使たちに腹をたてることはほとんどなかった。こんなことはめったに起こらなかったことは次のことでよくわかる、すなわち、私がこどものころ、召使がしかられ、父がどなっているのを立ち聞きしたとき、私はおそろしい出来事だと感じて、なんとなく恐怖感におそわれて二階へかけ上がったのを覚えているのだ。

〚注〛 **be angry with**「誰々に対して腹をたてる」。**it shows how seldom this occurred, that...** の構文は it は that 以下全文をうけ、this は前に述べた「召使に腹をたてること」をさす。であるから、how seldom this occurred is shown by the fact that... のように書きなおしてみればよくわかる。that 以下の節では主節は it impressed me... と I remember... である。**impressed me as**「～として私に印象を与えた」。

---

### ( 21 )

**196.** 年々数千の人々がスイスに行き冬季競技に参加したり、夏山に登ったりする。どの山も高いために、あるいはけわしいために、または近よりがたいために、登山者を恐怖させることはなく、ひとつまたひとつと峰々は征服され、登山者の数の多いこと今や秋の落葉さながらである。

〚注〛 **to make one's way**「行く」。**to take part in...**「...に参加する」。

**197.** 習慣という鎖は概してひじょうに小さいから、気がつかずにいる間にいつか断ち切ることのできないほど丈夫なものになってしまう。

**198.** 生活の必需品および富の原料をほとんど自給自足している国々は、食物や石炭や石油を海外から輸入しなければならない国々よりも安全である。——実際、力が弱くて自国の自然の富を守ることができないというのでなければ。

〚注〛 **self-support**「自給自足する」。**as regards**「...に関して」。regards は動詞。主語は as の中に含まれる。**be obliged to～**「～をよぎなくされる」。

**199.** ローマ人はその当時知られていただけの全世界を征服したけれども、その征服した民族から有益なる学問を学ぶことを恥としなかった。

〖注〗 **were masters of**...「...の主となった」とは「...を征服した」ということ、類例：—Hideyoshi *made himself master* of the Empire. (秀吉が天下を取った) **were not too proud to learn**=were not ashamed of learning. 類例：—He is *too proud to* ask questions.=He *is ashamed of* asking questions. (彼は自尊心が強くて質問しない＝質問することを恥としている)

**200.** さて、ある題目は文学の威厳を損ずるように考えられる、そしてこれらの題目のうちのあるものはつまらないから大詩人がとりあげるには足らないと君は思うかも知れない。

〖注〗 **be beneath the dignity**「威厳を落とす」、類例：—It is *beneath your dignity* to do such a thing. (そんなことをすると威厳にかかわる)

**201.** 彼はなかなか苦労人であったからそんなばかなことはしなかった。

〖注〗 **too much of**...「...の性質が多分である」。**man of the world**「世間を知っている人」。**know better** はさらによく知るところがあるから「そんなばかなことはしない」という意味、類例：—You should *know better* at your age. (君くらいの年ではもっと分別がありそうなものだ＝そんなことをするとは年がいもない) すなわち本題は He was too wise to do such a thing. などという意味。

**202.** 私が成功した一大秘訣(ひけつ)は、小さな点に細心の注意を払うという私の生涯の習慣であることは疑いない。どんな小さなことでも私の注意を受けないということはなかった。たいがいの青年が、実際あまりに小さなことと考えそうなことでも私にとってはけっして小さすぎるということはなかったのである。

〖注〗 **secret of the success that has been given me**「私に与えられた成功のひけつ」。**life-long**「生涯つづく」。**most young people seem to think** はカッコの中に入れて考えてみる。

( 22 )

**203.** 真実な、真面目な、重みのある人かどうかわからない人がふしぎな話をしたらば、あまり軽卒にこれを真(ま)に受けたり、または他へ受け売りするようなことをしてはいけない。しかしまたあまりさし出てそのいうことを反ばくするのもよくない。

〖注〗 **a person of weight**=a person of consequence.「(社会に)重きをなす人」「勢力家」。**relate**=tell. **report**「伝え知らせる」。**and yet** は but の強いもの。

**204.** 人は自分のあやまちを知らないではそれを改めることはできない。だからぼくは自分にあやまちを指摘してくれる人をば友人と見なし、けっしてとかく世間一般の人にありがちのように、不愉快に思ったり、怒ったりするようなことはなかった。

〚注〛 **mine**=my faults. **instead of** —ing 「しないで」、類例：—*Instead of going to* school, he idles away his time at home. (学校へ行かないで家でぶらぶらしている)　**be displeased**「不愉快に思う」、類例：—His father *is displeased* with him. (彼は父のごきげんをそこねている)　**people in general**「世間一般の人たち」。

**205.** 理論家はややもすれば事実をただちに言葉の上の考察で決定できるように思う傾きがある。プルタークはめんどりと鶏卵とはいずれが初めに生じたかという問題について、興味ある議論をしている。そして提出された一考案では、めんどりが初めに生じた、なんとなれば何人も卵のめんどりとは言わないで めんどりの卵と言うからであるというのである。

**206.** 彼らは彼女がやさしく彼らを呼ぶ声を聞くと よろこんでその命に従い、従順なこどものように彼女の言いつけのままに動く。

〚注〛 **come and go at her bidding**「彼女の言いつけどおり往(ﾜ)ったり来たりする」。

**207.** 彼は殿下と同じくらいの年かっこうでございますから、よろこんで殿下のお相手をいたすでございましょう。

〚注〛 **wait upon**〜「〜にはべる、仕える」。

**208.** それらの個人主義的国家——そこでは国家の利益が個人の利己的な利益のため あまりにもしばしば犠牲にされ、大臣や将軍や提督が功績のみによって任命されることはめったになく、戦時においてさえ汚職が起こり、実際に法律によって罰せられないことはなんでも許されると考えられている——そういう国家はこの国の実例から学ぶとよい、というのは、この国の偉大さと成功の原因は愛国心という一語にまとめ得ることは疑いのないところだからである。

〚注〛 **do well to**...「...するとよい、するのが賢明である」。

**209.** われわれ自身の世代は「虚偽の支配」というものをいやというほど知ってきた。ヒットラーとナチス党からこれを知り、それからレーニンとスターリンからこれを知った。

〖注〗 **the Reign of the Lie** は the Reign of Terror (恐怖時代)などにまねて造った言葉。

**210.** 一つの社会が十分運動することはけっこうなことだが、運動遊戯を第一にし、他の事がらをすべて第二にすることはよくない。現代の運動第一主義はたしかに極端に走っている。 適度の運動は精力を蓄積するが、過度の運動はそれを浪費する。

〖注〗 **subordinate~ to**...「~を...の下に置く」。

--------

( 23 )

**211.** 交際に関してわれわれが守る規則を書物にも適用し、近づきになる価値のない書物を近づけないように十分厳重にしなければならない。

〖注〗 **apply~to**...「~を...に適用する」。通例ならば apply the rules *to* books のようにするのであるが、本題では rules に形容詞節がついて長くなったから後へ回したのである。 **in regard to**...=regarding...「に関して」。 **refusing** も applying と同じ関係で be strict in へつづく。 **refuse our acquaintance to**...「...に対して知り合いになることを拒む」「交際を拒絶する」。 **those books** (which are) **unworthy of it** の it は our acquaintance をさす。

**212.** われわれは皆、何が起こるかわからないときにはもっとも悪いことを気づかいがちである。だから苦労や難儀を実際以上に大きく考えないようにいやが上にも注意すべきである、ことにこういうわが国にとって都合の悪い時世においては。

〖注〗 **are apt to**...「とかく...しがちである」。

**213.** 書籍は隣人にも譬(たと)えられよう、もし良いものならばどんなに長く続けてもさしつかえなく、もし悪いものならば一時も早く捨て去るべきである。

〖注〗 **compare~to**...=**liken~to**...「~を...に譬える」、類例:―Life is often *compared to* a voyage. (人生はしばしば航海にたとえられる) **get rid of**「(厄介を)除く」。

**214.** 出版言論の自由は、新聞発行者やラジオ、テレビの放送局管理者や、その他の方法で報道や思想を広める人々の便宜のためのものでないことは、いくたび思い起こしても、すぎる心配はない。出版言論の自由は公共のため、公共全体のためにあるので、他のもろもろの自由と不可分に関

連しているのである。

〖注〗 **remind** は to *remind* some one *of* something の形をとるときと of something のかわりに that-Clause がくるときとがある。**the press**「新聞、雑誌」すなわち言論機関のこと。**spread~abroad**「~を広く伝える」で abroad はここでは「外国へ」と考えてはいけない。

**215.** 運動に時間をさくことはできないと考える人がある。そういう人は、運動のための時間を作らなければならないということを、いくら早く教えても早すぎることはない。そうでないと彼らは病気のため時間をつくらなければならなくなるであろう。

〖注〗 **spare time**「時間を割愛(かつあい)する」、類例:—Can you *spare* me a quarter of an hour? (15分間おじゃまできますか) **find time for**...「...をする時間をつくる」。

**216.** 時間に余裕のない教師として、大英百科全書から得られる知識の価値はぼくには推賞しきれない[ほど とおといものである]。

〖注〗 **time at my disposal**「自分の自由になる時間」、類例:—This is all the money now *at my disposal*. (いま使える金はこれだけだ) If you wish to ride, my car is *at your service*. (乗りたいなら私の自動車を貸してあげます、ご自由にお使いなさい)

**217.** この勇気ある科学者のおかげでできた英国の最初の地質学的地図を、どんなに賞賛してもけっしてほめすぎにはならない。

〖注〗 **speak in terms of too high praise of**=speak too highly of.

**218.** 50年の研究と労力とを費してようやくガリレオはその振子の発明を完成した。この発明が時間を計り、また天文学上の計算をなすにどんなに重要であるかは、ほとんど言いつくすことができない。

〖注〗 **elapse** (=pass away) は時間の経過について用いる語。**an invention** 以下は the invention of his pendulum の同格 (Apposition)。**overvalue**「過大に評価する」。反対は undervalue.

**219.** 蚕(かいこ)は感覚がひじょうに鋭くかつ せん細な 動物であるから、いやが上にも注意してその住居を清潔にし、たえずきれいな空気を入れて元気づけてやらなければならない。私は、偶然の悪臭のため、蚕が弱って幾十匹も一度に死ぬのを見たことがある。

〖注〗 **in scores**「続々とたくさん」。

**220.** アメリカの生活において、自由な、競争的な(独占的でない)、個人企業の果たす 中心的役割は、いくら 重要視してもさしつかえあるまい。

しかしアメリカ文明の力の基本的源泉はもっと深いところにある、すなわち、その源は倫理的であり、精神的なのである。

**221.** 住所の選択はたといそこにただ二三年の短日月を過ごそうと欲する場合でも、知的見地から見てきわめて重要なる事がらで、その価値はどんなに重大視しても誇大ということはできぬくらいである。

〚注〛 a matter so important＝so important a matter. consequence 「重要さ」。

―――――

(24)

**222.** 現代に必要なことは印刷物を少なくし、読書を少なくし、思索を多くすることである。読書はたやすく、思索はむずかしい、前者は後者を伴なわなければ無益である。

**223.** 公職にある人はほとんど常に過度の非難をうけるか、または、過度の賞賛をうける。そして自己をよりよく知っていればいるほど、非難されたからといってむやみに悲観することも、またほめられたからといってやたらに得意になることも、少なくなるだろう。

〚注〛 the more...the less 「多ければ多いほど...それだけ少なく」、(16)参照。 the less likely 「それだけしそうではない」。 unduly 「不当に、過度に」。

**224.** われわれは、身体と精神との関係がひじょうに密接なものであることに気づかないわけには行かない、そして前者が後者にいかに影響するかに気づいたとき、われわれは健康を保つことが道徳的義務であることを認めなければならないのである。

〚注〛 cannot fail to...＝cannot but... 「きっと...する」。

**225.** この間ひとりの少年が嘲弄(ちょうろう)的な口調でその相手(の少年)に向かって「オイ貴様は年期小僧じゃないか」と言った。そういった方の少年は、身分はいやしいながらおのずから威厳のある相手よりは、身分が上だということは着ているものでわかった。ののしられた方は陽気な活発な少年で、年のころようやく12歳ぐらい、粗末なものではあるがきちんとしたなりをしていた。

〚注〛 attired＝dressed.

**226.** 1783年、アイスランドにおける一火山は二筋の溶岩を噴出した、一つは長さ40マイル幅7マイル、一つは長さ50マイル幅15マイルであった。

**227.** 女は押入れのところへ駆けて行ってきれいなさっぱりした前掛けと帽子とを取り出し、前掛けは腰のまわりに、帽子は愛嬌のある顔をつつむようにつけた。…そしていそがしく階下へ駆けおりた、するとそこに自分の夫と二人の紳士とが立っていた。かみさんは二人の客に別々にていねいに礼をした。

〖注〗 **good woman** ここでは「おかみさん」の意味。**first to one then to the other**「はじめ一方の人にそれからこんどは別の方の人に」。

**228.** こうして、ある者は牢獄に避難所を求めようとして窃盗(とう)の罪を犯し、ある者は自分にわずかの米を与えなかった友人の家を焼き、またある者は妻子を飢餓に任せて南国に逃げた。

〖注〗 secure は得がたいもの、ほしいものなどを得る、手に入れる意味に用いるが、ここの secure は seek refuge などとほぼ同意と見てよい、類例:—They *took refuge* in the embassy. (彼らは大使館に避難した) **refuse**「拒んで与えない」。類例:—I can *refuse* you nothing. (君には何を頼まれてもいやといえない)

―――――――――

( 25 )

**229.** 働くことと遊ぶこととは共に健康に欠くべからざるものである。これ(遊び)はわれわれに休息を与え、あれ(仕事)はわれわれに元気を与える。

**230.** 犬は猫よりも忠実な動物である。猫は場所(家)に執着し犬は人に愛着する。

**231.** 冬と夏とは[貴賤(せん)上下の別なく]だれにでも一様にくる、これ(夏)は花をもたらし、あれ(冬)は雪をもたらす。

**232.** 貧乏な人々は金持の持っている便益のあるものを持っていない、しかしそれだからといってわれわれは金持の人々を幸福と思い、貧乏な人人を不幸と思ってはならない。

〖注〗 **want**「欠く」。**account**=consider.「…と考える」。

―――――――――

( 26 )

**233.** 仕事が人間に対すると動物に対するとでは別物であるということ、また仕事が簡単な自然的な機能でなくなったということを、われわれは残念がる必要はない。またわれわれは仕事が競技の一種になることを望むべきではない、なぜならそうなると仕事は不生産的になるからである。

〚注〛 **has ceased to be**「...でなくなった」、類例：—It will *cease to be* novel. (めずらしくなくなる) **Nor should we**...=And we should not....

**234.** 病気の治療と予防が大いに進歩したといっても、人間のすべての苦痛が人間の知恵で征服できるということにはならない。

〚注〛 **affliction**「(病気などもふくめて)難儀、苦痛」。 **be overcome**「打ちまかされる」「征服される」。 類例：—He *is overcome with* sorrow. (ひどく悲しんでいる) He *was overcome by* their entreaties. (彼は彼らに拝みたおされた)

**235.** 自分のほんとうのところを知ることと、それを他人の口から言われるのとは別のことだ。

〚注〛 たとえば、自分の欠点はちゃんと欠点として知っていても、他人から、お前にはこういう欠点があるぞと言われると、いい気持ちはしない、ということ。 **have it told one** の it は truth で one は「その人に」で間接目的語。この構文については (71) 参照。

**236.** 諸君はもしだれに対してでも非難すべきところがあるなら、ほかの者にいわないで当人にその不平をいうがいい。人前と陰とで別の人間になろうとするほどあぶない芸当はない。

〚注〛 **to find fault with**...「...の欠点を見つける、...を非難する、とがめる」。 **tell him of what you complain**=tell him of your complaint. **behind one's back**「いないところで＝陰で」、類例：—You should not speak ill of others *behind their backs*. (陰で人をそしるものじゃない)

**237.** だれでも知っているとおり、金持であることと賢明で勇敢で人情のあることとはまったく別なことであるし、また一国民がいかにして金持になるかという問題と、いかにして自由に有徳に、あるいは文学、芸術、軍事、政治においてひいでるかという問題とは、まったく異なった問題である。

〚注〛 **humane** に対して human は「人間の」という意。 **enquiry**=inquiry. (質問)

( 27 )

**238.** 自分の着物にせよ他人の着物にせよ、着物のことをかれこれ言ってはなりません。たぶんあなた方はみすぼらしい身なりをした男の子か女の子を見かけるでしょう。しかしそれがなんでしょう。木綿も絹と同じこと清潔であり得るのです。

**239.** 広々した海面を眺めたとき、私の心は釈放された囚人の心のように踊った。私は心の中に消しがたい好奇心が燃え上がるのを感じた、それでこの機会を捕えて他の国々の風俗を見物しようと決心した。

〚注〛 **I cast my eye**「視線を投げた」「眺めた」。cast は現在、過去、過分とも同形である。この場合は過去。**waters** 具体的に海(または河)の水をさすときは複数形を使う。**that of**=the heart of. **I felt...kindle**「...が燃えるのを感じた」、(69) 参照。**manners** (複数)は「行儀」「作法」をさすときと「習俗」「風習」を意味する場合とある。

**240.** 北方諸国のいずれにも、熱帯繁茂の盛んな様($\frac{き}{う}$)に比すべきものは何もない。広々としたアメリカの風景における色彩は美しいものであるが、それも熱帯風景の色彩に比すれば壮麗という点においてほとんどゼロである。

〚注〛 **with which** の which は nothing を受ける。初めの方を any of the northern countries has nothing with which to compare... となおして見てもよい。**compare~with...**「~を...とくらべる」。**lovely as** (82) 参照。**as nothing to...**「...に比すれば無のようなもの」、類例:—My diligence is *as nothing to* yours. (ぼくの勉強などは君の勉強とはくらべ物にならない)

**241.** アメリカにおいてさえ、実際のところ、少女や婦人の教育は少年や成年男子の教育よりずっとおくれていた。女の子はわずかに最低の初等学校だけに、読み書きを学ぶために、自由に入学を許されていた。

〚注〛 **as a matter of fact**=in reality.

**242.** 人間が社交的生物であることはだれでも認めるであろう。このことは、人間が孤独をきらうことに、また自分の家族との交際以上の交際を欲することの中に認められる。

**243.** われわれの受けている困苦あるいは災難は、かりにわれわれが他人と境遇を換えることができるとして、その人の困苦災難を堪え忍ぶよりもいっそう たやすいものである。

〚注〛 この文は少々ややこしいが、大体は、「自分の困難よりも他人の困難の方が堪えやすいように見えるが、他人と位置を代えてその人の困難に当ってみると、最初の自分の受けていた困難の方がたやすいということがわかる」というような意味である。**we lie under**＝under which we lie として見よ、すなわち「われわれがこうむっている(困苦災難)」。 **would be** の次に easy to us を補ってみよ。 **in case**＝if.

---

( 28 )

**244.** ある人の概括的印象、しかも永続性の一番ありそうな印象は、主としてその人の日常生活から作られるもので、どれほどすばらしかろうとも挿話的な出来事のあれこれから形成されるものではない。

〚注〛 **however striking they may happen to be** 「挿話的出来事がたまたまどんなにいちじるしくあろうとも」。(93) 参照。

**245.** リチャード王は強壮な、じっとしていられない、肥大漢で、いつも心にただ一つの考えを持っていた、しかもその考えは人の脳天を打ち割ってやりたいというやっかいきわまるものであった。

〚注〛 **break one's head**＝kill a person by a blow on the head.

**246.** しかしわれわれは、いやしくも生存する限りは、国家をもつことを望む、あるいは少なくとも国家を持つ希望を持つことを望む、しかもそれは自由の国家でなければならない。

〚注〛 **while I do live** は while I live を強めるために do を入れたのだから、「いやしくも」などと訳してもよい。 **let me have a country**＝give me a country＝I want to have a country.

**247.** われわれは1マイル足らずを行くのに2時間もかかった、しかも時には河、時には岩山で、危険をおかしてなのだ。

**248.** 大天才が救貧院のやっかいになって死んだ例は往々(おうおう)あるが、これは人格というものを欠いていたからである。(これに反して)別段の才もない人々が富豪として、しかも世人から非常に尊敬される富豪として死んだのは皆その人の人格の賜物である。

〚注〛 **poorhouse**＝workhouse「貧民救助院」。 **on account of**＝owing to.

**249.** 彼は考えた、「どこか隠す場所を見つけなければならない、しかも二三秒のうちにだ、さもないと、万事休すとなるのだ」。

〚注〛 **with me**「私の場合に」「私にとって」の意味。 with＝in the case of.

in the world は強意の表現。(39) 参照。

**250.** 人は皆仕事に従事すべきもの、しかも自己の天性のなし得る最高の仕事に従事し、最善を尽したという自覚をもって死ぬことができるように努むべきである。

〖注〗 **let every man be...** =every man *should* be... と見てよい。**be occupied in...** =be engaged in...「...に従事する」。**be capable of ...**「...に堪える」、例:—His nature *is* not *capable of* this employment. (彼の性質はこの職に堪えられない)

---

( 29 )

**251.** 人間の ざわめき声やら、牛のなき声やら、豚の キーキーという声やら、道化役の呼び起こす笑い声やらで、市場は雑踏(ざっとう)をきわめていた。

〖注〗 **merry-andrew** 軽業(かるわざ)などで妙な姿をして出てこっけいを演じて見物人を笑わせる者。

**252.** 人口は増加するし、原料はないので、日本は高い生活費で苦しんでいる。

**253.** 食料品の高値やら、時々病気するやらで、この一家のものは自分たちの収入で生活するのが大いに困難になった。

〖注〗 **to live on...**「...を常食とする」意味と、「...で生活する」意味とある、類例:—We *live on* rice. (われわれは米を常食とする) He *lives on* his salary of 30,000 yen a month. (彼は3万円の月給で暮している)

**254.** むすこが無事で帰ってきたのを見た喜びやら、自分たちの幸運やらで、母親は二、三日で病気がなおってしまった。母親はたいそうむすこ自慢になり、自分をたずねてくる人たちに むすこの 冒険談をして 聞かせることにけっしてあきなかった。

〖注〗 **safe and sound**「まめで達者で」などと重ねるのに当たる。**get well**「平癒(へいゆ)する」、この反対は get ill=fall ill (発病する). **never tired of talking about...**「...の話をすることにあきなかった」。tire は「疲らせる」「あきさせる」という他動詞であるから、日本語の「疲れる」「あきる」は英語では Passive にして
　I *am tired* of reading. (読書にあきた)
　I *am tired* with walking. (歩いて疲れた)
などとなるのが通例だが、否定のときは tire を自動詞として

I *never tire* of reading Shakespeare. (私はシェイクスピアはいくら読んでもあきない)
I *never tire* of sea-views. (海の景色はいつ見てもよい)
のように用いることが多い。

**255.** 一つには怠惰のため、一つには気位が高いために、そのスペイン人は働く気にはなれない。

〚注〛 **bend** は「ひざを屈する」、すなわち「誇りを捨てる」こと。

**256.** 公私の用務[多端]で私はちっとも暇がない。

**257.** そこで暗がりにすわって波の音やら船の揺れるのやらで私は眠ってしまった。

**258.** 彼は税関の長官をしていた、そしてわいろやら、ゆすりやらで、ばくだいな金をためこんだ。

**259.** 私は裸になって着物を船に入れ、その船をひっぱって、徒渉(しょう)したり泳いだりしてブレファスキューの王[家御用の]港に達した。

〚注〛 **stript** (=stripped) **myself** (of my clothes) と補う、なお (**67**) 参照。

---

( 30 )

**260.** 卒業後も自分の教育に関心を持ちつづけてきた人ならだれでも知っていることであるが、高校や大学で学ぶことはせいぜい教育の一部分で、教育のほんの初めにすぎない。

〚注〛 **at best**「もっともよい場合でも」、「せいぜい」。

**261.** ひじょうに重要なことは、アメリカでは、正しいことをふつう一般の人が大事なことだと考え、真実が大事だと考えることである。

〚注〛 **matters**=is important.

**262.** 馬は全速力で駆け出した、そしてハンスは、自分がどうしているか気づく間もなく投げ飛ばされ、道ばたの溝の中に横たわっていた。

〚注〛 **what he was about**=what he was doing.

**263.** なすべきことはなそうと決心しなさい、そして決心したことは必ず実行しなさい。

〚注〛 **what you ought** (to perform) と補え。**without fail**「まちがいなく」「かならず」、類例:—I will pay you *without fail* by the end of the month. (月末までにはまちがいなくお返し申します)

**264.** 彼は朝晩近所のある人の仕事をしてやって、自分には大金と思わ

れるほどの金をためた、そしてその金を書物に費した。
　〘注〙 **night and morning** は晩と朝だけのこと、すなわち昼間は他の目的に費したものと見る。

**265.**　しかしけっきょく、外国の都会でもっともわれわれの興味を引くものは廃墟でも、教会でも、絵画でも、歴史や伝説の古跡でもなく、その地の日常生活——町の人だかりや、車馬の往来や、店頭である。
　〘注〙 **after all**「やはり」「結局」。

**266.**　過去のものを記憶することと未来のものを予期することは人間が他の動物ともっとも異なる二つの機能のように思われる。人間は、この二つの源から幸福を引き出そうと努力するし、またこの二つから大部分の不幸を経験するのである。
　〘注〙 **from these two sources** は happiness と miseries 両方にかかる。

**267.**　イギリス国民とアングロ・サクソン民族に対する歴史の最後の裁決が何であるかは、われわれの予想すべきことではない。しかしながら、われわれの言語上の試験、すなわち、文明の言語にわれわれが今まで付け加えたものを調査してみると、すくなくともわが民族の過去の業績については一つの意見を出すことができる。
　〘注〙　英語というものが世界の文化に貢献したことは認められるだろうという主旨の文。 **our linguistic test**「言語学上から見た功罪のためし」で次の **examination** 以下でくわしく説明してある。 **so far**＝up till now. (今まで) **enables** の主語は test, examination であるが、訳文では主語のところを副詞節にしてある。 **an opinion** は a favourable (好意的) opinion のふくみ。

**268.**　現代が必要とするものは、物的資源や知識技能の増加ではなく、それらを一部の利益のため利己的に用いずに、万人の利益のため無私の心をもって用いようとする動機と意志であることは、明らかである。

──────────

( 31 )

**269.**　読書しなさい、読んだことを熟慮しなさい、自分の判断を作りなさい、そしていわゆる学者なるものの言がどうであろうと、事実や証明によって自分の誤りを納得させられるまでは、自分の判断を固守しなさい。
　〘注〙 **in spite of**＝notwithstanding「にもかかわらず」。 **be offered** の be は is と同じだが、少し形式ばった用法。 **convince of~**「~を悟らせる」、類例:—
I cannot *convince him of* his error. (彼の誤解を悟らせることができない)

**270.** 旅客、らくだ、らくだ追いとがいっしょになって、いわゆる隊商というものを成すのである。

**271.** 彼の主義は簡易に、かつ常に自分のもうけた金額以内で生活することだった。彼が指摘したように、これは貧乏の心配をなくし、新事業に対する資金、いわゆる資本を供給する唯一の方法だった。

〔注〕 **the one way**＝the only way.

**272.** ふつうにいわれている平和はけっして（真の意味の）平和ではない。単に戦闘がないというだけでは平和ではない。かえって、平和を欲するものはそれを得んがために戦わなくてはならない。

〔注〕 **absence** は presence（存在）の反対で、「非存在」「欠乏」「無」を意味する。**on the contrary**「それと反対に」、**fight for it**「それを得んがために戦う」、すべて戦う類の動詞は相手をいうときに with を用い、目的をいうときに for を用いる、類例：—
　　to *fight with* the enemy（敵と戦う）
　　to *contend with* difficulties（困難とたたかう）
　　to *struggle with* adversity（逆境とたたかう）
　　to *fight for* liberty（自由を得るがためにたたかう）
　　to *struggle for existence*（生存競争する）
　　to *contend for* the prize（賞を得るために競う）

**273.** すべてこれら河、湖、大洋などの水はたえずいわゆる湿気、あるいは水蒸気となって空中に上昇している。

**274.** かおりのいいばら、あるいはすみれを、かぐのは快い。嗅覚(きゅうかく)は実際われわれが味覚と称するものの多くの部分を成すものであると、私は信ずる。

**275.** 彼らがラジオ・リベレーションから受けた印象はまったく否定的であった。いわゆるその悪罵(ばり)的な口調がいけないのだと彼らは公然とそれを非難した。

〔注〕 **Radio Liberation** ある放送局の名。**negative**「否定的」とは「感心しない」ということ。**for**「何々のかどで」。

**276.** 富むとか貧しいとかいうのはその人の人物いかんによるので、その財産によるものではない。黄金よりも名を重んじる人はすなわち富んでいるのだ。

**277.** 人間は何をするかによっていかなる人間になるかきまる、そのなすことをいかになすかが人物の性質を決定する。

〖注〗 人間というものは観念や主義というものに造られるのでなく、実践によって造られるのだという主旨。

**278.** われわれは首府ローマを瞥見(べっけん)せずにはイタリーを去ることはできそうもない。ローマはその現在によってよりもその過去によって有名な都市である。到る所でわれわれは、この都市が当時知られていたほとんど全世界を支配したローマ帝国の中心であったころの、古き栄光と権勢とを思い起こすのである。

**279.** どこへ君が行こうと、君の祖先がだれであろうと、どんな [中等] 学校や大学で学んでいようと、だれが君を助けようと、君の最上の機会は君自身の中にある。他人から受ける援助は君の外にある何ものかである。ところで重要なのは君の人物と君自身の行為である。

〖注〗 **No matter where**..., **no matter who**..., (no matter) **what school**..., (no matter) **who**... と補ってみよ。(**93**) 参照。

**280.** 私の生涯は半ば以上すぎ去った、おそらくその3分の2はすぎ去ってしまった。頭脳は以前どおりはっきりしている、おそらくまだ長い間はっきりしているだろう、しかし元気は以前のとおりではないし、またそうあり得ない、そして次第に衰えてゆく。

〖注〗 **my years**＝my life. **as~as ever**「相変わらず~」(**38**) 参照。

**281.** 人間は笑ったり泣いたりする唯一の動物である。それは、人間が事物の現状とそのそうであるべき状態との差異を感ずる唯一の動物だからである。

〖注〗 **is struck with difference**「相違に(心を)打たれる」、類例：—to *be struck with* wonder.（驚異の感に打たれる） to *be struck with* terror.（肝を冷やす）

**282.** われわれはただ彼がなしたことに対してのみならず、彼の人物に対して彼を尊敬する。

〖注〗 **for** は賞罰などの原因を示す、「...のかどで」などの意味。類例：—I praised him *for* his honesty.（私は彼の正直を賞した） He was punished *for* his misconduct.（彼は非行を罰られた） **not alone**...**but**＝not only...but. (**110**) 参照。

( 33 )

**283.** お客様を見ると彼はいすから飛び上がり、両手を差し出し心から歓迎した。というのはこの二人は旧友で高校 大学共に学友であり、二人とも自分自身をまたお互いを十分尊敬する人たちであり、そして必ずしもその結果として生ずるとは限らないことだが、お互いの交際を心から喜んでいたからである。

**284.** かくて前途多望の青年は自分も期し、また人からも期待されていた望みを裏切ったばかりでなく、何より悪いことには、年老いた父の心を裏切って失望させた。

〖注〗 **young man of promise**＝promising youth「末たのもしい青年」。**broke the promise** は約束を破った意味ではない、自らも偉い人になろうと期し、人もそう期していたその望みを空にしてしまった、すなわち自己および他人の期待にそむいたこと。the promise made to himself については次の例を参考せよ：—*I promised myself* a plesant evening. (愉快な晩を期待していた——今夜はおもしろいことをしようと待ちもうけていた)

**285.** なまけ者には休息の楽しみはわからない、なぜなら休むだけのことをして休んだことがないから。なお、一生けんめい働くことは肉体に休息を与えるのみならず、さらにいっそう大切なことには、心に平和を与える。もしわれわれが仕事の上に、修養の上に、全力を尽したら、われわれは安心して休むことができる。

〖注〗 **he has not earned it** (＝rest)「彼は休息を得るだけの働きをしなかった」、earn a holiday と言えば、「一日休むだけの働きをして休む」意味である。**tend to...**「...する傾きがある」。**to be**「[りっぱな人に] なりたいと」。

**286.** その上に、もし君が著作で成功しようとするならば、努力しなければならない。物を書きたいと言っている多くの人々は作家になりたいということにすぎない。つまり、仕事はせずに[作家という]地位を欲しているのだ。

**287.** 21歳の年に彼はすっかり自分の職の達人になってしまった。そしてなおよいことは、彼は一般の知識並びに学問上の知識をおどろくほどたくさんに集積した。

〖注〗 **was master of his trade** とは自己の職の奥義をきわめたこと。類例：—He *is master of* his business. (彼は自分の専門をきわめている)

**288.** 事態をいよいよ悪くすることには、われわれは呼吸という行為そのものによって、われわれみずから空気を汚すことを避け得ないことである。

〚注〛 **cannot help spoiling**「汚さざるを得ない、どうしても汚す」。(99) 参照。

---

( 34 )

**289.** もはや(金をくれという)すべての頼みに応ずることができないので、彼は金のかわりに約束を与えた。与えるべきものは約束のほかにはなかったのだ、しかし彼は(人の頼みを)断って人にいやな思いをさせるに忍びなかったのである。

〚注〛 **No longer able to satisfy**=as he could not any longer satisfy. **all he had to bestow** は had to とつけて、must と考えてはいけない。「与えるためにもっていた...」ということ。

**290.** 「ハリスさん」とエドワードが叫んだ、それだけいうのが精一杯であった。というわけは彼の恩人から受けた過去のいろいろな恩恵が心に浮かんで感謝の念で胸が一杯になり、それ以上に言葉が出なかったのである。

〚注〛 **farther utterance was denied**「それ以上言葉を発することができなかった」。

**291.** あの子はたった一分間——ほんのちょっとの短い間、歩哨(しょう)の持ち場で眠ったのです。私はただもうそれだけのことだということを承知しています、なぜなればペニーは自分の仕事をしながら居眠りをしたことはありませんから。

**292.** それらの天才たちが独自の職業を選ぶのは、その職業が一番よいと考えるからでもなく、その職業が もっとも 多くの栄誉や金銭や幸福を与える見込みがあるからでもなくて、そうしないではいられないからである。そして同じ理由で彼らは生命のある限りはその職業を固守する。彼らはただ、現にやっていることが好きであるということしか知らない、したがってそれに全精神を打ちこむのである。

〚注〛 **men of genius**「天才たち」。(1) 参照。**cannot help it**「それをせずにいられない」。**what they are about**=that which they are engaged in.

**293.** あますことを得たごくわずかの時間を私は必要上一刻の猶予も許

さないような法律上の諸点を調査するのに費しました。
  〖注〗 which admitted no delay「猶予を許させなかった」。
  **294.** 私たちが持ち合わせた金はようやく汽車賃にたりるだけだった。
  **295.** 彼はていねいに礼をしていった、「奥さん、私は医師です、ご近所の方があなたが病気だということを知らせてくれましたから、及ばずながら私の力にかなうことはしてあげようと思って参りました」。
  〖注〗 I am come.=I have come. 前者は「状態」に、後者は「動作」に重きを置いた表現。
  **296.** 書類が手許にないから覚えているだけのことからそのお話をしましょう。
  〖注〗 Being at a distance from...=as I am at a distance from...「...から離れているから」。 give account of them「その話をする」。
  **297.** わたしはさしあたって必要な荷物だけを下宿から持って行って、残りは運送屋に届けさせるようにした。
  〖注〗 carried...with me「いっしょに持って行く」。 was to be sent「送られる手はずにした」。
  **298.** 多くもないが、ぼくの持っている珍書は皆君の使用に任せよう。
  〖注〗 at your disposal「あなたの自由に」、類例:—I'll place any sum you may need *at your disposal.*(ご入用だけいくらなりとご用立ていたします)
  **299.** その災難を引き起こしたこどもたちは、だれもけがした少年の成り行きを知ろうとついて行く者はなかった、ところがすこし離れた所でその珍事を見ていたひとりのこどもがあって、できるだけのことをしてやろうと思って(けが人の家へ)行った。
  〖注〗 went の主語は who.
  **300.** 昼の明るさが苦痛であった、彼女はあらんかぎりの忍耐でそれをがまんせねばならなかった。
  〖注〗 summon は「呼び出す」が本来の意味で、courage, energy などを目的とすると「ふるい起こす」「出す」の意味になる。
  **301.** 孝心の深いむすこはわずかに残っていた力を用いて、自分が医者からもらってきた薬を犬の首に結びつけ、家に持ち帰らせたのである。
  **302.** 私は自分の限界を発見した、それで、その限界内でできるだけの優秀さをねらうことが唯一の賢明な策と思われた。
  **303.** 最初に私は業務をひどくやりそこなったので、しばらくの間は、

やった仕事に対して私が支払ってもらうべき金は多少あったが、資金が手もとに少しもなくなってしまった。どんなに正当な理由からであろうと、金を乞うと、それを相手に覚えていられて不利益をこうむるものである、だから私はふところにあるわずかの現金をありったけ元手にしてどうにかやり繰りをした。

〖注〗 **I found myself with some money**=I had some money. **have it remembered**「それを覚えられる」、(71) 参照。**against**「不利益に」「つごう悪く」、これに対し利益をあらわすには for を用いる、類例：—If you do so, you will act not *for*, but *against*, your own interest. (そんなことをすると君の利益にはならない、かえって不利益になる) **make shift**「やり繰りする」、類例：—to *make shift* to live (どうかこうか食べてゆく). to *make shift* with a small income. (わずかの収入でどうかこうかやってゆく)

---

( 35 )

**304.** 男性に礼儀のあるは女性に美のあるようなものだといわれる、礼儀は即時に人に好印象を与えるものである。

〖注〗 **instantaneous** は形容詞だが、副詞 in an instant (たちまち；ただちに) のように訳すと便利である。**in his behalf**=in his favour「彼のためになるように」、すなわち it 以下は it creates a favourable impression at once などという意味。

**305.** 動物で色を見ることができるものは少ない。たいていの哺乳(ほにゅう)動物でさえその見る世界は黒と白の世界で、彩られた世界ではないらしい。他方、嗅覚に関しては、われわれは多くの他の動物、たとえば犬やある種の蛾(が)よりはるかに不自由をしている。われわれの嗅覚は犬の嗅覚にくらべると、大きな動いている物をどうにか識別することのできる眼をわれわれ自身の眼とくらべたようなものだ。

〖注〗 **are much worse off than...**「...よりずっと困っている」。**in regard to**「に関して」。**just**「やっと」。

**306.** 角(つの)の水牛に対する、足の虎に対する、針の蜂に対する、ギリシアの古歌にいう美の女性に対する、この関係が欺瞞(ぎまん)のベンゴール人に対する関係で、それは天成の利器である。

〖注〗 天成の利器という語は原文にはないが前後の関係から見て補ったのである。

**307.** 国に銀行があるのは身体に心臓のあるがごときものである。銀行

は商業上の動脈を通じて貨幣を輸送し、全身が有効に機能を果すようにせねばならない。身体が心臓の適正な働きによるように、一国の商業は銀行の適正な働きによるのである。

〖注〗 **causing**=and cause と見よ、そして、**cause the body to function**=make the body function「身体を働かしめる」となる。

**308.** 恋が女性に作用するのは太陽が花に作用するようなものである。恋は彼らに色つやを添え、彼らを飾り、彼らをして輝かしめかつ美しくする。しかしそれが熾烈(しっ)にすぎると恋は彼らを焼き尽し、またはしぼませる。

**309.** 建物はその基礎が固くすべての用材が無きずであるとき、しっかりと立つものであるが、社会は一個の建物に似ている。信用のおけない人間の社会に対する関係は、ちょうどくさった用材の家に対するようなものである。

**310.** 彼は風景作品の種々の分野において定評ある大家たちを凌駕(りょうが)し、かつて試みられたことのない方面において自然風景の比類ない作品を残した。ターナーのその専門分野におけるは、シェイクスピアの文学におけるように、古今最高の名前である。

〖注〗 **in lines**「方面において」。**What Shakespeare...** は Turner is の補語。**the greatest name** は what Shakespeare... と同格。

---

( 36 )

**311.** 人生が短いのではなくて、われわれが人生を短くするのだ。ちょうど大きな富が不適当な所有者の手に入ると、またたく間にばらまかれてしまうのに、どんなに小さい富でも適当な人の手に委ねられると、利用によってふえるのと同じように、人生もそれを正しく用いる人にとっては長さに不足はないのである。

〖注〗 最初の文章は not A, but B,「A ではなくて B」の形。後の **him** は any man ということ。

**312.** 人によってはチューリップの花の色やちょうの羽に感心して見とれるものがあるように、私は生まれつき、にこにこしたうれしそうな人の顔を嘆美するものであった。

**313.** あらしまたあらし、波また波が真珠を含んでいる貝殻をますます

堅固にすると同じように、人生のあらしと波は人の性格をますます強固にする。

**314.** 現在は過去に根ざし、われわれの先祖の生活と実例が今なお大いにわれわれに影響しているように、われわれはわれわれの日常の行動によって、将来の境遇と性格とを形づくることに貢献しているのである。

**315.** 日光がきわめて小さい穴からでも見えるようなわけで、ささいな事で人間の品性がわかるものである。

〚注〛 will...「...するものだ」、(85) 参照。 illuminate=light up.

**316.** 気持のよい健康な住居は空気と日光を自由に室内に入れなければ得られないように、丈夫な身体とはればれした、または幸福そうな顔つきは、喜びと好意の念を自由に心の中へ入れることによってのみ得られる。

〚注〛 the free admittance into the mind of thoughts of...「...の念を心の中へ自由に入れること」。

**317.** 健康と財産のめぐみ、これらに初めがあるように、終りもまた必ずある。すべてのものが起こるのはただ倒れ、増すのはただ衰える、ためにすぎない。

〚注〛 as they have... の they は前の blessings をくり返したもの。

———

( 37 )

**318.** 人間の場合も土地の場合と同じように、往々(おうおう)所有主の知らない黄金の鉱脈 [長所・天才] の潜んでいることがある。

〚注〛 knows not of は does not know of の古い語法。

**319.** ベーコンは常にいっていたが、処世のことは道を行くのに似ている——もっとも近い路は概してもっとも悪い道である、ゆえにもしもっとも良い路を行こうとすれば多少迂回(うかい)せねばならないと。

〚注〛 business 事業。 and that の that は to say に続く。 would=wishes to. なお (92) 参照。

**320.** もし無作法が伝染するとすれば、よい作法もそうである。快活な人を不愉快に感ずる人はない。作法は天気と同じである。「よい天気ほど私の心をはればれさせるものはない」とキーツは言った。そして快活な人はどんな陰気な人にもいくらか晴天の幸福と言ったものをもたらす。

〖注〗 **a cheerful person descends on**... は「快活な人はもっとも陰気な人の上にさえ幾分の晴天の幸福をもって降下する」というのであるから本文のような意味となる。 **something of** は少量をあらわす、(**40**) 参照。

**321.** 言葉は太陽の光線と同じようなものだ。圧縮させればさせるほど深く焼きつくものである。

〖注〗 太陽の光線を一点に集めれば熱の強くなるように、言葉もつづめていえば含蓄深く意味深長となるという意味である。

**322.** 書物は砂金採掘の場合の金塊のようなもので、鉱夫は根気よく 1 トンというほど多量の塵土(どろ)を洗い、もしその骨折りののち選鉱なべの中にたった一塊の金を見いだせば十分満足するのである。

〖注〗 **alluvial** は alluvium (冲積(ちゅうせき)土)の形容詞、alluvial gold (砂金)、alluvial mining (砂金採取)などに用いられる。 **a ton of**「1 トンというほどたくさんの」。 **well content**「十分満足して」と上へかかる関係だが、上文のように訳し下してよい。

**323.** このことは個人の場合と同じように国家についてもあてはまる。ふつうの個人々々がその精力と金銭とを節約する、すなわちそれはそれらを賢く費すということに等しいが、そういう国家は常に繁栄する国家となるのである。

〖注〗 この例題は他のものと、it が this になり、また、前の方にも as がある点で異なっているが、類似型として掲げた。 **true of** の of は with とほとんど同じこと。 **which means the same thing** は、前に述べた事がらと次に述べる事がらを「同じ意味だ」といって結ぶ慣用法である。

---

( 38 )

**324.** 奥さん、人間のつらよごしになるような悪党も多かったでしょうが、こんな申し分のない悪党はありません。

〖注〗 **you see in him**...「彼において...を見る」とは he is...「彼は...である」というのに同じ。類例:—We *see in him* a good model for imitation. (彼はわれわれがならうべきりっぱな模範だ) We have *lost* a good teacher *in* Mr. A. (A 先生という良教師を失った) **disgraced humanity**「人間をはずかしめた」。

**325.** 四方幾マイルもの間、あたりの眺望は、こんな美しい所はいまだかつて人間の眼をよろこばしたことはないと思われるほどの美しい土地に展開していた。

**326.** 彼〔自分のむすこ〕はそのとき軍服姿のりっぱな様子をしてはいってきた、そして自慢じゃないが(私は自慢などするような人間じゃないから)彼は〔今まで軍服を着けた〕軍人の中でこれほどりっぱな者はあるまいと思われるほどりっぱに見えた。

〘注〙 **I am above it** の it は vanity をさす, to be above... は「...以上の人間だ」すなわち「そんなことはしない」意味となる, 類例:—Though poor, they were *above selling* their country. (貧乏ではあったが彼らは国を売るような人間じゃなかった)

**327.** 彼〔犬〕は今まで森を駆けまわったいかなる犬にも劣らないほど勇気のある犬であった。

**328.** オールド・アイアンサイズの全体の経歴は海軍でよくいう「運のよい船」の経歴であった。このことはたぶんこの船が常にすぐれた艦長をもち、また古今のどんな軍艦にも劣らぬ優秀な乗組員をもっていたという事実によって説明することができよう。

〘注〙 **Ironsides** は「堅牢物」「剛の者」などの意味。

**329.** わたしはそのピンクの塵(ﾁﾘ)がなんだか知りたくてしかたがなかった。急にその名前が思い浮かんだ、もっとも以前にそれを聞いたことはなかったのだが。それは火というものだった。わたしは、およそ物に確信がもてる人なら、だれにもまけないほどそれを確信したのであった。

〘注〙 これはイヴが初めて火を発見したという話のことである。**could be** の次に certain を入れて解する。

**330.** 私こそだれよりも第一にそんな説を反駁する権利がある。

**331.** スクルージはロンドンの市中でも一番いわゆる空想なるものを持たない男である。

〘注〙 **about him** は「身のまわりどこやらに」などの意味、類例:—He has something peculiar *about him*. (彼にはどこか変わったところがある)

**332.** 彼は身のまわりの習慣においてはすこぶるつきの汚い方で、同宿人こそいいつらの皮であった。

〘注〙 同宿人を気の狂うほどいやがらせた汚い人間中でももっとも汚い人間という意味。**to drive to distraction**＝to drive mad. 類例:—He nearly *went mad* with vexation.＝Vexation nearly *drove* him mad. (彼はくやしがって気が狂いそうだった)

**333.** 〔女というものは〕ほんとにかわいらしい者どもだ、彼らはお世辞は大きらいだとみずから称している。それでももし諸君が「ねえ、あなた、

あなたの場合についてはお世辞ではありません、明白なまじめな事実です、ほんとに掛け値のないところ、この世に足跡を印した人間の中であなたぐらいお美しい、親切な、かわいらしい、神様のような、完全な人間はありはしません」とでもいってごらんなさい、彼ら(女ども)はいかにもごもっともですというようなもの静かな笑い方をして、君の男らしい肩によりかかって、やっぱりあなたはいいお方ですわと、口の内につぶやくでしょう。

〖注〗 **so they tell you** 「彼らはおへつらいはきらいだと諸君に告げる」。**darling** は親しんで呼びかける語。**in your case** 「あなたについていう場合は」。**that ever trod this earth** 「この土を踏んだことのある」は that ever lived などいうのと同じ。trod は tread の過去。**smile a...smile** 類例:— to *laugh* a hearty *laugh*. (心から笑う) to *dream* a strange *dream*. (ふしぎな夢を見る)

**334.** 「私はアテネあるいはギリシアの市民ではなく、世界の市民だ」。これは古代ギリシアの哲学者で、おそらくはかつて生をうけた最大の賢者であるソクラテスの言葉である。

〖注〗 書き出しの文章は not A, but B, 「A ではなくて B」の形。

**335.** 世人はみな幸福の探求に汲々(きゅうきゅう)としているが、しかし一般の様子から判断してみると、幸福の探求に成功したものはごくすくない。ある者は金に、ある者は名誉に、ある者は野心の満足に、ある者は地位または目的の達成に、幸福を求めようとしているが、しかし彼らを幸福にしそうなものが手にはいると、幸福は依然として遠くにあることを知るのである。

───────

(39)

**336.** いったい全体どんな用があってあなたは彼に話をしているか。

**337.** だれがまあこんな事を思ったろう。

**338.** ドナルド[スコットランド人のこと]は世界中で一番実際的な人間である。

**339.** 自分の死後にどんな記憶を残していくか気にかける者など、まったくないのだという考えが、彼の心に浮かんだ。

〖注〗 **left behind him** 「死後に残した」、類例:—A tiger *leaves* a skin *behind him*. (虎は死して皮を残す) A man *leaves* a name *behind him*. (人は死して名を残す)

**340.** 彼はひじょうにつき合いやすい。たいそう人に好かれている。しかし友だちはない。彼はゆかいな仲間であるが、親しくしてもらおうとも親しくしようともしない。彼が心の底で無関心でないような人はただの一人もない。彼の幸福は他人にではなく自分自身に依存しているのだ。

**341.** 全体として見て、彼はたぐいない尊厳な顔つきを持っていたのではなかったが、見物人たちは彼の容姿に何か人間以上の神々(こうごう)しいものがあるかのように彼を凝視した。彼の顔の輝きのため目がくらむかのように、小手をかざして眺めさえした。

**342.** 「おとうさんは貧乏で私に何もくれることができませんでした、ですから私は天にも地にも着物が2枚しかありませんでした」。

〘注〙 but に打消しの意味を含むと見れば、in the world が打消しに伴なうといった規則がここにも当てはまる。

**343.** 商人が叫んでいった、「まあウェストさん、あなたはどんな気がして壁いっぱいこんなに絵をかけておくのです。全体あなたはこの絵をどこから持って来たのです」。

〘注〙 **Friend** はクエーカー宗の人々が Mr. のかわりに用いる敬称。 **thou, thy, thee** もやはり同派の人々の用いるもので、you, your, you に等しい。 **what has possessed thee to...?** 「...するとは何があなたの心に取りついたのか」、「気でも狂ったのか」、possess は「魔がさす」「きつねがつく」などというのに似て、病気にかかるのを be seized with というのにならい be possessed with ということがある。類例:—He was *seized with* an illness. (病気にかかった) He is *possessed with* (or *by*) a queer notion. (妙な考えにつかれている) What has *possessed* you to think of such a thing? (そんなことを考えるとは気でも狂ったのか) **didst** の -st は二人称単数の主語に対する動詞の語尾で、今は普通の場合はなくなっている。

**344.** 彼女はさけんだ、「これは大へんなことになった。いったいこれを彼女にどう説明したらいいだろう。第一、あなたにあのお金をやるようなばかなことをすべきじゃなかった、あなたの言うことを聞くなんて、私はなんてばかだったろう」。

〘注〙 **should have known better than** know better (than)=be wise enough not. 類例:—You ought to *know better* than (*i.e.* ought not be so foolish as) to go swimming just after a big meal! (たくさんごちそうを食べた後ですぐ泳ぎに行くようなばかなことをしてはならない) **in the first place**「まず第一に」

**345.** 病んでいる母には上等な味のよいみかんほど結構なものはないと

いうことを彼は知っていた、しかも彼はただの一文も金を持たなかったのである。

〚注〛 grateful について次の二つの用法を比較せよ：——
$\begin{cases} \text{I am }\textit{grateful to you}\text{ for your sympathy.} \\ \text{Your sympathy is }\textit{grateful to me.} \end{cases}$（ご同情ありがたい）

**346.** いったいどうして彼はそれを発見したのだろう。

**347.** 「いったい全体これは何事だ」と彼はいった。

**348.** 私は彼の名がいったい何というのか知らない。

**349.** 「なんだ！」と彼は飛び起きざまにさけんだ。「このまぬけのとんまめ！ 何だってもっと自分のする事に気をつけねえんだ？ いったいなぜ陸へ上がって着物を着ねえんだ？ 貴様は船に乗ってるがらじゃねえ」。

〚注〛 cuckoo=simpleton「ばか者」. **You're not fit to be in a boat.**「お前はボート内にいるに適しておらぬ」。

———

( 40 )

**350.** レーマーはちょっと学問はあったが、ほんの植字工で、印刷業にかけては何も知っていなかった。

**351.** 彼はまたたいへんな政略家であった。

**352.** 春(人の名)は嫉妬(と)をすべき原因があった。しかしすぐにその原因を推測するにはまだあまりにこどもであった。また召使たちも大へん春をすいていたからその事をほのめかして[春に心配させる]ことをあえてしなかった。

〚注〛 too...to については (21) 参照。

**353.** 彼女は、夫の方がまじめで、あまりじょうだんなんか言わない人だったから、ことに進んで下宿人たちにおしゃべりしたのだと、私は思っている。

〚注〛 one=a man.

**354.** もちろんのことだが、もらった猫に真先きにしてやるべきことは名をつけることである、で、ジャック・ハーマンはあれでもちょっとひょうきん者で、ちょうどそのころニューヨークの評判になっていた大象の大のひいきであったところから、[その名を取って]こんど手に入れたかわい

いやつをジャンボーと名づけた。

〖注〗 **an adopted cat**「もらった猫」。類例：—an adopted son（養子）。**in his way**=after a fashion.「彼一流の」「一種の」「あれでも」。類例：—He is kind *after a fashion*.（彼はあれでも親切なところがある） **stir**「評判」「さわぎ」。

**355.** ツルゲネフははっきり散文詩と言っているものでは、小品や小説より詩人的要素がはるかに少ない。そのわけは、自己意識は真の詩をそこなうものだからだ、つまり、真の詩は、気分や感情がわれ知らずほとばしり出ることなので。

〖注〗 **which** は true poetry をうける。**in spite of itself** とか spite of oneself と言えば、「われ知らず」、「そうしまいと思っても自然に」などの意味。

**356.** 私の友人サー・ロージャーはいろいろのよい性質があったが、とりわけ、少々こっけい家であった。

**357.** 英国の政治家は少々討論家に過ぎ、印度の政治家は少々随筆家にすぎる。

**358.** 丈夫な子供ではなかったが、彼には臆病（おくびょう）らしいところがすこしもなかった、そして幼いころ彼は絶対に物を恐れない精神を現わした、それが後年彼にあのような国への偉い功労をたてさせたのである。

**359.** その婚約はフロレンスの社交界に多少のセンセーションを起こした、そしてこの若い二人のためにいくつかのパーティが催された。

---

( 41 )

**360.** 自分の考えを口に出しさえしなければ、人間はなんでも好きなことを考えるのを妨げられはしない。彼の心の働きを制限するものは経験の限度と想像力の大小だけである。

〖注〗 **hindered from**=prevented from.

**361.** リンカーンは顔に微笑を浮かべつつ一国民の悲しみの重荷をになって一生を通した。生きている間、彼は勇敢な全国民の導きの星であった、そして彼が死んだ時はいたいけなこどもでさえ街上で泣いた。

〖注〗 **a people** は「民族」「一国民」。**the little children**=even the little children; the very little children. the に stress を置いて読む。

**362.** とにかく、アメリカ、ソ連、イギリスはおたがいに、くりかえし

くりかえし、核兵器実験を停止する協定を結ぶことが何よりも欲することであると、言っているのだ。しかしまた同時に、そういう協定ができないかぎりは、実験をやめることはできないと公言している。

〖注〗 **end** 他動詞で、「終わらせる」。

**363.** 容易に混合しない二種類の液体を同一の容器に入れると、軽い方の液体は重い方の液体の上に浮かぶ。重い方の液体を軽い方の液体の上に浮ばせることもたぶんできるが、これは両方の液体をすこしも攪乱(かくらん)しないときに限って初めて可能なのである。

**364.** 眼の及ぶかぎり、見えるものはただ砂ばかりだ。

〖注〗 **is to be seen** は can be seen の意味。

**365.** 蒸汽船は河筋を通って、乗客や貨物を上下に運び、ときにはその出発点から3千マイルも遠くまで行く。

〖注〗 **as far as** の次に地名の来るときは「どこそこまで」だが、本題のように里程の来る場合は「…マイルという遠距離まで」の意味。

**366.** 人類の歴史は人間活動の歴史であって、人間性と人間の物質的条件が現状のままであるかぎり、いつまでも、経済的産業的要因は政治的社会的生活の進行に有力な影響力をもつにちがいない。

〖注〗 **what they are**「それらが現在あるもの」。(32) 参照。**so long** は、前の so long as に応じて、「それだけ長く」と期間を明示している形。この so long という副詞句が前に出たので must...have と助動詞が主動詞と離れて主語の前に来たのである。

**367.** もっとも簡単な時間の尺度は、軸の周囲をまわる地球の回転である。この回転はわれわれの知るかぎりでは一定不変で、完全に規則的である。そして人間の観察のいかなる時期においても速さを変えていない。

**368.** 私は暇な時間を多く絵をかいて過ごす。それはひじょうな楽しみである。しかしそれだからといって傑作を制作しているとは考えない。才能の乏しい人に関するかぎり、その人の作品の優秀さの性質は、大芸術家の作品中に見られる優秀さの性質に本質的に劣っている。

〖注〗 **that of**=the nature of.

**369.** 私の少年時代でもっとも楽しかったのは、6歳そこそこのごく幼いころ、乗馬のために自分専用の小馬を持っていて、好きなだけ長くその馬にまたがり、好きなだけ遠くへ行くことを許されていた時期であった。

〖注〗 **that early period, (which was) little past the age of six** この

that はこれから six まで全体が次の when の先行詞であることを示すだけで、「あの」というほど強くない。 little は (19) に述べたように打消しの意味であるから「6歳をほとんど出ていなかったこどもの時分」となる。

**370.** 眼の点からいうとその少年はすでに老人であった、そして彼の祖父にめがねが必要であったとほとんど同じように、めがねがなくてはならなかった。

〘注〙 **almost as much as...** は「祖父にめがねが必要であるとほとんど同程度に」という意味。

**371.** 将来、知的職業につこうという人々に関するかぎりは、従来からの外国語と文学と数学とヨーロッパ史の教育が一番よい一般教育であると、ヨーロッパ人は固く信じている。

〘注〙 **languages** ここでは、ラテン、ギリシアの古典語や、近代語では主として外国語のことを意味している。

**372.** この広大な宇宙には理性や目的や向上心を賦与されている生物がほかにもあるかもしれない。しかしそれについては何も知られていない。われわれの知識の及ぶかぎりでは、人間の精神と人格とは唯一独自のもので、宇宙によって今までに成就された最高の所産である。

〘注〙 **so far as our knowledge goes** 類例：—It leaves nothing to be desired *so far as the style goes* (=*so far as the style is concerned*). (文体だけは申し分がない)

**373.** 上着と帽子とくつと手袋は明らかにだいぶ古いものであった、しかし、つくろいやブラッシュをかけている点では、人前に出してはずかしくないように、ちゃんと行き届いているようであった。

〘注〙 **have seen better days** は「かつてはもっとよかった」ということで、今はひどくなっている、おちぶれている、老衰している、などの意味となる。everything had been done apparently「見たところあらゆることがなされていた」だから、訳文のようになる。**presentable**「人前に出せる」「見苦しくない」。

---

( 42 )

**374.** しかし、たいていいつもこの葉は緑色である。それは広くて平ったく、大きな広がった表面をもっている。そしてこの表面は、それにさす太陽の光をできるだけ多く捕えるように、水平にひろがっている。

【注】 **as much as possible of the sunlight** の much は of the sunlight につづく。

**375.** 科学の目的は事物を説明するにあるというのが一般の考えである。実際のところ、いわゆる科学の説明は、通常観察された事実の相互の関係を明白にわかりやすくするために、できるだけ単純な言葉でこれらの事実を記述する以上にはあまり出ていない。

【注】 **so-called**「いわゆる」、(31) 参照。 **the simplest possible terms**「ありとあらゆる語のうちもっとも単純な語」。possible は simplest を強めるために用いたのである、類例:—This is *the best possible* method. (これはあらゆる方法のうちで最上だ)

**376.** 万一諸君がスコットランド人といっしょにエディンバラからロンドンまで旅行するようなことがあったら、諸君はその男が汽車の通過する地方を眼を離さず見つめているのに気がつくだろう。彼は自分の座席に支払った賃金の一文の価をも損しまいと窓から始終外を見ているのである。

**377.** 第3日に晴雨計がいちじるしく下ったから、それによって船長は大風が来るということを信じた。そこでその大風が襲来した場合に対処すべきあらゆる準備をした。

【注】 **so low as to induce...to believe**「...をして次の事を信ぜしめるほど低く」。 **should it come on**＝if it should come on. なお (96) 参照。

**378.** いったいどういうふうにして小説家は、このように互いに矛盾する性質を結び合わせて、いかにもそういう人物がありそうに見せるような、もっともらしい調和を作り出すのか。

【注】 **so to combine...as to...** は to combine...in such a way as to... となおしてみよ。 **plausible** [plɔ́:zəbl]「なるほどと思わせる」「もっともらしい」。 **credible** は「信用し得る」で、これと credulous (信じやすい、人の言うことをすぐ真[ま]にうける)と混同しないこと。

**379.** 私たちが着物を着たり脱いだり、ものを食べたり、飲んだり、会ったり別れたりするときにあいさつをしたりすること、私たちのふつうの話の大部分の形式さえ、反復によって固定しているので、ほとんど反射作用の部に入れてよいほどである。

( 43 )

**380.** そのあたりの土地は大へん肥えていたので私は野菜園を作ろうと決心した。熱帯地方では園芸は楽しい仕事であって、ぞうさなく利益があがるから、ふたたび昔のジャーナリズム(文筆業)を始める必要はあるまいと思った。

〘注〙 **would be..., it might prove** の would や might はそのときの気持を間接話法で述べたので、直接話法にすれば、それぞれ will, may となるわけ。

**381.** ちょうどこの朝にかぎって、一つの考えが私の頭に浮かんだ。ひじょうに簡単で合理的で行いやすいものなので、今までこういう計画を思いつかなかったことに私はおどろいてしまった。

〘注〙 **this particular morning**「この特別な朝」「(ほかの朝もあるのに)とくにこの朝にかぎって」。**presented itself**＝appeared. 類例：——Soon a good opportunity *presented itself*. (やがてよい機会が現われた) An idea *presented itself* to my mind. (一趣向が胸に浮かんだ)

**382.** 人気がひじょうに出て、すべての機が熟したので、もうこれ以上待たずに、さっそく、この際始めなければ、大失敗になると知った。

〘注〙 **strike** は例の "Strike while the iron is hot."(好機を逸するな)とあわせ考えればよくわかるだろう。**would be a mistake not to strike** は not to strike の中に、if we did not strike という条件がふくまれているので、would となっている。

**383.** そのつもりではなかったけれど、彼は私をひじょうに楽しませてくれたので、こんどは私の方で彼をもてなすために何かするのが当然だと思った。

〘注〙 **so much did he amuse me** は he amused me so much よりも強調した言い方、did については (62) 参照。**only**「まったく」。**in my turn**「こんどは私の方で」、類例：——I was surprised *in my turn*. (こんどはこちらがおどろいた)

**384.** つまらない作品(記事)を発表してやって[投稿者に]示す慈悲心は、むかしの追剝(おいはぎ)の気前よさのようなものである。彼らは貧乏人に同情するあまり、貧乏人を助ける資金を手に入れるために金持から金品を強奪したのであった。

〘注〙 **shown** which is shown と見る。**relieving them** の them は the poor.

**385.** 街で人々がふりかえって彼をじっと見るほどに彼を目立たせたものは、濃い毛髪で、それが大きく波うっていて、濃い赤色であったことだ。

**386.** 水はきわめて浅かった、だから、たとい氷が破れても、ちょっと水につかるくらいで、それ以上別に心配することはなかった。

〖注〗 **in the event of the ice giving way**「氷が破れるということがあっても」。**give way** は重さなどのためにおちこむ、くずれること。**ducking** は duck(家鴨)—to duck(頭を水に突っこむ)からできた語である、類例:—to *give* one *a ducking*. (人を水へつっこんでいじめる)

**387.** 彼は働いた日のことも病気で働けなかった日のことも毎日日誌を正確につけた、だからある年に幾日働かない日があったか、(知ろうと思えば)知ることができる。

〖注〗 **those** = the days. **prevent~from**...「さまたげて...させない」。類例:—*Prevent* him *from* drinking. (酒を飲ませるな)

**388.** 放浪者の役割が、寒冷な幾月かの間、必要の上から、多くの鳥に大いに課せられるのだ。冬は他の季節より食物がずっとすくないから、十分の餌(き)を得るために、ずっと広範囲の地域を毎日飛び回らねばならないからだ。

〖注〗 **to a large extent** 大いに。 **sufficient** ここでは名詞。

**389.** わたしは毎晩、目をさましていられるかぎり、起きていて星を眺めるつもりです。そして、あの輝やく天(き)の原をわたしの記憶に刻みつけておいて、やがてその星の原がとり去られたときに、想像の力で、まっくらな空にあの美しい幾百万の星をとり戻し、ふたたび輝かせ、わたしの涙のにじみで倍の数にすることができるようにしたいのです。

**390.** 彼は学校の課業よりも釣(き)その他の娯楽が好きであった。しかしついに彼は、資産のすくない自分の父が自分に教育を与えるために多大の犠牲を払っているということをさとった。

〖注〗 **preferred...to~**=liked...better than~「~よりも...を好んだ」。**he might obtain**... の he は前の he と同一人で、すなわち「むすこが教育を受けるために」が文字どおり。

**391.** むかしなら大寺院の建立に大金を寄与した金持は今日では巨大な実験所を建造する、そして、そこでは学者が黙々として隠れた人類の敵と戦い、未来の人々がより大きな幸福と健康とに恵まれるように、自分の生命をもしばしば犠牲にするのだ。

【注】 silent men 無口な人々、訳文は少しかえた。 hidden enemies とは「病源」のこと。

**392.** 良い計画とは収入に応じて支出することであり、けっして得たもの全部を費さないことである。病気や老齢のため働けなくなったとき困らないように、われわれは幾分かを貯蓄すべきである。

【注】 **in proportion to**「比例して」「釣り合って」、類例:—A man will succeed *in proportion to* his perseverance. (人は忍耐に準じて成功する) **lay by**「貯蓄する」、類例:—He *lays by* a part of his income. (収入の一部を貯蓄する) **in the event of...**「...の場合に」

**393.** 船長は動きさえしなかった。彼は船員に前と同じように肩ごしに、同じ声の調子で話しかけた、へや中に聞こえるようにすこしばかり高いが、しかしまったく落ちついた調子で。

【注】 **never so much as**=not even. (47) 参照。 **calm and steady**「落ち着いてしっかりした」、tone of voice にかかる。

**394.** この原子時代に人間が生きてゆく方法を知るために、毎日何千となくはつかねずみやうさぎが犠牲にされている。これらの実験用動物は、原子の爆発から出てくるおそろしいガンマ線にさらされている。

【注】 **by thousands**「何千となく」、この by は「...を単位にして」または「...を単位にして数えるほど」の意味、類例:—Time is measured *by* the hour. (時は時間を単位に計られる)

**395.** 終夜われわれは、馬のしっぽを北極星の方に向けて、ゆっくり進んだ。雪の中に(人馬の)通った道がたくさんあった、それで騎兵の一隊がそっちの方を通ったことにだれも気づかないようにこれらの道の上をたどって行った。これらのことはちょっとした用心であるがその(率いる)士官が経験ある人であることを示している。

【注】 **track** は定まった通路でなくて人畜が勝手に「通った道」。 **we kept to the line of these**「これらの路の線からはずれないようにした」。類例:—*Keep to* the left. (左側通行) 上の keeping our horses' tail to... では keep が他動詞。 **that way**=that direction (その方向), passed の副詞的目的語。 **mark the experienced officer**=mark that the officer is (*or* was) experienced.

**396.** 気候の異なる地方は皆それぞれ特有の産物を有するから、われわれの自然の欲求を満足させるために相互の交際というものが生じる、したがって貿易によって遠隔の地も諸国の産物を供給されるのである。

【注】 **produce** は産出されたもの、ことに「農産物」。動詞は [prədjúːs].

**397.** この老紳士はひじで人を押しのけ、からだをあちこちにごろつかせながら、群集のまん中を押し分けて歩くので、人の2倍も場所がいるのであった。

〘注〙 elbow aside は push aside (押しのける) の push のかわりに elbow (ひじ)を動詞として用い、ひじで押しわける意味をあらわしたもの。**force one's way through**... 「無理に...を押しわけて通る」 類例：—to *make one's way* through difficulties (困難を排して進む). to *push one's way* through the crowd (群集を押しわけて通る). to *fight one's way* through the world (奮闘生活をする). **twice as much as**...「...の2倍」。類例：—The new ship is *three times as large as* the former one. (こんどの船は前の船の3倍ある) He has *twice as many* books *as* I have. (彼は私の倍も本を持っている) **room** はここでは space (余地、空間)の意味。

---

( 44 )

**398.** 遊ぶこと、または遊ぶ時間が禁ぜられているのではなかった。仕事の習慣がこわれ、なまけ癖がつくといけないから、休日は与えられなかったけれど、彼は毎日じゅうぶん娯楽の時間を持ち、運動の要求は散歩で満たされた。

〘注〙 **It is not that**... については (111) 参照。**amuse himself**「遊ぶ」「楽しむ」。

**399.** この所は水流の突進がおそろしいほど激しいので、だれも粉砕されるのを恐れて、丸木船に乗ってさえあえてそこに近寄るものはなかった。

〘注〙 **no one ventured to approach it**＝no one dared to approach it「それに近づく危険を冒す人はなかった」。

**400.** ロンドンには彼は二、三人の知人しかなかった、その知人から彼は遠ざかっていた。それは必要上、または誘惑されて、なけなしの金を使うことになるといけないと思ったから。

〘注〙 **could not spare**「割愛(かつあい)できなかった、なくては困る」。

**401.** 私は彼が私を見はしないかと思ってメリーに話しかける勇気も出なかった、というわけは彼の眼は始終私を見まもっていたから。

**402.** 私があんなに警戒していなかったらあんなばかな事はしなかったでしょう、しかし私はあなたに本当の事を知られはしまいかと、ほとんど半狂乱になっていたのです。

**403.** この問合わせ(アンケート)を始めたセン・ジョン・アーヴィン氏は

(こどもにくれる)おこづかいは既定の慣例で、疑問の余地ないものと考えていた。彼がただ一つ懸念したことは、この慣例が、親のだらしなさや無分別な気前よさによって、濫用されはしまいかということであった。

〚注〛 **accepted**「是認した」「賛成した」。**liable to**「~を免かれない」「しがちな」「しやすい」、類例:—It is *liable to* danger. (それは危険にさらされている)  Difficulties are *liable to* occur. (めんどうな事は起こりがちだ) **parental** は parent の形容詞。

**404.** われわれはこの前あわてて退却したときのように不意討ちを食わされていやな思いをしないように、軽く用心深い歩調で、炬火(たいまつ)を前に振りかざして進んだ。

〚注〛 **as we had been** (surprised) と補ってみよ。

**405.** 夫が化粧べやに出入りし、いろいろの小つぼや小びんなどに鼻を突っこむことをけっして許しなさるな、あなたの美しさ、あなたの美しい顔の色の秘密を見ぬかれるおそれがあるから。

〚注〛 **frequent** の発音は、形容詞(ひんぴんたる)は [fríːkwənt] で、動詞(しばしば訪問する)は [frikwént] である。

**406.** 私が自分のすぐれた知識を見せびらかしたがっているのだと、彼に思われはしないかと、私は恥ずかしいほどであった。

**407.** 女は彼の真剣な様子に恐怖し、かつ彼が狂乱のあまり自分に害をしはしないかと怖れて、大声を立てた。

〚注〛 **affright**=frighten.

**408.** 彼が野生の花を愛するのはほとんど一種の情熱であった。彼は年年草花の芽を出すのを待ちかまえており、その周辺何マイルかのところは、どこに一番先に花が咲くかということを知っていた。野生の花をつむにも彼は将来の発生を害することをおそれて、一カ所からたくさん取らないようにした。

〚注〛 **wild** は domestic に対する、類例:—domestic animals (家畜), wild beasts (野獣). **watch for** は wait for (待つ) の類で、気をつけて「待ちかまえる」こと。**their annual return**「花の年々の帰来」すなわちいったん枯れた花がまた翌年芽を出し花を開くこと。**refrain from —ing**「—することを控える」、類例:—Kindly refrain from smoking. (喫煙はごえんりょください)

**409.** 私がこの町の金持になったときに、私はまず第一に心配しました、だれかが私の家へ押し入って金を強奪するか、あるいは私の身体に危害を加えはしまいかと。

〘注〙 **break into...**「(盗賊が)...へ押し入る」。類例：—His house *was broken into* last night. (彼の家へ昨夜泥棒がはいった)　**seize upon**「ひっつかむ」「略奪する」。**do me personal harm**「私に身体上の害を加える」。

**410.** 旅人がコトガーに来たときには、リスペスは、シムラまたは名も知らない異国に連れて行かれるかと思って、自分のへやの中に閉じこもっていた。

〘注〙 **used to lock herself into...**「...いつもみずからを...に閉じこめた」、used to については (63) 参照。

**411.** 私は、彼が「おじゃまをしてすみません」と自身でわびに来るのを必要と考えはすまいかと、まだ大いに心配していました。

〘注〙 **lest he might...** は fear の同格である。**in person**＝personally. 代理や書面でなく「自身で」「親しく」。**apologize for "bothering" me.**「私を悩ましたことに対してわびをいう」。

**412.** 私はやがて、この家の宝庫にまだ何かめぼしいものがあることを知った——たしか、何か宝石が——そして彼女は、私がまた腰をぬかすといけないと思って、まともにそのことを話すのをさけようとしていることを知った。

〘注〙 これは彼女が家にある宝の話をして私という人をびっくり仰天させたということにつづく文である。**and that...** は discovered that とつづくもの。**get around** は「さける」こと。lest があっても、should をつけないこともある一例。

## (45)

**413.** ある本が有名であるというだけで、ある人々は恐れをなして遠ざかる。ところがそういう人々も、勇気を出してその本を開いてみれば、そこに喜びと利益を見いだすであろうに。

〘注〙 関係代名詞 who は、必ずしも下から訳しあげてこなくてもよい。**The fact...is enough to scare off some people** は「...という事実が人々をおどかして追い払うに十分である」が直訳になる。

**414.** 彼が幸いにして私の治世に生まれていたならば私は彼を首相としたであろうに。

〘注〙 **had he had**＝if he had had. (96) 参照。

**415.** しかし彼は不幸にも同級生のたいがいよりも年が二つ上だった。

**416.** 彼はどんなに長い間自分の城を留守にする場合にも、この村がいざといえばすぐさま30名の壮漢からなる一団を提供することを考えて、気が休まった。この人数は城を守って余りがあった。

〚注〛 **on the slightest notice**「もっともわずかの知らせで」。類例：—They were ready to start *at a minute's notice*. (通知があり次第すぐに出発する用意ができていた)

**417.** ドナルドはそんな計略にかかるようなとんまではなかった。

**418.** 私は本問題について自分でも二、三の論文を公にした。その論文は一向売れなかったので、私はそれは幸福なる少数の人にのみ読まれたのだと思ってなぐさめるのであった。

〚注〛 **which** は some tracts を受け、were read の主格となっている。**they never sold** の they も tracts をさす、「その論文が売れなかった」、sold はここでは自動詞 sell の過去、類例：—This book *sells* well. (この本はよく売れる) The house *sold* at a good price. (家がいい値で売れた)

**419.** ああ、なつかしきドナルドよ、私がうれしくもあなたのもとに過ごすことを得た数ヵ月の間に、どんなによい物語をあなたは私に語ったことだろう。

**420.** できるならいつも自分よりすぐれた友と交わるがよい、不幸にして自分より劣った人々と交わる場合には、もし好い機会をつかんで相手を自分の水準まで引き上げる——これは愛情と共に賢明さを必要とするが——ことをしなければ、必ず相手は遠慮なくあなたを彼らの水準まで引き下げるにちがいないということを、けっして忘れてはならない。

〚注〛 **move amongst** (=among)「(人と)交わる」。**this** は次の that 節をあらかじめ指示しているもの。**which** は to draw...level という内容を指す。**be not be slow**「のろのろしていない、すぐに...する」。

**421.** 独創的な画家で世人の理解と報酬とをあてにするものはばかである。ふとした風の吹きまわしで同情ある有能な批評家によって見いだされるような幸運をつかむことはあるかもしれない。

〚注〛 **count on**=expect 当てにする、類例：—You had better not *count on* an increase in your salary at present. (今は月給の上がることを期待しない方がいいよ) **to be found out**「見いだされる」、もちろん「才能を認められる」こと。**blows...in his direction**「彼のいる方角へ吹きよこす」。

**422.** 娘どもは自分たちがもっとも近代的と思うような話題で彼を喜ばそうと努めた。ところがモーゼズは反対に古代の作家から一つ二つ質問を

出し、おかげで大いに嘲笑されるという満足を得た。

〚注〛 **the ancients** はふつう古代文明の民をいう、ここでは古代ローマなどの作家中から何かを引用したのであろう。**for which**「そのことのために」。

**423.** 妻もまたいつか自分の家にこの人を招いて[きょうの]親切に報いてよろこびたいと期していた。

**424.** 勘定の談判をするに先だち、彼らは用心深くも荷物車をば、いっしょにつれて来た中国人の若い者に託して先へ送り届けさせた。

〚注〛 **in charge of...**「...に託して」、類例：—I will *take charge of* the goods. (私が品物を預かりましょう) I am *in charge of* the goods. (私が品物を預かっている)

**425.** オーツはこんどの告発人と組になって、かわいそうに、女王(というやんごとなき御方)に大逆罪の罪を帰せるという大胆不敵な事をあえてした。

〚注〛 **accuse...of~**「...に~の罪を負わせる」。**herself** は emphasize するために入れた語、常人でない女王という御方などいう意味。

**426.** そなたのむすこは運よく町で私に会い、私のもっとも勇敢な士官の一人の寡婦(やもめ)が貧と病いとに苦しみ、なんら救助の手段をも得ずにいるということを私に告げ知らせた。

〚注〛 **informed me of the fact that...**「...という事実を私に知らせた」。**was suffering from...**「...に苦しんでいる」。

---

( 46 )

**427.** 私は翌朝になって友だち同士が顔を見合わせても恥ずかしくないような楽しみが好きだ。

**428.** 私たちは道徳的あるいは田園的の娯楽にその年をすごした。近所の金持を訪問したり、または貧乏な人々を救済したりなどして。

**429.** 単語は真の意味で生き物である。実際、単語はたえず生まれたり死んだりしている。世の中が進むにつれ言語もこれに伴なって進まなければならない、新しい思想をあらわすべき新しい単語を取り入れ、過去のものとなった思想や事実に属するような単語を後へ残して。

**430.** 学術上の用語は諸君が今まで出くわしたことのないようなのが多いから、よい辞書を座右に備え、意味のわからない語に出くわしたらすぐ

辞書をひいて見るがよいと思う。

〚注〛 **terms of science**=technical terms「術語」。**at hand**「手近に」。**consult** は consult with... といえば「...と相談する」意味であるが、他動詞としては専門家の意見を問う意味である、類例：—to consult a lawyer（弁護士の鑑定を乞う）. to consult a doctor（医師の診断を求める） to consult a dictionary（辞書をひく）. **a word you do not comprehend the meaning of**=a word *the meaning of which*（=*whose meaning*）you do not understand「諸君がその意味を理解しない語」。

**431.** そのころは、実際、もし人が自分の観察か、ふつうの談話から得られる以上の知識を求めるならば、まず第一に必要なことはラテン語を学ぶことであった。

〚注〛 多少でも学問的なことは、ラテン語で書かれた書物からのみ得られた時代のことを述べている。

**432.** くせはつきやすい、ことに悪いくせはつきやすい。今日小さなことと思われるものも、じきに大きなことになり、いかり綱のような強さをもって人をつなぐのである。

〚注〛 **habits are formed**「くせがつく」、参考：—to *form* a good habit.（良習慣をつける）to *contract* a bad habit.（悪習がつく）

**433.** 教育の目的は児童を生活に適させることであるべきだということはすでに言い古された言葉なので、人々は、その明白な常識にはもっともだと賛成しながら、その平凡さをふふんと鼻で笑うのだ。

〚注〛 **fit~for...** ~を...に適合させる。 **commonplaceness**「平凡さ、陳腐(ちんぷ)さ」。

**434.** 歯に対する注意というようなつまらない事がらと思われることさえ、人生の安楽に少なからざる影響を持つかもしれない。

───────

( 47 )

**435.** 昆虫は人間のむかしから変わらぬ大敵である。世界の食糧供給に対する破壊は、悪い人々よりもむしろ害虫によって行なわれる。年々、平時戦時を問わず、われわれは有害な昆虫と戦わねばならない。

**436.** 学校教育の大きな効用は、諸君に物事を教えるということよりもむしろ学問の方法を教えることである。それで学校を出てからいかなる事項を研究しようと欲する場合にも、自分でその方法をそれに応用するようになるためである。

【注】 for yourselves「自分で」、(8) 参照。 any matter to which you choose to turn your mind「諸君が心をそれに向けることを欲する事がら」。

**437.** もっとも多く生きた人とはもっとも多くの年を数えた人ではなくて、人生の意義をもっとも痛切に知り得た人をいうのである。

【注】 number the most years「もっとも多くの年を数える」とはもちろんもっとも長く生きること。

**438.** アーノルド博士が少年についていった言葉は、成人の場合にも等しくあてはまる——すなわち、ある少年と他の少年との差異は才能の点にあるのでなく、むしろ精力の点にあると。

【注】 is equally true of men「成人についても等しく真である」。consists in=lies in「...にある」、類例:—Happiness *consists in* contentment. (幸福は満足にある＝満足すればすなわち幸福)

**439.** 木綿やリンネルのぼろが製紙原料としてヨーロッパに輸入されてからは、他の植物性の繊維は幾世紀もの間全然、あるいはほとんど全然、使用されなかった。しかしこれは植物性繊維が不適当なためではなくて、ぼろの方が製紙にきわめて適している上に、ほかのいかなる材料よりも安価であったからである。

【注】 introduction は introduce の名詞で、新しいものなどの「輸入」「採用」などをいう、類例:—When was Buddhism *introduced* into Japan? (仏教はいつ日本に伝来したか) *introduction* of foreign capital (外資導入). give up「やめる」、類例:—If my eyes do not get well, I must *give up* my studies. (眼病がなおらなければ学問を断念しなければならない)

**440.** ヘンリー・フォードは自分の富を誇らず、いっそう安価な自動車を作り、いっそう労働賃金を高くし、いっそう機械学の奇蹟を生みだすためでなければ、その富を使わない。彼は庶民に属していて、社会的差別について、無関心であるというよりむしろそれを知らない。

【注】 have no use for them の use は「使い道」「用途」の意味である。bring...to birth「...を生み出す」。

**441.** イギリス人は (むかしから) いつも自分の家庭に愛着を持っている、これは家族に対する愛情によるというよりは、他人から干渉されることをきらうためと、ひとりになって自分自身のことは自分で勝手にすることを好むためである。

【注】 minding his own business の business は「商売」「実業」の意味でなくて「自分にかかわること」という広い意味、類例:—*Mind your own business!* (大きなお世話、自分の頭のはえを追え)　That is *none of your business.* (お前の知った事じゃない)　*Go about your business!* (ここには用がないからさっさと帰れ)

**442.**　彼らはそれ以上物を言わないで、暖かな黄昏(たそがれ)の中にすわりつづけていた。そしてとうとうおたがいの顔が見分けがつかないようになってしまった。考えていると言うよりはむしろ、なだらかな動かない心の静寂(じゃく)にひたって、我を忘れていたのだ。こうもりが1匹パタパタと飛び過ぎた。

〚注〛 **lost in ...**「我を忘れて」「途方にくれて」、類例：—He is *lost in* thoughts. (思案にくれている)　They are *lost in* wonder. (仰天している)

**443.**　世に立つ人の助けとなるものは偶然の出来事ではなくて、(強固なる)意志と不撓(とう)の勤勉である。

**444.**　真の意味の法律は、自由で理性ある人間を、むしろその正当な利益にみちびくことであって、これを制限することではない。

〚注〛 **in its true notion** は in its true sense などと同類の用法である。**limitation** の動詞は limit；**direction** の動詞は direct で、前者は of a free ... man まで、後者はさらに interest までつづく。

**445.**　その山脈はその背後にある大きなふしぎ(な物)を守っている壁のような印象を与えた。私は景色を嘆賞する念より、むしろその壁の背後にあるものを見たいという好奇心でいっぱいになった。私の心はまだ明らかにされない物事に向かって熱心につき進むのであった。

**446.**　国によって異なっているのは、専門教育というよりはむしろ専門研究に先だって施される(一般)教育の方である。

〚注〛 **It** は **that** 以下を代表する。**provided**＝which is provided. **prior to**＝before.

**447.**　彼女が暗がりをさがしまわり、ついに自分の着物を見つけそれを着て、わたしたちのものは針一本さえ取らずに立ち去ったという事実には、なんとなく奇妙なしかも感動すべきところがあった。

**448.**　もし君がぼくの何者であるかを知ったら、ぼくに口もきくまいが。

**449.**　ほんとに私はこのお方に今が今までお目にかかったことはありません——この方は私の目にはいったことすらないんです。

〚注〛 **to set eyes upon** は単に see の意を強くいったもの、類例：—I never *set eyes on* his like in my life. (彼のような人は生まれてからまだ見たことがない)

**450.** 一人の男が私に近づいて、ある町の名を挙げてその方面へわたしが行くところなのかときいたが、その町の名さえも耳にしたことがなかったので、私は一向に知らないと答えた。私は地図を持っていなかった、というのはその地方の良い地図がなかったし、悪い地図ではない方がましであるから。

**451.** 彼はぞうりをぬぐ暇もなく(そのまま)急いで姫の跡を追って一番奥のへやまではいって行った。

〖注〗 **without so much as waiting to remove...**「...を脱ぐために時間を取ることさえしないで」。

---

( 48 )

**452.** 私は一向におどろかなかった、そうあろうとはじゅうぶん予期していたから。

**453.** なるほど妻があるということは医者にとって効能がある。妻があるとその医師は信用すべき者と極印がつく、だから医師に妻があるということがわからないうちは、その医師にかからない人が多い。けれども白髪もそれと同じく効能があるものだ。

〖注〗 **Yes** は後の **but** と応じて「なるほど...であるがしかし」となる、(109)参照。 **Marriage helps a doctor.**「結婚が医師を助ける」とは結婚した人だと信用があるという意味。**respectful** は通例「うやうやしい」の意味であるがここでは respectable (尊敬すべき、信用ある)の意味に用いたのであろう。**consult a doctor**「医者の診察をこう」。

**454.** 長たらしい前書を書いた、むかしの小説家は気の毒にも、雷のさなかにアコーディオンをひくようなもので、人に読まれる機会はきわめて少ない。

〖注〗 **long-winded**「息の長い」、ここでは「長たらしい」。**preparation** はここでは小説の本筋にはいるまでに、前置きのように種々なことを書くことをさしている。ふつうの「準備」の意味ではない。**about** ほとんど。**chance**「(読まれる、聞かれる)機会」。

**455.** リヴァプールへ着いたとき、私は 一人の 男と知り合いになった。その男は数年前にアメリカへ渡ったことのある男で、そのときは希望が達せられなかったので、絶望して英国へ帰ったが、新しい希望を得て、再度の試みをしようとしているのだった。その熱心さは、他の人々が最初の試

みに示す熱心さに、まさらないまでも、すこしも劣らないものであった。

〖注〗 with as much enthusiasm, if not more, than others は本来ならば than を as と書くべきところを、すぐ前の more に引かれ than で as をも兼ねさせている。厳密に言えば不都合だがふつうに用いられる形である。

**456.** 政党というものは人がこれを使えばよいものだが、これに使われると困る。政党は常に手段であって、それ自身を目的として扱ってはならない。これだけのことなら一般論として明白であるけれども、いよいよ実践となると政党の手綱(たづな)をどの程度に締めるかゆるめるかを決定することはたやすくはないだろう、そしてこの手綱の締め方は事実、時によって大いに変化があった。

〖注〗 **good servants, bad masters** のところはもちろん諺(ことわざ)の Fire is a good servant but a bad master. を思わせる。**be treated** 扱われる。**in general** は「一般として」で、これに対するのは in particular である。本文で **in practice** となっているから、本来、これに対するものは in theory (理論上は)である。

**457.** われわれは15分間櫂(かい)を一生けんめい漕(こ)いだ、それがわたしには15時間も漕いだように思われた。

**458.** 人は自分の弱点を知らないといって非難されるが、しかし自己の力量を知る者も同様すくないだろう。

**459.** 人は世間の評判よりずっとすぐれていることが往々(おうおう)ある、また人は外見よりもはるかに劣っていることも同様にしばしばあるものだ。

〖注〗 **It sometimes happens that...** の It は that 以下を代表する、すなわち「...のことが往々あるものである」。**have credit for being** (good)「(良い)と世間から思われている」、類例:—I *gave* you *credit for* more sense. (君はもっと物がわかると思っていた[のに案外わからずやだ]) They *give* him (=he *has*) *credit for* being wise. (彼は賢いという評判だ)

---

( 49 )

**460.** 人は数カ月または数カ年の生命を得るため[生きのびるため]に大金を費すことがある、しかしだれか1年いくら(の値)で年[生命]を切り売りする者があるのを聞いたことがあるか。

〖注〗 **fortune**「大金」、類例:—He has made *a fortune*, and lives in clover. (彼はひと財産をこしらえてぜいたくに暮している)　He has spent *a small* *fortune* on it. (彼はそれにちょっとひと財産——大金——をかけた) 本題で複数にいったのはいく財産というほどの大金の意味。 **who ever heard?** は裏に No one ever heard. (だれも聞いたことはあるまい)を含むことはもちろん。

**461.** 今は、工員はボタンを押し、輪転機をまわすだけで、完成品を作ることをしない。部品のところで単調な仕事をする——1日機械の操作何時間と計算するが、その総和である結果は工員個人の仕上げたものとはけっしてならないのである。

〚注〛 **so many hours of machine-driving a day** は前にある work の内容を説明したもの。 **which** の先行詞は hours of machine-driving.

**462.** イギリス人は自分の細君に家政の費用として1カ月なにほど、衣服費としてなにほど、小づかいとしてなにほどというように金を渡す。

**463.** 1枚の絵はいろどられたカンヴァスの何平方インチで出来上がっている、けれども、一時に1平方インチずつ、つぎつぎにずっと見て行って全部見てしまったとしても、(そんな見方をしたのでは)その1枚の絵を見たことにはならない。

〚注〛 **these**=these square inches. **one at a time** 「いちどに1平方インチずつ」、これは副詞句。 **covering~** 「~に及んで」。

---

( 50 )

**464.** そして一瞬つかの間に私は百本以上の矢がわたしの左の手に射かけられたことを感じ知った。その矢がさながら針のように私を刺した。

〚注〛 ガリヴァーが小人国へ行き小人の矢に射られた話である。

**465.** われわれの街路はみんな並木になっていて、葉と枝の間にさながら星のように街灯が輝いている。その下を通るとその光がそれにもっとも近い部分の葉を緑灰色に染めているのに気がつく。

〚注〛 **are lined with trees**「木を並べられている」「木が並んでいる」。

**466.** 自由はその国民にとってけっして幸福とはならなかった。人民は世間へ放り出された子供のように全然どうしていいかわからなかった。彼らは今まで久しいあいだ、国防や政治については統治者に依頼することに慣れきたったので、この二つの仕事のどちらにも取りかかるすべを知らなかったのである。

〚注〛 **anything but** が強い打消しにひとしいことは **(102)** を参照せよ。**help-**

less は足腰の立たぬ病人のようにどうすることもできない無力の状態をいう。**turned loose upon the world**「世間へほうり出された」、類例:—It is dangerous to *let loose* such men *on* society. (ああいう人間を世間へ出すのは危険だ) **rely upon**「信頼する」。**government** は govern (治める)の名詞で、「政治」あるいは「政府」。**they knew not**=they did not know.

**467.** 気候の方が軍務よりもいっそう多くの損害を与えた。2千人の中で半分以上は病気になり、あとのものもさながら幽霊のようになってしまった。

〚注〛 **proved more destructive**「いっそう有害であった」。参考:—to *be destructive of* (or *to*) human life. (人命を損ずる)

**468.** その少女は食卓の準備をし、こどもたちを暖炉のまわりにすわらせ、まるでおなかをすかせた小鳥のように、彼らを養ってやった。

**469.** 彼は美人の奴隷となることを自慢に思っていた。で、ヴァンデラー夫人の命令をば、あたかも好意のしるしかなんぞのように受けたのである。

〚注〛 **take a pride in**...「...を自慢の種とする」。類例:—He *takes a pride in* his country. (彼はお国自慢だ) **servility** は servile (奴隷のような、卑屈な)という形容詞からできた名詞、すなわち servility to...「...に屈従すること」「...の奴隷となること」。

**470.** 私はとまったんです、というのは、ほんとうですよ、私は息が切れたからです、そして、ふしぎなことに、連中はだれひとり動くものはなく、みんなまるで羊のようにわたしをじろじろ見ているだけでした。

〚注〛 **I tell you**「いいですか」というように相手に念を押す表現。

**471.** 彼らは宗教にせよ、政治にせよ、はっきりとして確立した原理の支配を受けないできたものだから、すべての物事をただそれだけの現象として語るのであった。

〚注〛 **under the influence of**「〜の影響(感化)をうけて」。**religious or political** は principles の形容詞。本題の主旨は、諸種の現象を原理に結びつけて考えないということ。

───────────────

(51)

**472.** 犀(さい)は非常に猛烈狂暴で、土人はししをおそれる以上にこれをおそれるほどである。

〚注〛 **rhinoceros** 語尾の s は複数のしるしではない、複数は rhinoceroses

である。**so much so that**=so fierce and savage that.... **they do**=they dread.

**473.** 秋になると青虫はすっかり食欲を失ってしまった。食欲のなくなったことは、どんなにやわらかい、またどんなに汁(しる)の多い葉でも、もはや食い気を起こさせることができないほどであった。

〖注〗 **could not tempt it to eat**「食うようにそれを誘うことができなかった」。

**474.** 胴体も頭同様おそろしく切りきざまれていた——胴体はほとんど人間の形をとどめぬまでに切りきざまれていた。

**475.** 時によるとひじょうに寒気が強くて、なまの卵がまるで茹(ゆで)玉子のように堅く凍ってしまうほどであった。

**476.** わたしは自分が世人の大きな関心のまとになっていることを知った、それがはなはだしかったので、運転手は、私たちの道順を秘密にしておかねばならない、記者達をまくためにだ。さもないと記者達が待ちぶせしているから、と私に話した。

〖注〗 **that would otherwise awaited** の otherwise は if he did not keep our route secret を簡単に言いあらわしたもの。

**477.** 「私はサー・ウィリアム・ソーンヒルが国じゅうでも屈指(くっし)の気前のいい、そのくせ気まぐれな人、ひじょうに慈善に富んだ人だと評されているのを聞いたことがあります」。——「時によるとおそらく慈善が過ぎるでしょう、少なくとも若い時には極端に慈善をやりすぎたのです」。

〖注〗 **a man of benevolence**=a benevolent man. (1) 参照。**too much so**=too much benevolent として解する。**carry benevolence to an excess**「慈善を極端な程度まで持ってゆく」。

---

( 52 )

**478.** 小石とか砂利(じゃり)とかいうものは、もしいくらかでもそんなものがあったとすれば、みな舗装の中に閉じこめられているか、あるいはまったく溶けてしまったらしい。

**479.** スコットランド人こそ共和政治の下に生きるにもっとも適する国民である——すなわちまじめで、冷静で、理解がよく、法律を遵奉(じゅんぽう)するし、その上に他人の意見をすすんで尊重しようとする。

**480.** もし人間がうれしさのあまり狂気したことがあったとすれば、それはすなわちそのときの私であった。

**481.** もし世界語といわれる価値ある言語があるとすれば、英語こそそういわれる価値がある。

〚注〛 **deserve to be so called**「そういわれる価値がある」、この **so** は後の the universal language をさす。本文をコンマのところで前後転倒して見ればその関係がよくわかる。**claim** は「当然の権利として要求する」意味であるから **may claim to be called**... ＝is entitled to be called... ＝deserves to be called... と見てよい、すなわち「...と呼ばれる価値がある」となる。

**482.** セイロン島くらい自然が気前よくその恵みを与えた所は、たとえあるとしてもごくすくない。ほんのすこししか働かないでどんな貧しいものでも、じゅうぶん食べてゆくことができる。海は魚類に富んでおり、陸地は産物を豊かに産出するから、カレーや米の不足することはない。

〚注〛 **the poorest can keep themselves sufficiently supplied**「一番の貧乏人でさえじゅうぶん食糧を得たべてゆくことができる」。**curry and rice** はふつうライスカレーのことだが、ここでは「カレー粉と米」の意味。**run short**「欠乏する」、類例：—Provisions *ran short*. (食糧が欠乏した)

**483.** およそ世の中にアビゲール嬢とキティー・コリンズぐらい仲の悪そうな人たちはまたとなかった。(そのくせ)またアビゲール嬢とキティー・コリンズぐらい仲の良いものも世間に類がなかった。二人はしじゅう小競(ぜり)合いをするか、そうでなければ仲よくいっしょにお茶を飲んでいた。

〚注〛 **skirmish** とはちょいちょい言葉争いなどをすることをいったのである。

**484.** どちらかというと、彼は年齢より若く見えた、それはおそらく、いつも若い人々といっしょに住んでいた結果であろう。

〚注〛 **a result** の前に which was のようなものを入れて解する。

**485.** レニングラードの私の第一印象——中心は23年の後でも大した変化はない、どちらかと言えば、23年前より荒廃し疲弊した感じである。

**486.** 現代生活には、いやしくもそれが愉快なものになり得るものならば二つの徳がひじょうに必要である。その徳とは誠実と生活の簡易である。そして注意すべきはその徳のうちどちらかを実行すれば、他方がいっそう容易になるということである。

**487.** 彼は一時の怒りで人を不親切に扱うようなことはまずなかったといってよい。

〖注〗 **was seldom provoked into...ing**「...するほどに怒らせられることはめったになかった」、類例:—I *reasoned* him *into* compliance. (説いてきかせて承知させた)  You cannot *talk* me *into* doing such a thing. (君がいくら説いてもぼくにそんなことをさせることはできない)

**488.** 本当の偉大ということは階級とか権力とかいうものとはほとんど関係がない。

  〖注〗 **to have to do with**「関係がある」、類例—This *has nothing to do with* that. (これとあれとは関係がない —— まったく別だ) I *have nothing to do with* that affair. (私はあの事件には無関係だ)

**489.** フランス人はボートをこいだり、船を操縦する術にかけてはほとんど英国人に劣っていないが、この二者に対するフランスの嗜好(どう)はきわめて狭い範囲に限られている。

  〖注〗 **pursuits** 職業、娯楽など何でも人の従事するもの。

**490.** 大多数の場合は、非常に重態の患者が自分の死期が近づいているらしいということを知るのは当然であり、適当なことだ。ほかの理由はとにかく、身のまわりを処理することができるという理由からだけでも、そうなのだ。

  〖注〗 これは死期の迫った重症患者に死期のことを聞かせるべきか否かの問題を扱った文の一部である。ここは if anything とはちがって否定語が来ている例で、**if for no other reason than**=even if there is no other reason (for it) than つまり、「ほかに理由がないとしても」。

───────

( 53 )

**491.** 世人は、悪疫流行地から来た人といえば、必ずそれを迎えることをきらい避けるものである、たといその人がどんなに健康そうに見えても。

  〖注〗 **rage** は荒れ狂うという意から流行病などの「猖獗(しょうけつ)する」ことをいう。

**492.** 生きている植物や動物は、どんな平凡なものでも、研究のしがいのないものはないし、聡明に観察すればひじょうにおもしろい物語を語らないものはない。くもとその習慣とはどこか遠い国のめずらしい動物にすこしも劣らぬ興味をわれわれに与えるし、毎日ありや蜂の生活の中に演じられている以上におどろくべき物語は、いまだかつて人間の想像から生まれたことはない。

**493.** 「そんなものに私はさわりもしません、大丈夫です。いくらおなか

がすいても、私はあんなみすぼらしい、干からびたざくろなどは食べようとは思いません」と彼女は言った。

〚注〛 **I assure you** は「きっと...だから安心なさい」などという心持ちで用いる。**think of ... ing**「しようなどと思う」、類例：—You must not *think of leaving* at this time of night. (こんなに夜ふけて帰ろうなどとはもってのほかです——[ぜひお泊まりなさい])

**494.** 正直な人はいかに貧しくとも人の中の王である。

〚注〛 **for a' that**=for all that. 類例：—He is very rich, but he is not happy *for all that*.=He is not happy *for all* his wealth. (あんなに金があっても心は楽しくない)

**495.** 信念は、いかにそれがりっぱでも、行ないに変わるのでなければなんの価値もないものである。

〚注〛 **convert ~ into ...**「~を変じて...とする」、ゆえに convert itself into ...「変じて...となる」。

**496.** 婚約した二人が、たとい何年かかってどんなに一生けんめい努めようとも、どうしておたがいを知ることができよう。

〚注〛 他人同志ならば冷静な批評眼をもって相手を見ることができるかもしれないが、婚約した者がどうしてお互いに知り合うことができよう。

**497.** なんといってもやはり女性のこの特質がわれわれの女性に対する興味をいよいよ深くするものであろう。

〚注〛 **what makes her ever so interesting to us**「女性をわれわれに対しひじょうに興味あるものとするところのもの」。

**498.** どんなに博学であっても金で雇われる牧師などを得てなんの益があろう。

〚注〛 **what would it avail us to ... ?**=it would avail us nothing to ...「...することはすこしも我らを利することはないだろう」。 **though** (he be) **never so learned**=however learned he may be.

**499.** 彼女はひじょうに博学かもしれないが、けっして学者ぶる人ではない。

---

( 54 )

**500.** 「だれか のこぎりを持っているか」とフランクが言うと、「ぼくが持っている」、「ぼくも持っている」と子供らの中の3人が(口々に)答えた。

**501.** きたない壁、天井、床などは空気にかび臭い、重くるしい臭気をつける。きたない着物、泥のついたくつ、料理、洗濯物などもまたそうだ。

**502.** われわれが庭で見るばらのやぶは灌木(ぼく)である。ぶどう、すいかずら、きづた、およびその他の匍匐(ほふく)する蔓(つる)類もやはり灌木である。

**503.** トルストイがこれらの言葉を書いてから半世紀近くにもなる。その間に科学はいちじるしい発展をした——独裁政治もまたそうだ。

**504.** 従順と徳行とについて少年のまず学ぶべきことは観察の習慣——すなわち眼を用いる習慣である。何を見るのに眼を用いるかはあまりかまったことではない、用いさえすればよい。人は知識は力であるという、また実際そのとおりである——しかしその知識というのは観察によって得たものに限るのである。

〚注〛 **It matters little.** は It does not matter. (どうでもよい)をすこし弱く言ったのである。 **what you use them on**「何に眼を用いるか」。 **provided=if. but only...** 知識は力であるというのは観察によって得た知識に関するので、そうでない知識は力にならないということ。

**505.** フランクリンもこうであった——君もまたそうあり得るのだ。フランクリンは賞を得ようと努めて賞を得た。君もまたそうあるように。

〚注〛 **with**=in the case of「...にあって」。 **So may you!** の may は祈願の意味をあらわす。

**506.** 諸君はこれは小娘にとってはきわめて寂しい家であったと考えるでしょう。実際そのとおりであったのです。娘は子猫1匹犬1匹のほかには遊ぶ友だちもなかったのです。

---

( 55 )

**507.** イングランド人とスコットランド人とが同胞のようにいっしょに生活することができるようになったのは、長い歳月を経てからであった。

**508.** 夜がだいぶふけてからようやく彼らは止まった。

**509.** 彼は涙の乾かない中にすぐ笑い出すことがよくあった。

〚注〛 **would**—(63) 参照。

**510.** 彼の作家としての名声は徐々に築かれ、彼の真価は長年月を経てからようやく認められた。生涯の終わりにおいてさえ、彼の著書はほんの

わずかの人気を得ていたに過ぎなかった。

〘注〙 **a limited popularity**「限られた人気」すなわち「すこしの人気」、類例:—*a limited quantity* (少量).

**511.** 貧しい食物のために、かわいそうにこの男の健康がひじょうに衰えて、学業が終わらないうちに死んでしまった。

〘注〙 **to give way**「屈する」。

**512.** われわれは無思慮という愚行を行なっているのだ。間に合わなくなるまで立ちなおれなかったなどということにしてはならない。愚行を捨てて現実に直面するだけの洞察(どうさつ)力と真剣さと勇気とをふるい起こさなければならない。

〘注〙 **in thoughtlessness** の in は in the form of ということ。**it must not happen** の it は that 以下を代表する形式主語。**summon up**「(勇気、元気などを)喚起する、ふるい起こす」。

**513.** 彼女は蒼白(そうはく)な顔をして彼をじっと見た、そして二度つばをのんでからようやく物がいえた。

〘注〙 あまりびっくりして急には物がいえなかったこと。

**514.** おそろしい獣どもは今まで駆けた余勢で氷の上をよほど先まで行ってからようやく方向を変えることができた。

**515.** 書物の代金を払ったとき、私は船が私の着かないうちに出てしまいはしないかと心配してひじょうに急いでいたので、つい勘定書を調べなかったのです。

---

## (56)

**516.** 朝食がすむやいなや捕虜どもは軍曹ひとり伍長ひとり兵8人に監視されて、サヴァナに向け送られた。彼らが出かけてから間もなくジャスパーは兄に別れを告げ、用事にかこつけてそこを出発した。

〘注〙 **be gone** は「行ってしまう=いなくなる」ことをいう、ゆえに本文は「彼らが出かけてからまもなく」という意味である。もし been を除いて had not gone long とすれば「あまり遠くへ行かないうちに」の意味となる。**set out**=started. **on some pretended errand**「何か偽りの用事で」、類例:—I have come to town *on business.* (用事で上京した) The boy has gone *on an errand.* (こどもはお使いに行った)

**517.** その後まもなく私たちはまた偶然に会った。私たちは、私の近所の通りのかどでばったり出くわしたのである、そして私は彼の変わりようにびっくりした。

〚注〛 **come face to face**「顔と顔とむきあいになる」。**was struck by...**「...におどろかされた」、strike は変わった様子などが人の心を打つ意味、類例：—The likeness of the two boys *struck me*. (ふたりの少年が実によく似ていると思った)

**518.** ある日その紳士は象や子供らが何をしているかと思って行って見た。...スープ[象の名]も釣をしていた。象は鼻で大きな竹の釣竿(つりざお)を持って子供らのそばに立っていた。紳士がいくらも待たないうちに象の釣竿のえさに魚がついた。

〚注〛 **the elephant had a bite** 象のたれていた糸に魚がついたことをいう、a bite は魚がえさを食うこと。

**519.** あまり遠くまで行かないうちに鐘の音が風のまにまに聞えて来た、するとどういうわけか、理由はわからないけれど、その音を聞くと私はがっかりしてしまった。

〚注〛 **my heart sank within me**「意気沮喪(そそう)した」。この場合は heart は気力、勇気のことである、類例：—My *heart* fails me.＝My heart dies within me. (落胆(らくたん)する)

**520.** 半マイルも行かないうちに、ペゴティが突然いけがきからあらわれたので私はびっくりした。

〚注〛 **astonished to see...** (68) 参照。

**521.** 私たちがその動物の難儀をかわいそうだなどと考えている暇もないうちに、(幾頭かの)犬と馬に乗った人たちとがその動物[が通った]と同じ道をとって飛ぶようにやって来るのが見えた。

〚注〛 **the very path**—(12) 参照。

---

( 57 )

**522.** 現在にいたるまで人間はある程度機械の奴隷であった。人間が自分の仕事をするために機械を発明するやいなや、人間が飢えはじめたという事実には何か悲劇的なものがある。

〚注〛 **to a certain extent**「ある程度まで」。

**523.** さもしい人間は恩を施してもらいたがっているくせに、いったん恩を受けてしまうとすぐ恩人を忘れてしまう。(これに反して)高潔な人は人から恩を受けることを躊躇(ちゅうちょ)するが、もし受ければその恩を返さなければ義理がすまないと感じるのである。

〖注〗 **mean man** を「小人」とすれば、**noble man** は「君子」。**if so**=if he receives favours from others. **he feels** (*himself to be*) **under obligations to**...=he feels *that he is* under obligations to...「...する義理があると感ずる」。**them** は favours を受ける。

**524.** それで、どれが原因でありどれが結果であるにしても、地球上いたる所の人口増加と産業組織の勃興(ぼっこう)とが――各国民が人口の稠密(ちゅうみつ)を加え産業主義への道に相当進出して行くやいなや、必然的に感ずるあの複雑な一連の避けがたい必要事物と共に――あらゆる近代の戦争の主要な原因である。

〖注〗 **No matter which is cause, which** (is) **effect**「どちらが原因でどちらが結果であろうとも」。

**525.** その家の外に出るやいなや私は封筒を開いた、するとその中にお金がはいっているではないか。あの人たちに対する私の考えは変わった、ほんとだよ。少しの間(ま)もおかずその手紙とお金をチョッキのポケットに押しこんで、もよりの簡易飯屋へとかけ出した。

〖注〗 **I can tell you.** 相手に念を押す気持をあらわす。**lost not a moment**「一刻の猶予もなく、たちどころに」。I lost not a moment but でけっきょく I immediately *or* at once と同じことになる。**break** はそれまでの状態を変えて急に別な状態になるという意味。ここでは begin to run に近いもの。

**526.** 王が多年の間ひじょうに苦心をし、それがためずいぶんうそもつ いたすべての計画は、王の崩(ほう)ずるとほとんど同時に、中のからな砂山のようにくずれてしまった。

〖注〗 **all** 以下を解りやすく書きなおせば、all the plans and schemes *at which* he had laboured so long and *for which* he had lied so much となる。**labour at**=work at.

**527.** その言葉が口から出るやいなや、その言葉が聞き手に起こしたうれしさを私は見てとった。聞いた人はためらい、不本意であるとつぶやいた、けれどもやがて、私の申し出をありがたく受け入れ、その本を受けとって、よろこびのあまり顔をほてらした。

〚注〛 cause は double object をとる。ここでは delight の次に省略された which と hearer が目的語である。 **murmured reluctance** たとえば、「そんなことをしていただいてはこまりますなどとつぶやいた」という意味。

**528.** 私たちが宿屋に帰るとすぐに私の教区の人々が大勢私の成功したことをきいてお祝いにやってきた。

〚注〛 **no sooner...but...**=no sooner...than.... **numbers of**「沢山の」、類例:—*Great numbers of* students come to Tokyo every year, but very few of them attain their object. (年々多数の学生が東京へ出るが目的を達するものは実にわずかである)

**529.** 少年は紙を取った、そしてそれに書いてある文句を一見するやいなや驚喜の叫び声を発した。

**530.** ニコラスは目がさめるかさめないうちに家に近づいてくる馬車の音をきいた。

**531.** 私が出かけるか出かけないうちに、一人の男がつかつかと寄ってきて、あなたは誰々さんと思いますがそのとおりでしょうかと私に聞いた。

〚注〛 **asked me** の次のところを直接話法にすれば、"Am I right in thinking your name is so-and-so?" となる。もちろん so-and-so のところに本当の名前がはいるわけ。

**532.** けれどもある日彼は彼がまだ見たこともないし、また彼の軍隊が征服したこともない場所のあるということを聞いた——その場所はすなわち楽園であった。けれども彼はそういう所のあることを聞くやいなや、「わしはその国も征服しよう」という決心をした。

〚注〛 **his resolution was taken**=he made up his mind.

**533.** 私がすわるかすわらないうちに、丸っこくてたけだけしい黒い眼をした大きな茶色の獣が、足元から6ヤードのところで流れの表面に浮かび上がってきた。それからす早く私の姿を見つけてザブンとまた水中に飛びこんで、そこに映っていたはっきりした姿をかき乱してしまった。

〚注〛 **catch sight of...**「...を見つける」。

**534.** その思いつきが彼の心に浮かぶか浮かばないうちに、小道が突然曲りかどになった、それで彼は敵から姿をかくしたことになった。

**535.** こういう動機から私は牧師の職について1年たつかたたないうちに、まじめに結婚問題について考えはじめた。

〚注〛 全体を I had scarcely been in orders a year when I began to... となおしてみよ。

**536.** 「お前の鼻の頭へソーセージがぶらさがればよいのに」。彼がこういうかいわないうちにソーセージが彼の細君の鼻の頭からぶらさがっていた。

**537.** 大統領が大事な書類を調べてそれに署名する朝の仕事にかかろうと席につくかつかないうちに、案内をこう声もなく入口の戸がすうとあいた。

〖注〗 **but just** は「何々したばかり」の意味だから scarcely に等しいと見てさしつかえない。 **seated himself**=sat「すわった」。 **look over**「調べる」。

**538.** 鷹(たか)は鳥を見るやいなやそれを追いかけて飛んだ、そしてすみやかにそれを(捕えて)地面に持ってきた。

**539.** 岡の頂上にたどりついて、(木も何もない)ただ草だけはえている所に出たとき、彼女はもう身体が熱くそして息を切らしていた。そこに腰をおろすかおろさないうちに、彼女は疲れを忘れてしまった、それほど眼の前の景色は美しかったのである。

〖注〗 **by the time** (when)...「の時までに」。

**540.** おかあさんに本当のことを話したいという欲望が彼ののどまでおし上げてきた、しかしそれを言葉にあらわそうとするやいなや真実でなくなってしまった、だから彼が黙っていたのはうそを言わないためであったのだ。

**541.** 何百万というちっちゃな赤蟻(あり)が私の種子を大がい運んで行ってしまった、そして蟻が見のがしたのがたまたまあれば、それが緑の芽を出したその瞬間に、陸がににちょん切られてしまった。

**542.** なぜあんなに多くのおとなしい人たちが、自動車の運転席に乗るやいなや気が大きくなるのか、私にはまったくわけがわからない。彼らが日常生活の束縛から本当に解放されたのはこの時だけだというのか、それとも、飢えている自己を満足させてくれるというのか。

〖注〗 この文はふつうの時は上品に振舞っているような人も一たび自動車に乗ってドライヴするとなると、無鉄砲な運転をするのが、どうもふしぎだといっている。**It may be...** の It は前文の内容を受ける、つまり、「そのことは」である。**they feel...life** は the only time を修飾する形容詞節である。when を前に入れて見ればよい。**starved ego** というのは、平生の「満たされない自我」ということ。

**543.** その婦人は青年を見るやいなや叫んだ。「もしあなた、なんとかし

てください。私を離させてください。私のこどもが——かわいそうに私のこどもがおぼれようとしています、それだのに皆さんが私を離しません」。

---

( 58 )

**544.** あるとき小川を飛び越そうとしたが川が広かったのでトライは水の中へ落ちた。それでも彼は泣きはしなかった。彼はもうすこし大きくなってからもういちどやってみようと決心した。そしていくらもたたないうちに川のどんな広い所でも飛び越えることができるようになった。

〚注〛 **jump across**=jump over. 類例：—Can you *swim across* (or *over*) this river? (君はこの河を泳いでわたることができるか)

**545.** 知識が増したおかげで政府は今日では以前よりも多くの意図した結果を達成することが可能である、そして近いうちには今なお不可能の結果が可能となることと思われる。

〚注〛 **owing to**...「...のために」、類例：—*Owing to* my illness I could not attend the meeting. (病気のため会に出られなかった)

**546.** しかし彼が自分の国を出て他国を旅行することになるとすぐに、世間には自分の見たこともないものがひじょうに多く、また聞いたことすらないものもかなり多いということがわかってくる、そこでまもなく自分の国のふしぎなものの話などはしなくなる。

〚注〛 **home** 母国。**directly**=as soon as. **wonders** と複数にいうのはどこそこの七不思議などいう類をいう。

**547.** けれど、まもなく古い根から新芽が生ずる、で久しからずして土人はまた[バナナ]の一ふさを得るのである、一ふさまた一ふさとすみやかに相次いでできるから、一ふさ食いつくさないうちに後のが熟すばかりになっている。

---

( 59 )

**548.** ある人が暇をどう費やすかがわかって初めてその人がわかるとちょうど同じように、一国民の人生の楽しみが何であるかがわかって初めてその国民がわかる。人の品性があらわれるのは、しなければならないことをすることをやめて、自分のしたいことをする時である。

**549.** その世紀(十九世紀)の中ごろになって初めて、海上に出た汽船のトン数が帆走船に追いつきはじめたのである。その後は海上輸送の発展は急速であった。

〖注〗 that of sailing ships の that は the tonnage.

**550.** 私は沙漠の自由な良い空気を吸うとたちまち、今まで背負っていたとはほとんど感じなかった大きな重荷が心からおろされたように感じた。約3週間私は死の危険の下に生きてきた。危険は終わった、そしてその時になって初めて自分は今まで実に戦々兢々(きょうきょう)たる思いをしていたことを知った。

〖注〗 no sooner...than... (57) 参照。 did I know は knew を強めて言ったのである。

**551.** しかし彼らは翌朝になってようやく陸を見た、しかもそれは彼らが見るだろうと期待していた島ではなかった、なぜならば、彼らは潮流のために約30マイルもちがった方へ押し流されていたからである。

**552.** 彼がしっかり縛(しば)られてしまうまでは、人々は私に彼のところへ行かせようとはしなかった。(自由にされると)私はかわいそうに皆から侮辱されたこの男の体にわが身を投げて、彼の胸に私の悲しみを泣いて訴えた。それを見て父と家族のものはみな私を嘲笑(ちょうしょう)し、男へは脅迫(きょうはく)の言葉とひどい悪口を浴びせていた。

〖注〗 **would they let** の would は wanted to の意味。 **heap**「つみ重ねる、さかんに[悪口などを]浴びせる」。 **shameful epithets**「恥になるような形容辞」とは、「このどろぼう野郎」とかいうようなことをさす。

**553.** 母船に乗っている人たちには、どんなことが起こったのかわからなかった。人々はもちろん、その潜水艦が3時間以上は水中にとどまっていることができないということを知っていた。それでこの時間の制限が近づいてきてはじめて、何か異状があるらしいという疑念が起こってきた。

〖注〗 **on board the mother ship**=in the mother ship. **had no idea of...**「全然わからなかった」、類例—The dwellers in temperate zones can *have no idea of* the luxuriance of tropical vegetation. (温帯の住民には熱帯植物の繁茂は想像できない) **all was not well**=something was wrong.

**554.** 夕方になると彼はいとまを告げた、しかしそれに先だって彼は(近日)ふたたびわれわれを訪問する許可をこうたので、先方が大家さんのことであるから、われわれはさっそくその請(こ)いに承諾を与えたのである。

〖注〗 **at the approach of evening**=when evening approached「夕が近づいた時に」、簡単に towards evening (夕方)という副詞句を用いても同意味である。**but** 以下を (it was) **not till he had requested permission to renew his visit** (that he took leave) と補ってみよ、すなわち、「訪問を繰り返す許可を請うてから後にいとまを告げた」ということである。**landlord** は「地主」あるいは「家主」。**which we agreed to** は to which we agreed としてみた方がわかりやすいかもしれない、which は his request と見るべきだから we agreed to his request (われわれは彼の請いを承諾した)ということになる、類例：—I cannot *agree to* such a proposal. (そのような申し出に応ずることはできません)

**555.** さて、そこで、前置きとして、人類史上のこの事実に気を留めていただきたいとお願いする、すなわち、多くの偉大な画家の功績は彼らが餓死した後に至るまで、けっして認められなかったという事実である。

〖注〗 **starved and dead** は starved to death という言い方もあるが、後の方は餓死の動作の気持が多いし、前者の方は状態の方に重きを置いている。

---

( 60 )

**556.** 寸を与えれば尺を望む（負うといえば抱かるという）。

〖注〗 **ell** 反物を測る尺度の名、英国では 45 インチ。**will take** は「取らなくては承知しない」の意味。(85) 参照。「1 インチくれると、ぜひ 1 エル取るという」とは「すこし親切にすればすぐつけ上がる」こと。

**557.** 小事に注意すれば大事はおのずから成る。

〖注〗 5 円、10 円という小額に注意していれば、5 千円、1 万円という大金はみずから大事にするようになるという意味。

**558.** 諸君は天が諸君に命ずるところの者となれ、そうすれば成功するであろう。もし他のものとなるならば無きに劣ること幾千倍であろう。

〖注〗 **intend for**...「...にしようと思う」、類例：—His father *intends* him *for* a physician. (彼の父は彼を医者にするつもりだ) Nature *designed* him *for* a poet.=He *is designed* (by Nature) *for* a poet. (彼は天成の詩人だ)

**559.** 動物の肉体の単純反応を試験してみると、それが明らかにある特定の目的にかなうものであることがわかる。眠っている子供の足に軽くさわると、子供は足を引っこめる、猫の耳をくすぐると、猫はその耳を振る。

**560.** われわれは地球が太陽から正確に適切な分量の輻(ふ)射熱を受けていればこそ生存しているのだ。過多でも過少でも、どちらへでもこの均衡

を破ってみよ、そうすれば生物はこの地上から姿を消してしまわねばならない。

**561.** 運輸と生産は引き離すことができない。生産者から消費者へ品物が自由に流れる場合には、生産者が生産し得る有用な品物の量が多ければ多いほど、当事者各人は楽にやってゆける。しかしこの流れをどこかでじゃまするとだれもが損害をこうむり、流れをまったく止めてしまえば文明が崩壊してしまうであろう。

〚注〛 **flow**「流れ」。**better off**「いっそう暮し向きがよく」。**everyone concerned**「関係する各人」すなわち この場合は生産者と消費者両方である、類例：—the authorities *concerned*. (当局者) the parties *concerned* (利害関係者、当事者)

**562.** もしあなたが徒歩旅行か自転車旅行に出たことがあるならば、早起きが仕事の秘訣だということを知っているでしょう。朝、早立ちにすれば、予定も運命もこちらの自由になる、おそ立ちをすれば、時間の奴隷となってしまう。疲れた足で時間を追っかけて歩くのだ。

〚注〛 **have been on a walking tour** 現在完了形で、経験をあらわしている。**master** と servant は「使う者」と「使われる者」としてよく用いられる語であるが、ここでは servant のかわりにもっとひどい **slave** が使ってある。

**563.** 求めよ、そうすれば与えられるであろう、捜せ、そうすれば見いだすであろう、門をたたけ、そうすればあけてもらえるであろう。

〚注〛 **ye** [jiː] 二人称、複数の主語(古い形)。新約聖書、ルカ伝 11 章 9 節。

**564.** 人が言葉を信ずることはおどろくべきほどである。たとえば、もし人にばかだと言われたら、その男は自分はばかでないかしらと思って悲しくなるだろう。もし りこうな男だと言われたら、たとえ諸君がその男から買った品物の代価を払わないで行ってしまってもうれしく思うだろう。

〚注〛 **believe in**...「...を信ずる」。

**565.** 第一流の通訳というものは両国の文化にほんとうに通暁(つうぎょう)しているから、たとえて言えば、純粋に文字どおりの翻訳よりはるか高い空に飛び上がることができる。たとえば博識のロシア人がクリロフの書いた動物物語をあげたとすれば、一流の通訳ならイソップの中から同類の物語をさっそく出してくるだろう。

〚注〛 **top-notch**=first rate. **be at home**「慣れきっている、通じている」。**figuratively**「比喩的に」、これに対し「文字どおりに」は literally となる。**soar** は「鳥などが空中高く飛ぶ」ことだから、比喩的にと断ったわけ。Krylov はロシアの動物寓話の作者の名。

## (61)

**566.** ただ一歩を誤るか、すべるか、倒れるかしたならば、のこぎりの歯のような下の岩に粉砕して無惨な最後を遂げるほかはない。

〖注〗 文頭に If one makes (takes) を補い、**and**=then としてみよ。

**567.** もう数日たつと、このりっぱな蔵書はもはや存在しなくなるのだ。これらの書物は多くの見知らぬ人の手に移り、このへやを去る、ここではやさしい心づかいをもって大事にされていたのであるが。

**568.** 眠っている間にちょっとでも動いたが最後、彼は(崖(がけ)から)ころげ落ちて下の岩にぶつかって粉みじんになってしまったにちがいありません。

〖注〗 **The least movement**...=if he had made the least movement.

**569.** 一瞬後には私は、私(の飛行機)を導き、私が正常な状態にあるのかそれともさかさまの状態にあるのかを教える計器盤の上で踊っている針のほかには何もない、真暗な灰色のかたまりの中に完全にのみこまれてしまった。

〖注〗 これは飛行中真黒な雲の中にはいったときの状態を述べたもの。**Another moment and** はここでは Another moment passed and とか A moment later という意味で、前の問題とすこしちがった例である。**to guide** ... は needles の修飾語と見る。

**570.** 最後の足音や馬車の車輪のとどろきが遠く消え去った。その後の静けさを破って、敵に占領された地点からまた新たに射撃が起こるようなことはなかった。ドイツ軍はフランス軍が退却したのを知っていたのだ。数分後にはドイツ軍は放棄された村を占領するだろう、彼らの接近してくる騒音がこの小屋にも聞えてくるだろう。その間おそろしい静寂がつづいた。台所に残されたあわれな負傷兵たちさえ黙って自分の運命を待った。

〖注〗 **renewal of firing**「射撃をふたたび始めること」。**take possession of** ...「...を占領する」。**in the meantime**=in the meanwhile「その間」。

## (62)

**571.** だれにでもはっきりわかることであるが、大きな飛行機を飛ばせるには小さい飛行機より余計動力を必要とするし、また一定のエンジンの

動力で支え、かつ推進させ得る全重量には必ずある限界がある。たしかにわれわれはゼロの動力で無限の重さを運ぶことは望めない——石は空中には浮かばないのだ。

〘注〙 **keep it going**「それを進ませつづける」。**does a little one**=a little aeroplane requires.

**572.** 「よい公民」という言葉は多額納税者とか、慧眼(けいがん)な政治家とか、学識ある人とかを意味するのではない、またすぐれた芸術家を意味するのでもない。それは、自分の義務をできるだけ良心的に果たす一般庶民をこそ意味するものなのだ。

〘注〙 **a good citizen** が引用符でくくってあるのは「a good citizen という言葉」という意味。**tax payer** は納税者で、税額の多少で high, heavy とか、low, slight などの形容詞を用いる。

**573.** 彼はいったい ひじょうに遠慮がちではあるが、しかしいちど口を開けば必ず適切なことを言う。

〘注〙 **generally**「特別の場合でなく、概して」すなわち「平常は」の意味となる。**to the purpose**=to the point. 類例:—He speaks drily but *to the point*. (彼のいうことは乾燥無味だが要領を得ている)。His answer is *nothing to the purpose*. (彼の返事は不得要領だ)

**574.** もし分析的に読書することを心がけなければ、いくらたくさんの物語を読み、筋の詳細をいくら多く覚えており、いくら多数の登場人物の名をあげることができようと、有益な結果が得られることはあやしいものだ。

〘注〙 **no matter how**「何々はどうであれ、いかに...であろうとも」、譲歩の構文に使う。(93) 参照。

**575.** エックス光線は、破壊もせず、すこしの損傷も与えずに多くの物の内部を調べ、それについて多くのことを知る手段をわれわれに与えてくれる。この科学を産業に応用する多大の価値は実にこの点にあるのだ。

〘注〙 **provide~with...**「~に...を供給する」。 **see into**「調査する」。seeing into と learning...about は共に the interior につづく。

**576.** 土と雨と露とが樹木にやわらかい若芽を出させるように、本と勉強とは心を養いその隠れた力を開かせる。

**577.** 彼女は親しげな微笑をうかべてはっきり言った、「わたし自身花をあの人たちのところへ持って 行ってやります。 あなたの 言うとおりでした、花をやるとみんなが喜ぶのです。そしてわたしも幸福になります。何

でわたしが(病気がなおって)元気になって行くのかお医者さんにもわかりません——わたしにはちゃんとわかっています。生きる目あてがあるからなのです。」

〘注〙 the people といったのは「病人や貧しい人」で、すでに話題に上がった人たちなので定冠詞がついている。what is making me well は日本語ふうには why I am getting well であるが、前者の方の用法によく慣れること。

---

( 63 )

**578.** くじらが静かに水面に横たわっているときにはあまり胴体は見えない、しかし時々彼は水からおどり出すことがある。

**579.** 時間の合わないような時計ならだれでもうっちゃってしまうか、手放してしまうだろう、しかも自分の心がまちがった事と本当の事との区別がつかないほど病的になり、虚栄のためにほとんど役にたたなくなり、またおそらく自分がいかなるものか教えてくれないようになっても、それで満足していることが往々あるものだ。

〘注〙 **part with** は惜しいものなどを「手ばなす」に用いる、類例：—I will not *part with* this at any price. (これはいくらいい値でも手ばなさない)。**keep time** は時計の時間が合うこと、類例：—Does your watch *keep good* time?—No, it *gains* (or *loses*) a little. (君の時計はよく合うか——いや、すこし進む[あるいは遅れる]) **content** (形)=contented. (他動過分)、類例：—He is *contented* (or *content*) with his lot. (彼は自分の運命に甘んじている) **distinguish—from~**「—と~とを弁別する」。

**580.** 私の兄弟と私とでいつも家の中を散らかしたものです、子供というものは皆そうしたものですが。

**581.** 地震は大昔から一般の注意を引いてきた、そしてその破壊力のために、以前には超自然現象とみなされていたのはおどろくに当らない。

〘注〙 **be regarded as** とみなされる。**on account of...**「...のゆえに」。

**582.** 彼は必ず毎日外出した、そして、常にいっていた、「自分は天気のお世話にならないから医者のお世話にもならない」と。

〘注〙 **make it a rule to...**「主義として...する」「必ず...する」、類例：—I *make it a rule to* side with the weaker party. (ぼくは弱者にくみする主義だ) **consult** は対等の人と相談する意味のときは to *consult with* some one *about* some matter (何々のことについてだれだれと相談する)のように用いるが、専門家と相談する、すなわち意見を聞く意味には to *consult* a doctor

(医者の診察をこう), to *consult* a lawyer (弁護士の鑑定をこう), to *consult* a dictionary (辞書をひく) などと用いる。consult the weather とは天気と相談、すなわち好天気ならば出かける、雨天ならば出かけないというようなこと。

**583.** 彼の健康は日一日とよくなった。「ああ」彼はよく私に向かってさけんだものだ、「島の生活にはよそに見られない魅力がある。 人間の病苦の半分は、医者や薬はなくても、こんなよい所に住むだけで、振り落せるだろう」と。

**584.** わたしは 言うことがわかるように 口がきけるようになるやいなや、朝食の時にはみんなの給仕の役をよくしました、そして、何か欲しいものがあればベルを押すことをせずに、私が召使頭のところへ使いにやらされました。

〚注〛 **so as to be understood** は so that they could understand me のようになおして見ればよくわかるだろう。なお **(42)** 参照。**ask for**「求める」。**whatever was wanted**「何でも必要なもの」。

**585.** いつもはおだやかに始まり、それから次第に勢いを増して快い軟風となるのを例とした海風が、今は突然にしかもものごい勢いでやって来た。それで波は巻き上がり砕けて、見渡すかぎり、一面の白波と化した。

**586.** その音は飛行機のエンジンのうなりのようにひびいた。だれかが「おい、聞け」と言う。そこでわれわれは聞き耳を立てるのだった、心臓をどきどきさせながら。するとその音は止まってしまう、そして将軍のいびきにすぎないことを知るのだった。

**587.** ごく小さかったころあなたは何もおかしいことがないのによく腹をかかえて笑ったものだ。それは、余分の精力がたくさんあって、その一部が笑いとなってわき上がったからだ。

〚注〛 **energy to spare**「余分の精力」、類例:—time *to spare* (暇)。

---

( 64 )

**588.** ぼくはうそつきなどといわれつけてはいない。

〚注〛 平常うそつきといわれつけていれば慣れて腹も立たないが、そうでないから、うそつきなどといわれては腹が立つという意味。

**589.** もしあなたが厚着をし暖いへやに住むことに慣れているのなら、急に薄着になり、へやを冷くしておこうとするとひどく寒く感ずるでしょ

う。そして注意しないとかぜをひくかもしれない。

〘注〙 **catch (a) cold**=take (a) cold.「かぜをひく」、類例:—to *have* a cold. (かぜをひいている)

**590.** 土曜日は午後の取引の後はぼくの自由の時間であった、それでぼくはその時間を小湾に小さなボートを浮かべて過ごすことにしていた。

〘注〙 **Saturdays**=on Saturdays. **put it in**=spend my time.

**591.** それでもアイダは楽しかった、というのはおとうさんがたいそう自分をかわいがってくれるし、また[さびしい]灯台の中に住むことにもなれてしまったから。

---

( 65 )

**592.** 私の父の蔵書は主として小説であった、で私はたいがいそれを読んだ、そして後になってしばしばあんなに知識欲に渇いていた当時もっと適当な書物に出くわさなかったということを悲しんだ、というわけは私は今では文学者になるまいと決心したのであるから。

〘注〙 前の **since** は「その後」の意味の副詞、後の **since** は seeing that すなわち「...であるから」の意味。 **it was resolved** あるいは it was decided などの次には should がつづく、類例:—*It was decided* that he *should* go abroad.(彼を洋行させることに決定した) **a man of letters**「文学者」、(1) 参照。**fall in one's way**「ある物が偶然出てくる=人があるものに偶然出くわす」、類例:—I will do anything that *comes in my way*.(何でもあり次第の仕事をする)

**593.** 彼は非常に日本の事物が好きだということであった。彼は日本の家族制度の大賛美者で、謙遜(けんそん)とか礼儀とかいうような日本人に特有の美徳は家族制度の産物であるといった。

〘注〙 **He was said to have** は It was said that he had ... の縮まったもの。**things Japanese**「日本の事物」、こういう意味のときは名詞は複数で形容詞が後につく、類例:—things western(西洋の文物). **saying**=and said として見よ。**peculiar to**...「...に特有な」。

**594.** われわれは、われわれの生まれた場所、またわれわれの生涯を過ごす場所を好むものである、いな、おそらく好む以上のあるものがあるだろう。同様にわれわれはまた、すべての外国に対立した場合のわれわれの国全体に対して愛をもつべきである、そして国を守るために全力をつくす

べきである。

〖注〗 as opposed to... 「...に対立せしめられた場合に」。ought to= should. everything that lies in our power 「われわれの能力中に存するすべて」すなわち all we can などというのに等しい。preserve it from harm 「害にかからないように国を守る」。

**595.** 彼は利口な人間、つき合っておもしろい相手、軽卒な学生だった、借金をするのがたいそう好き、それから酒屋がことに好きだった。

〖注〗 had の主語は文頭の he. セミコロンの使い方はこの筆者の文体的特色。

**596.** 私はあなたにギリシア語の天才があると確信する、ですからその方に熱心になったら前途には赫々(かくかく)たる光明があると思います。

〖注〗 feel sure 「たしかにそう思う」。have a brilliant future before you は前途有望なことをいう、類例:—Japan *has a bright future before* her. (日本の前途には光明ある未来がある=前途洋々)

**597.** 翌日は地主が来訪するはずになっていたから、妻は鹿肉パイの料理にとりかかった。娘たちも他の者と同様にいそがしそうに見えた、私はややしばらく娘たちが火の上で何か煮ているのを見ていた。最初は何か母親の手伝いをしているのだと思っていた、ところがディックが小声で姉たちは顔に塗る化粧水をこしらえているのだと内通に及んだ。私は生まれつき化粧水はどんな種類のものでもきらいであった、というのは私は化粧水というものは顔の色をよくしないで、かえって悪くすることを知っていたからである。そこで私はいすをそろりそろりと火のそばに近づけ、火ばしになおすところでもあるように、それをつかんで粗相(偶然)のように見せかけて、その調合物をことごとくひっくり返してやった。そしてもういちどこしらえなおすにはすでに時がおそかったのである。

〖注〗 equally...with~ 「～と同じに」。Washes of...=I had a natural antipathy to all kinds of washes. by slow degrees 「すこしずつ」。

**598.** すべてのフランス人のようにナポレオンにもひじょうに芝居気があった。

〖注〗 stage-effect 舞台上の効果を欲することは大向うの喝采(かっさい)を博そうとすること。

**599.** 1年もたたないうちに私たちはまた一人娘をもうけた、そして私はこんどこそグリッスルという名にしようときめていた、ところが一人の金持の親類が名づけ親になろうという気まぐれを起こしたので、2番目の

娘はその人のいうとおりになって、ソファイアと名づけられた。

**600.** 彼は私の肩をなで、お前はいい子だ、私はすっかりお前が気に入ったと言った。

〚注〛 **told me** 以下を直接話法にして書き直せば he said, "You are a good boy; I have taken quite a fancy to you."

---

( 66 )

**601.** 「あら、こんなにかわいらしいのがあってよ、その小さな黒い頭の所をつまんで早く召し上がれよ」。

〚注〛 **Do take** の do は強勢。

**602.** ある画廊の入口に配備された一人の兵士が、最初につえを預けない者はだれも通してはならないという厳命を受けていた。一人の紳士がポケットへ両手をつっこんではいって来た。兵士は紳士の腕をつかんで言った。「止まれ、つえはどうした」「つえは持っていません」「それでは戻ってつえを取ってこい、それまでは通せない」。

〚注〛 **allow~to...**「~に...を許す」。

**603.** スクィーヤズはそのへやを出て行ったが、すこしたつとスマイクのえり首をつかまえて引きずりながら帰ってきた。

**604.** スクィーヤズはひどく怒って、彼につばを吐きかけ、顔に真っこうから一撃をくわした。

**605.** 彼は私の頭をなでてくれた。しかしどういうものか私は彼がきらいであった。

**606.** フランクリンはいかなる人であったか。活版職工！かつては一活版所の雇人であった。貧困は正面から彼にせまった、しかし貧乏の神の空白なうつろな目つきも全然彼をおどすことはできなかった。彼は世の大部分の人の戦わねばならない潮流よりもさらに困難な潮流と争った。それでも彼はこれに屈伏しなかった。

〚注〛 **Poverty** を女性とし **her** で受けてある。**could nothing daunt him**「すこしも彼[の勇気]をくじくことはできなかった」、nothing は not at all の意味の副詞。**daunt**=discourage.

**607.** われわれは直面しなければならない混乱について実際的に見つも

ることが必要である。あるいくつかの事実がわれわれの面前に迫っている。戦争はすべてが国家主義的であるとは限らない。国家主義的主権を廃止したところで、社会階級の戦争がま近かにあるだろう。

> 〚注〛 working「実行的な、実際に使える」。All...is not... 部分否定の文。nationalist (形容詞)「国家主義の」。abolish...and「命令形+and」の構文、(60)参照。on hand「目の前に」。

**608.** 自己の財政には臆せずに直面して、金銭上の収入支出を常に計算しておくことは、各人の当然なすべき本務である。

> 〚注〛 **bounden duty**「ぜひしなくてはならぬ義務」。**look his affairs in the face**「自己の財政を正面に見る」とはたとい自分に負債などがあっても、それを恐れて財政状況をなるべく考えないようにしているなどという卑劣なことをしてはならないということ。

---

( 67 )

**609.** 彼は自分さえ楽しみが得られれば、だれの楽しみをうばったってかまわない。

> 〚注〛 so that は so long as, if only などの意味。

**610.** 貧乏なら貧乏らしくする勇気をお持ちなさい、そうすれば貧乏の一番苦しいところはなくなるのです。

> 〚注〛 **disarm poverty of its sharpest sting**「貧乏というものからもっとも鋭いとげという武器を奪うことになる」。

**611.** 患者は折々理性の働きを失った。

> 〚注〛 正気を失ってうごとなどいうこと。

**612.** 彼を追いはらって、私の書斎を独占したくてたまらなかったので、もうそれ以上一刻も待っていられなかった。

> 〚注〛 **get rid of...**「...をとりのぞく」。**at intervals** 間隔をおいて。

**613.** 彼女がそれまで気がかりになっていた秘密を打ちあけて、胸の重荷を下ろしたのはよほどたってからであった。

**614.** もし私があなたの町からねずみを駆除したら、あなたは私に千ギルダーくれますか。

**615.** ゆえなく約束の時間を守らない人は、自己の時間と同様に他人の時間をも浪費して顧みないものであるということを示す。多忙な人にとっ

ては時間は金である、こういう人から時間を奪う者は、その人の懐中物をとるのと同様の損害をその人に与えるのである。

**616.** 諸君が英国の停車場に着くとすべて赤帽は「さあお客様が来た、親切に取り扱ってあげよう」というようなふうに見える。それで、どの赤帽に諸君の荷物を持たせるか、またこちらのききたい質問をだれに答えてもらうか、これが問題なのだ。

〖注〗 **it is who shall...**=the question is who shall...「問題はだれに...してもらおうかということである」とは皆がわれもわれもと親切をつくしたがっているから、そういう問題が持ち上がるという心持。

**617.** 当時の彼の態度は、その後もずっとそうであったが、さっぱりして男らしく人に頼るところがなかった。彼は人といっしょになって自分も話をしたが他人の領分をおかすことはなく、教養がないため口の出しようのない話題が出たときは、注意と敬意を払ってじっと耳をかたむけているように見受けられた。

〖注〗 **He took his share in conversation.**「彼は会話において自分の分け前を取った＝会話に加わって話をした」。**but not more than belonged to him**「しかし彼に属する分け前以上は取らなかった＝他人の分け前までおかすことはしなかった」。**apparent** の訳出に留意。

**618.** 父を失い、夫を失い、子供を失い、[その上に]所有物は自分の住んでいる家のほかはことごとくうばわれてしまっても、スロウカム夫人はその谷間を去ることができなかった、というのはまだ頑是(ガンゼ)ない9人の子供をかかえていたからである。

〖注〗 **the house that sheltered her**「後女の宿となる家」、shelter は雨露をしのいで保護する意味の動詞。**helpless** 自分で身の始末のできないのをいう。

**619.** 私の経験でお前の経験の足らない所を補い、若いお前の前途にあるいばらを取り除いてやりたい、いばらのためには私も若いときにひっかかれ醜い傷を負わされたのだから。

〖注〗 **which scratched and disfigured me**「そのいばらが私をひっかき容貌(キリョウ)をそこなった」、ここではもちろん比喩的に用いられている。**mine**=my youth.

**620.** へやが明るくなった、彼女は起き上がり、小さいひびのはいった鏡のところへ行って、自分の顔を長い間眺めた。自分が美しいということをかつては知っていたとしても、時には虐待され、いつもろくな着物も着

せられず、何かかにか不足がちな夫との生活が、この知識を彼女からうばってしまっていたのである。

　〘注〙 **more or less**「多かれ少なかれ」。

**621.** 古ぼけた誤報の断片がいまだにわれわれの考え方をごたごたさせているし、ごく最近わずかの間、中国を訪れた人々が新しい(誤った)報道を積みかさねる。われわれの(頭という)屋根裏べやから百年間もの残存物をすぐにきれいさっぱり掃き出すことは不可能かもしれない、けれども、大きなじゃまになる伝説のようなもののいくつかは、永久に放棄されてもよさそうなものだ。

　〘注〙 著者 Pearl Buck が西欧人が中国に対する見解を誤っていることを指摘した文。**a new accumulation ladled out**「くみ出された新しい蓄積」となるが、訳文のようにしてみた。**attics** ここでは「頭」とか「心」というものをたとえて言ったもの。初めの方の **clutter** も「がらくたなどで取りちらかす」という意味で、全体の比喩が一貫しているわけ。**for good and all** for good だけでもよく、「これっきり、永久に」ということ。

**622.** しかし、親類の中に評判の悪い人物とか、うるさい客人とか、あるいはかかり合いたくないような者があった場合には、そういう人たちの帰る時に、私は必ず乗馬用の外とうとか、長ぐつとか、また折々は値の安い馬などを貸してやるようにしていた。するとそういう連中はけっしてそれを返しに来ることのないのを見て私は満足に思った。こういう方法で私たちは好かない人たちを家から追い払ってしまった。

　〘注〙 **upon his leaving**「彼の去るにあたって」。**I ever took care to...**「いつも忘れずにきっと...した」。**have the satisfaction of~** (45) 参照。**such as**=those whom.

( 68 )

**623.** エイカーズ氏はジョンの成功を聞いてひじょうによろこんだ。わが子は何の天才もないにしても、いつかは有用な人物になるだろうとたのもしく思った。

　〘注〙 **in time**「相当の時節が来れば」「いつかは」「そのうちには」。

**624.** それから数カ月後に、その女性がまた来たので、事務員はびっくりした、こんどはその女性は自動車を運転して来たので、二重におどろいたのだった。

〚注〛 この話の前後は、この前に来たときは、婦人はもう余命いくばくもないという重病人であった。もちろん人の運転する自動車にのせてもらって来たのだった。

**625.** ハーマンは自分よりははるか下だと考えていた自分の父の徒弟が、自分と同程度の知識を持っているということを考えて、ちょっとの間はおどろきとくやしさとで黙っていた。

〚注〛 **be possessed of**=possess.—(75) 参照。**equal to his** (knowledge)「自分の知識に等しい」。

**626.** もっともりっぱな作家のもっともすぐれた章句に親しんでいない人は、いつかは、自分の一番よいと思った考えが、そういう大家の思想のなかでは、むしろつまらぬ思想に当るものであることを知って、くやしく思うであろう。

〚注〛 **be familiarized with~**「~に親しんでいる、精通している」。**his best thoughts** で best が斜体になっているのは、自分では best と考えているという気持をあらわす。**indifferent** は「可もなく不可もなく」「平凡な」と、さらに進んで「つまらない」の意味にもなる。

**627.** 王子は翌朝深い眠りからさめてあたりを見まわすと、わが身は〔いつかしら〕わらぶきの納屋にひとりいるのを知ってひじょうにおどろいた。

**628.** 彼は3等船客として汽船に乗りこみ、1900年合衆国に上陸したが、身には1文の金もなく、こんな名もない若い日本人には学問研究の当てなどほとんどない有様であった。

〚注〛 これは野口英世の話である。**with little research opportunity waiting for~**「~を待っている研究の機会はほとんどなく」。**obscure** は「名もない、世に知られない」。

**629.** 彼らは英語を勉強していて、英語を練習したがった。彼らは私にレニングラードの印象をたずねた。私が工学者でないことを知って失望した。そして私は政治学の教授だと言うと急に立ち去ってしまった。

〚注〛 これはアメリカ人の訪ソ旅行談の一節である。**abruptly** = suddenly, quickly.

**630.** 人間は常に物の性質を変えている、そして自分が変えた物が変える前と全く同様に作用しつづけるものといつも考えている、だから新しい予期しない物が出てくるとびっくりする。

**631.** 人間は人類に昔からついて来た三つの懲罰のうちの二つ、すなわ

ち、戦争と悪疫とを除去しようとしているが、けっきょく、その第三の懲罰、飢餓によって死滅せねばならないのだろうか。

〖注〗 **rid itself of** (63) 参照。scourge=anything which causes much suffering. よく「天罰」などの意味に用いる。

**632.** 彼は生きているうちに、感謝している世界の人が贈り得るすべての名誉をもって、彼の仕事に報いられた。彼は自分の意見と研究が全世界の思想と行動に影響を与えるのをまのあたりに見た。もし偉さが自分の同時代人のためになした善の程度によって測られるならば、彼の名は永久に高く位するであろう。

〖注〗 **have his work rewarded**「彼の仕事は報いられた」、(71) 参照。**for all time**「永久に」。

**633.** 春はおずおずとした足どりで徐々に近づいてくる季節だ。時には一日うれしそうに踊り出してくることもあるが、翌日はまた引っこんでしまう。冬のまん中にも晴れ晴れした、暖かい、快晴の日があり、自然がその眠りから目ざめたように思われ、日陰の寒さと裸の木の枝のみが春なお遠いことをわれわれに思わせる。

〖注〗 **on occasion**=occasionally「時折」。

**634.** 最後にわれわれは反逆門を見た。この門をくぐってふたたび帰らぬ旅におもむいた有名な人々も多いのである。

**635.** 人間を一室内に閉じこめ、すき間をすっかりふさいでしまい、中に炭火の起こった火ばちを置けば、その人は眠りについたら再びさめることはない。

---

(69)

**636.** 彼がその旅行談や、見(聞)談をするのを聞くほどおもしろいことはなかった。

**637.** 太陽が遠い丘のかなたに沈むのを眺めたり、帰りのことを考えずに大きい森の中をどこまでもさまよったり、岸に立って小舟が遠い島々に隠れてゆくのを見送ったり、雲間に見えつ隠れつする雁(かり)の旅路に思いをはせたりすることは、心楽しいことである。

〖注〗 **with no thought of**=without thinking of. **far-off**=distant.

**638.** 私はレプリコーンというもののあることをしばしば聞いた、が隠さず正直のところをいうと、私はそういうもののあることをしかとは信じなかった。

〖注〗 of=that there are として見よ、類例:—I never heard *of* (=that there is) such a man. (そういう人のあるということを聞かない) **Leprechaun** は Ireland のおとぎばなしに出てくる一寸法師のくつ屋。**believe in**...「...の存在を信ずる」、類例:—I don't *believe in* ghosts. (私は幽霊があるものとは信じない) I *believe in* God. (神の存在を信ずる) believe in はまた人物を信用するに用いることもある、例:—The students *believe in* their teacher. (学生は先生を信じている)

**639.** ハムレットは王すなわち 彼の叔父(訳)がこの言葉を聞いて 顔色を変えたことを認めた。

**640.** 二人は互いに抱き合って泣いたり笑ったりした、うわさに聞くとその後二人は互いに楽しく暮したということである。

**641.** それゆえに私は二十世紀人が宗教回復の探求に出発するのを見ようと期待している。きっとそれを回復するだろうと思っている。

〖注〗 **quest** の類例:—They went out to Australia *in quest of* gold. (金を捜しにオーストラリアへ出かけた) his perpetual *quest for* a new experience (新しい経験に対する彼の不断の追求)

---

## (70)

**642.** 私は喜んでお前にフットボールをやらせる。私は荒っぽい男らしいスポーツをよいと思っている。しかしそれが人の一生の唯一の目的となることは感心しない。学課をよくやることをどんなスポーツの犠牲にもしてもらいたくない。言うまでもないことだが、世に成功するには人格が頭や身体のどちらよりもはるかに大切だ。

〖注〗 **standing well**「よくできること」。**count for**「勘定にはいる」「物の数にはいる」「重要さがある」。類例:—We *count for* nothing in the world. (われわれは物の数にもはいらない)

**643.** スープは非常にたけの高い象でした。そして時々子供らはスープを木の下にとどまらせて、その木の枝からいろいろの果物を取りました。

〖注〗 **would**—(63, d) 参照。**nuts** はくり、くるみのような堅果。**berry** は漿果(しょう)。

**644.** 私たちは街道に近く住んでいたから、旅人や異郷の人などが、し

ばしば私の家の名物になっているすぐり酒を味わいに立ち寄った。

〚注〛 gooseberry-wine すぐりで造った酒。**for which we had great reputation**「その酒で私たちは大なる名声を持っていた」、有名になる事がらをいうのに for を用いる、類例：—What is Japan *noted for?*（日本の名物は何か）Japan is *famous for* its scenery.（日本は景色で有名）

**645.** 君は、それをどうやるのか教えてもらうような地位にいる時より、むしろ自分で積極的にやる場合の方がよく上達するだろう。君がしたいと思うことを他人がやっているのをただ見ているのはあまり足しにならない。君はそれをやってみなければならない。

〚注〛 **acquire skill**「熟達する」。**if** はこの場合 when と同じような意味である。

**646.** 私は学生がみんな、その国の言葉の正確な知識がなくては文学も文化も徹底的に鑑賞できるものでないことを、悟ってもらいたい、そして、それが早ければ早いほどよいのだ。

〚注〛 **come to know**「知るようになる」。**the language**「その国の国語」の意味で定冠詞がついている。

**647.** 自分の欲することを人にしてやるように努めよ、そして時にあるいは人が自分の欲することをしてくれなくても、それがために落胆するな。

〚注〛 **be discouraged** は be encouraged の反対で「勇気をくじかれる」。**if** (=even if) **they fail** (to do to you as you would have them do to you) と補って見よ、すなわち「たとい諸君が彼らにしてもらいたいと思うことを彼らがしてくれなくても」の意味、fail to... は「...しない」、類例：—I will *not fail to* pay you at the end of the month.（月末には必ず払います）

**648.** あの俳優たちに父王殺害に似たところを演じさせよう。

**649.** 子供たちはいつでもさるが遊んでいるところをながめるのを喜ぶ、そしてこれらの小動物(猿)もまた、実に、人々に訪問されるのを喜んでいるらしい。

**650.** そしてもしわたしがお暇を出されてしまうと、ジョウエットさんもまた、わたしに推薦状を下さらないでしょう。わたしどうしたらいいでしょう。わたしの一生はどうなるでしょう。わたしはあなた様のために一生けんめい努めたのですのに、こんなことをされるのは我慢できません。

〚注〛 **be dismissed**「解雇される、くびになる」。**After all I've tried to do** all の次に関係代名詞を入れて解する、「私がやろうと努めたすべてのことの後で」となる。after all の独立した意味「結局」の用法ではないことに注意。

**651.** 私はあなたに書物をあげて学校にやり、なおあなたの喜ぶようなことは何でもしてあげたいんですが。

〖注〗 attend school「学校に行く」。

**652.** マルカムは自分の子供にそのような危険な旅をさせたくはなかった、というのは綿をちぎったような雪が降りしきり、日もとっぷりと暮れかけていたから。

**653.** 「ある人が今日たきぎをあのおばさんのところへ持ってきたが、ぼくはおばさんがその人に、もし今夜だれかにそれを切ってもらわなければ、あすの朝火をたきつけるものがないと言っているのを聞いた」。

〖注〗 to make a fire with は with which to make a fire の which を略した形、類例:—a chair to sit on=a chair on which to sit.

**654.** 「あなたは私が皿を渡すときナイフとフォークを皿から取っておけといいましたね」——「私はナイフやフォークに落ちられて、それをお前に拾ってやるのはいやだからね」。

**655.** 「では、アリスさん、あなたは私があなたをかわいがっていて、あなたに来てもらうのをいつも喜んでいることをご存じなんですね、もし私の力でそうすることができるなら、私はきっとあなたを始終ここに置きますよ」と、リードさんが言った。

〖注〗 were it in my power=if it were in my power—(90) 参照。

**656.** 彼はすべての遊戯に先立ちになり、そして子供が上ぐつ取り、音楽いす、家族馬車などにあきたときに、皆に腰をかけさせておいてなぞをかけた。

〖注〗 hunt the slippers 大勢が一人を囲んで車座になり上ぐつを甲から乙、乙から丙と回すのを中央の一人が取る遊戯。musical chairs 人の数を 10 人とすればいすを 9 脚置き、音楽につれてぐるぐる回り、音楽が急にやむと同時に皆急いでいすに腰をかける、一人残ったものが負けになる。family coach 各人が馬、手綱、車など馬車に縁のあるものになり、別に一人馬車の話をする人がおり、その人が話の際に馬といえば馬になった人が立ち上がり、手綱といえば手綱になった人が立ち上がる、立ちそこなった人が負けとなる。

( 71 )

**657.** 人はあることにほねを折ってそれがうまくいくと、ちっともほねが折れなかったように人に思われたいというばかげた望みを抱くものである。

〖注〗 **a happy effort** とは「好結果を得た努力」のこと。**is possessed with ...** はとんでもない考えなどに「とりつかれる」という意味、類例：—He *is possessed with* a strange notion. (妙な考え——謬見(びゅうけん)——を抱いている) **have it thought** の it は that 以下を代表する。**it cost him nothing** の it はそのうまくいったという仕事をさす、すなわち「その仕事には何の犠牲も払わなかった」「わけなくできた」という意味、類例：—The invention *cost him* five years' labour. (この発明に彼は5カ年を費やした)

**658.** 人間の眼も浮世の様(さま)をながめ[つかれて]老衰してしまえば、眼に眼帯をかけられるということもさしておそろしい不幸とは思われない。

〖注〗 **the ways of the world**「世人の常になすところ」「世の習い」、類例：—Inscrutable are *the ways of Heaven*. (天のなすところははかりがたい＝人間万事塞翁(さいおう)が馬)

**659.** 蒸気機関を理解したいと思う人は技師のところへ行って各部分を説明してもらえば理解することができる。しかしもし蒸気機関の歴史を知りたいと思うなら、最初に造られたものまで後戻りし、その後に生じた新しい改良を一々研究しなければならない。

〖注〗 **do so**＝understand.

**660.** その動物の後脚の一本は折れたか、またはほかのけがをしていた、それで妙なふうにびっこをひいていた。しっぽはなく、耳はつけ根のところまで切られていた。全体としてみると、それは、戦争で体のあちこちを撃ち取られた上に、さんざんに打ちのめされて、みじめな姿で帰ってきた老兵士のようであった。

〖注〗 **otherwise**＝in other ways. **close to his head**「頭に近いところまで」。 **altogether**＝on the whole. **had～shot away**「砲弾でうたれてちぎりとられた」。

**661.** ある母が娘の肖像画を描かせるために有名な画家のところへ娘を連れて行った、そしてやっと肖像画ができ上がったとき彼らはそれを見に行った。画家が肖像画を彼らの前に置くと、母は顔に不興の色を浮かべてそれを見ていたが、一語も言わなかった。画家もまた口を開かなかった。

娘はついに不愉快な沈黙を破って、「お母さん、どこへかけましょう」と言うと、婦人は「面(つら)を壁に向けてかけておくのならどこへかけておいてもいいでしょう」と答えた。

〖注〗 at length「ついに」「やがて」。 so long as...「かぎり」、(41) 参照。

**662.** どんなに罪にけがれ悲しみにくもった心といえども、寛大にして親切な行ないを見て、胸底のもっとも気高い情を呼び起こされないものはない。

〖注〗 **There beats** は There is というところを heart であるから鼓動という語を用いたのである。全体は Every heart that beats has its noblest impulse aroused... というのにひとしい。

**663.** 夜は[形勢が]いっそう悪かった——というのは、手または足を凍傷せずに甲板に止まっているということはほとんどできなかったのであるから。

〖注〗 甲板に止まっているとたいがいは凍傷にかかるということ。

**664.** 帝は、看護人の一人に命じて、オーナノウの死に関することをくわしく取りしらべさせた。看護人は念のために死体をもう一度もって来させた。ところがおどろいた、死体はまだあたたかく、オーナノウ将軍は生命があったのである。そこで看護人は将軍をあたたかい毛布に包んで本営へ運ばせた。

〖注〗 **orderly** に二つの意味がある。 1. a soldier in attendance on an officer, to carry orders &c.; 2. an attendant in a ward of a (military) hospital.

**665.** ヒットラーの約束はこうであった、ドイツ民族は世界で最善の、最優秀の、しかももっとも虐待された国民であるから、彼を通して、全世界に君臨し、ユダヤ、スラヴ、有色民族のような劣等な人種を足下に踏みつけるべきである。

〖注〗 **wronged**「不当な扱いをうけた、虐待された」。should は約束とか予言の場合によく用いられ、主節動詞が現在ならば shall となる。 **be put in authority over~**「~に対して権威者の地位につけられる」。 **have~trodden**「~を踏みつぶす」。trodden は tread の過去分詞。

( 72 )

**666.** 公平に評すれば彼女(自分の妻)は性質のよい、家政のじょうずな婦人であった。

**667.** 手短かに話すならば、1952年の5月、アイスランドはその漁場の限界を、一番長い二つの岬(みさき)の間に引いた線と、小島と岸にある岩の間に引いた線から4マイルの周囲まで外に向かって移動させ、そのようにして、以前に公開されていた豊かな漁場をとり囲んだのである。

〚注〛 **to cut a long story short**「長い話を短くすれば、手っとり早く言えば」。**thus enclosing** は and thus enclosed のように訳せばよい。

**668.** 一口にいえば、私は自分が厳格な一夫一婦論者であるということをほこりとした。

〚注〛 **to value oneself upon**＝to pride oneself upon. 類例：—He *prides himself on* his attainments. (彼は学識が自慢だ) He *values himself on* his skill in teaching. (彼は教授法がじょうずだと自負している) **monogamist** に対して、polygamy は「一夫多妻」ということ。

**669.** 貧窮は人生のいかなる状態においても大きな不幸である、しかし俗にいわゆる「むかし ならした人」ほど貧窮を痛切に感じる者はない。

〚注〛 **those who have seen better days**「よき日を見た人＝幸福な時代を経た人＝むかしは何某といわれた人々」。比較：
{ He *has seen better days* (in his time).
（今こそ零落(れいらく)しているがむかしはたいしたものだった）
He *has seen his best days* (already).
（あの人はもう盛りを過ぎてしまった）

**670.** これはある親たちの言うところであるが、なお悪いことには、新しい型の試験——いわゆる心理学的テスト——が用いられている、そしてこれは学業とははっきりした関係は何もないのである。

〚注〛 **so some parents have said** これはこの文全体を so でまず代表させている。**that** の先行詞は type.

**671.** 森林の気候に及ぼす影響については、大森林は気候をやわらげる傾きがあると言ってよい。夏には森林の中は外の開けた土地よりいつも涼しく、そして奇妙なことだが、冬には森林の中は開けた場所より暖かい。

〚注〛 **large bodies of timber**「樹木の大きな団体＝大森林」。

**672.** 話は元へもどって、私はこんなふうに引きつづき2年間、すなわ

ち私が 12 になるまで父の仕事に従事しておりました。

〚注〛 **that is** (to say)「換言すれば」「すなわち」。

**673.** 卒直に申しあげると、私はあなたのお顔つきや、なさることが気に入らないのです、そしてあなたがこんなぐあいにして私の家へ来られたのは、何か悪い計画でもあるのじゃないかと思うのです。

〚注〛 **thus**「このようにして」。 **introduce oneself** 自分はこういう者だとみずから名のり出ること。

**674.** そこは小じんまりとした気持ちのよいところで、楽ないすがあり、気持ちのよい灯火があり、よく枯れたオリーヴの木の親しみのある開いた炉の火があった。何一つ欠けたところがないように、戸外には岸によせる波のかすかな音が聞えてきた。

〚注〛 **seasoned olivewood**「枯れたオリーヴの木材」、まきにするもの。

**675.** 重ね重ねの難儀のあげくに夜が近づいてきた。

〚注〛 **be at hand** まぢかにある。

**676.** だれかが幽霊を見たという事実を確証するには、まず第一に、随時に起こるほかの出来事を立証するに必要であるのとまったく同じ種類の証拠が必要である。

〚注〛 **To establish** は不定法の名詞用法で文の主語となり、その述語動詞が requires である。 **occasional** 時折の。

**677.** 天国の門は、いわば中からだけ開くことができるのである。

〚注〛 **from within** 本来前置詞である within が他の前置詞に支配されている。

**678.** 妙な話だが、私がロンドンへやって来たのは、人間に会うためではなく、さらに多く孤独を求めてであった。というわけは、それまで住んでいた町の中ではあまりによく顔を知られているため、一歩外へ出れば必ずほとんどその瞬間に人と会話を始めるという有様であったからだ。

〚注〛 **could not...without~**「...すれば必ず~」、(105) 参照。

**679.** もし手紙というものがなかったならば、商品を注文するにも、勘定を支払うにも、金を借りるにも、クラブに入会するにも、招待状をもらって承知したと言うにも、勤め口を申しこむにも、どんなに不便だろう——日常生活のきまったようなことの、ほんの三、四の例をあげてみても、このようなわけである。

〚注〛 **If it weren't**=if there were no=but for. **(94), (107)** 参照。 **to name**「名をあげるならば」。

( 73 )

**680.** 「ああ頭の痛いこと！胸の痛みはいうまでもないことだが」と彼女は物うげにいった。

**681.** ここから窓に達することさえだれにも不可能であったろう、ましてへやの中にはいるなどということはなおさらである。

**682.** 財宝名誉はいうに及ばず、衣食すら手をわずらわし額に汗するのでなければ得られないのである。

〚注〛 **raiment**=clothing.　**come at**=gain; obtain.

**683.** スコットランド人あるいはアイルランド人もその生国をかくすことは困難である、ロンドン人はもちろんのこと。

**684.** 大発見家といわれる価値のある人々は、実際、ある時期には、狂人といわないまでも、空想家と考えられたものである。

〚注〛 **as a matter of fact**「事実上」。**discoverers worthy of the name**「その名にふさわしい発見者」すなわち「発見者といわれるに値する発見者」。**at one time or another**「いつかは」。

**685.** 「その事実たるや奇々怪々とまではいかなくとも、まずふしぎなものだ」とホームズが言った。

〚注〛 **singular**=uncommon; strange.

---

( 74 )

**686.** 植物は人間のことに興味を感じているような様子は少しもない、われわれは7の5倍は35であることをばらにわからせようとはけっしてしないであろう。そして樫(かし)の木に米の値段の上がり下がりを話してみたところで何にもならない。

〚注〛 **get a rose to understand**「ばらに理解させる」。

**687.** ある人々はいわば現在の危機的事態に慣れすぎてしまうという危険がある。こういう人たちは毎日、新聞で危機的事態のことを読み、ひじょうに錯雑(さくざつ)したものであることを知るが、しかしどういうわけか、おそかれ早かれ世の中はまた万事具合よくなってくるだろうと考える。そんなあやふやな物——結構なご時世の到来——を待ったところでむだである。

〘注〙 **come right**「よくなる」。類例:— Things will *come right* in the end. (結局はことはよいようになるだろう)

**688.** (子供の)しつけは過度になってはいけない——禁止のための禁止というものは好ましくない、それにまた、気まぐれであってはならない——今日禁じたことを明日は許すというのでは何もならない。

〘注〙 **prohibition for prohibition's sake** これに類した成句は種々ある。art for art's sake (芸術のための芸術). これに対して art for life's sake (人生のための芸術).

**689.** 動物がその親たちの経験の結果をどういうふうに承け継ぐかは当然な疑問のように見えた、それで、この答を出そうとしてばく大な時間と精力が費されてきた、ところが、こんな質問をするのはなんの益もない、つまり(生得でなく)生後習得した性質の遺伝などというものは存在しないという簡単な理由でなのだ。

〘注〙 **acquired** は inborn と反対で、前者は、経験とか練習とか努力で「手に入れる」、「身につける」、後者は「もって生まれた」「天賦の」である。

**690.** ヘイスティングズの筆と争うことはとてもできないことであった。

**691.** だだっこの思うとおりにしてやることはとてもできない。水おけにうつった月を見れば彼らはぜひそれを取らなければきかないのである。

**692.** もし彼がその非難を引っこめなかったら、彼の妻は何をするかしれたものじゃなかった。

---

( 75 )

**693.** 私は生まれつき書物が好きで、またひじょうな読書家であった。

**694.** 人間はだれでも若いうちにいつか数日間、急に目が見えなくなり、耳が聞えなくなると仕合せなのだがと、私はしばしば考えた。盲目になってみれば目明きのありがたさが一層わかるようになり、耳が聞えなくなってみて耳の聞えるよろこびを教えられるのである。

〘注〙 **be appreciative of...** は「...のありがた味をしみじみ感じる」。

**695.** むしろ自分自身が所有したいと思うものを持っているということで他人を賞賛する点では、凡俗も識者も一致する。賢い人はもっとも有徳だと思う人を賞賛するし、その他の連中はもっとも富裕な人を賞賛する。

〚注〛 the vulgar「俗人」、(4) 参照。 men of sense「分別のある人」、(1) 参照。

**696.** 彼の顔は輪郭がきわだって、口とあごとは鉄のような意志を示していた。

**697.** ネルソンはこのときバスチカにおいてよりは責任が軽かった、それに事を共にする人は、けっしてほね惜しみしない、ネルソンの理想にかなった人であった。

〚注〛 **was never sparing of himself**「けっして労を惜しまなかった」、類例:—to be sparing of time (時間を惜しむ).

**698.** 私は読書にあきて眠かった。

**699.** 彼女は彼からわれわれの不幸についての話をいくらか聞いていた、しかしソーンヒルの若主人がその原因であるということはまだ知らされずにいた。

〚注〛 **be kept ignorant of...**「...について無知の状態におかれる」。

**700.** 自分ではどうすることもできない者が、知らない土地を長く放浪するのだから、衣食の窮乏と風雨にさらされることで、死よりほかには待ちもうけられなかった。

〚注〛 **want**「衣食の窮乏」。 **the best**「それがまあ最上のもの」、つまりことによればもっとひどい死に方もあろうという気持ち。 **so helpless a creature**「それほどたよりない人間」。

**701.** この連中を相手にした経験で、私には容易に解けそうもない疑問が残った、つまり、このことは単に若者の非協力にすぎないのか、それとも何かもっと根の深いことの徴候を示したものか、と。

〚注〛 これは筆者のソ連印象の一つである。青年たちが政府のやり方などに批判的であったのを見ての話である。 **youthful**=of the young people.

**702.** 人がある不善を行なうか、またはばかな行ないをしたときに、その人のなし得る最善の罪滅ぼしは、同じあやまちに陥らないように他人に警告することだと私は思う。

〚注〛 **be guilty of**=commit.「(罪を)おかす」。

**703.** ボナパートはたびたび大いに談じた、時にはすこししゃべりすぎることもあった。しかし彼ほど気持ちよく興味深く話をすることのできるものはあるまい。彼の議論好きなことといったら、議論に躍起となってい

る最中には彼がぜひ内緒にしていたいと思う秘密さえ彼からたやすく聞き出すことができるほどであった。

〚注〛 **be anxious to**...「...することを切望する」。

**704.** 自覚している人は往々自分の価値を知ることがあるが、うぬぼれている人は概して自分の無能を悟らないものである。

---

### ( 76 )

**705.** 物を言う前にまず考えよ、事が重要なときはとくにそうだ。用いようとする文句の意味を熟考し、その文句をして意味あるもの、適切なもの、人の気にさわらないものにせよ。

〚注〛 **of moment** = of importance.　**weigh** は重量をはかる意味から、前後を考量する、軽重を考えるなどの意味に用いられる、類例:—to *weigh* one's words (よく考えて物を言う、一言も軽卒に吐かない). **expressions**「言葉づかい」「辞句」。**that they may be**...「その文句が...であるように」と目的を示す、**(43)** 参照。

**706.** 人が従事するいろいろな型の活動の中で、もっとも多数の筋肉を使うものが、一般の肉体的発達の見地から見ると、明らかにいっそう重要である。

〚注〛 **those**=forms of activity.　**from the point of view of**...「...の点から見て」、類例:—*from this scientific point of view* (この学術上の見地から見れば), *from my point of view* (ぼくの目から見れば). **physical** に対するのは mental (精神的).

**707.** その種類は何であろうと、実際生活における成功は、単に知識にのみ基づくとはいえない、いな主として知識に基づくともいえないのである。学問的職業においてさえ、単なる知識というものはとかく世人の考えたがるほど重要なものではない。

〚注〛 **is dependent upon**...=depends upon...「...による」。**solely**「単に」「全然」。 **or indeed chiefly** は solely といったのをさらに言いなおして、全然知識によるといえないどころか、主として知識によるとすらいえないという意味。 **learned professions** とは法学、医学、神学などの職業。

**708.** しかし彼は言った、それはかまいません、そんなわずかなものはこの次で結構ですと。で、私は、長いことこの近所には来ないかもしれないよ、と言った。けれども彼は、そんなこと一向かまいません、いつまで

も待てますよ、と言った。

〖注〗 **let the trifle stand over**「そのわずかな支払いの金をのばしておく」。**for a good while**=for a long time. **of no consequence**=of no importance, not important at all.

**709.** 読書の際 役に立ちそうな格言に出くわしたならば、それを取ってわが物とし、ただちにそれを実際に応用することにしなさい、あたかもわざわざ友人の意見を求めた場合に、その忠言を取り用いるように。

〖注〗 **take it for our own**「わがものとして取る」、類例：—He took Maugham *for* his model. (彼はモームを手本にした) She *chose* him *for* her husband. (彼女は彼を夫に選んだ) **make an immediate application of it**=apply it immediately「ただちに それを実際に応用する」。 **as we would** (make an application) **of**... と補ってみよ。 **purposely**=on purpose.「わざと」。

**710.** 彼は父から短気以外にほとんどなにも承け継がなかったが、母からは後になって彼にひじょうに役立った芸術的才能を承け継いだ。

〖注〗 **from his father he derived**...「父から...を承け継いだ」。derive ~from ...は「...から~を引き出す」。 **a quick temper**「短気」、類例：—to have *a bad* (or *quick, short, hot*) *temper* (おこりっぽい). to have *a good* (or *sweet*) *temper* (がまん強い). **proved of great service**「たいへん役に立った」。prove は「(どう)なる」の意味で次のように使う、類例：—The last wound he received *proved mortal*. (最後に受けた傷が致命傷となった) Our boy has *proved of service* to his country. (せがれがお国の役に立った)

**711.** 歴史が現代の舞台に光を投げ与えることができてこそ初めて 役に立つのとちょうど同じように、過去の文学も今日意義を持っている限りにおいてのみ価値があるのだ。

〖注〗 **in so far as** p. 101 参照。

**712.** 同じように、われわれの知性は、貧弱な精神性と道徳性に比してあまりに大きくなりすぎたゆえに、われわれもまた死滅を免れることができないだろう。おそらくこういう見こみは正しいだろう、もし果たしてそうだとすれば、われわれの叫びもむだであり、人類にもっと賢くなれ、もっと人間的になれと訴えてみても役に立たず、こんな均衡を失った人類というものの絶滅は防ぎようがないだろう。

〖注〗 **In the same way** と言ったのは、体ばかり大きくなって、その割合に脳が小さくて、ついに死滅した古代動物を例にあげたので、「それと同様に」となったもの。 **outcries**「(人類の危険を)さけぶこと」。 **of no avail**=of no use. **ill-balanced** つまり、「知性ばかり大きくて精神方面、道徳方面の力がこれに伴なわない」。 **species**「種族」、ここでは「人類」。

**713.** 芸術家の生命と彼の芸術の生命との関係はひじょうに密なので、彼の衰退の各段階は彼の作品という記録の中にはっきりとしるされる。それゆえ、芸術家は創作力のために最高度の活力ある状態に自分を維持することがもっとも重要である。

〖注〗 **So close is the relation...that...** = the relation...is so close that... (43) 参照。 **the stages of his decline** は第一期、第二期というような「衰退の全段階」。 **a man should** の should は (90) を参照。 **for the sake of...**「...のために」、類例:—*for convenience' sake* (便宜上)。

**714.** 遺伝と進化との諸法則は生物界を今日ある状態にし、なお将来どうなるかも決定する。近年われわれはこれらの法則をますます理解するにいたり、これに関するわれわれの知識は理論的に興味深くなったとともに実用的に重要となった。

〖注〗 **world of life**「生物界」。 **what it now is** は「今日の有様」、**what it may yet be** は「将来の状態」、(32) 参照。 **of recent years**「近年」、類例:—*of late* (近頃), *of old* (昔)。

**715.** 富は名声への権利とはならない。現在生きている大金持のうちには、とるに足らない人間にすぎないものがすくなくない。彼らの多くは比較的無知である。彼らは道徳的にも社会的にも物の数にはいらない。

〖注〗 **of no account**「重要でない=つまらない」、類例:—a man *of account* (重要な人), a matter *of no account* (つまらないこと)。

---

( 77 )

**716.** 内側の壁はきれいにのろで白くぬってあった、そして私の娘たちは自分たちの考案になった絵で壁を飾ろうと企てた。

**717.** 自分でかいた絵を除いては、これらがベンの見た初めての絵であった。

**718.** われわれ相互の所見、批評、訂正などによって進歩に資するために、次の会合には、自作各々一篇を出そうという提案があった。

**719.** 人が運命と呼ぶものは、通例その人みずから紡(つむ)ぎ出した糸から、みずから織り成したものである。

**720.** われわれの用いる単語は大部分自分で選ぶものだ、けれども文章の方はめったに自分では作らない。文章はすぐ前の、また、遠い、さらにずっと遠い過去から、承け継いだのである。

〖注〗 ここで sentences というのは「文章の型」のような意味である。

**721.** 私は来世に天国があるということは信ずるが、地獄があるということは信じない。しかし私は現世においては両方とも存することを固く信ずる。そしてこの世の天国および地獄は人がみずから作るものである。

〖注〗 **believe in a heaven** は believe in the existence of a heaven と同じく、「天国の存在を信ずる」ということ。

---

( 78 )

**722.** 快活な性質は大いに生まれつきの気質のものであるが、他の習慣と同じように訓練し涵養(かんよう)することもできる。われわれは人生を利用することも悪用することもでき、われわれが人生から歓喜を引き出すのも不幸を引き出すのもそれは主として自分次第なのである。

〖注〗 **is capable of being**＝can be.

**723.** 紳士は意志が強固であるばかりでなく心が正しいものである。紳士はよくすべきことはよくする。紳士は許すべきことは許し、怒るべきことは怒る、しかし恨みをいだくことはない。紳士はこの点においてソクラテスを学ぼうとする。ある人がこの哲人に向かって言った、「わたしはお前に恨みを報いなければ むしろ 死にたい」 と、ソクラテスは答えて言った。「わしは君を友としなければむしろ死にたい」と。

〖注〗 **the gentleman** はいわゆる代表単数で、紳士たるものはの意味。**as well as** (110) 参照。**resent** は侮辱などを「憤慨する」こと。**duly**＝properly すなわち 怒るべきを怒り、許すべきを許すなどの意味。**may I die**＝I wish I may die 「死ぬことを願う」、類例:—May you succeed!＝I wish you may succeed! (ご成功を祈る) **be revenged upon...** は「...に恨みを報いる」こと、revenge という動詞は to revenge one's wrongs upon the offender のように用いる、wrongs は受けた仇(あだ)、offender は仇をなした人をいい、one's wrongs のかわりに oneself を用いて、I am determined to *revenge myself upon* him (彼に対して恨みをはらす決心だ)といい、それを受動態にして、I am determined to *be revenged upon* him というのである。

**724.** 47人の忠臣——これがわが国の普通教育ではひじょうに重んじら

れている——は世俗には四十七義士でとおっている。

〖注〗 in common parlance「普通のいい方では」。

**725.** あなたはまさか私をただ手先に使っていたんじゃないでしょうね。私は手先に使われることはまったくもってきらいですからね。

〖注〗 I hope はよいことについて I think のかわりに用いる語、類例:—*I hope I shall succeed this time.*(こんどは成功だろうと思う) **make a cat's paw of one** は、ねこがさるにだまされて熱い灰の中のくりを拾ってやったという寓話(ぐうわ)から起こった文句で、「人を手先に使う」こと。**'pon (=upon) my soul** は upon my word (余が一言にかけて、たしかに)の変体で、「本当に」という意味。

**726.** 公正とは公明な処置、法律の前の平等、および男女各人がその人生を最も多く利用する機会を得ること、を意味する。これが本質的に民主主義の理想であって、日本ののりこうな人々はどこまでもこれを志している。

〖注〗 **by justice is meant...**「...が justice によって意味されている」ということ。 by justice we mean... としてもよい。

**727.** 私の資産は親からゆずり受けたものではない——みな私が自分で作ったものだ。(だから)湯水のように浪費してもかまわない。

〖注〗 **to make ducks and drakes of**=squander「浪費する」、ducks and drakes は小石あるいは平たい物を投げて水面をかすめる水切りの遊びをいう。

**728.** 日本人は、ヨーロッパ人には一番美しい花として気に入るような花のあるものをほとんど好かない、そしてヨーロッパ人がほとんどかえりみないような花を珍重(ちんちょう)する。

〖注〗 **care but little for...**「...をほとんど好まない」、「...をほとんど望まない」、類例:—I don't *care* much *for* him. (あまり彼を好かない) He does not *care for* money. (金はほしがらない) **to Europeans commend themselves as the fairest**「ヨーロッパ人にもっとも美しいものとして自分自身を気に入らせる＝ヨーロッパ人にもっとも美しいものとして気に入る」、commend はふつう「推せんする」意味であるが、無意志の主格のときは「気に入らせる」となる、類例:—Honesty will *commend* a man *to* his employer. (正直にすれば雇主の気に入る)

**729.** われわれは、ひじょうに愉快に時を過ごして、どんな難儀も物ともしなかったあの時代のことを、たびたび考えたり、話したりする。

〖注〗 **had such a good time of it**「たいへんおもしろかった」、of it は訳さないでよい、類例:—I *had a bad time of it.* (つらい思いをした) **make light of**「軽んずる」。

**730.** 人々は仕方のないことは[あきらめて]運命にまかせ、できるだけ

努力して逆境を善用しようと決心した。

〘注〙 **to make the best of a bad bargain** 不幸な境遇からできるだけの幸福を引き出すようなことをいう。

**731.** その会議の方針は——これはなかなか賢明なのだが——わたしたちはすべて不完全な人間だ、だから、それをいかに善用してすこしでも完全に近づけるかということだ。

〘注〙 この文は女性の衣裳についての会談のことなので、衣裳をくふうしてすこしでも美人になろうというのである。

**732.** 彼は私の名をたずね、それからその書いたものを見て、すっかりそれを私に読んで聞かせたが、私はちっともわからなかった。

〘注〙 **all over**「すっかり」。

**733.** 奥さん、あなたは何か妙なことをおっしゃいましたね、だが私は何が何だかさっぱりわかりませんでした。

〘注〙 **You did say** は you said の意味を強く、なるほどおっしゃることはおっしゃいましたなどという口調。 **ma'am**=madam. **couldn't make head or tail of**=could make nothing of. 類例：—I can *make nothing of* what he says. (あの人のいうことは一向わけがわからない)

───────

( 79 )

**734.** 大きな木の下の地面に腰をおろすと、近づいてくる暴風に、かん高い呼び声や叫びのまじったような混乱したもの音が聞えはじめた。

〘注〙 **Sitting**=when I sat. **as of**=like the noise of. **coming**=approaching「近づいてくる」。

**735.** その小鳥たちはいそがしそうに虫をさがしたり追っかけたりしていたが、わずか数分で、私の近くの木々をしらべつくして飛んで行ってしまった。私は今目撃した光景では満足しないで、飛び上がって、その鳥の群れを見失わないようにかけ出した。

〘注〙 **searching for** は the insects につながる。 **be satisfied with~**「~に満足する」。 **rushed after~**「~の後を追ってかけ出した」。

**736.** 私は自由の国に生まれ早くからその価値を知っていたので、どこの国においてでも、圧迫されている国民が自由の旗をひるがえすのを見るときは、私の同情心はそれに引きつけられるのを禁じ得ないのである。

〖注〗 whensoever...「...する時はいつでも」。unfurl は巻いてあるものを広げる。

**737.** 一人の一生のうちに2回の世界戦争の勃発(ぼっ)のあったこと、人類の経験上もっとも破壊的な爆弾の発明と使用のことに言及して、彼はこうつけ加えざるを得ない。

〖注〗 be compelled to...「...を余儀なくされる、やむを得ず...する」。

**738.** 心気は爽快になり身体も休まったから、アリはなつめやしの実を取って食い、飢えをいやすことができた。その間にミーク・アイ[らくだの名]はその辺の草や葉を食いはじめた。

〖注〗 was able to=could. satisfy his hunger on...「...を食って飢えを満足さす」、on は We *live on* rice.(われわれは米を食って生活する)の on と同じもの、feed on も同類、類例:—Horses *feed on* hay.(馬は草を食って生きている)

**739.** 彼は20歳以後は独立独行のほかなくなったので、技術者として身を立てる考えでベルギーとフランスで勉強した。

〖注〗 left...to his own guidance「彼自身の指導に残されたから＝独立自営のほかなくなったので」。

**740.** アメリカの教育の特長は大学に行っている青年の全人口に対する割合が大きいことだと言われるのを時々耳にする。そういう言い方をすると、これはまったく誤解を招く言葉になる。その本当の特長というのは、全日制で勉強している18歳から20歳までのアメリカ青年の比率がひじょうに大きいということなのである。

〖注〗 hears it said that it は that 以下を代表する。youth = young people. attending 他動詞だから前置詞は不要。So phrased=if it is expressed in such words. full-time は part-time に対するもので、前者は学校に行くことを本業とするが、後者は夜学などのように、勤めの余暇に学校に行く、ということ。

**741.** するとついに、たくさんの種類の鳥、たいていは小がらのものだが、その大群が木々に密集してくるのが見えてきた、そしてあるものは幹や大枝を走りまわり、あるものは飛び続けていた。

〖注〗 swarm「群がる」「密集する」、類例:—The beach is *swarming with* bathers.(岸は泳ぐ人たちでいっぱいだ) keep on the wing「(とまらないで)飛んでいる」。

**742.** ねずみやはつかねずみを家畜と考えることはできないが、これら

は人間によって世界の各地に運ばれたもので、北や南の寒冷地にも熱帯の島々にも勝手にはびこって住んでいて、今日では他のいかなる齧歯(じっ)類よりもずっと広い範囲に及んでいる。

〚注〛 free は「拘束されないで自由勝手に」の意味で living の補語。climate は「気候」「風土」。

---

## (80)

**743.** このようにわれわれはまったく世論によって支配されるものであるから、ひじょうに注意して社会人心の純潔を保つよう努めるべきである。

〚注〛 the utmost care should be taken＝we should take the utmost care.

**744.** 比較級の語と最上級の語の前に the を用いることは、実際形容詞や副詞を修飾して名詞を修飾しないから、他の the の用法にほとんど関係がない。だからそれを全然別種の語と考え、副詞として分類してもしごく妥当(だとう)であろう。

**745.** 実際われわれは世界各地からくる外人のために避難所を開いているのだから、誰も彼も公平に迎え入れてやるべきである。

**746.** さて、このように英国は(英)文学の流れ出る源泉を持っているのであるから、それを仲介として〔英米両国民間に〕温厚にして雅量のある感情を生ずるようにすることは、すこしも遺憾なくできることでもあり、またそうするのがほんとうに英国の義務である。

〚注〛 前の二つの it は to make を、最後の it は fountainhead を代表する。her は England をさす。

**747.** 彼は金をもうけようというよりは、むしろ自分の(探偵)術を愛する心から働いたのであるから、異常な、いや一歩進んで、奇怪という方面に傾いていないものだと、どんな探偵(たんてい)にでもたずさわることを拒んだのである。

**748.** この事件は実際世間が異常にだれているときに起こったので、実の価値以上に人の注意をひいたのであろう。

〚注〛 a period of exceptional dullness「例外的沈滞の時期」とは、耳目を聳動(しょう)するような事件がなくて、世の中が非常にだれている時ということ。

## ( 81 )

**749.** 太陽と地球の距離は、大ざっぱにいえば9千3百万マイルある。もし太陽へ汽車に乗って旅行できるとしたら、夜も昼も止まらず1時間40マイルの一定速度で走って、目的地まで265年以上かかるだろう。

〘注〙 **If it were**... は現在の事実に反対の仮想である。(**94**) 参照。

**750.** 事実、物の比例で言うならば、脳のうちの未調査の領域は、地球上の未踏査の地域、いやそう言えば、太陽系の未調査の領域よりも、はるかに大きいのである。

〘注〙 **relatively speaking**「比較して言えば」。**by far**「はるかに」、これは比較級や最上級といっしょに使われる、by far the best「ずばぬけて最良」など。**for that matter**「そのことなら」「そう言えば」で、この成句はよく用いられる。

**751.** 単に自己観察からいえば、私自身の場合は、茶やコーヒーの方がたばこよりもはるかに危険である。

**752.** つづけて射った24本の矢の中で、10本は的(まと)に当り、その他はきわめて的に近かったから、的の距離を考え合わせて、これはじょうずな弓術と考えられた。

〘注〙 **in succession**=successively. **range** は矢、弾丸などが的に対して、とどくことをいうのに用いられる、例:—The shot *ranged* too far. (弾丸があまり的から遠かった)

**753.** 厳密に言えば、俳優は劇芸術の媒介物の一つにすぎない。生きた媒介物であるため俳優は厳格に言うと誤解を招く立場に立つ。劇の歴史はその全盛衰を通じてたしかに劇作家が俳優によって食われた歴史である。

〘注〙 **a false position** 誤解を招く立場、自分に逆らわねばならない立場、生きものでなければ創作家の定めたとおりになるが、生きものだからそうはいかない、ということ。**rises and declines**「栄枯盛衰」。**the dramatist's sure eclipse by the actor**「俳優による劇作家のたしかなる光りの喪失」とは劇作家が俳優のはなやかさの陰にかくされるという意味である。

---

## ( 82 )

**754.** 若くはあったが彼はその仕事に堪えなくはなかった。

〘注〙 **was not unequal to the task**=was equal to the task. 比較:—

{ He is *fit for* the post. (彼はその位置に適任だ)
{ He is *equal to* the task. (彼はその任に堪える)

**755.** 貧しくはあったが、この人が生きていたために世界がいっそうよくならなかった日は一日もなかった。

〖注〗 **the better because...**「...であるがため、それだけよく」。the は副詞。

**756.** 私の科学論文は短かったのに、その中にたくさんあった文章の上の誤りを、彼はたいへん親切に訂正してくれた。

〖注〗 **literary** はふつう「文学的」であるが、ここでは言い回しとか用語とかをさしている。つまり、内容である科学のことを別にしての意味。literal は「文字どおり」などの意味で、すこしちがいがあるから混同しないこと。

**757.** 案内者たちは荷物を負うていたのであるが[それでも足が早くて]、私は彼らにおくれないようにするのが少々むずかしかった。

〖注〗 **to keep pace with...**「...と歩調を共にする=...におくれない」すなわち to keep up with とほぼ同じ。類例:—I try to *keep pace with* the times. (ぼくは時世におくれないように努める) It is hard for me to *keep up with* my class in English. (ぼくには英語で級の者におくれずについて行くのは困難だ)

**758.** 最近10年間に世間に起きたことはよく知らないが、ぼくはだまされてそんなばかげた話を信ずるようなことはしないよ。だがわかった、君はぼくの無知をからかうつもりなんだね。

〖注〗 **have a mind to...**「...する気がある」。**sport with...**「...をもてあそぶ」。

**759.** そういう推論はあまり好まないけれども、承認せざるを得ない、すなわちそれは、芸術作品はその果実によって判断されなければならない。だからもし果実がよくなければ、その作品は価値がないということである。

〖注〗 "The tree is known by his fruit." (木のよしあしはその実によってわかる)という言葉は聖書(マタイ伝、12:23)にあって有名。ここは画家の意図がよいとか悪いとかで絵は判断できないという文意。

**760.** 疑いもなく、りっぱな友人というものは人生の幸福と価値とをひじょうに増すものではあるが、われわれは主としてわれわれみずからの力によらなくてはならない、そして人はみな自分のもっともよい友となるか、そうでなければもっとも悪い敵となるものである。

〖注〗 **add to**=increase.

**761.** ラスキンもしくはティンダルのような文士と同じく風景を見るこ

とのできる者はまれである。山の景色に対する彼らの美しい描写は、彼らの英語に熟達していたこと(それももちろん非常なものであったが)よりも、むしろその眼前にあるものを見得る力によるのである。

〘注〙 **It is not every one who...**「みながみな...ではない」という意味から転じて「...である者はめったにない」という気持ちに用いられる、類例：— It is *not every man* who can appreciate poetry. (詩を味わい得る者は多くない) Such things do *not* happen *every day*. (こんな機会は毎日はない——千載一遇) **did**=saw. **depend less on~than...**「~よりもむしろ...による」。 **mastery**「熟達」「通暁」。 **the English language**=English. **as that is** の that は mastery をさす。

**762.** 彼らは彼の人気を、相当なものだったにかかわらず、ばかにしていた。しかし、その人気がひじょうに高くなって、もう打ちこわしかねるようになったとき、彼らは、もうおそすぎたのだが、物事の初めはどんなささいなものでも、おろそかにしてはならないということを悟った。

〘注〙 **made light of**「...を軽んじた」(78) 参照。

**763.** ギリシア人は、人間の活動のほとんどあらゆる部門においてすぐれていたが、科学の創造にはおどろくほどわずかしか貢献しなかった。

〘注〙 **did surprisingly little for...**「...のためにおどろくほどすこししか尽さなかった」、do for は人のため、国のためなどに「尽す」こと、類例：— He has *done much for* his country. (国家に大いに貢献している)

**764.** 彼は貧しかったけれど、金で名誉を売るような卑劣な人間ではなかった。

〘注〙 **was above selling...**「...を売るようなさもしいことはしない」、類例：—He must be *above* such meanness. (彼はそんな卑劣なことはすまい) **at any price**「どんな値段でも＝どんな大金をもらっても」。

**765.** ある偉い人が先日われわれに語った、「現代は発明の時代として歴史上に知られるだろう。今日の王者は技師である。現在存在する機械類はおどろくべきものだが、それもまだだれも夢想さえしなかったような機械類によって凌駕(りょうが)されるだろう」。

**766.** 世界は疲弊しきっていたけれども、やはりいろいろな事件があるものだから、大小各国は大なる常備軍を維持し、また破産のおそれあるにもかかわらず、費用のかかる平和的軍備の拡張を計らねばならなかった。

〘注〙 **exhausted**=tired out「疲れきって」。 **events still compelled states to~**=states were compelled (*or* obliged) to~by events.「いろいろ

な事件のために～することを余儀なくされた」「～せねばならなかった」。 **state** は政治的に見た「国家」をいう、地理的にいえば country である。 **great and small** は states にかかる形容詞。 **standing forces**「常備軍」、参考：—standing army（常備陸軍）, standing squadron（常備艦隊）. **in the face of**...「...の面前において」の意味から「...にもかかわらず」となる。

**767.** 社会はせっせと速い勢いでたえず前進していながら、またたえずなつかしく惜しむ気持で過去をふり返って見ているが、これはちょっと見るとふしぎな気がするだろう。しかし、この二つの傾向は、矛盾しているように見えようが、同じ原理に容易に帰着せしめられるのだ。すなわち、両方とも実際の現状にじっとがまんしていられない気持から生まれるのだ。

〚注〛 **should** は it is strange... の文によく使われるもの。 **propensity**「傾向」「性癖」。

———

( 83 )

**768.** 詩人が落下する雪片が地上の汚れにまだ染まないとき、これを清浄と純潔の表象としようとするのはまことにもっともなことだ。

〚注〛 **look to～for**...=「～に...を求める」、類例：—to *look to* a person *for* assistance.「人に助力を待つ、世話になるつもり」。

**769.** やさしい婦人は有頂天になってよろこんだ、そして婦人がわが子のことを鼻高く思ったのもけっして無理からぬことであった。それはわが子のかいた絵には、一生をこの業(絵画)にたずさわった老画伯が(自分でかいたといっても)恥ずかしくないような筆のはこびがあったから。

〚注〛 **of which** の of は ashamed につくもの、類例：—Don't *be ashamed of* your shabby clothes.（弊(へい)衣を恥じるな） Don't *be proud of* your fine clothes.（美服に誇るな）

**770.** 科学は解決した問題と同じ数の新問題を提出する。科学はその発明品をわれわれの戸口に置く、それでこれを用いるのはわれわれの責任である。この議論は当然水素爆弾に関連したものと考えたっていいわけだが、それのことではなく、実はもっと身近な発明品に関するものなのだ。

〚注〛 responsible for と連語するので、**responsibility** と名詞になっても、for がつく。「～に対する責任」となる。 **we make of them** は use の修飾節。 **inventions nearer at home** は具体的には電気器具、テレビ、ラジオなど。

**771.** ハーディング氏は運のよい男だと言われるのももっともだ。それというのは富貴に生まれたのではないのに、今は鉄道会社の取締重役だからだ。しかしそれだからといって苦労がないわけではない。

〚注〛 **born to wealth**=born rich「金持に生まれる」。

**772.** その事業の初めは困難だらけで、ふつうの男なら参ってしまっても無理はなかった。しかし奴隷の幼年時代から学問と教養への道を奮闘して切り開いて来た人にとっては、これらの困難は打ち勝つべき障害がすこしばかり数を増したにすぎなかった、そしてみごと彼はそれらを征服しおおせた。

〚注〛 **were beset with difficulties**「困難になやまされた」。**fight his way** は make one's way の変化で「奮闘して進む」こと。**overcome them he did** は he overcame them を強く言ったのである。(63) 参照。

**773.** その講演そのものはきわめてありきたりの正統派の流儀に従ったもので、実際、この同じ講演がスターリン時代になされたとしてもちっともおかしくないものだった。

〚注〛 **under Stalin**「スターリン統治下」。

───────────

( 84 )

**774.** 剣術の先生からブルースやウォレスのような大愛国者を作り出すことを期待することができないと同様に、ただの論理学者から大思想家を作り出そうなどとは思いもよらないことだ。

〚注〛 **a Bruce or a Wallace** のように固有名詞に a をつけるのは、Bruce のような人、Wallace のような人の意味。類例:—He is *a Newton* of the age.(彼は当代のニュートンである——大数学者) **make of**=make out of— (78) 参照。

**775.** 君があの巣にとどこうなどと試みるのは、月の黒点を取ろうとするようなものでとうていできることじゃない。

**776.** あまり遠い以前のことではないが、ある方面では次のように言う傾向があった——科学的発見は、毒ガス・爆撃機・潜水艦等々の、破壊的なおそろしい用途に向けられているから、もし科学が全然なかったとしたら、文明はもっと具合よく進んでいたかもしれない、と。しかしこれは明らかに皮相の速断である。石炭ガスが自殺用に供され、ラジオがジャズ音

楽の放送に使われるからこの二つとも禁止してしまう方がよいというようなものである。

〚注〛 tendency to... 「...する傾向」。 had been put...uses 「...の用途に供せられた」。 fared better 「いっそううまくいった」、類例：—I *fared well*. (上首尾だった) The enterprise *fared ill*. (事業は失敗した) with no science at all は if there had been no science at all の省略された形であるから、これを受ける本文は might have fared の形をとっている、(98) 参照。

**777.** 「では一つうけたまわりたいものだが、石炭は 一種の 石でなくて何ですか、それからまたバタは脂肪、小麦は種子、革は獣皮、絹は一種の毛虫の糸ではないか、そしてまたわれわれは虎を猫の種類の動物と呼んでもいいように、猫を虎の種類と呼んでもよくないだろうか」。

〚注〛 what is coal but...? (100) 参照。 is not butter, grease? 「バタは脂肪ではないか」。

**778.** 私に主張を捨てよとおっしゃるのは財産を捨ててしまえとお勧めなさると同様です。

**779.** 人に算術の問題をやってもらうのは人に飯を食ってもらうようなものだ。

〚注〛 人に飯を食ってもらって自分の腹のたしにはならない、人に算術を解いてもらっても自分のためにはならない。 to do sums 「算術の問題を解く」。類例：—He is good at *sums*. (彼は算術がじょうずだ) He *did* a rapid *sum* in his head. (彼はす早く暗算をした)

**780.** 人類の大運動に同情し、またこれを援助するために何事をか言い得ないような者は、口をつぐんでいる方がましだ。

**781.** (そんなことをするのは)土螢(つちぼたる)が電光と光を競うようなものだ。

〚注〛 to match oneself against... 「...に自分を対抗させる＝...と張り合う」。

**782.** 多くの若い人たちは生まれつき優雅でないからといって相変わらず無作法をやっている、(ちょうどそれは)われわれが生まれたばかりに大学にはいるに適していなかったからといって(下級)学校に行くのを拒むようなものだ。

**783.** 事情を明らかにするために、私はあったことをすぐ説明した方がよいでしょう。

(85)

**784.** 自然の理法にはそむきがたい。

〖注〗 自然はぜひ人から服従されねばやまない、人は自然に従わねばならない。

**785.** 飛行の大胆な試みが、初めて行なわれたのは、そんなに昔のことではない。大胆なのだ、当時はだれも飛ぶ術を知らなかったのだから、それに発動機がお粗末で、なかなか円滑に動かなかったのだし、機体の翼やそのほかのあらゆる部分が堅牢でなく、また形が正しくなかったのだから。しかも、飛行が行なわれる場合はたいがい、地上に近接したほんの短距離飛行で、それもまったくの無風状態の場合であった。

〖注〗 **were wrongly shaped**「形が正しくなかった」。**short hops**「短距離飛行」。**dead calm** は「大凪(なぎ)」で、これを最上級にした型、めずらしい用例。

**786.** ラセラスは行きたいと思った、けれども彼の妹もイムラクもどうしても同意しなかった。

**787.** 彼はさっさと現金を払うが、しかし(そのかわり)払った金の価値だけのものはぜひ取らなければ承知しないという人間である。

〖注〗 **pays prompt cash** とは出ししぶらずにさっさと現金を出すこと。

**788.** 今日世間の求めるのは、米国の工場で出来た「英国製の毛織物」を提供することをしない青年、ニューヨークで出来た「アイルランド製リンネル」を売ることをしない青年である。

〖注〗 **mill**=factory.

**789.** 人はパンのみで生きるものではないが、しかし考えることのみで生きるものでもない。私は考えたり、しゃべったり、感じたりすることを好むが、しかし役に立ててくれとさわぐ手と、何もしないでぶらさがっていたがらない腕とを、私が持っていることを忘れることはできない。

〖注〗 **clamour to be**...「...してくれとやかましく言う」。**put to use**「役に立てる」。**hang idle**「何もせずにぶらさがっている」、類例:—to *lie* (*sit, stand, remain*) *idle* (何もせずにいる、遊んでいる)

**790.** 女は押し入れの鍵(かぎ)が血で染まっていることに気がついたので、二、三度それを拭き取ろうとした、けれどもその血はどうしても取れなかった。洗っても、せっけんや砂をつけてこすってもむだで、血はなお消えないでいた。

( 86 )

**791.** おれが不自由する前に貴様に不自由させる。

〖注〗 盗賊がこういって人の物をうばう。**Thou shalt**＝you shall＝I will make you.  **ere I shall**＝before I shall want.

**792.** あなた方が道に迷われたのならば、この洞穴〔自分の家〕でできるかぎりの便宜はよろこんで与えてあげます。

〖注〗 **You shall be supplied with**...＝I will supply you with...「諸君に...を供しましょう」。

**793.** 私の店からどれでもあんたが好きな書物を10冊選びなさい、それをあんたが持っている2冊とあわせて、あんたに進呈しましょう。

**794.** ぼくは翻弄(ﾎﾝﾛｳ)されるような人間じゃないということを彼に知らしてやる。

**795.** 「ああ、あっぱれな、エドワードや」と老紳士が言った。「ではあんたは力になる人がほしいのだね。よろしい私が力になってあげよう」。

〖注〗 **needed** 助動詞でなく、本動詞の用法。 **You shall have one.**＝You shall have a friend in me.＝I will be a friend to you.

**796.** わが血管の中に血が1滴でも残っているかぎりはわが主君の血は流させはしません。

〖注〗 **have a drop left** 「have＋目的語・補語」の型。 left は過去分詞。

**797.** むち打ちという土台からまちがっている方法によらなければ教えることができないなら、私のせがれは学校へはやらない。

〖注〗 **flogging** 英国の学校で whip, birch, rod などというむちをもって子供のしりを打つ刑罰が行なわれたことがある、**fundamental** は表面の意味は「根本の」、というのだが、fundament に「しり」という意があるから、「しりをむち打つような誤ったこと」という意味をきかせたしゃれである。

**798.** 「私が自身で格子(ｺｳ)のところに立っていましょう、そして外の出来事をできるだけあなたに申し上げましょう」とリベッカがいった。するとアイヴァンホーが「それはいけません、私がさせません、各々の格子、各々のすき間はじきに射手の的(ﾏﾄ)になります」。

〖注〗 **as I can**「できるだけ」。 **passes**=happens「起こる」。 **without**=out-of-doors; outside the house.

**799.** この世紀の初め以来普通教育は急速に発達した。人々は次第に良い教育の価値を認めるようになった。今日、自分の子弟にできるだけ良い教育を受けさせたいと望まない父兄はほとんどない。

---

( 87 )

**800.** 世に財産を目あてに結婚する男ほどいやしむべき人物はない。それならば財産を目あてに結婚する女性がなぜいやしむべき者でないだろうか、そういう理由は私にはわからない。

〖注〗 **fortune-hunter**=a man seeking a rich wife.

**801.** 貧乏人はわれわれの助けを待たないで楽しく暮している、そうすればわれわれも彼らの助けを受けずに生活してゆくようにしたって何も悪いことはあるまい、[むしろそうすべきではあるまいか]。

〖注〗 **The poor**=poor people. **theirs**=their help.

**802.**「君のおとうさんは君を牛乳屋にしようというのだね」——「したっていいじゃないか」。

〖注〗 **Why not?**=Why should your father not make a milkman of you? =There is no reason why he should not make a milkman of you.「君のおとうさんが君を牛乳屋にしてなぜわるいか、何も悪いことはないじゃないか、いいじゃないか」。

**803.** 幽霊が他の場所よりもよけいピラミッド[金字塔]に出なくてはならないという理由はけっしてない。

**804.** 首相オクセンスティールンは、若い女王がこの奇怪な使節を一目見られたら、すぐさまぷっと吹き出されるか、さもなくば彼らの異常な容姿を見て、こわがられるだろうと気づかった。「なんでこわがるわけがあろう」と小女王はいわれた。「してその方は私には笑うような失礼なことしかできないと思うのですか」。

〖注〗 **burst out (a) laughing**「急に笑い出す」。a は on の意味の古い用法で、今では不要。**at the first sight of** . . .「. . . を見るとすぐさま」。**manners**「礼儀作法」、用例:=He has no *manners*. (彼は行儀を知らない) Where is (or are) your *manners*? (お前は行儀を知らないのか) これは子供などをたしなめる言葉。

( 88 )

**805.** 「まあなんとこの子は 美しい 顔つきをしていること！ こんなかわいらしい笑顔がいつまでもつづかないとはなんと残念なことだろう」とベンがひとりごとをいった。

**806.** ああ、人間が、わが脳みそを盗み去るようにその口に敵を入れるとは。

〖注〗 気違い水という酒を飲んで正気を失うことをあざけったのである。

**807.** 彼女は言った、「ほんとに、変わったもの見たさに何もかばを見に行くことはないでしょう。豚をごらんなさい。豚の顔には何かおそろしいものがありますよ。星をつくったと同じ力が豚の顔をつくったと考えると(おどろくことではありませんか)」。

〖注〗 **created it** の it は the face of a pig. **that created** の that の先行詞は the same power. これは「神様」の意味。

**808.** そもそも人間は何物なれば自然の理法に逆らおうとするのか。

〖注〗 大胆不敵にも自然に逆らおうとする人間とはいったい何者ぞとおどろいたのである。

**809.** あわれむべきかな寡婦(やもめ)たち！ いったい彼らは何をしたからといってやり玉に上げられて笑いの種となるのだろう。

〖注〗 **jokes that are made at their expense** 「彼らを犠牲にしてなされるじょうだん」、類例：—They are making merry *at my expense*. (彼らは私のことを笑っている)

**810.** 「ねえ、ラルフ君、おとうさんの言いつけにそむいて遊ぶなんて、だいたい君が間違っていたんだよ」と、ラルフの家へ行く途中でサー・ヘンリー・アラビは言った、「君は 良い 子供だから、君がそんなことをしたとは意外だ。親友として私は心から君に言うのだが、両親に服従することは子供の第一の義務だよ」。

〖注〗 **it was very wrong of you to...**「...するのは君がよくなかった」、類例：—*It is wrong of you* to waste time. (時間を浪費するのはよろしくない) **on their way**「途中で」、類例：—I met him *on my way* to school. (学校へ行く途中で彼に会った)

(89)

**811.** 人は常に死の覚悟をしているべきものだ。

**812.** ふつうの人は必ず、自分の生涯の起きている時間の大部分を生計の資を得ることに費やす。人の仕事はその人の一番の楽しみとなるべきで、それから彼は生活のよろこびの大部分を引き出すべきである。

〚注〛 **from it he should derive**...=he should derive...from it.

**813.** りっぱな男子たる者の目標は、生活を楽にすることではなく、どんな緊張にも耐えられるように生活を強靱(きょうじん)にすることであるべきだ。人間の大きさはその人のもつ動機の大きさで計られる。

〚注〛 **manhood** は成人男子を総称する場合と、人間たること、男らしさなど抽象名詞として使う場合とある。**stand the utmost strain**「極度の緊張に耐える」。stand は他動詞。

**814.** まことに、富が力であり、できるだけ金持になることがあまねく人々のいだく野心の目的である間は、それを達成する道はえこひいきや不公平なしに、万人に対して開かれていることがもっとも適当である。

〚注〛 本文の骨子は It is most fitting that the path to its attainment should be open to all. である。**to grow as rich as possible the universal object of ambition** は possible の次に is を補う。

**815.** 慈善は近きより始めて、衆に及ぼすべし。

〚注〛「慈善はわが家より始まる、しかしそこだけでとどまるべきでない」。この諺は前半だけをいうことが多い、他人に慈善を施すよりまずもって一家のことを考えねばならないということ。

**816.** われわれは暇の時間をば、ことごとく仕事か娯楽に利用することを努むべきである、なぜならば何もすることなく費やされた時間は、自分にとっても、また公衆にとっても純然たる損失であるから。われわれは「暇つぶし」という文句さえわからない方がよい。

〚注〛 **one** は we と書いても同じこと。**his** は前の one に応ずるのだから one's と書くのを正しいとする文法家もある。**spare time**「よけいな時間」、「閑暇」。**time simply idled away**「単に浪費された時間」。類例:—He idles his time *away*. (何もせず遊んで日を暮す) **even** は understand 以下全体にかかる、すなわち "to kill time" という文句を理解することさえすべきでないという意味。

**817.** こういう時間には、こどもの周囲に、こどもがさわっていけない、高価な、こわれやすい品物を置いてはいけない。壁もあまり上品な色にし

て、こどもの汚れた指の跡がつくようなものであってはいけない。

〖注〗 **these hours** これはこどもが室内で遊ぶ時間のこと。**should not be surrounded** こどもを主語にして、「とり囲まれてはならない」となっている。訳文では別にしてある。 **exquisitely coloured** は「上品な色にする、上品な壁紙をはる」こと。**on no account must dirty finger marks appear upon them** は、「どんなことがあっても汚された指の跡がその壁に現われてはいけない」となる。つまり、汚れた手でさわっても跡がつかないような色の壁にせよという意味。

---

( 90 )

**818.** けれどもベンは猫が暖かくしているということよりも自分が絵筆を手に入れる方がずっと必要だと思った。

〖注〗 猫の毛を刈って絵筆をこしらえた話。

**819.** それらの事実は明るみへ出した方がよいだろう、というのは、彼女の継父の死についてはうわさが広がっていて、それが事件を真相以上におそろしいものにしかねないと思われるふしがあるからだ。

〖注〗 **I have reasons to know** 「知るべき理由がある」が言葉どおりの訳。**which** の先行詞は rumours.

**820.** 健康状態はただ肉体の安楽と活動とに必要なるのみならず、また精神の安楽と活動とにも必要である。したがってわれわれは肉体の健康を増進するために、できるかぎりの手段をつくすのはもっとも必要なことである。

〖注〗 **is necessary to...** 「...に必要」、類例：—Sleep *is necessary to* health. (睡眠は健康に必要) **of the greatest importance**＝most important. (76) 参照。 **take every means in our power** 「力にあるだけの手段をことごとくつくす」。means は本来複数だが、単数の扱いをして every などをつける。

**821.** 話をするもの[著者]と読者との間に、できるだけ早く相互の了解が成り立つということは望ましいことである。

**822.** だれでも自分の国を愛すべきである。

## (91)

**823.** もちろん原始時代の猟人にとっては、商売が今日都会人に対するとちょうど同じように、狩猟は仕事であった。できればすこしも骨を折らずに獲物を捕えたいと思った。そして屠殺(とさつ)所で家畜を殺すような近代のやり方は原始猟人の場合だったら全生活問題の解決と思われたことだろう。

〚注〛 **practice**「(実際に行う)こと」。**domestic animals**「家畜」、類例：— *domestic fowls*（家禽(かきん)）.

**824.** われわれが注意と同情とをもって読み、理解し鑑賞するために苦心するならば、われわれの心の滋養となる書物を発見し、書物のない宮殿よりもむしろ書物ある屋根べやに住みたいといったマコーリーの意見に賛成するであろう。

〚注〛 **with care**＝carefully; **with sympathy**＝sympathetically. この二つはいずれも「with＋名詞」を副詞句として用いた例。**taking**＝and take と見て訳してよい。**take pains**「骨を折る」「苦心する」。**agree with...**「...と一致する」。**he said that he would rather...**＝he said, "I would rather..." **garret** は貧乏文士などの住む所。**a library**＝a collection of books（蔵書）。**one**＝a library.

**825.** 自分の本棚の本より図書館の本で読んだ方がいいと言っている人人を知っている。私にはわからない話だ。第一、私は自分の本は一さつ一さつその独特のにおいで知っている、そしてページの間に鼻をつっこみさえすればあらゆる連想をよび起こすのだから。

〚注〛 **in a library copy** の in は「その本で」の意味で、同じものを読むのに、どれで読むかという時に in が使われる。in translation なら「翻訳で」となる。**in one**＝in the copy. **for one thing**「一つには」。**have but to put**＝have only to put. **be reminded of**「〜を思い起こさせられる」。

**826.** いやしい人と交わるよりはむしろひとりでいる方がよい。友だちは自分と同等の者か、あるいは自分よりすぐれた者であるべきである。なんとなれば、人の価値は常にその人の友だちの価値によって支配されるからである。

〚注〛 **Let your companions be...**＝your companions should be ... と見てよい。**that of...**＝the worth of.

**827.** 彼が私を食事に呼びにくる時間だ。どうしてこんなにおそいのだ

ろう。何か起こったにちがいない。どうしたのか行ってみた方がよいと思う。

〖注〗 **It's time he came**... の came は一種の仮定法で特別の使い方、意味は he should come... と同じ。

**828.** 一行中の一人は、近道を取るのが一番いいという説を出した。

〖注〗 **remark** 意見などを「言う」。

**829.** 私はヴァムボージ夫人といっしょにいるくらいなら囚人船に住む方がよほどよい。

〖注〗 **galley** むかし罪人奴隷などにこがせた橈船(とうせん)。

**830.** 君は家へ帰り、そのことについては何も言わないでいる方がいい、金を取り返えそうなどという努力はかえって君の愚を暴露するばかりだから。

**831.** 顧客とか泊まり客とかの勘定を催促する段になると、その(催促するという)重荷はきっと私の肩にかかるんです、うちのだんなときたら、あの杯をかじればっても自分で催促になんぞ動きもしません。

〖注〗 これは宿屋の主婦が客の勘定を催促するについて夫の無能なことをののしるところ。**he'd**=he would. **burthen**=burden. **budge after them** とは customers や guests を追って動く、すなわち催促に従事すること。**himself** 「自分で」。

**832.** 「救貧院へ行かれない人がたくさんあります、またそんな所へ行くくらいなら死んだ方がましだと思う人もたくさんあります」。——「死んだ方がましなら、死んで、ありあまる人口を減らしたらいいだろう」。

**833.** こうもりはその前脚——むしろ腕と呼ぶ方がいいのだが——に長い細い指がある。

**834.** 私は悪の天幕におるよりはむしろわが神の家の門番となりたいと思う。

〖注〗 「罪業の天幕の中に住まんよりはむしろ神の宮殿の門番をする方がましだ」ということ。旧約聖書の詩篇、84：10 にある。**I had rather** は今の言い方にすれば I would rather.

(92)

**835.** 英国王でかなりの艦隊を建造したのはこの王が最初であると信じられている。彼はまた、陸上で安全であることを欲するものは海上の覇権(はけん)を握らなければならない、という金言を後継者に残したということである。

〖注〗 **This King is believed to have been...** は it is believed that he *was*... をちぢめたもの。(he was) **the first ruler to...**「彼が最初に...した王」、類例:—He was *the first man to come* (＝he came first). (彼が一番先に来た) **it is said of him that...**「彼に関して...ということがいわれている」、類例:—People *say of* him that he is mad. (世間では彼を評して狂人といっている)

**836.** 魚を捕えようと欲する者はぬれることをいやがってはいけない。

〖注〗 虎穴に入らずんば虎児を得ず。

**837.** われわれがもし祖先の歴史を学んで益を得ようと欲するならば、歴史の中の国はわれわれが生存している今の国と異なる国であることを忘れてはいけない。

〖注〗 **the country of which we read**「そういう国があったとわれわれが歴史で読む国」。

**838.** 忍耐と要領とは、高い地位に登ろうと欲するすべての人にとって、特に衆に抜きんでる必要を感ずる人々にとって、もっとも大切な二大資質である。

**839.** 我らはエジプトの地において主(しゅ)のみ手によって死んだならばよかったのに。

〖注〗 旧約聖書、出エジプト記、16:3.

**840.** 私の召使が皆お前のようでありたいものだ。

---

(93)

**841.** どういう動機からにもせよつねに用心にしくはない。

〖注〗 **be on the side of caution**「用心の側に立つ」。

**842.** 平野は、たといそれがどんなに美しいものであれ、私の目にはけっしてそうは見えない。私は奔流と、岩石と、もみの木と、こんもり茂った森と、山と、上ったり降りたりするけわしい道と、私のそばにおそろしいような深淵とが、必要なのだ。

**843.** 適度に脳を使うことは疑いもなく健康的であるが、過度に脳を使うことはその正反対である。頭を使いすぎる人はすべて——数学家、哲学家、法律家、著作家、あるいは実業家、そのいずれを問わず——それがために身体の健康を損ずるものである。

〘注〙 Brain work in moderation=moderate brain work「適度なる脳の仕事」。brain work in excess=excessive brain work「過度になる脳の仕事」。the very reverse「正反対」。who work their brains too much の work は他動詞、「脳をあまり多く働かせる人は」。do so at the expense of... の do so は work their brains too much をくりかえすかわりである、すなわち、「...を犠牲に供して過度の脳の仕事をするというものだ」。

**844.** 現にその島はほとんどあらゆる野菜類の栽培を許すような気候をもっているから、島内の農業は容易であり、また有利であろうと期待されるかもしれない。しかし実際はそうではない。ほんとうの原因はなんであろうと、農夫は一般に自己の労働に対して ごくすこししか 収穫しないことはたしかである。

〘注〙 Possessing, as the island does=as the island possesses. (80) 参照。both easy and profitable「容易でもあり有利でもある」、(110) 参照。such is not the case「そんなわけではない」、類例:—*Such being the case*「そういうわけだから」。

**845.** 旅行者がどの道を選ぼうとも、ずっと登りつづけさえすれば、別別の谷から出発しても、山の頂上でいっしょになるだろう。

〘注〙 これは真理に到達することを登山にたとえた話。keep on=continue.

**846.** われわれはけっして人をいやしむべきでない、たとえその人の境遇がいかにいやしかろうとも。

〘注〙 despise [dispáiz] 軽べつする。humble いやしい。

**847.** たとえどんなに健康であっても、強くても、あるいは幸運であっても、あなた方だれしもひじょうな苦痛にたえることを覚悟しなければならない、そしてその苦痛を善用できないものかどうか自問してみることはむだではない。なぜなら苦痛はそれを利用する方法を知っている人にとっては、ひじょうに大きな価値を持っているからである。

〘注〙 it is worth while for you to...「あなたが...することはするだけのかいがある」、類例:—Would it be *worth while* to read this book? It is *not worth while* reading. (この本を読む価値があるか。そんなものを読むのは暇つぶしだ) put...to good use「...を善用する」、類例:—to *put* money *to a bad use* (金を悪用する).

**848.** 私の連れはどうしてもその[こっけいな]出来事を見て笑いをおさえることができなかった。

〘注〙 **do what he could**「笑いをおさえようとできるだけのことをしたけれども」。

**849.** 一事をよく知ろうと欲する人は、ほかに自分の心を引きつけ誘うたくさんの事がらを、知らずにすます勇気がなくてはならない。

〘注〙 **would**=wishes to. (**92**) 参照。**be ignorant of...**「...を知らずにいる」。**a thousand** はたくさんの意味をあらわす。**however attracting and inviting** (they might be)「いかにそれらが自分の注意を引き心を誘うようなことであろうとも」とは、おもしろそうで研究してみたいようなことでも、ということ。

**850.** 人の一生は、その間に行なったこと、その間に考えたり感じたことによって測るべきである。人は有益な仕事をすればするほど、考えたり感じたりすればするほど、ますます真の生活をするのである。怠惰な、役に立たない人間は、いくつまで生きのびたところでただの植物にすぎない。

〘注〙 **the more...the more**「...すればするほどますます」、(**16**) 参照。**to what extent**「どの程度まで」。

**851.** およそ一つの論文がいかによく書かれていようと、また一つの演説がいかによく報道されようと、話す言葉の中には、生きた人間の発声の中には、文体のいかなる美もまねられず、言葉のいかなる配列も及ばない魅力がある。

〘注〙 **any article...any speech** は an article...a speech よりも強調的な言い方。

**852.** 小児の行儀作法はその小児の社会上の地位に従ってその必要の程度はちがう。小児の徳性に至っては、その小児の身分はどうであっても、早きが上にも早くから(この涵養(かんよう)に)注意しなくてはならない。

〘注〙 **cannot...too**―(**23**) 参照。**attend to** は pay attention (注意する) の意味から、勤むべきことを注意して勤める意味に用いられる、類例:―*Attend to* your business first. (まず本務をつとめよ)

**853.** 最初は薄給で満足しなさい、そうすれば、それに対し少しずつ増額されるたびごとに、そのありがた味を感ずるであろう。しかしながらその給料がどんなに少額でもけっして給料以上の生活をしないように決心しなさい。

〚注〛 appreciate 鑑賞玩味(がんみ)する意味から「真価を知る」「ありがた味を知る」の意味となる。 **never to live above it** を裏からいえば to live within it である、参照:—

{to live *within one's means* （身分相当の暮しをする）
{to live *beyond one's means* （身分不相応のぜいたくをする）

**854.** ありがたい、とにもかくにも、そのことがすんだのだ。そう言って自分に言い聞かせ、固い決心をとりもどした。私はいつもより、ありありと夢を見ていたにすぎなかったのだと信じこむにいたった。

〚注〛 **reason** の動詞の用法の例:—I tried to *reason with* him. (私は彼を道理で説きふせようとした) He *was reasoned into* compliance. (彼は説きふせられて承諾した)

**855.** 世界自由諸国は、他の多くのことでもそうであるが、青年に対する計画を立てる場合に、たえず連絡を保っていなければならない、というのは、方法はいろいろあろうとも、基本的目標は同じであるからだ、すなわち、個人の自由の維持と拡大という共通目標なのだから。

〚注〛 **be in communication** (with) は「～と文通している」「連絡をとっている」意味によく使われる。 **however diverse their methods** may be と補ってみる。 **remain** は自動詞、したがって、**the same** は補語。

**856.** 食(英国人は食物のことを食というのが好きだ)の問題は英国人にとっては限りなく興味あるもののようである。英国人はいつ会ってもきっと、まず天候のことを話し合い、それから身体に合うもの——というのは食物の種類のことなんだが——のことを話し合うのが常である。

〚注〛 **diet** は通例 vegetable diet (菜食), meat diet (肉食)などと連語で用い、あるいは病人などの「規定の食」をいうのであるが、英国人は food のかわりに diet という語を好んで用いるというのである。 **one** (=a subject) **of unlimited interest**「無限に興味ある問題」、すなわち a very interesting subject の意味。 **ready to**=willing to と見てよい。 **that is to say** は上を受けて、「...というのは次のようにいうに等しい」で、「換言すれば」「すなわち」の意味である、to say を省いて単に that is ということも多い。 **agree with** は気候、食物などが身体に適することをいう、類例:—Does the climate of Tokyo *agree with* you? (東京の気候はおからだに適しますか) The shrimps I had at dinner *disagreed with* me. (晩餐(ばんさん)に食べたえびがあたった)

**857.** 出勤の往復に乗物に乗るならば、周囲がどんなにやかましく、あるいはこんでいても、目を閉じてそれを休め、その時間を沈黙と冥想(めいそう)に当てなさい。

〚注〛 **ride to and from work**「仕事へ行くと、仕事から帰りに乗る」で、こ

のrideは汽車、電車に乗ること。**rest them**のthemはyour eyes。**allow**はここでは「割り当てる」「とっておく」に当たる言葉。**interlude**は元来芝居の「幕間」または、「あいの狂言」の意味であるが、ここでは通勤の「途中の時間」という意味。

**858.** 書物はすべてどこかに肝要な箇所を持っている。一読してこれらの急所をつかみ、有用な知識を理解することのうまい人は、真に、良い読書家と言ってよい。人はどんなにいそがしかろうと、貧乏であろうと、読書の時間をみつけ、また書物を手に入れることはできる。

〚注〛 **skilled in**...「...に熟練した」。**at first sight**「一目見て」。

**859.** 外の世界はどうなろうとご勝手次第、国が興ろうと国が滅びようと、(そんなことはお構いなし)勘定を払うだけの金さえあれば、当座は自分の見渡すかぎりの所を支配する主権者である。

〚注〛 この文は宿屋に着いた旅人の心をいったものである。**so long as** = if. **(41)** 参照。**the wherewithal to pay** = the money with which to pay「払うべき金」。**all he surveys**「見渡すかぎり」とは宿屋の室内をいったのである。'monarch of all I survey' は William Cowper (1731-1800) という詩人の言葉。

---

( 94 )

**860.** われわれは野球で打者にストライクを三つ許し、その三つをどう始末するかを見る。もし12のストライクを許したら、だれも勝負をしようと思わないであろう。機会が多すぎると野球を台なしにしてしまう。

〚注〛 **do with**...「...を処分する」、類例:—I do not know *what to do with* it. (どうしてよいかわからない)

**861.** もし芸術(絵画)が自然の外観の単なる記録であるとすれば、一番よく模倣したものが一番満足な芸術品となるだろう。そして写真が絵画にとってかわる時が急速に近づいてきていることになるだろう。

〚注〛 **replace** = take the place of. 例:—Buses are *replacing* trams. (バスがだんだん市街電車にとってかわる)

**862.** もし彼がその(小説家としての)職業に完全に身を投じていたら、小説家として高い地位を占めることができたろうか、ということは疑問である。なぜなら彼の欠点は勤勉や練習ではほとんど減少させ得ないようなものであったから。

863. 実際、科学のどの分野についてでも、若い研究家がなした発見を一切除外してしまって、書物を書くことになったとすれば、書くことはほとんど何もなくなってしまうだろう。

〚注〛 科学上の発見の大多数は若い学者によってなされるものだという主旨。**in which** の which は book をうける。**little left to write about**＝little left about which the author should write.

864. 私がもういちど こどもになれたなら、私は注意の習慣を養いたいと思う。自己と当面の問題との間をば、何物にもへだてさせまいと思う。氷すべりの名人はけっして二つの方向に滑走しようとはしないということを、忘れないようにしようと思う。

〚注〛 **school** を動詞として「訓練する」などの意味に用いる、類例：—to *school oneself to* patience (忍耐に身をならす)

865. ある花形選手がかつてぼくに言ったことがある、「ぼくはチームから抜けられる方法があったらいいと思うよ、なにも蹴球をやめたいというのではない。そりゃ好きなんだ、けれども、まるで命をそれにかけたように試合をするのが不愉快でたまらないんだ。あんまり真剣すぎる。楽しさがまったくない」。

〚注〛 **it isn't that** は it isn't because とか、I don't mean that などの意味になる。

866. もしたいていの人が着たとすれば、彼の服はひどく見すぼらしく見えたであろう、ところがこの男にはどこか、衣裳のことなど かれこれ言わせないようなものがあった、それで、私があげたような服装のこまかい点は、実は後から思い出したのであった（その時には気がつかなかった）。

〚注〛 **On** は If they had been put on と補ってみればよくわかるだろう。**prevented one from criticizing**「人に批評することをさしひかえさせた」。**the details**「こまかい点」とは、上着がどうであったとか、ズボンがどうであったと言って、そのみすぼらしさをあげたわけである。

———

(95)

867. 諸君に対してこんなことを言う必要はあるまいと思うが、へや中で一番よい席をとるとか、あるいは食事の際にまず人にとってあげましょうとも言わないで、傍若(ぼうじゃく)無人にすぐ自分の好きなものをぶんどるということは、いかにも無作法千万なことである。

〚注〛 **I dare say**＝I suppose; perhaps.「たぶん」、類例：—You are hungry, *I dare say* (＝*I suppose*). (さぞおなかがすいたでしょう) **how rude it is** の it は to take... と to seize との二つの不定詞を代表する。**seize upon** は「つかみかかって」うばい取る。**at table** は「食事の際」の意味、用例：— Religion and politics are forbidden topics *at table*. (食事の席に宗教と政治の話題は禁物である) **help others** (to something)「人に何か取ってやる」、類例：—Please *help yourself to* anything you like. (なんでも好きなものを取っておあがりください)　Shall *I help you to* more cake? (もっとお菓子を取ってあげましょうか)

**868.** 蹴球は楽しみでやるのでない、ひどく真剣な仕事としてやる、そして、選手は、次の試合は人生の一大事であるかのように、毎日何時間も練習しなければならない。

〚注〛 **hours of attention** の attention は仕事などに「従事する」意味の attend の名詞。ここでは「注意」では当らない。**the sole interest**「唯一の関心事」。

**869.** 太陽は立ち去るのがいやのようであったが、ある見えない力が太陽を地平線のかなたへ引きおろしていた。しかし太陽は消える前にその光輝を放射しつくそうと欲するかのように、生きた火の長い、赤黄金色の光線を送り出し、この光線が地球を夢の国に変化させた。

〚注〛 **as if eager** eager の前に it were を補ってみよ。

**870.** 12時が鳴ると、電気にでもうたれたように急に道具を放すような職人は、義務をつくしているかもしれないが、それ以上は何もしていない。単に義務をつくすだけで大成功したものはいまだかつてない。義務をつくし、なおそれ以上のことをしなくてはならない。仕事を愛するならば「以上」はわけもないことである。

〚注〛 **tools** は大工や左官などの道具のように手で使うもの。**may** は後の **but** と応じ、「...ではあろうがしかし...」という気持ち、類例：—He *may* be a scholar, *but* he is not a good teacher. (学者かもしれないが良い教師ではない) **make a success of one's life** は「自分の一生を成功にする」すなわち to succeed in life などの意味である、類例：—to make a success of it (うまくやってのける). to make a failure of it (しくじる).

**871.** そしてもしわれわれが心配か怒りか恐怖で心が緊張していると、その疲労はせっせと木を切っていたとちょうど同じである。もしこの疲労を十分の睡眠で取り除かないと、われわれの行動にその影響が現われるのは否定できない。

〖注〗 **busy chopping**「いそがしく切っている」、busily chopping と言わないでこのように使う方が慣用。**its effect upon our behaviour**「われわれの行動に及ぼすその影響」で、effect には on や upon がよくつく。**is undeniable** =cannot be denied.

**872.** 燃える船から上る火焰は炎々としてものすごく、そのため海は水平線までも明らかに照らし出され、物体は白昼のようにはっきりと見えるようになった。
　〖注〗 **broad daylight**「白昼」、参考:—broad distinction (明白な差異). broad facts (明白な事実).

**873.** われわれが仰いで空にただよう白雲をながめ、あるいは伏して足もとに咲くさまざまな花の燃え立つような色をながめるとき、われわれは突然自然のふところにいだかれるような感じがする。
　〖注〗 **gaze at**「つくづくながめる」、参考:—to glance at (ちらと見る、ちょっと見る); to glare at (にらむ); to stare at (じろじろ、あるいはきょろきょろ見る).

**874.** 現代はこれまでの時代のどれよりも、もっと扱いにくい専制というものを見いだしたかのように見える。むかしの専制はこれにくらべれば単純であった。むかしの暴君は、国民のためを思って国民を治めているのだなどというふりは、まず見せなかった。
　〖注〗 むかしの暴君は自分の利益をはっきりと標榜(ひょうぼう)して政治をしたが、現代の政治は一種の専制で、それが国民の福祉を標榜しているように見せかけるから、やっかいなものだという主旨。**a form of tyranny**「ある形の暴政」。**any** =any form of tyranny. **by comparison** に with the present one と補ってみよ。**pretence**「ふり、よそおうこと」。

**875.** まるで雲から降ってきたかのように、奇妙なかっこうのびっこの犬が突然その場に現われ、おどろきと恐怖におそわれた羊の後から元気よくびっこを引きながら行って、羊どもをまっすぐ羊の囲いの中へ追いこんだ。
　〖注〗 **drove home and into the hold** まず大ざっぱに「家の方へ」と言って、それからもっとこまかく「囲いの中へ」と言っている、これが英語の慣用。

**876.** そうしまいと思っても、彼の眼は、物に魅せられたように、幾度も幾度も炉だなの上にかけてある銃の方に向いたのである。
　〖注〗 **in spite of himself**=in spite of his effort not to do so. 類例:— I laughed *in spite of* myself. (笑うまいと思ってもとうとう笑ってしまった) **mantel**=mantelpiece「炉の上の飾りだな」。

**877.** それから彼女は、何かおそろしいものでも払いのけるように片手を振って、そして倒れて死んでしまった。

**878.** 霊感は宗教に特有のものではないということはほとんど言うまでもない。霊感とは、突然に、そして言わば外から、人の頭にはいってくるように思われる思いつきである。

〚注〛 **it goes without saying that...**「...は言うまでもない」。from without の **without** は「...のそと」という前置詞であるが、ここでは from という別の前置詞に支配されている。

---

( 96 )

**879.** 広告から得られるばく大な収入がなければ、新聞はそう安く売ることはできない。会社でその製品を日刊新聞に広告するため毎年数千ポンドを投じているものもある。

**880.** 高い望みをいだいて人生にうって出た人々の中に、こうも失敗が多い理由を一言で述べよと求められたなら、躊躇(ちゅうちょ)なく答える、彼らは意志の力を欠いていたのであると。

〚注〛 **to call upon~to...**「~に...することを求める」、区別:—
{ The country *calls upon* us *to* defend her.
(国家はそれを守ることをわれわれに求める=われわれは国家を守らなければならない)
He *called on* me yesterday. (昨日彼がぼくを訪問した)。

**881.** 彼が偉くなったのも、彼が身を滅ぼしたのも、ともに野心のためであった。彼には種々の短所もあったが、また偉いりっぱな資質もそなえていた。だから、もし彼がよく適当の分(ぶん)を守っていたら死にいたるまで彼に匹敵する者はなかったろうに。

〚注〛 **To ambition he owed...**=he owed...to ambition. 類例:—He *owes* his success *to* good luck.=His success is *due to* (or *owing to*) good luck. (彼の成功は僥倖(ぎょうこう)だ) **with all his failings**「たくさんの弱点をもっているにもかかわらず」、類例:—*With all* his faults, he is a great man. (いろいろ欠点はあるが偉い人だ) *For all* his wealth, he is not contented. (あんなに金があっても満足していない) **keep within due bounds**「適当の限度内にいる」、すなわち「度を越えない」、類例:—You should *keep within* (due) *bounds*. (程度を知れ) You must not *go beyond* (all) *bounds*. (度をすごすな、あまり欲ばるな) **equal**「匹敵する者」、類例:—He has no *equal* in the knowledge of English. (英語の知識にかけては彼に匹敵する者はない)

**882.** 雨がたくさん降らなければ、日本はもっとも住み心地のよい国の一つなのだが。

**883.** どなたにお会いするのか前もってわかっておりましたら、つばさに乗って飛んでくることができてもまだおそいと思ったほどでしょう。

〚注〛 これは相手が会ってひじょうにうれしい人だったので、それとわかっていれば飛んでくるのだったのに、という気持ちの文。**wings could not have conveyed me swiftly enough**「つばさでも十分に速くは私を運ぶことはできなかったであろう」が文字どおりの訳文。

**884.** もし私が21歳のとき、健康と生活の諸法則を今と同じだけ知っていたら、たしかに2倍の仕事をもっと良くもっと気楽に仕遂げることができたと思う。

〚注〛 **with greater ease to myself**「自分自身に対するいっそう大きな気楽さをもって」。**as I do**＝as I know.

**885.** ネルソンが再び起き上り得ないうちに獰猛(どうもう)な獣は、彼に乗りかかり、今にも打ち下ろそうと恐ろしい手をあげていた。その一撃が下ったならば、ヨーロッパの全歴史はそのために全部変わっていたかもしれない。

〚注〛 このときネルソンが猛獣のために倒れたならヨーロッパの歴史は現在のようではなかったろうという意味。

**886.** 田舎(いなか)へ出かけて行く暇があったら、ひじょうに彼のためになったろうに。

〚注〛 **to do one good**「人を益する；ためになる」、類例：—Exercise *does one good* (＝is good for the health). (運動はからだのためになる＝健康に益がある) Too much wine will *do you harm*. (あまり酒を飲むとからだの毒になるぞ) Such men will *do you more harm than good*. (ああいう人は君にとって有害無益だ)

**887.** 彼がいつも私の上に残した印象は、もし彼がもっと身分の高くない階級に生まれたとしても、公生活のどんな部門でも同様にりっぱにやってのけただろうということであった。

〚注〛 **acquit oneself**「(任を)果たす」。

**888.** アフリカの土人はひじょうにだちょうの卵を好み、それを食料に供する。卵を採るのに彼らはひじょうに用心深くしてやる、というのは、もし鳥が彼らを発見すれば、ことごとく卵を破って巣を立ちのくからである。

〖注〗 **they would** の they は the birds を受ける。

**889.** 旧文化の上に新しい文明を加えることはもちろん大事業である。そして日本はそれを試み、その完成に成功したことはただ感服のほかはない。もしこの偉業が、どちらの文明の美点も少しも失うことなくして成就されたならば、それはまさに奇蹟であろう。

〖注〗 **nothing short of a miracle**=quite a miracle. 類例:—His escape was *nothing short of* (=quite) a miracle.  It was *little short of* (=almost) a miracle.

---

( 97 )

**890.** その半島はこのように長い海岸線を持っているから、そうでない場合より気候は温和である。

**891.** いうまでもなく、実業家というものは相当な抵当なしに金を貸すということはめったにありません、さもなければたちまち貧乏になってしまうかもしれませんからね。

〖注〗 **reduce** は「元に返す」の意味から転じて「...にしてしまう」。「...に帰せしめる」などの意味となる、類例:—The house was *reduced to ashes*. (家は灰燼(かいじん)に帰した)  He was *reduced to a skeleton*. (やせて骸(がい)骨のようになってしまった)

**892.** 茶の木は6フィート以上には延ばさない、さもないと容易に葉に手がとどかないからである。茶の木は延びるままにしておくと高い木ぐらいの高さに延びる、だから中国のある地方ではさるを慣らして茶の木に登らせ、葉を摘ませるということである。

〖注〗 **is allowed to**...「...するままに放任される」。**grow to a height of**...「...の高さに達する」、類例:—Snow fell *to a depth of* more than one meter. (雪が1メートル以上積った)  **otherwise**=if it were allowed to grow to such a height.  **The leaf could not be reached.**=We *could not* (=should not be able to) reach the leaf.

**893.** 彼の時間厳守は彼の数々の習慣の中でももっとも注意深く養われたものの一つであった。そうでなかったとしたら、あんなばく大な文学的労作をなしとげることは、とても不可能であったろう。彼は受取った手紙は一通残らずその日に返事を出すことにきめていた、調べてみたり慎重に考慮したりすることの必要な場合を除いては。

〘注〙 **cultivated** 次に ones (=habits) を補って見よ。 **made it a rule to...**「...するのを常例としていた」、類例:— I *maks it a rule to* side with the weaker party. (ぼくは弱い方の肩を持つ主義だ)

**894.** いうまでもないことであるが、富と安易とは、人間の最高の教養には必要でない。さもなければ、世界はあらゆる時代において卑賤の階級から身を起こした人々にこれほど負うことが大ではなかったであろう。

〘注〙 **had not the world been**=the world would not have been. **indebted to...**「...に負うている」、類例:—For the following account, I am *indebted to* Bakin. (次の記事は馬琴翁に負うている) **in all times**「あらゆる時代に」。

**895.** 人が、自分以外にたしかにだれもけっして見ることはないと思って日記をつける場合には、その人はたぶん完全にほんとうのことを書くだろう。そうしないための動機は全然ない[からだ]。

〘注〙 **being otherwise**=being not truthful, つまり、「うそを書くこと」。

**896.** 陸海軍を維持するに必要な税金のため、男女各人は、そうでない場合に働く必要のあるよりは、すくなくとも1日1時間ずつ余計働かなければならない。

〘注〙 **compels...to work** の主語は The taxation である、すなわち「税金が彼らをしいて働かせる」、類例:—They *compelled* me *to* drink. (彼らは無理じいに私に飲ませた) **need** (to work)=must work.

**897.** フランス人はアングロサクソン民族(英米人)より食物にはぜいたくである、けれどもこの食物の点でぜいたくにふける傾向は、食物のぜいたくをしなければ、とうてい満足できないような不備な住居でがまんすることで、埋め合わせになっている。

〘注〙 フランス人は食物にぜいたくをしているので、住居の方はあまりよくなくても、食物をおごっているのだから、しかたがないとあきらめている、というような主旨の文。**is counterbalanced by**「～で埋め合わされている」。**satisfaction** はここでは「がまんすること」「辛抱すること」。**more inadequate dwellings than would otherwise content them** の more inadequate はけっきょく less adequate としてみればよい。otherwise は if they were not luxurious in their food で、「食物までつましくしていたならば」となる。

**898.** これらの誘導弾には核弾頭がとり付けられるが、その核弾頭は着弾すると人間の社会を全滅させ、これのみが生存を可能にさせている微妙な環境を粉砕するだろう。これが、もし事情がちがっておれば、人類史上

人間の知性の最大の勝利ともなり得るはずのものの不幸な意味あいなのである。

 〖注〗 最初の文の主語は nuclear cargo. **nuclear cargo** は誘導弾の先頭へつける原子爆弾のこと。**on arriving**=when it arrives. **delicate conditions** とは神経の働きとか細胞の機能のようなものをさしているのであろう。**what might...man** とは「科学の粋」とでもいうべきもの。平和的利用をすればすばらしい手がらであるのに、破壊武器として使われるから、不幸となるのである。

**899.** 彼らがこんなに近くにい合わせたのはよい仕合せであった、そうでなかったら母は子供の後を追って[河に]飛びこみ二人とも命を失ったであろう。

**900.** お前はただあたり前のことをしたまでのことである。もしそうしなかったら、お前は不正直であったのだ。

 〖注〗 **nothing more** (than what was right) と補って見よ。**If you had acted otherwise.**=If you had not acted so.

**901.** すべて世の中のけっこうなものは辛抱して待たなければならない、そして通例1滴ずつよりほかは来ないものである。

 〖注〗 **drop by drop**=little by little.「すこしずつ」。

**902.** 彼はひどい打撲傷を受け、また足首の骨をはずした、しかしそのほかにはけがはなかった。

 〖注〗 **had his ankle dislocated** については (71) を参照せよ。dislocate は「脱臼させる」。

---

( 98 )

**903.** いわゆる「不可能」な行為が遂行されたとき、他の人々もこれならばやろうとさえ思えばとうの昔にやることが出来たのであるということを知った。

**904.** やつはこうも言いそうな様子をしている:—「オイ君、いい人だから、ちょっと聞いてくれたまえ、君は金がある、ぼくはない、1ペニーくらいはぼくにくれてもよさそうなものだね」。

 〖注〗 **might give me**「くれようと思えば容易にくれられる」という意味。

**905.** 彼の性質には人によっては怠情とでも呼びかねないところがあった、が、実はそんなものではなかった。

〖注〗 **not quite that**=not exactly that, *i.e.* laziness.

**906.** 彼女はその死骸を自分の家へ移したかったのであるが、移すことはできなかった。

〖注〗 **her home** の次に if she could を補って解せ。すなわち移すことができさえすればよろこんで移すのであったということ。

**907.** その中の一つや二つなくなってもけっして勘づかれることはなかったでしょう、で私は［そうしようと思えば］露見の心配もなくふところを肥やすことが容易にできたのです。

〖注〗 **one or two of them** の中に「たとえ一つや二つ紛失しても」という仮定を含む。**miss** は「ないのに気がつく」こと。**might have enriched myself** に if I had wanted to を補って解せ。

**908.** 花とこん虫は手袋と手のようにおたがいに適合している。多くの場合花はその訪問者を得なければおそらくなくなってしまい、こん虫はその花がなければなくなってしまうであろう。

**909.** 地球と大きさのほぼ同じくらいの星も多少知られているが、大多数（の星）はひじょうに大きく、その各々の中に地球を何十万詰めこんでもまだ余裕があるほどである。あちこちでわれわれは地球を何万億も入れ得るほど大きな巨星に遭遇する。

〖注〗 **hundreds of thousands**「幾千という数の幾百倍」「何十万」、**millions of millions**「百万の百万倍」。 **room to spare**「余地」。

---

( 99 )

**910.** 私は彼女［妻］がこのいばった調子で話をするのを聞いて笑わずにはいられなかった、しかし私は自分たちの心をよろこばせるような罪のない空想をたいして不愉快とは思わなかった。

〖注〗 **be displeased with...**「...を不快に思う」、類例：—I am very much *pleased with* my new man. (ぼくはこんどの男がひじょうに気に入った) His father is *displeased with* him. (彼はおとうさんの不興をこうむっている) **tend to...**「...する助けとなる」。

**911.** 私は昨夜9時と10時の間にこの場所を散歩していた、そしてここは幽霊の出るにはもってこいの場面だと考えざるを得なかった。

〘注〙 **fancy it** (to be) **one of**... と補ってみよ。**appear in** の in は a house to live *in* (=a house in which to live) などの in と同じ性質のもの。**for a ghost** の for は不定詞の意味上の主語を示すもの、すなわち「幽霊が現われるには」、類例:—It is difficult *for a Japanese to* learn European languages. (日本人がヨーロッパ語を学ぶのは困難だ)

**912.** 母は隣村より遠く自宅から離れたことはなかった、それで彼女の夫がそんな長旅に出ることを考えると、すこしばかりおどろかないわけにゆかなかった。

〘注〙 **at the thought of**...「...を考えると」、「...を思い出すと」、類例:—I was grieved *at the thought of* leaving school. (退学することを思い出すと悲しかった)

**913.** 地下鉄の美麗さと乗客のくすんだ衣服との対照はほとんどあきれるほどであった。地下鉄はすばらしい技術的偉業であるという感銘を受けざるを得なかった。

〘注〙 **almost violent**「ほとんど不自然と言ってもいい」。**the Merto** ここではモスクワの地下鉄のこと。**One could not help** の could は仮定法とも考えられる。しかし、この One は I と言ってもよいわけで、そうすれば仮定法と考える必要はない。

**914.** 人はだれでも他人に影響を与えざるを得ない、たとえどんなに影響を与えまいとしても、あるいは自分のしていることにほとんど覚えがなくても。何人もどっちつかず(善でも悪でもない状態)であることはできない。もしその人が善をなしているのでなければ、ある意味で悪をなしているであろう。

〘注〙 **is conscious of** 前に however little he を補ってみよ。be conscious of~ は「~を自覚している」、類例:—I *am conscious of* my want of ability. (才能の足りないことは十分承知している)

**915.** どんなことを彼が言おうとも聴衆は彼のいうことを信ぜざるを得なかった。

〘注〙 **had no choice but to believe**=could not (choose) but believe.

**916.** 正直と真実とは、こどもにおいてさえも[こどもの正直真実でも]、その周囲の人々に良い影響を及ぼさないということはない。

〘注〙 **cannot fail to**...=cannot but...「きっと...する」。

**917.** 彼は彼らが発揮した嘆賞すべき自助の精神に感動せざるを得なかった。

**918.** ディーン・ラムゼイの回想録中の美しい逸話はウイスキーに関するものである、で私はそれを引用することを控えることができない。

---

### (100)

**919.** そこで彼女[孟子の母]はまた引越した、自分のむすこが学生や学者ばかりを見ることができるように。

〚注〛 scholar「学問をする人」。 men of learning=learned men.

**920.** 教師は児童を打つよりほかに知識を授ける方法を知らなかった。夫は、上流のものでさえ、妻をなぐることを恥としなかった。

〚注〛 二、三世紀前までのヨーロッパなどの習慣を述べたもの。

**921.** 人っ子一人そこらには見えなかった。そうかといって、遠く村まで行って警報を与える暇はない。来るべき危険を阻止し得るのはただこの少年のみであった。

〚注〛 all the way「はるばると」。

**922.** なるほど、その船自体がいわば一塊の陸地にほかならなかった。そしてわれわれはこの上でふつう生活とはなはだしくはちがわない生活を送ることができたのであった。

〚注〛 in a sense=so to speak「いわば」。 surprisingly「おどろくほど」。 customary one=ordinary life.

**923.** そういう殺人の背後にあるものは自殺的無謀のみである。国民安全協議会発表の数字は致命的大衝突の 75 パーセントは見通しのきく、直線道路において起こることを示している。

〚注〛 suicidal recklessness そんな無謀な運転をすれば自分も死ぬことになるという意味。 lies behind the slaughter=is the cause of the slaughter. smashup=violent collision 激突。

**924.** 袋の中にあったものでなければ出てこない。

〚注〛「ないそでは振れない」という意味。

**925.** ある朝ウイルという無考えな、遊ぶことよりほかは何でもいやという子供が、1日なまけて暮そうと思って、うららかな野べに出た。

〚注〛 care for「...に意をとめる」「...を欲する」、類例:—Don't *you* care *for* wealth or fame? (君は金も名誉もほしくないのか)

**926.** 自然が注意深く研究されればされるほど、秩序があまねく行きわたっていることが発見されてきた。これと同時に、無秩序と思われたものが複雑さであるにすぎないことがわかってきた。

〚注〛 **the more..., the more...** (16) 参照。**order** は主語で、その前に助動詞が来ている。**has proved to be...**「...であることがわかった」。

**927.** 彼は途中こじきをしながら行かねばならない、そしてそれは公道以外のところではできないだろう。

**928.** クリスマスおめでとうがくそくらえ。クリスマスが何だ、金がないのに勘定を払わなけりゃならず、取ったものは年ばかりで相変わらず貧乏な不めでたい時じゃないか。

〚注〛 **Out upon...**＝fie upon...「...もへちまもあるものか」などという意味。**a year older and not an hour richer** 年は1年とっても1時間分だけも金持にはならないということ。

**929.** 実際の人物以外に何と人が彼を見よう。ああいう行ないの結果は零落(れいらく)のほかに何があろう。

**930.** 義務という題目については全国民がただ一つの考えを持っている。小学生はだれでも、この題目について質問されると、次のように答えるだろう、「各人の義務は国を強くし富ませることに努め、そしてわが国の独立を守りそれを保持することに尽すことだ」と。

〚注〛 **if he is questioned** と補ってみる。

**931.**「手前どものはほんのお粗末な食事で」とダドルストンが言った。「ただ焼肉とプラムプディングくらいしか差し上げられませんから」。

〚注〛 **ours**＝our fare. **humble fare** はまた poor fare ともいう。人を招待したとき「何もありません」などいうところを You must put up with poor fare.(あなたはまずい食事を辛抱しなければならない)という。**plum pudding** は干しぶどうなどを入れてこしらえた蒸しまんじゅうのようなもの、この場合は plum は「梅」でない。

**932.** 一、二度一行中に遠くの方にしゅろの木のこずえが見えると思った者があった。しかしそうではなかった、それはただ地平線上の一片の雲にすぎないということがわかった。

〚注〛 **fancy** そうでないことを空想でそうと思う。 **turned out**＝proved; was found.「後になって見たら...ということがわかった」。

**933.** 手短かに言えば、人間は活動のためにつくられたもので、人生は心の活動の舞台にすぎない。どんな重要な仕事でも、いわばただ比較的ま

じめな種類の娯楽にすぎないのであって、ある目的の追求を楽しむかぎり、それを達しなくても、あるいは達せられたとき消えうせても、そんなことはほとんど問題ではない。

〘注〙 **the most important occupations** = even the most important occupations. (**13**) 参照。**take pleasure in**...「...を楽しむ」、類例：—He *takes pleasure* in reading.（彼は読書が好きだ）

**934.** 道具は人間の手の延長にすぎず、また機械は単に複雑な道具にすぎない。だから機械を発明する人は人間の力と人類の幸福を増大するものである。

---

## (101)

**935.** まごまごするのしないのってなかった。だれがへやへはいってくるかと思えば、あの都からの二人のえらい知り合いだったから。

〘注〙 **confusion on confusion**「狼狽(ろうばい)に狼狽を重ねる」意味。

**936.** 早馬をもって報を伝えてきたのは、だれあろうジョン[王]自身であった。

**937.** ああしゃくにさわると心に思いながらじっと彼を見送っていると、私のひじにさわる者があるから、だれかと思うと前に述べた小さな僧であった。

〘注〙 **when** は前から訳して来て、「その時に」となる。**touch me on the elbow**「私のひじにさわる」、(**66**) 参照。

**938.** ある大通りを通っているとだれに会ったと思う、最初にあなたが私を推薦してくれたそのいとこだからふしぎじゃありませんか。

---

## (102)

**939.** ベーカー家の人々は親類や友だちによって囲まれるのが何よりも好きであった。それはお金がたくさんあったからではなかった。金持どころではなく、彼らが提供したような歓待を準備するためには、ベーカー夫人の乏しい財布を、幾度か最後の6ペンスまでもはたかなくてはならなかった。

〘注〙 **not that**=not because. **empty of**...「...をからにする」。

**940.** [世間には] 人の仕事なら進んでやるけれど自分の仕事はいっこうにしないという人間がある。

〖注〗 **are ready to...** は「進んで、よろこんで...する」すなわち are willing to... とほぼ同意。 **attend to** は仕事などを注意して勤める意味、類例:—You must *attend to* your business. (務めを大事にしなくてはいけない) The student should *attend to* his studies. (学生は学問に身をいれるべきだ)

**941.** 彼は自分の貧乏を人のせいにして自分の罪とはどうしてもしない。

〖注〗 **to lay...at another's door**「...を人の罪に帰する」。

**942.** 彼らは疲労ははなはだしく、ただ寝たいと思うばかりである。

〖注〗 本題の **anyting but** は too...to 中に含まれる打消しの意味と合して前章で述べた nothing but の意味をなすもので、本章に説いた anything but ではないから特に注意を要する。すなわち全体を書きなおせば They are *so* tired *that* they care for *nothing but* bed.

**943.** ワイパード・ホーキン師の説教はほかに何と評してもよかろうが、なんぼなんでも短いとはいわれない。

〖注〗 **none of the shortest, whatever else they may be**=anything but the shortest.

**944.** 火焔ははじめ遠く離れているように見えるが、だんだんに近寄ってきて、ついにかわいそうな象たちはどちらを見てもみな火で、火のないのはただ一方だけになる。

**945.** 父はぼくをいつも金に不足させておくから、ぼくと父の間がらは今では円満どころじゃない。

〖注〗 **stand on good terms**「仲がよい」、類例:—to be *on bad terms* (仲が悪い). to be *on speaking terms* (会えばたがいに物を言う仲). **short of...**「...が不足」、類例:—to be *short of* hand (手不足). to be *short of* goods (品不足).

**946.** クロムウェルは王の名はないが王の実力を有していた、そして実際のところヘンリー八世以後のどの王にもまさるほどの権力を有していた。

**947.** 英国においてはこういう種類の教授法はほとんど知られていない。

**948.** 今でも覚えているが、私は彼のわざとらしくないいばった、殿様

らしい様子をほとんど崇拝せんばかりであった。
　〖注�〗 easy「固苦しくない」。 swagger 肩で風切るような態度。

**949.**　それはその当時秘密にされたので、今はもうみんなに忘れられ、ただ私たちのような二、三の老人が覚えているばかりです。

**950.**　少年は燃える甲板に立っていた、彼一人のほかはみな甲板から逃れてしまったのである。

---

## (103)

**951.**　われわれが足の下に踏む［つまらぬ］ものでも、何か簡単にして妙味のある教訓を与えないものはない。

**952.**　城内の人で万一の時の覚悟［討死の覚悟］をしていない者は一人もなかった。
　〖注〗 not a soul は no man の意味を強くあらわすもの、「ただの一人もなかった」。

**953.**　ロンドンではくつなおしのような者でも奥の部屋にピアノを置いていないものはない。

**954.**　見つけさえすればどんな法律にでも穴［欠点］はある。

**955.**　世の中から見てはどんなにつまらない職業でも、この世のもっとも価値のある人がそれにたずさわって名誉を与えなかったものはない。
　〖注〗 どんないやしい職業の人からもりっぱな偉人傑士が出てそのためにその職業の名誉となったということ。

**956.**　15世紀終りごろの人にとっては、ほとんど毎年、それまで世間に通用していた考えがまた一つと廃物として捨てられ、何か新発見がもう古いと言われて捨てられるか、もっと新しい発見でそれまでの意義を減少させられたのであった。
　〖注〗 文芸復興時代のことで、思想界も科学界も年々新しいものが世に現われ、古いものがどんどん捨て去られたことを述べたもの。 there was scarcely a year but「～しない年は1年としてないほどであった」。 bring to the scrap-heap「ごみために捨てる」。 found itself surpassed「自分自身が凌駕（りょうが）されたのを知った」。 lessen=make less.

---

## (104)

**957.** 人はどんなに年老いても今1年ぐらいは生きられると思っているものである。

**958.** どんなに獰(ど)猛な獣でもいくらか憐みの心を持たないものはない。

**959.** なるほど文学の一形式としては新聞は永続性の要素を欠いているが、読者に鼓吹しようとする思想は永続的な効果を生ずる。新聞はほとんど普遍的な唯一の読み物である。自己の天職とする業務にいかに熱中している人でも、新聞を読む暇がないという者はないのである。

〖注〗 **it is true..., but** (109) 参照。**inspire~with...**「...を~に吹きこむ」。**is occupied with...**「...に従事している」、「...にいそがしい」、類例：—He *is occupied with* literary work. (著述に従事している、著述にいそがしい)

**960.** どんな悪人でも[世間から]善人と思われたいと願わないほどのものはおそらく見当たらないであろう。

**961.** どんなにささいな行為でもそれ相応にそれからそれと連続して結果を生じないものはない。たとえば、どんなに細い毛髪でもやはりそれ相応の陰影を投ずるようなものである。

〖注〗 **train of consequences**「結果の引きつづき」。

**962.** 人生はいかに短かいといっても礼節をつくすだけの時間は必ず常にある。

〖注〗 **but that**＝but.

---

## (105)

**963.** 降るといえばきっとどしゃ降りだ。

〖注〗 It never rains without pouring. としてもよい。Events, especially, misfortunes always come together. (不幸などは必ずいくつもつづいて起こるものだ)という意味で、Misfortunes never come single. と同じような場合に用いられる。

**964.** 私はかんの強い強情(ごうじょう)な子であったが、このような気持ち[腹の立つすねたいような気持ち]が起こると、いつでも私は彼女[お母さん]が

存命中いつもなされたようなやさしい、涙をふくんだ眼で私をじっと見ておいでなさるような心持ちがした。

〚注〛 frame=a mental condition.「心の状態」。come upon「襲ってくる」。

**965.** 私はモツアルトやヘンデルの曲を聞くと必ず、それを初めて好きになったときに歌ってくれたあの美しい声が、またもどってくるのが聞えるような気がする。

〚注〛 Handel は英語読みでは [hǽndl] で、ドイツ生まれの音楽家。in which 「その声で」、すなわち、その声で歌われて初めて好きになったとつづくわけ。them=the airs.

**966.**「自慢じゃないが」とか何とかいう前置きの後へすぐに何か自慢の出て来ない例は聞いたことも見たこともない。

〚注〛 introductory words「前置きの言葉」、参考：—introductory remarks =introduction（緒言、はしがき）. &c.=et cetera=and so forth.「等」「うんぬん」。

**967.** 妙なわけだが、どんな病気でもお医者を呼んで見せると、きっともう1日手おくれになると とうてい回復の見込みがなかったという場合でないことは、ぼくはいまだかつてこれを聞かないのである。

〚注〛 case 病症、患者。render cure hopeless「治療を望みなきものとする」。

**968.** どんな小さな鳥が、どんな大きな木にとまっても、一番遠くの果ての繊維(末梢)までその震動を伝えないということはない。だれの心でも時々はきわめてささいな言葉に対してまったくこれと同じように敏感なことがある。

〚注〛 the smallest, the greatest の前に even を付けてみよ。(13) 参照。light upon...「...にとまる」。at times=now and then「時々」。no less sensitive=quite as sensitive.「すこしも劣らず、まったく同じくらい敏感な」、類例：—He is *no less* clever *than* his brother.=He is *quite as* clever as his brother. (兄にすこしも劣らずりこうである)

**969.** 彼は成長してえらいこどもとなり、経験によって賢くなった。というのは、どんな事件が起こっても必ず彼は何かしら価値のある教訓をそこから学ぶのが彼の特性の一つであったから。こうして彼は多くの人々が世にも幸運な事件から得るよりも、さらに多くの利益を彼の不幸から得るのが常であった。

**970.** このような待遇に満足するほど心の卑劣な人間があり得ることを見ると、実に憤慨せずにはいられません。

**971.** 死と戦い危険を冒す勇士の英雄的行動を読む者は、何人も尊敬、嘆称の念を起こさないではいられない、けれども英雄的行動はつねに必ず辛労と献身との結果である。

**972.** エマスンの肖像を見るとだれでもきっと彼が賢かったばかりでなく、親切な人であったことを感じる。その顔をよく注意して見てごらん。それは愛すべく信頼すべき顔だ。諸君はこの人を諸君の友人の一人に数えたくなるだろう。

〖注〗 **not only wise but good** の構文は (110) 参照。

**973.** エマスンは言った、「幸福というものは人にそそいでやればその数滴は必ず自分の身にもふりかかる香水である」と。

**974.** アメリカとらのほえ声は他の獣の間に恐怖と狼狽を生じ、彼らを四方に遁走(とんそう)させる。土人はそのほえ声を聞けば必ず恐怖の念をいだくが、それもふしぎはないのである、なぜというに毎年多数の人々が獰猛(どうもう)なこの獣の犠牲とならないことはないのであるから。

〖注〗 **a number of** は元来 some (若干) の意味だが a great number of (多数の) の意味に用いられることもある。**fall victims to**...「...の犠牲となる」、類例:—He *fell a victim to* an assassin. (彼は刺客の手にたおれた)

**975.** どんな職業でも長い間やっていれば、だれしも自分の毎日やっていることが、善悪いずれの傾向を持つかを、つくづく考えさせられるようになるものだ。

〖注〗 **trade** 広い意味では「職業」。**tends to**...「...に向かってゆく」、「...になる傾向がある」。

---

### (106)

**976.** いったんすぎ去った時間はけっして返らないということ、失なわれた瞬間は永久に失なわれたものであるということは、だれでもよく知っている。であるから時間というものは、他のすべての種類の財産にもまして、侵すべからざるものである。ところが、他人の権利であるこの時間を浪費する権利を主張しない者は一人もない。

〖注〗 **above all**...「...にもまして」。 **ought to be free from invasion**「侵略をまぬかれるべきはずである」。 **free from**...は...を免除されるの意味から、...のない意味に移る、類例：—No man is *free from* faults. (欠点のない人はない)　**and yet** = nevertheless「しかも」「それにもかかわらず」。 **claim the power of**...「...の権利を要求する」「...の権利があると主張する」。

**977.**　われわれは働くことが生きることの条件となっている世の中にいる。1回の食事といえども、だれかが作り出すために働いたのでなければだれの口にもはいらない。働く人々は食べる資格がある、働かない人々は飢える資格がある。生きて行く道は三つしかない —— 働くことによってか、盗むことによってか、ないしは、こじきすることによってである。

**978.**　だれでもピット氏の私室に入った者はそのへやを出る際には、以前よりはさらに勇敢な人となった心地のしないものはなかった。

〖注〗 **closet** = private or small room, especially for interviews or for study.

**979.**　幸運は必ずしもことごとく利益ではないように、不運も必ずしもことごとく損失ではない。ローマはギリシアを征服したが、しかしギリシアの文明はローマの文明に打ち勝った、そしてある大作家が言ったように、「今日ヨーロッパには源をギリシアに発しないものは何一つない」。

〖注〗 **not necessarily**「必ずしも...ない」。

**980.**　平易は勤労によって得られる[ほねを折っているとしまいに平易になる]。何事でも最初からやさしいものはない、歩行のようなものですらそうだ。

**981.**　何かしら支配的欲望[たとえば大望のような]に駆(か)られずして世界に足跡を印したものはない。

〖注〗 **master passion** = a predominant passion. 脳中において主となっている情、類例：—Ambition was his *master passion*. **be possessed by** (*or* **with**)... とはきつねにつかれるなどというように、「...につかれる」ことをいう、類例：—He *is possessed by* a devil. (彼は悪魔につかれている)　What has *possessed* you to think of such a thing? (君は何につかれてそんなことを考えるのか = 気でも狂ったのか)　本文では野心というようなものがついてその人を駆っていろいろなことをさせるということ。

**982.**　17世紀の歴史や軽い文学で、われわれの祖先が子孫たちよりも人情がなかったことを証拠立てる記事のないページはほとんど1ページもない。

**983.** 人はそのあわれな生を切(せつ)に愛しているから、ただ生きることができるなら、どんな境遇にも甘んじて屈従する。

〖注〗 **are enamoured of their lives**=love their lives「生命を愛する」。

---

## (107)

**984.** もし彼に快活の気性がなかったならば、あんなか弱い体格でみずから求めて引きうけたあんなに多くの仕事を、やり通すことはできなかったろう。

**985.** 倹約と勤勉と天才との結合は、もし彼のあわれな健康が彼の出費を増加させると同時に、何度も働くことを不可能にするいうことがなかったならば、まもなく彼を成功させたことであろうに。

〖注〗 **disable~for . . .** ~を...ができないようにする。

**986.** その怪獣の尾は、倒れた大木のように 3, 40 フィート地面に横たわっていた、で、彼女はその尾から怪獣の背に登れると思った、けれどもそれはまちがいだった。彼女がその急な坂のところにきたときに尾はつるつるしていたのでドーンとおっこった。もし私がいなかったらけがするところだった。

**987.** それまで発見されたただ二つの鳥の標本は、その骨格がふつうの鳥とまるで違っているので、もし幸運な偶然で、そのつばさの痕跡(こんせき)がわれわれにも見られるように、きめの細かい泥岩に化石として残っているということがなかったならば、いったいそれらが鳥類であったかどうか疑いをはさんだであろう。

〖注〗 **so far found**「それまでに発見されたところの」。**so unlikely . . . that** so . . . that の関係になる。**if it were not for the lucky accident**「幸運な偶然がなかったならば」。訳文ではここを副詞句のようにした。**their having been embedded**=the fact that they had been embedded. 化石になっていることを言う。**in such fine mud that** such . . . that の関係になる。**the imprint is still preserved to us**「その痕跡が今なおわれわれに残されている」。

**988.** 彼はびっこのため停車場へ歩いてゆくのにたっぷり時間の余裕を見ておかなければならなかった。ちょうど彼が出かけようとしたとき、彼の友だちが話をするためにひょっこりはいってこなかったなら、万事うまくいったであろうに。

〚注〛 **on accout of**...「...のために」。**in stepped a friend** は a friend stepped in を転倒させたもの。それは「ひょっこりはいってきた」というような強調的な言い方と、a friend を修飾する長い Clause があるから。

**989.** この前の秋にたくわえておいた穀物のたくわえがなかったならば、じきにそれは餓死するであろう。

〚注〛 **die of**...「...で死ぬ」、類例：—What did he *die of*? (彼は何病で死んだか) He *died of* consumption. (肺病で死んだ)

**990.** 希望をもって延ばすのでなければ人生は短いものである。

**991.** 彼女は、違約金の束縛がなかったなら、ミス・シャープを解雇したであろう。

---

### (108)

**992.** 彼がその顔と会話とをオリヴィアの方へ向けたのであるから、彼を私たちの家へ引きつけたものはオリヴィアであるということは、もはや疑いをいれなかった。

**993.** それはとにかく、ひょうは [われわれとひょうとの間を] へだてている火が燃えきってしまったら、すぐさま [われわれに] おどりかかったろうということは、ほとんど疑いがなかった。

〚注〛 **intervening**「間にはさまっている」。

**994.** 1909年の末数カ月間に、東京および横浜でゴム輪を人力車に用いることがにわかにはやってきた。この流行が地方のほとんどすべての大都会に広がるだろうということは疑いがなかった。

〚注〛 **solid rubber tyres** は pneumatic tire (空気入れタイヤ)に対し空気入れでないのをいう。tyre=tire.

**995.** 私はこの頃たびたびあなたのことを聞き及びました。定めしあなたも私のことをお聞きになったでしょう。私は陸軍少佐オールックです。

〚注〛 **have heard much of you** こういう場合の much は「何度も」と訳してさしつかえない、類例：—Have you seen *anything of* him lately? (近ごろあの方にお会いですか) I have seen *nothing of* him of late. (近ごろいっこう会いません) **of late**=lately.

**996.** ニュートンの老祖母は、孫のことをかれこれと話すことはけっして飽(あ)きなかったであろうと思う。「家の孫はそのうちにりっぱな職人に

なるでしょう。アイザックはきっと出世をして死ぬまでには金持になるにちがいありません」などと言ったことであろう。

〚注〛 **weary of**=tired of. 「倦(う)む」。**make** はここでは become の意味、類例：—You will *make* a good worker. (あなたはりっぱな勤労者になるでしょう) A good daughter will *make* a good wife. (孝行な娘は夫に仕えて貞淑な妻となる) **one of these days**「遠からず」「その中に」。

**997.** それよりもなおいいことは、就眠前1時間くらい散歩するか、あるいは仲よしの友と愉快に雑談するがいい。そうすれば、身体は、そのまま放任しておくと別に人為を加えなくても、きっと必要なだけの休息を取るものである[から心配はない]。

〚注〛 **chat** 打ちくつろいだよもやまの話をいう。**nature** はここでは飲食休養などを要する人間の肉体の意と見てよい。**she** は nature を受ける。

## (109)

**998.** なるほど、義務の念は時折自分の仲間に不愉快な思いをさせるようなことをあなたにさせるかもしれない。しかしあなたが親切な心を持っていること、利己主義を超越していること、仲間の幸福を促進するためには自分の個人的便宜を喜んで犠牲にすること、が了解されれば、あなたは友だちに不足することはないであろう。

〚注〛 **make sacrifice of**...「...を犠牲にする」。

**999.** その知識がなくても、あるいは2に2を加えて場合によっては5になるかもしれないと信じていても、政府をくつがえすことはできるかもしれない、けれども一つの機械を製作することは けっしてできないし、もし舟を所有していたとすれば、その舟をどこの港へでももって行くことは全然不可能であるだろう。

〚注〛 政体の変革などということは数学的論理によらなくてもできるかもしれないが、数学がなくては機械もできず、舟を運転することもできないという主旨。**that knowledge** とは 2+2=4 ということをさしている。**in a certain environment**「事情によっては」。**government**「政府」「政体」。**were in possession of**=possessed.

**1000.** なるほどナポレオンは一人しかなかった。しかしまた一方から考えれば、ふつうのアメリカ青年の前途をさえぎるアルプスはかのコルシカ人が越えた峰ほど高くも、危険でもないのである。

〔注〕 the Alps「アルプス山脈」。the Corsican とは Napoleon をさす。

**1001.** 私としては、実際雨季を好む、なるほど、雨季にはむしろまったく気持ちがよいとは言えないほど内に閉じこもっていなければならない、しかしその時われわれは少なくともそこで目をさまして活動しているし、また外出し得る時には戸外の世界がそれだけにいっそうおもしろい。

〔注〕 **for my part**=as for me; so far as I am concerned「私としては」。**rather more than is agreeable** の more than は not の意味で、rather disagreeably と言うのに等しい。

**1002.** 自分の服装や風采(ふうさい)に無頓着(むとんじゃく)でだらしのない人は他の事についても無頓着のことが多い。なるほど、偉人には時に自分の風采にまったく無頓着の人があるが、しかし彼らはそれにもかかわらず偉大なのであって、それがために偉大なのではない。

〔注〕 **personal appearance**「容貌」「風采」。**in spite of this**「これ(=無頓着)にもかかわらず」。**in consequence of it**「その(=無頓着の)結果として」。

**1003.** だれでも自己の身中に金鉱を蔵していて、その富はただ自己の勤勉(の程度)にのみ制限される。もっとも、時としては、ほかによい名がないからわれわれが運と呼んでいるところのものを欠いている場合には、勤勉も用をなさないことはある。

**1004.** 書物に対する大きな愛着とは何であろう? それは、あらゆる過去の時代の偉大かつ善良な人々と、親しく知り合うようなものなのである。なるほど、本はたなの上にあるのを見ると黙っている。しかし黙ってはいるが、図書室にはいると、私はまるで死んだ人たちがそこにいるような気がする。そしてこれらの本に質問を発すれば答えてくれることを私は知っている。

〔注〕 **personal introduction**=being personally introduced「親しく紹介されること」。**silent as they are**=though they are silent. (82) 参照。**the dead**=dead people.

---

### (110)

**1005.** 実務においてと同様、芸術および知識のあらゆる分野においても、自己の精力を浪費し、また正しい方面に費せば自分自身のためにも世

間のためにも偉大な結果を生み出すような能力を濫費(らんぴ)している人々を、われわれはいかにたびたび見いだすことであろう。

〖注〗 **in the right lines would produce great result** は「正しい方面に費されたならば偉大な結果を生ずるだろう」の意味で, in the right lines が条件の文句である。(98) 参照。

**1006.** 働かないで、しかも働くことを恥と思うような人は非難すべきであると共にまたあわれむべきである。(世の中に)無知とぜいたくほどおそろしいものはない。

〖注〗 **thinks himself** (to be) **above it**=thinks that he is above working 「自分は労働するような人間じゃないと考える」、参考:—Though poor, I am *above selling* my country. (たとい貧乏でも国を売るような卑劣な人間じゃない) He is *above asking* questions. (彼は質問することを恥と思って質問しない)

**1007.** まず第一に、彼は旅行に対する計画を立てた。地図を買った、本を読んだ、そして、十分熟考の後、一番ためにもなりまた愉快も得られそうなある道すじを選んだ。

〖注〗 **afford**=furnish; bestow「与える」「供する」。

**1008.** 真昼の 太陽の 一番暑いときには、砂は 旅行者の 眼をくらまし、ちょうど天に太陽があるように砂の下にも今一つの太陽があるように思わせる。

**1009.** どんな 種類の 食物でも 食後 2 時間以内に 食べるものではない。そしてきまった食事と食事との間隔は少なくとも 4 時間なければならない。夕食は就寝前 2 時間になすべきである。それは睡眠中、からだの他の諸部分と同様に、胃にも休息を与えるためである。

〖注〗 **food** は「食物」、**meal** は朝食夕食などいう「食事」。**that...may** が目的をあらわすことは (43) に詳説した。

**1010.** 私は、簡素な生活は愛国者の義務でもあるが、またキリスト教徒の義務だと信じている。フランス人は生活のしかたをわれわれよりもよっぽどよくわきまえている、彼らは浪費をほとんど本能的に避けるのだ。

**1011.** 健康に必要な条件は実に簡単明白である。規則正しい習慣、日々の運動、清潔、および万事につけ——飲物においても食事においても——節度あること、これらを守ればたいていの人は健康を保てる。

**1012.** 善に対しても、悪に対すると同様に非常に大なる資質が彼の性質

中にある。前者を発展せしめるか後者を発展せしめるかは事情次第だ。

〚注〛 capacity「才能」「器量」、類例:—*a capacity for* tolerance (人を入れる雅量) *a capacity for* great achievement (大事をなす器量). **rest with...**「...次第」、類例:—It *rests with* you to decide. (君の意見(<small>いかん</small>)次第だ) **the one, the other** については (24) 参照。

**1013.** 母の温順なる性質と共に父の勇気をことごとく承け継いだこの少年たちのために、りっぱな出世の道が開かれた。

〚注〛 career はここでは将来の進路、出世の道などの意味、類例:—In Japan, all careers are open to the poorest boys. (日本ではすべての出世の道がどんな貧乏人のこどもに対してでも開いている=どんな貧乏人でもどんな出世でも望める)

**1014.** 音楽の耳のない人たちに関するかぎり、彼らが音楽を学ぼうとするのは、自分や他人の絶えざるかんしゃくのたねになるばかりでなく、時間と金の浪費であろう。

〚注〛 **ear** 聞き分ける力。**so far as...are concerned**「...の関するかぎり」、(41) 参照。it would be 以下の文章は、as well as...to others をカッコに入れて考えれば、it...for...to の形である、類例:—*It* is necessary *for* you *to* go there. (君がそこへ行くことが必要だ)

**1015.** 召使の待遇はよくすべきだ、人情がそれを必要とするばかりでなく、よく待遇しないと不愉快な不正直な召使となるからである、こういうことを口にするのはたやすい。

〚注〛 **humanity requires** こういう抽象名詞を主語にした語法をよく覚えること。「人道上...を必要とする」とか「慈悲心がそうさせる」などの表現になる。**otherwise**=if they are not treated well.

**1016.** 私はと言えば、私にもっとも考えさせた本からもっとも多く利益を得たし、またもっとも多くの楽しみをも得た。そして困難がひとたび征服されると、これらの本が、私の記憶と理解力との中のみならず、私の愛情の中にも、もっとも深く根を張った本となるのである。

〚注〛 **strike the deepest root**「もっとも深く根を張る」。

**1017.** 私はいくつかの教室を参観して、学校生活を規制していると思われるきびしい規律に感心もしたがゆううつにもなった。

〚注〛 **impressed and depressed** にはごろ合わせの妙味がある。この文はソ連の教育の話である。

**1018.** 英国が18世紀にあのように有名になったのは、なかんずく、そ

の自由のためであった。大陸からの観察者はそこに自由国家の模範と、個人の自由の本家と、この両者を見いだしたのである。

〚注〛 **in it** の it はもちろん England.

**1019.** 君が金持であろうと貧乏であろうと、けっしてだれからでも何でも借りることをするな。買う余裕のないものはなくてすませよ。これはまったく習慣の問題で、この習慣を養うことのできない者はただに他人を害するばかりでなく、また自己にとっても幾多不幸の種をたくわえるものである。

〚注〛 **allow oneself to**...「自分を抑制せずして...する」こと。**owe** の用法:—I *owe you* 100 yen. (ぼくは君に 100 円負債がある)　**afford** は財政が許す許さぬ、余裕の有る無しをいう語、類例:—I *cannot afford* such extravagance. (私はそんなぜいたくはできない)　I *cannot afford* to buy such a thing. (そんなものを買う余裕はない)　**fail to**=cannot.　**lay up**=store; put by「蓄積する」。**a store of** は a lot of などにならって「たくさんの(蓄積)」の意味、類例:—He has *a store of* wisdom. (彼は豊富な知恵がある)

**1020.** その見知らぬ人の話は、愉快で また同時に有益であったので、私はその話をつづけてもらいたいと思った、けれども、だいぶん夜もふけて、もはや翌日の疲労に備えるために寝て休息すべき時刻となった。

〚注〛 **which was**...=because it was... として of it の次へ回してみよ。**induced me to wish for continuance of it**「私の心を誘って会話の継続を願わせた」。**it was time to**... は「...すべき時間であった」の意味、high が加わると、「もうとっくに...すべき時刻」の意味となる、類例:—It is *high time* the boy should be put to school. (もうとっくに学校へ出してよい時分だ)　**retire** は retire to repose, retire to rest, retire to bed, retire for the night などとも用いられ、寝室に退いて床につくこと。**refreshment** ここでは「休養」の意味。

---

## (111)

**1021.** わたしはシーザーを愛する心が薄かったのではない、ローマを愛する心がもっと深かったのである。

**1022.** ぼくはおもな役はみな自分でやった——というのは何もぼくがほかのこどもより芝居がじょうずであったからというのではない、芝居小屋がぼくの物だったからである。

〚注〛 これはこどもが芝居のまねをして遊んだときの話。

**1023.** 彼はこう言った、「ただあなたがおもしろい気質の方で、服装の点で世間の人たちをからかって見たかっただけのことで、あなたのようなお金持の紳士を信用するのを恐れるつもりはありません」。

〚注〛 **he hoped he wasn't...** は直接話法にすれば、"I hope I am not afraid..." となる。**play larks on**「～をからかう」「～にふざける」。**the public**「世間の人」。この文は、大金持が、こじきのようなぼろ服を着ているとの話である。

**1024.** 人々はこれらの英雄を、彼らの人格と性格が完全であったためではなく、彼らが勇敢で、非利己的で、すばらしい行ないをなし得たがゆえに、愛し尊敬するのである。

**1025.** たまたま少年が強壮でないからといって、必ずしも海上生活がその少年に適しないという結論は出て来ない。海上生活はその少年を強壮な人にするのにちょうど持ってこいのことであるかもしれない。

〚注〛 **it** は that 以下を代表する。**follow** は「つづく」「ついで起こる」の意味から論理上（結論として）つづいてくることをあらわす、類例：—If he writes poetry, it *naturally follows* that he must understand poetry.（詩を作るなら詩がわかる道理だ）**the very thing required to...**「...するために必要であつらえ向きのこと」。

**1026.** 鳥類は生来世界中でもっとも喜びに満ちた生き物である。それは諸君が鳥を見たり、さえずるのを聞いたりするとき、鳥がいつも諸君に喜びを与えるからではなく、鳥がほかのどんな動物よりも喜びを感ずるからである。ほかの動物はふつうまじめで厳粛そうに見える、そしてその多くは物悲しそうにさえ見える。ところが鳥類はたいがいその動作や様子できわめてうれしげに振舞うのである。

〚注〛 **in the world** は the most を強めるに用いたもの、(39) 参照。**for the most part**＝mostly. 類例：—The students are, *for the most part*, from the provinces.（学生はたいてい地方出だ）**show themselves joyous**「うれしそうに振舞う」、類例：—to *show oneself (to be) a gentleman*（紳士らしい振舞いをする）

**1027.** ある意味で世界の均衡が変わろうとしている。それは単に時間単位で測った距離が極端に短縮されるということではない、また、奥地の町が頻繁な交通の要路に浮かび上がってくるというだけではなく、灯台に匹敵するようなものが帝国の前哨（しょう）として遠く大洋の真中に建てられることになるだろうというだけではない。

〖注〗 この文は **not merely that** だけ出ていて、後にあるべき **but that** のようなものは現われていない。

**1028.** われわれはもはや案内書どおりには生活しないで、むしろ案内書にほめてある名所を除外し、案内書には出ていない多くの物が、博物館や大寺院のように、特記されている新しいその土地の地図を自分で作り上げた。だからといって一般の案内書を悪く言うつもりはない。

〖注〗 **that the guidebook exalts**「案内書がほめちぎるところの」で、sights の修飾節。**stand out prominently**「特に目立つ」。**not that**=it is not to be inferred, however, that.

## (112)

**1029.** どんな長い夜でもいつかは明ける。

**1030.** どんな良馬でもつまずくことがあるように、どんな良妻でもぶつぶついうことはあるものだ。

**1031.** 最初のうち金のはいってき方がおそくとも失望してはならない、運の悪いのもそういつまでも続くものではないから。またひょっと初めに金がどんどんはいるようなことがあっても、それをみな使ってしまってはならない。よいことも、悪いことと同じようにいつまでも続くものではないということを思い、また年月を経るにしたがってだんだん金がたくさん要るようになるかもしれないということを思って、若干を貯蓄して不幸の日に備えねばならない。実業に従事するもので最初あまり運がよかったために産を失ったものはたくさんある。

〖注〗 冒頭の **if** は though の意である。**come in**（金が）「はいる」、これを名詞にしたのが income（収入）である。**if it happens that...**「たまたま...ということがあれば」。**lay up**（=save）**for a rainy day**「不幸の日のためにたくわえておく」、for のかわりに against を用いて、「備える」意味をあらわしてもよい。**demand on your purse**「財布に対する要求」、すなわち「金の必要」。**many a man** は many men よりもかえって意味が強い。**be ruined**「倒産する」。

## 索 引 凡 例

△索引中の数字はページ数ではなく、例題の番号であり、括弧を施した数字は章の番号である。章を掲げた場合はその章中にある例題番号は省いた。たとえば as soon as は (57) をもって代表させているから、その章中 as soon as を含む例題 522, 523, 524 等は省略してある。

△索引は成句を主としたけれども、単語の重要なものも加えた。なお文法上の術語及びいわゆる「公式」をも掲げて各方面から本文をさぐるに遺憾のないことを期した。

△たとえば Participial Construction のことを知ろうとすれば索引 P の部に

     Participial Construction ............................................(79)

とあることによって第 79 章 (page 204) を見ればよい。同様に 'have＋Object＋Past Participle' の公式に従うものは第 71 章を見るべきだというふうである。(本文では日本語に直したのが多いから照会されたい。)

△動詞はすべて原形をもって挙げたが、動詞の sign である to は後に移した。たとえば索引に

     attend to, to .........................................................940

とあるのは to attend to の to を後に移したもので例題 940—"...who are ready to *attend to* anybody's business..." とあるのに応ずるわけである。

△動詞 to be も多くは後に移した、たとえば索引に

     ashamed (of), to be ...............................................769

とあるのは to be ashamed of の to be を後に移したので、例題 769—"...need not have *been ashamed of*" とあるのに応ずるわけである。

△ただし to be の to だけを後に移したものもあり、to be fond of を be fond of, to としている。

△冠詞もまた多く後に移した。たとえば a man of the world を man of the world, a とし、the incarnation of を incarnation of, the としたよ

うにである。

△代名詞はすべて one をもってあらわした、たとえば本文中に " after *his* own heart " とあるのを索引では after *one's* own heart とし、本文中に " devote *ourselves* to ... " とあるのを索引では devote *oneself* to, to と したようにである。

# INDEX

( )内の数字は各章の番号、( )のない数字は例題番号を示す。

## A

abandon oneself to, to ...... 150
a bit of .......................... 354
able to ........................289, 1024
above reproach, to be......... 50
above selling, to be............ 764
Absolute Infinitive ............ (72)
Absolute Participle ............ (81)
Abstruct Noun+itself ...... (5)
according to ............28, 140, 276
accustomed to, to be .........
 ..................139, 170, 319, 466
acquiesce in, to ............... 74
Adjective + of = Present
 Participle ..................... (75)
a few ............................... (19)
after all .................265, 333, 497
after one's own heart......... 697
against .......................... 303
a good many..................... 546
a great deal of...............351, 847
a great many ..................33, 546
a great number of ............ 129
agree with, to .................. 856
alike...and ..................... (110)
a little ............................. (19)
all+Abstract Noun ............ (5)
all attention, to be ............ 36
all at once...................... 7

all but.............................(102)
all...but ..........................(102)
all+ears, to be................. (5)
allow...to, to ..................... 602
all+Plural Common Noun (5)
all (that) one has............... (34)
all the better...for ............ (17)
all the way........................ 921
all through ..................... 149
all too .............................. (22)
a man of learning ............ (1)
a man of his means ......... (1)
and that........................... (28)
and yet .......................203, 345
an oyster of a man........... (2)
anxious about, to be ......... 84
anxious to..., to be.........523, 703
anything but...............466, (102)
appeal to, to ..................29, 142
apply to, to ..................... 153
apt to, to be ......34, 141, 204, 212
as (=though)..................... (82)
as a matter of fact ...241, 375, 684
as...as any ........................ (38)
as...as ever ..................280, (38)
as far as............364, 365, 369, 585
as few............................... 458
as for ............................... 157
ashamed of, to be............... 769
as if ......87, 106, 341,865,(95), 1008

[ 459 ]

| | |
|---|---|
| as it is | (80) |
| as it were | 63, (95) |
| as lief as | 831 |
| as long as | (41), 389 |
| as many | (48) |
| as much | (48) |
| as much as | 85 |
| as regards | 198 |
| as...so | 307, (36), 576 |
| as so many | (50) |
| as so much | (50) |
| as soon as | 40, (57), 993 |
| as soon as possible | 821 |
| a sort of | 20 |
| as though | (95) |
| as to | 6, 153, 819, 987 |
| as well as | 177, 420, 466, 474, (110) |
| at a distance | 296 |
| at any rate | 362 |
| at best | 260 |
| at first | 944, 980, 1031 |
| at hand | 430 |
| at last | 176, 390, 442, 661 |
| at length | 661 |
| at night | 663 |
| at once | 352, 783 |
| at once...and | (110), 1020 |
| at one's bidding | 206 |
| at one's disposal | 216, 298 |
| at one's expense | 809 |
| at one's instigation | 90 |
| at present | 42 |
| at the age of | 287 |
| at the expense of | 843 |
| at the mercy of, to be | 137, 150 |
| at the thought of | 912 |
| attend to, to | 940 |
| at times | 968, 998 |
| awake to find, to | (68) |
| aware of, to be | 704 |
| away (=constantly) | 83 |

## B

| | |
|---|---|
| be able to, to | 293 |
| be + Adjective + of, to = Verb | (75) |
| be after, to | 104 |
| be back, to | 58 |
| be capable of, to | 134, 722 |
| be fond of, to | 134, 693, 703 |
| before | (55) |
| before long | (58) |
| behind one's back | 40, 236 |
| be liable to, to | 110, 403 |
| believe in, to | 564, 642, 721 |
| be put in authority over, to | 665 |
| be to, to | 132 |
| bereft of | 618 |
| beside | 518 |
| besides | 184 |
| be so kind as to, to | (45) |
| bestow...on, to | 290 |
| be the matter what it may | (93) |
| better off, to be | 140, 561 |
| be used to, to | (64) |
| both...and | 844, 881, 884, (110) |
| bound to, to be | 32 |
| brave as he was | (82) |
| bring...to birth, to | 440 |
| busy oneself with, to | 200 |
| but for | (107) |
| but (=only) | (100) |
| but that | (107) |
| but that, do not deny | (108) |
| but (=that+not) | (103) |

# INDEX

but too ........................(22), 207
but (=who+not)...............(103)
by accident .................178, 597
by degrees........................ 597
by far ............................. 750
by means of ..................... 396
by no means..................... 6
by oneself ........................ (7)
by the time ..................... 539
by virtue of ..................... 101

## C

cannot afford to ............... 1019
cannot but........................ (99)
cannot fail to .........224, 916, 917
cannot help—ing .........288, (99)
cannot refrain from............ 918
cannot...too ..................... (23)
cannot...without ............... 678
care for, to...............728, 925, 942
cast one's eye on..., to ...... 239
catch sight of, to............... 533
cause...to, to .................... 307
cease to be, to................... 233
chance upon, to ............... 178
clad in, to be .................. 126
clear...of, to .................619, 622
come right, to .................. 687
come to light, to............... 819
come what may.................. (93)
commend one to, to ......... 728
compare to, to................... 213
compare with, to............... 240
compete with, to............... 92
composed of, to be............ 63
Concessive Clause ............ (93)
Conditional Clause............ (98)
conform to, to .................. 168

conscious of, to be............ 914
consist in, to...................140, 438
consist of, to..................... 592
consult, to ...............430, 582, 709
content with, to be ...98, 579, 853
count on, to ..................... 421

## D

dare not............................ 401
dashed to pieces, to be ......
................................566, 568
delivered of a child, to be... (67)
dependent upon, to be ...... 707
depend on (or upon), to ...
.....................307, 340, 722, 761
deprive...of, to .................. 661
derive...from, to ......710, 812, 879
destined to, to be............... 123
devote oneself to, to ......... 84
die of, to........................... 989
directly .......................(57), 538
displeased with, to be......... 910
distinguish...from, to ......155, 579
do (as Pro-verb)............472, (62)
do for, to ......................... 763
do (of Emphasis)...............
.............313, 504, (62), 601, 772
do sums, to ..................... 779
do well, to.....................208, 996
do without, to ...............52, 1019
do with, to........................ 860
drop by drop..................... 901
due to................... ......... 54

## E

each other ........................ 483
ease...of, to ..................... (67)
else ........................101, 102, 899

| | |
|---|---|
| embodiment of, the | (5) |
| engaged in, to be | 678, 706, 740 |
| ere long | 547 |
| even if | 496, 623 |
| ever so (=however) | (53) |
| ever so many | (53) |
| expressive of | (75) |

## F

| | |
|---|---|
| fail to, to | 112 |
| fall asleep, to | 257 |
| fall a victim to, to | 974 |
| fall back upon, to | 137 |
| fall in one's way, to | 592 |
| fall into abuse | 403 |
| fare well, to | 776 |
| far from | 80 |
| feed on (*or* upon), to | 738 |
| few | (19), 335, 482 |
| few, if any | (52) |
| fight one's way, to | 772 |
| find fault with, to | 236 |
| fix one's eyes on (*or* upon), to | 106, 401 |
| fond of, to be | 693 |
| for a good while | 597 |
| for a moment | 625 |
| for a while | 303 |
| force one's way through, to | 397 |
| for ever | 976 |
| for example | 153 |
| for fear...may | (44) |
| for good and all | 620 |
| for instance | 305, 564 |
| for itself | (8) |
| for its own sake | (8) |
| forget...in, to | 17 |
| for my part | 1001, 1016 |
| for oneself | (8) |
| for one thing | 825 |
| for that matter | 750 |
| for the first time | 66 |
| for the most part | 1026 |
| for want of | 1003 |
| free...from, to | 54 |
| from the point of view | 706 |
| from time to time | 219 |

## G

| | |
|---|---|
| gaze at, to | 312, 873 |
| generally speaking | (81) |
| get around, to | 412 |
| get nowhere, to | 5, 24 |
| get+Object+Past Participle | (71) |
| get on with, to | 340 |
| get rid of, to | 622 |
| get through, to | 893 |
| get together, to | 129 |
| give attention to, to | 202 |
| give up, to | 51 |
| give way, to | 386 |
| glad to see one, to be | (68) |
| glance at, to | 529 |
| go ashore, to | 58 |
| going to, to be | 57 |
| go on, to | 97, 1031 |
| go to the devil, to | 51 |
| go without, to | 140 |
| grateful to, to be | 345 |
| grind away, to | 83 |
| guilty of, to be | 702 |

## H

| | |
|---|---|
| had best | (91), 828 |
| had better | (91) |
| had it not | (96) |

happen to, to...... 1025
hardly ......174, (20), 862, 909
hardly...before ...... (57)
hardly...when ...... (57)
hardly...without ...... 278
have a dislike to, to ...... (65)
have a genius for, to ...... (65)
have a liking for, to ...... (65)
have at hand, to ...... 430
have call on, to...... 142
have got, to ...... 42
have in common, to ...... 102
have no choice but, to ...... 915
have no idea of, to...... 553
have + Object + Past Participle ...... (71)
have+Object+Root Infinitive ...... (70)
have seen better days......373, 669
have some one come, to...... (70)
have the+Abstract Noun+Infinitive ...... (45)
have the+Abstract Noun+of+Gerund ...... (45)
have to, to......
......58, 78, 127, 176, 215, 435, 901
have to oneself, to ......93, 94
hear say, to ......(69), 640
hear tell of, to......(69), 638
he shall ...... (86)
he that ...... 934
he who ......276, 780, 835
his royal highness ...... 207
hold one's peace, to...... 780
hot from the oven ...... 83
however...may......244, (93), 914

# I

I can tell you ...... 169
I dare say ...... 867
if any ...... (52)
if at all ...... (52)
if ever...... (52)
if I were...... (94)
if one were...... (94)
ignorant of, to be......700, 849
Imperative...and ...... (60)
Imperative...or ...... (60)
impersonation of, the......(5), 49
impossible to overpraise, to be...... (23)
in addition to ...... 793
in a sense ......922, 933
incarnation of, the ...... (5)
in consequence of......219, 1002
indeed...but ......(109)
in excess of ...... 128
in fact......105, 111, 456
in general ......204, 844, 456
in great haste ...... 51
in itself ...... (6)
in life ...... 964
in one's behalf...... 304
in one's life ...... 66
in one's power...... 295
in one's turn......383, 956
in one's way...... 178
in order that...may ...74, (43), 919
in order to......228, 718
in person ...... 411
in proportion to ...... 392
in regard to ......211, 305
in scores...... 219
in short......80, 933

| | |
|---|---|
| in sight, to be | 921 |
| inspire one with, to | 69, 959 |
| in spite of | 1002 |
| in spite of oneself | 355, 876 |
| instead of | 55, 75, 204, 289, 597 |
| interested in, to be | 137 |
| in the case of | 129 |
| in the course of | 33, 366 |
| in the darkness | 447 |
| in the event of | 392 |
| in the first place | 1007 |
| in the meantime | 570 |
| in the world | 115, 249, 329, (39), 1026 |
| in time | 623 |
| introduce oneself, to | 673 |
| in vain | 790 |
| it happens that | 1003, 1031 |
| it is an ill wind that | (112) |
| it is impossible to overpraise | (23) |
| it is in...as in | (37) |
| it is no use crying | (74) |
| it is right that one should | (90) |
| it is true...but | 149, 959, (109) |
| it is with...as with | (37) |
| it matters not (*or* little) | 123, 504 |
| it transpires that | 967 |
| it was a long time before | (55), 507 |
| I wish I were | (94) |

## K

| | |
|---|---|
| keep...for oneself, to | 82 |
| keep...in sight, to | 735 |
| keep...to oneself, to | 95 |
| keep to, to | 395 |
| keep within bounds, to | 881 |

| | |
|---|---|
| know better, to | 344 |

## L

| | |
|---|---|
| last of all | 634 |
| laugh at, to | 422 |
| lay by, to | 392 |
| lay down one's life for, to | 166 |
| lay up, to | 989, 1019, 1031 |
| learn to, to | 149 |
| leave behind, to | 339 |
| left to oneself | 96, 997 |
| lest...might | 404 |
| lest...should | (44) |
| let the matter be what it may | (93) |
| like so many | (50) |
| likely to, to be | 5, 136, 153 |
| listen to, to | 904 |
| little | (19), 369, 710, 763, 933 |
| little dream, to | 188 |
| little imagine, to | 185 |
| little, if any | (52) |
| little, if anything | 488 |
| little, if at all | (52) |
| little know, to | 187 |
| little think, to | 186 |
| live above, to | 853 |
| live upon, to | 184 |
| living, as I do, | (80) |
| load one with, to | 85 |
| long before | 903 |
| look around, to | 45, 627 |
| look one in the face, to | (66) |
| look one's affairs in the face, to | 608 |
| look upon...as, to | 20, 111, 204 |
| lose not a moment, to | 525 |
| lost in, to be | 442 |

| | |
|---|---|
| not so much as | (47) |
| not so much...as | (47) |
| not that...but that | (111) |
| not the less for | (17) |
| not the less that | 152 |
| not till | (59) |
| not to mention | (73) |
| not to speak of | (73) |
| not until | (59) |
| no use crying, it is | (74) |

## O

| | |
|---|---|
| obliged to, to be | 198 |
| occupied with, to be | 959 |
| of + Abstract Noun | (1), (76) |
| of consequence | 185, 707 |
| of course | 99, 163, 354, 553 |
| of eminence | 1 |
| of importance | (76), 706 |
| of it | 729 |
| of late | 995 |
| of no account | 715 |
| of no avail | 712 |
| of old | 384 |
| of oneself | (9) |
| of one's own accord | (9) |
| of one's own free will | 88 |
| of one's own head | 90 |
| of one's own —ing | (77) |
| of value, to be | 711 |
| on account of | 248, 581, 988, 1018 |
| on all sides | 944 |
| on board the ship | 553 |
| once more | 181 |
| one after another | 196 |
| on earth | (39) |
| one day | 532 |
| one of these days | 996 |
| one more...and | (61) |
| oneself | (11) |
| one...the other | (24) |
| one thing...another | (26) |
| on good terms, to be | 945 |
| on hand | 606 |
| only to | (68) |
| only too...to | (22) |
| on no account | 817 |
| on occasion | 633 |
| on one's part | 145 |
| on one's way | 810 |
| on the contrary | 422 |
| on the other hand | 305 |
| otherwise | ...76, 476, 660, (97), 1015 |
| ought to | 50, 102, 594, 723 |
| out of | 924 |
| out upon | 928 |
| owe to, to | 217, 881 |
| owing to | 248, 441, 545 |

## P

| | |
|---|---|
| Participial Construction | (79) |
| part with, to | 579 |
| pat one on the..., to | 600, (66) |
| personification of, the | (5) |
| personified | (5) |
| play larks on, to | 1023 |
| plenty of | 988 |
| point of view | 80 |
| possessed by, to be | 981 |
| possessed of, to be | 625, (75), 695 |
| possessed with, to be | 657 |
| prefer...to, to | 390 |
| prepared for, to be | 811, 952 |
| present itself, to | 381 |
| Present Tense | (63) |

# INDEX

## M

| | |
|---|---|
| make a cat's paw of, to | 725 |
| make a man of, to | 60, (78), 1025 |
| make allowances, to | 38 |
| make ducks and drakes of, to | 727 |
| make hard or tail of, to | 733 |
| make it a rule to, to | 582, 893 |
| make light of, to | 729, 762 |
| make much of, to | 724, 728 |
| make one's claim for, to | 71 |
| make one's way, to | 196 |
| make sacrifices of, to | 998 |
| make shift, to | 303 |
| make the best of, to | 722, 730 |
| make the most of, to | 726 |
| make up one's mind, to | 544 |
| make use of, to | 81 |
| man of letters, a | 592 |
| man of sense, a | 4, 695 |
| man of the world, a | 201 |
| many a | 939, 1031 |
| master of one's trade | 287 |
| may as well | (84) |
| may well | (83) |
| might as well | (84) |
| might have been | 127, 402, (98) |
| more or less | 620 |
| much of | 357, 374 |
| much the more | 145 |

## N

| | |
|---|---|
| necessary to, to be | 229, 896 |
| Negative + Comparative = Superlative | (15) |
| never...but | (105) |
| never so | (83) |
| never to return | (68) |
| never...without | (105) |
| no...but | 93, (103) |
| no doubt | 828 |
| no fear but that | (108), 997 |
| no fear but what | 996 |
| no good trying | (74) |
| no little | 182 |
| no longer | 143, 289, 567 |
| no matter | 279, 524, 573, (93) |
| no more...than | (18), 492 |
| none but | (4), (100) |
| none the less | (17) |
| none the worse | 151 |
| no one but | (100) |
| no rule but, there is | (103) |
| no rule that has not, there is | (106) |
| no...so...but | (104) |
| no sooner than | (57), 550 |
| not a few | (19) |
| not a little | (19) |
| not alone...but | 282 |
| not at all | 241 |
| not...because | (111) |
| not...but | 63, 144, 311, 334 |
| not every | 761 |
| nothing but | (100) |
| nothing can be simpler | (15) |
| nothing can be so simple as | (15) |
| nothing of | 372, 450 |
| nothing short of | 889 |
| nothing...so...but | (104) |
| not in the least | 452 |
| not...long before | (56) |
| not more...than | (18) |
| not necessarily | 979 |
| not only...but | 50, 285, (110) |

prevent one from —ing, to ..................................387, 866
proud of, to be...............254, 769
provide...with, to............116, 575
pull oneself together, to...... 512
put...in order, to............... 490
put on, to......................... 447

## R

rarely ............................... 208
ready to, to be...................
...............479, 547, 723, 856, 940
reduced to poverty, to be... 891
refrain from, to.................. 408
regard...as, to .........103, 581, 684
relieve...of, to .................. 616
rely upon, to..................... 466
revenged upon, to be......... 723
rid...of, to.....................(67), 630
rob...of, to......................... (67)
run into debt, to............... 595
run short, to..................... 482

## S

say to oneself, to ............91, 805
scarcely ......(20), 190, 474, 519, 550
scarcely...before ............... (57)
scarcely...when.................. (57)
seize upon, to .................. 867
seldom .........................(20), 891
seldom, if ever.................. (52)
set about, to..................... 466
set oneself to do, to ......... 55
set out, to......................... 516
shift for oneself, to............77, 78
short of, to be.................. 945
should I fail..................... (96)
should (of Duty or Obligation) ...745, 688, (89), 1009, 1015
should (of Surprise)............ (88)
should have done............... (89)
shrink from, to.................. 2
show off, to ...................... 406
so (also) am I .................. (54)
so as to........................(42), 583
so...as to ......................(42), 758
so-called........................375, 670
so far ............................... 987
so far as ...............(41), 711, 1014
so (indeed) I am .............. (54)
so long as.........(41), 661, 859, 933
so many........................... (49)
somehow .......................... 7
some...others.................... 77
something of ...............320, (40)
so much so that ............... (51)
so...that......158, 192, (43), 587, 744
..., so that...............191, (43), 585
(so) that...may .................. (43)
so to speak....................677, 687
spare of, to be.................. 127
speak ill of, to...............27, 1028
stand by, to ..................... 269
stand over, to .................. 708
stare at, to........................ 513
stare one in the face, to...... 606
strange to relate (or say)...671, 678
strike one on the head, to... (66)
strip...of, to ..................... 618
strive after, to .................. 34
struck with, to be ............ 281
Subjunctive Past and Past Perfect .........344, 413, 679, (94)
subordinate...to, to ............ 210
succeed in, to .................. 3
such as ..................428, 765, 862

such...as ........................... (46)
such...that ........................ (46)
suffer from, to ................ 252, 426
Superlative+that ever ...... (38)
supplied with, to be ......... 396

## T

take advantage of, to ......... 44, 103
take a look, to ................... 73
take a walk, to................... 911
take care of, to................... 557
take leave of, to ............... 516
take one by surprise, to...... 121
take one by the hand, to... (66)
take one's share, to............ 617
take pains, to................... 175, 824
take part in, to................... 196
take possession of, to......... 570
take time, to...................... 181
talk to oneself, to............... (10)
tend to, to............... 285, 671, 975
that is to say...................... 856
that of .................. (27), 368, 826
that...may .................. (43), 1009
that...may not ................... (44)
the aged............................ 26
the+Adjective .................. (4)
the better for .................. 144
the bravest that ever lived... (38)
the+Common Noun=Abstract Noun .................. (3)
the + Comparative ... the + Comparative ...76, (16), 223, 850
the first...to ...................... 835
the incarnation of ............ (5)
the instant........................ 543
the last person to............... (14)
the letter ......................... 18

the moment ..................... (57)
the more the better............ 42
the one...the other ............ (24)
there is no —ing............... (74)
these...those .................. 230, 232
the sooner the better...... (16), 644
the sweeter for.................. 34
the truth is that ............... 33
the very ........................... (12)
the wisest man.................. (13)
think of, to....................... 77
this...that ........................ (25)
those of............................ 4, (27)
those who ........................ 1019
thousands of millions......... 31
throw light on, to ............ 711
tire of, to ........................ 254
tired of, to be ............... 656, 698
to be plain with you......... 673
to be sure...but ............... (109)
to do one justice............... 666
to express it in one word... 668
to make matters clear......... 783
to make sure..................... 664
to the purpose .................. 573
too apt to ........................ 204
too...for .......................... 6, (21)
too much so..................... 477
to oneself ........................ (10)
too...not to...................... (21)
too ready to ..................... (22)
too...to ........................... (21)
to return ........................ 672
to say nothing of............... (73)
to tell the truth ............... (72)
to the purpose.................. 573
to use a common phrase ... 669
turn...into, to ................. 60

twice as much as ............ 397

## U

unfit one for, to ............... 105
up to ............................. 522
used to ............... 40, 410, (63), 964
used to, to be .................. (64)

## V

value...above, to ............... 276
Verbs of Causation............ (70)
Verbs of Perception ......... (69)
very (*adj.*) .........39, (12), 120, 131

## W

wait for, to........................ 901
wait upon, to..................... 207
watch for, to..................... 408
well one may..................... (83)
well-to-do ........................ 30
were it not........................ (96)
what (=all the...that)......... (34)
what (=that which) ...... (30), 385
what (=what little)............ (34)
what a pity...should ......... (88)
what by...and what by ...... (29)
whatever the matter may be (93)
what is better ............... 65, (33)
what is called .................. (31)
what is the same thing...... 120
what is worse .................. 284
what makes the matter worse ........................... 288
what one is ............ (32), 366, 714
what sort of ................. 153, 339
what the dickens? ............ 348
what to do with ............... 165
what we call.................... (31)
what with...and what with ................................. 14, (29)
what X is to Y, that is A to B............................ (35)
what you call .................. (31)
whistle one's life away, to... 96
who are you that you should...? ..................... (88)
who should...but...? ........ (101)
why should I not?............ (87)
why the deuce...? ............ 317
will (of Insistence)............ (85)
will (often)........................ (63)
willing to, to be ............ 983, 998
will not (of Refusal) ......... (85)
with all ........................... 881
with care ........................ 824
with impartiality ............... 745
without ........................... (98)
without fail ..................... 263
without so much as............ (47)
worth while, to be ........... 847
would (=I wish)............... (92)
would (=wish to) ......... (92), 849
would as lief...as.............. 831
would as soon...as ........... 829
would (often) ............... 35, (63)
would rather...than............ (91)

## Y

You shall ....................... (86)

## 新々英文解釈研究
(新訂新版)

昭和33年 3月20日 第105版　昭和40年 5月 1日 改訂第31版発行
昭和40年12月25日　新訂新版発行

| 著　者 | 山　崎　　　貞 | |
|---|---|---|
| 改訂者 | 佐　山　栄太郎 | |
| 発行者 | 小　酒　井　益　蔵 | 東京都新宿区神楽坂1の2 |
| 印刷所 | 研究社印刷株式会社 | 東京都新宿区神楽坂1の2 |

発行所　研究社出版株式会社　東京都新宿区神楽坂1の2
替振口座東京83761番

定価 450 円

# 研究社・高校英語参考書

## 新々英文解釈研究
山崎貞著・佐山栄太郎増訂　¥450

収録された数百の構文成句，110余節に分った詳細な解説『山崎の新々英解』の呼称で受験生間に好評の名著。

## 最新英文解釈
佐山栄太郎著　¥330

内容の把握，英和両様の説明，書き換え，設問応答等の形で英文解釈の本道を明かにし自分の力を試せる。

## 英文解釈と構文の研究
小宮山久之助著　¥250

大学入試に出題される傾向にある現代作家を中心に長文50篇を分類，訳し方，単語，熟語，文法的盲点を解説した

## 英文解釈の徹底的研究
志賀武男著　¥380

入試の必勝は，まず与えられた英文を構文と語句の両面にわたって研究する事で，英文構成の知識を身につける

## 英文解釈の道
田中菊雄著　¥180

英文解釈上の根本要素に関して出来るだけ確実に理解力をのばすことを主眼に，例題，演習問題は実力涵養に資す

## 英文解釈一日一題
清成孝著　¥320

精選された360題の練習問題を一日に一題ずつ配当し，語法の習得に重点をおいて英文解釈力を鋭意養成する

## 新自修英文典
山崎貞著・毛利可信増訂　¥480

抽象に傾きやすい英文法を実証的に一般学生を標準として明快に説明，さらに作文，解釈にも応用した問題つき

## 英文法・英作文
太田朗著　¥380

英文法と英作文を別にやることは断片的な知識の寄せ集めに終る難がある両者を有機的に結合させた絶好の書。

## 英文法の知識
毛利可信著　¥320

段階的に知識を整理し，日本語とは大いに異なる構文を理解することを主眼に新しい時代の文法書として好評

## 演習本位活用英文法
松川昇太郎著　¥350

文法事項の講義説明だけでなく，実際問題に役立つことに留意して，反復練習する書として好評の書である。

|  |  |  |  |
|---|---|---|---|
| 高校初年 英文法教室 | 小宮山久之助著 | ¥250 | わかり易い例やユーモアを織り込んで興味を覚えさせ、文法事項や例文を通して解釈力を養わせるもの。 |
| 新自修英作文 | 毛利良雄著 | 予¥450 | 高校生が常に陥る和文英訳・英作文の誤りについて、まったく新しい方法によって解決した、待望の書。 |
| 英作文一日一題 | 岩田一男著 | ¥250 | 一日一題、360日分、ヴァラエティに富んだ事項別の問題に対して解説。文法的な注意を行い、訳文には工夫した。 |
| 添削式英作文の研究 | 中西秀三著 | ¥250 | まず「基礎篇」で文法の総ざらいをし英文の組立てを練習させ「実力篇」で最後の磨きをかける工夫をしている |
| 英作文基礎研究 | 岡村 弘著 | ¥270 | 基本的例文を暗誦する、文法上用法上の知識を例文ごとに理解する、入試から厳選した問題を練習する書。 |
| 自由英作文 | 矢吹勝二著 | ¥220 | 英文を書く実力をつけるには和文英訳より自由英作文の方が効果が大であると20年の体験によりこう著者は説く |
| 入試英作文の急所 | 毛利良雄著 | ¥260 | どんな文章でもそれがどんな基本文型に還元できるかが分れば、和文英訳は十中八九、成功であると説く。 |
| 高校初年 英作文演習 | 青木常雄著 | ¥270 | まず英語の語法をわからせようとつとめ、さらにそれを活用する練習問題を与えて、これに習熟させるもの。 |
| 新和文英訳講義 | 久保田正次著 | ¥380 | 天候・四季・時間など20項目にわたって、それぞれの場合に必要な表現と語句とを集め、短文を作る工夫を示す。 |
| 新和文英訳の工夫 | 青木常雄著 | ¥230 | 和文英訳に不得手な諸君のために、原文の内容の大体を文法的に誤りのない正しい英文に表現する力を養わせる |
| 公式応用 和文英訳研究 | 渡辺秀雄著 | ¥350 | 百数十にのぼる基本公式を古今の名文600余題について詳細に検討説明し、公式を中心に文法的解説を施す。 |

|  |  |
|---|---|
| 和文英訳の知識<br>小島 嶽著 ¥180 | 前半の基礎篇において重要な基礎構文の英訳を示して説明し、後半の応用篇においては75題の練習題をあげた。 |
| 正誤問題の徹底的研究<br>志賀武男著 ¥250 | 活きた英文法を知りたい人、英文に対する鋭いセンスを涵養し真に正しい英語の知識を身につけたい人はぜひ! |
| 英語書き換え問題の急所<br>毛利良雄・佐山栄太郎著 ¥180 | 大学受験生が、これだけはぜひ暗誦しなければならぬ問題を系統的にまとめ、自信と実力を養成する。 |
| 組織的 受験英語の完成<br>小宮山久之助著 ¥270 | 90項目にわたって厳選された二千余の重要問題を文法、解釈、作文及び背景のあらゆる面の実力涵養に資する書 |
| 英 語 一 日 一 題<br>植木五一著 ¥250 | 文法力養成をモットーとし、わずかの時間に英語の実力を涵養させ、受験準備を着々と完成させる定評の書。 |
| 高校英語の総合研究<br>佐々木 学著 ¥380 | 基本的文型、重要語句及び節の研究を中心とし、殊に文型の徹底的理解を先決条件とした、能率的学習書。 |
| 高 校 英 語 の 基 礎<br>池谷敏雄著 ¥320 | 高校英語の基礎を固め実力を伸ばすために、また、本格的受験参考書を読む前のウオーミング・アップの書。 |
| 英 語 自 習 帖<br>寺西武夫著 ¥290 | 中学の基礎から説いて足固めを十分に行い、次第に高校の真実力を養成、大学入試の難関を突破できるよう導く。 |
| 基 礎 英 語 の 復 習<br>佐々木高政著 ¥100 | 高校初年のために中学の英語を総復習して基礎を固め、英語の基本的な構文を覚えさせ、応用自在の力を与える。 |
| 誤り易い 英語の熟語と類句<br>山田惣七著 ¥350 | ごく普通使用される熟語や慣用句の中で、学生に誤られやすいものを選び、その意義と用法の異なる点を説明。 |
| エース英単語・熟語<br>金口儀明著 ¥200 | 大学入試最近の傾向を考慮して、活用の仕方と文例を示し、基本語と重要語を区分して段階的に覚えやすくした |

| | |
|---|---|
| 高校英語の基礎問題集<br>池谷敏雄著 ￥120 | やさしいものから，手ごたえのあるものまで，全ての問題にわたり実力を試し，完璧を期する問題集である。 |
| 英語標準問題 300 選<br>佐山栄太郎・梶木隆一・岩田一男編 | 大学受験の標準英語力を示す問題を選定し，これに徹底的な解説，指導を加えて実力養成の限界を示したもの。 |
| 段階的英文法問題集<br>安藤貞雄著 ￥100 | 過去数年間の大学入試英文法問題を易から難へと段階をふんで分類し，体系的に把握できるよう編さんした。 |
| 大学入試 精選客観テスト<br>奥 幸雄編 ￥100 | 客観テストの生命はその多様性にある。発音，語い，内容理解，空所補充など実力判定の場は広い。ぜひ活用を！ |
| 大学入試 新分類英語問題集<br>研究社編集部編 ￥150 | 入試問題の解釈，作文，文法を項目別に分け，代表的な問題を厳選し，やさしいものから難しいものへと配列。 |
| 大学入試 英語問題の徹底的研究<br>奥 幸雄監修 ￥400 | 問題のすべてに解説・急所・ヒントを添えて，高校生なら誰にでも完全に理解できるよう徹底的に研究した。 |
| 就職試験英語問題集<br>〈高校用〉研究社編集部編 ￥130 | 全国有名 300 社にわたる最近 4 か年の問題を綿密に分類し，「傾向と対策」「重要構文 100 選」を添えた。 |

## 進学英語シリーズ

| | |
|---|---|
| 基本動詞の整理と活用<br>岩田一男著 ￥180 | 動詞とそれに前置詞，副詞の結びついたフレーズの活用を覚えることは英語熟達の急所であることを説いた。 |
| 英語正誤問題の急所<br>毛利良雄著 ￥180 | 受験生として知っておかねばならない基礎英文法を整理するために，必要な「正誤問題」を系統的にまとめた。 |
| 図解英文の構成<br>西尾 孝著 ￥180 | 英文の構造を図解法を利用することによって視覚に訴え，効果的・能率的に英文の構造が分るよう工夫した。 |

| | |
|---|---|
| **誤り易い前置詞の急所**<br>　　　　　毛利可信著　￥180 | 前置詞の用法を生きた姿で捉え，前置詞の持ち味を明らかにすると共に，他の前置詞との関係をも解明した。 |
| **語い・発音・アクセント問題**<br>　　　　　小栗敬三著　￥180 | 実戦本位にして，問題を掲げ急所をつき，要点を説明し解答を付し，大学入試突破の線まで到達するための書。 |
| **適語選択完成問題の急所**<br>　　　　　池谷敏雄著　￥180 | 大学入試の最大難関である選択問題と補充問題を系統的に分類して，さらに要点・急所を指摘してある。 |

## 高校英語副読本

| | |
|---|---|
| **Fifty Famous Stories**<br>（五十の物語）<br>　　　　佐山栄太郎編注　￥100 | 今もなお教養の糧として万人の読むべき古典の一つである同名の書から面白く，しかも親しみやすい12篇を選ぶ。 |
| **Biographical Stories**<br>（伝記物語）<br>　　　　梶木隆一編注　￥100 | 文豪 Hawthorne がニュートン，フランクリンなどの逸話を語りつつ，高潔な教訓と批判とをこめた名著。 |
| **The Happy Prince and Other Tales**（幸福な王子他）<br>　　　　石井正之助編注　￥100 | 同名の書から‘The Happy Prince’他3篇を収録。簡潔な言葉による感覚的表現や，純粋な愛情などが心を打つ。 |
| **Tales from Shakespeare**<br>（シェイクスピア物語）<br>　　　　荒木一雄編注　￥100 | 名作 Tales from Shakespeare より喜劇‘A Midsummer Night's Dream’と悲劇‘Hamlet’を収録した。 |
| **A Tale of the Ragged Mountains, etc.**（のこぎり山物語 他）<br>　　　　海江田　進編注　￥100 | 山の中を散策していると，突然インドの光景が出現し，そこで起こった事件で主人公が死ぬという催眠術の話。 |
| **The Snow Image and David Swan**（雪人形 他）<br>　　　　沢崎九二三編注　￥100 | 幼い子供の夢の世界と純真な母親の共鳴を描き，人生の運命を幻想曲ふうにつづった寓話的・象徴的作品二ツ。 |
| **Japanese Strange Stories**<br>（日本奇談）<br>　　　　藤井一五郎編注　￥100 | 「雨月物語」，「御伽百話物語」などの原文に忠実に Hearn は日本人の思考・感情・風習を正確に観察してある。 |

| | |
|---|---|
| **Tom Sawyer and Other Stories** (トム・ソーヤの冒険 他)<br>刈田元司編注　￥100 | *The Adventures of Tom Sawyer* の最も有名なペンキ塗りの章, 他2篇に人間性に対する深い理解と観察をみる |
| **Adventures of a Scientist, etc.** (科学者の冒険 他)<br>研究社編集部編注　￥100 | アメリカの少年少女向け教育雑誌 *Uncle Ray's Magazine* より, 興味深々の9篇を選んで収めたものである。 |
| **David Livingstone**<br>(アフリカ探険王リビングストン)<br>小西友七編注　￥100 | 一世紀前アフリカの奥地に入りこみ, キリスト教文化を導入しつつその全貌を明らかにしていった偉人の物語 |
| **Five Historic Speeches by U.S. Presidents** (アメリカ大統領演説選)　原沢正喜編注　￥100 | ワシントン, ジェファソン, リンカーン, ルーズヴェルト, ケネディの演説から, 最も記念すべきものを選ぶ |
| **A Sermon on Shaving and Other Essays** (ひげそりの談義他)<br>研究社編集部編注　￥100 | 英国の随筆家 R. リンドとガードナーの, 日常生活に身近かなことの観察と意見をのべた軽妙なエッセイ7篇。 |
| **Select Readings from American Journals** (アメリカ新聞・雑誌選)　髙部義信編注　￥100 | *The Christian Science Monitor* 紙の「世界世論の鏡」欄掲載のものと他の米紙から選んだもの27篇を収めた。 |

## 研究社英語物語双書〈上級用〉

| | |
|---|---|
| **Around-The-World**<br>(世界一周物語)<br>矢吹勝二注釈　￥120 | Reese 氏が世界各地を歴訪してその地の珍らしい見聞を, 印象深く甥に書き送った手紙形式の書である。 |
| **Silas Marner**<br>(サイラス・マーナー物語)<br>研究社編集部注釈　￥120 | 苦心して蓄えた金を盗まれて, 絶望のドン底におちいったサイラスが, 金髪の幼児の愛で更生する物語。 |
| **School Topics** (話題の泉)<br>髙部義信注釈　￥130 | High School 課外読本として有名なアメリカのアンクル・レイズ・マガジンから実益の読物32篇を抜すいした。 |
| **Necklace & Other Stories**<br>(頸飾 他五篇)<br>研究社編集部注釈　￥130 | モーパッサンの「頸飾」の他, トルストイの「神はみそなわす」, ホーソンの「大紅玉」「あざ」他1篇を収む。 |

| | |
|---|---|
| **The Scarlet Letter** (緋文字)<br>研究社編集部注釈　¥120 | 姦通罪の緋文字を胸につけながらも贖罪の道を歩み抜く，人妻の雄々しい生涯を語るホーソンの傑作である。 |
| **The Biggest Men in Letters, etc.** (現代文芸偉人伝)<br>小山喜久弥注釈　¥120 | トーマス・マン，ヘミングウェイ，フォークナー，サルトル，ピカソ，ストラヴィンスキー，などの伝記。 |
| **Three Popular Tales from Tolstoy** (トルストイ民話集)<br>伊賀上謙編注　¥130 | トルストイの民話は，彼の深い思想を親しみやすい形式に盛った珠玉の芸術品となっている。好短篇3篇収む。 |
| **Trapp Family Singers**<br>(菩提樹)<br>富田美彦・本庄寛編注　¥120 | 音楽愛好一家が，コンテストに1等賞を得た場面を中心として，原書第1部から6章を選んで注を添えた。 |
| **Tales from Chaucer**<br>(チョーサー物語)<br>梅崎秀雄注釈　¥150 | 「カンタベリー物語」の中から三ツの物語と，テニソンの叙事詩「国王牧歌12巻」から1篇を劇形式で再現した |
| **Captain Scott & Robert Owen** (スコット伝・オウエン伝)<br>広瀬和清注釈　¥130 | 南極探険に一生を捧げたスコット大佐と，産業革命当時の社会思想家であるロバート・オウエンの伝記である。 |
| **Albert Schweitzer, etc.**<br>(シュヴァイツァー伝・パスツール伝)<br>森　三重雄注釈　¥120 | オックスフォード大学版　Medical Scientists and Doctors から2篇を選んで，高校生向き副読本とした。 |
| **Letter From Peking**<br>(ペキンからの便り)<br>富田美彦・広瀬裕子共編　¥130 | エリザベス夫人が動乱のペキン大学総長の夫からの手紙を待ちわびる内容で，家庭内に起こる様々な悲喜を描く。 |
| **It Seems To Me**<br>(ルーズヴェルト夫人の人生案内)<br>出口泰生注釈　¥120 | 「レイディーズ・ホームジャーナル」に連載された，ルーズヴェルト夫人の人生案内欄をまとめた興味ぶかい読物 |
| **Hamlet** (ハムレット)<br>植田虎雄注釈　¥150 | シェイクスピアの名作「ハムレット」を，原作にできるだけ忠実に分り易く書き直し，巻末に詳注をほどこした。 |

大学受験英語雑誌　**高校英語研究**　毎月14日発売　定価　120円